SIR ELDON GORST

The Overshadowed Proconsul

Sir Eldon Gorst, 1907
(*Courtesy of Mrs. K. R. Thomas*)

SIR ELDON GORST
The Overshadowed Proconsul

PETER MELLINI

HOOVER COLONIAL STUDIES
Edited by
Peter Duignan, L. H. Gann,
A. H. M. Kirk-Greene

HOOVER INSTITUTION PRESS
Stanford University, Stanford, California 94305

Hoover Institution Publication

© 1977 by the Board of Trustees of the
   Leland Stanford Junior University
All rights reserved
International Standard Book Number: 0–8179– 6781-8
Library of Congress Catalog Card Number: 76-51878
Printed in the United States of America

Contents

List of Illustrations

Photographs

Cartoons of Gorst

(All cartoons were found in the Gorst press cuttings.)

About the Author

Peter Mellini is Associate Professor of History,
California State College at Sonoma, and Director
of The Historic Preservation Program. He earned
his master's degree and his doctorate in history
from Stanford University and was instructor in
history at Stanford, 1968-1970. He was the recip-
ient of the Leverhulme Fellowship in 1966 and the
National Endowment for the Humanities Summer Stipend in 1971.

Dr. Mellini is a native Californian who has
traveled extensively in Europe, the Middle East,
South Asia, and Australia.

He is coauthor with Roy Matthews of *The New
Vanity Fair Album* (Scolar Press, 1977) and a con-
tributor of book reviews to *African Historical
Studies, The Annals of Political and Social Science,*
and *American Historical Review.*

Foreword

Hoover Colonial Studies Series

The last three decades or so have seen a revolution
in the historiography of modern Africa. Historians
once devoted their attention largely to the conquerors
and builders of empire; their colonial subjects went
mainly unrecorded. Then the pendulum started to swing
the other way. Imperial history began to fall from
academic favor. Scholars attempted to write the annals of modern Africa in African terms, with the colonial period no more than a cruel but short-lived interlude. Some academicians went even further. The
historians of Africa were to assume a political mission: they were to assist in nation-building and to
lend their skills to bring about the triumph of a particular ideology or a particular class. The term
"Eurocentric" became a word of abuse beloved by re-
viewers anxious to denigrate those authors whose political philosophy they happened to dislike.

Yet the history of the Europeans in Africa cannot
be separated from the history of Africa at large. No
reputable historian of Eastern Europe, for instance,
would deny historical legitimacy, say, to a study of
the Ottoman conquerors of Albania or the Austrian invaders of Bosnia. Similarly, the policies of a British governor in what is now Tanzania or the exploits
of a Belgian military leader in what is now Zaire
belong to the history of Africa just as much as they
belong to the annals of Great Britain or of Belgium,
respectively.

Students concerned with the history of the Europeans in Africa, moreover, enjoy advantages today that
were not available to their predecessors half a century ago. A mass of new archival material has recently
become accessible in depositories both of the former
metropolitan powers and of the independent African

x   SIR ELDON GORST

states. In addition, colonial historians can now
draw on a great body of sociological and anthropolog-
ical material largely unavailable in the early days
of European colonization.

   To take advantage of this new material and to re-
analyze the colonial period as a phase of Euro-African
history, the Hoover Institution has launched a new
program of scholarly inquiries organized around the
theme of African colonial studies.

   One major series, directed by Peter Duignan and
Lewis H. Gann, will deal with the men who modernized
Africa—*Agents of Empire*. This project, interdisciplin-
ary in approach, will cover all colonial powers in
sub-Saharan Africa. It will be concerned with the
transference to Africa of Western institutions and
modes of production, techniques and skills, ideas and
ideals—in short, with the total Western impact on
Africans. The project will seek to answer the following questions: What were the situations faced by the
agents of colonialism both in their efforts to govern
Africans and in their ideological justifications for
doing so? How did African societies react and respond
to foreign rule? What effects did Europeans have on
African societies? What were the sequences of adjust-
ment and change?

   Complementing this project will be a series of
biographies and of edited versions of primary sources
(diaries, letters, journals and reports). We have
also planned a volume of contributed essays on notable
colonial governors as well as one on Belgian governors
of the Congo.

   We are pleased to introduce Peter Mellini's political biography of Sir Eldon Gorst, the successor
to Cromer as his Majesty's Agent and Consul General of
Egypt. Mellini throws light both on the history of
British colonialism and on political and cultural contacts between the Western and the Islamic world.

   We trust that this and subsequent studies will
help to elucidate and reinterpret the colonial past.

                              Peter Duignan
                              Lewis H. Gann
                              A. H. M. Kirk-Greene

Acknowledgments

The cooperation of Mrs. K. R. Thomas of Castle Combe, Wiltshire, Sir Eldon Gorst's daughter, who allowed me to use her father's papers, made this biography possible. Her friendship, hospitality, and sense of humor are among the most pleasant memories of a task that consumed much of my spare time the last several years. Her son and daughter-in-law, Paul and Magarit Lysley of Castle Combe, were also most helpful and hospitable. Mr. Archibald Hunter of Castle Combe shared his childhood memories of Egypt, the Anglo-Egyptian milieu, and his uncle "Jack" Gorst with me; his observations were most enlightening.

This biography developed out of a doctoral dissertation in history at Stanford University. The initial stimulus to study the career of Sir Eldon Gorst came from the enthusiastic teaching of the late Professor Christina Phelps Harris. My advisor, Professor Wayne Vucinich, was a source of sound counsel, constant encouragement, and friendship. Dr. George Rentz and Professor Richard Lyman supervised the relevant parts of my professional training. Professor Peter Stansky read my dissertation critically, and urged me to work further on Gorst.

The History Department at Stanford was generous in its assistance during my graduate career. The Graduate Division, the Overseas Campus Office, and the Committee on International Studies, all of Stanford University, and the Leverhulme Foundation made it possible for me to do the initial research in England. Professor P. M. Holt of the School of Oriental and African Studies in the University of London was generous with his time and advice. I am particularly grateful to Miss Elizabeth Monroe, of St. Anthony's College, Oxford, who placed the resources of the Middle East Centre there at my disposal, and made a number of invaluable suggestions.

A summer stipend in 1971 from the National Endowment for the Humanities enabled me to return to En-
gland and go to Egypt to work further on Gorst's life.
Earlier, two grants from the Hoover Institution made
possible some necessary background research. A vari-
ety of officials and librarians gave me access to
their collections: The Keeper and staff of the Public
Record Office, London; the staff of the Bodleian,
Oxford; the University Library and Pembroke College,
Cambridge; the British Museum, the Church Missionary
Society, the National Liberal Club, the Historical
Manuscripts Commission, the Royal Commonwealth Society,
and the Royal Geographical Society, all in London; the
Sudan Archive at Durham University, particulary Mr. I.
J. C. Foster, all were most generous with their facil-
ities and time. At the Middle East Centre, Oxford,
Mr. Albert Hourani, Dr. Derek Hopwood, Miss Jo Kadera,
and Mr. Lionel Dix made me welcome and comfortable at
all hours. Colonel T. E. Ingram, the archivist of the
Baring Brothers, gave me access to some obscure letters of the first Earl of Cromer, and Baron Rennell of
Rodd allowed me to see his father's papers at the Rodd,
his family's home. Mr. Gordon Phillips, the archivist
of *The Times*, let me rummage carefully through that
newspaper's records, and provided me with some tidbits
on Gorst, Cromer, and *The Times*. Mrs. Clare Talbot,
the librarian of Hatfield House, allowed me to see
relevant material in the library of the Marquesses of
Salisbury.

Crown-Copyright material is reproduced or quoted
by permission of the Controller of H.M. Stationary
Office.

The photographs of Sir Eldon and his wife
appear through the courtesy of Mrs. K. R. Thomas.
The cooperation and advice of the eleventh Baron and
Lady Monson and the interest and hospitality of Mrs.
Prudence de Lobinière, daughter of Sir Eldon Gorst's
godchild, Margaret Turnure Bevan, produced the photo
of Romaine Stone Turnure, later the ninth Lady Monson.
At the last moment, Mr. Christopher Simon Sykes found
a photo of his great grandmother, Lady Jessica Sykes.
Dr. Khalid Baaba translated the three Egyptian cartoons about Gorst with sensitivity and precision.

Several individuals provided materials or made
suggestions that enhanced my understanding of Gorst
and his era. I am especially grateful to Dr. Neil

Daglish, Dr. Roger Adelson, Mr. Joachim O. Ronall, Mrs. Guistina Ryan, Dr. Samir Seikaly, Dr. Nancy Newman, and Dr. Myron Turbow. My colleagues in the History Department at Sonoma State College encouraged me in my work. I am beholden particularly to Dr. Stephen Watrous who somehow found the time to read almost all the manuscript and to make some essential and perceptive suggestions. Dr. Alice Wexler made some helpful comments and Miss Carolyn Zainer's critique refocused my work. Ms. Elizabeth Flory edited and typed the first complete manuscript with discernment, wit, and patience. Dr. Peter Duignan's comments sharpened the final text. Mrs. Sally Jaggar Hayes and Mrs. Betsy Brandt edited the copy with speed, accuracy, and diplomacy. Ms. Andrea Bond proofed the bibliography and end notes, and indexed the book with care and good humor. Mrs. Jeanne Nickerson typed the final copy speedily and precisely. Mrs. Mickey Hamilton, general manager of the Hoover Press, exercised her talents for organization to give the book its final shape.

Dr. Lenore Terr, Ms. Verna Adams, Mr. Stephens VanDenburgh, Mr. C. J. Carey, Mr. and Mrs. Keith Wallace, Mr. S. J. Rushton, and Dr. and Mrs. James Driscoll all deserve special thanks for their advice and friendship. Other colleagues and friends gave their counsel and support when it was needed and I am very grateful to them.

Mr. Christopher Sykes, Gorst's nephew, wrote to me recently about his uncle: "His work in Egypt has been very much, and I think unfairly, criticised, and too many conclusions are drawn from his last years of office when he was a very sick man." I hope what I have written does Sir Eldon Gorst (1861-1911) the justice he deserves.

This book is dedicated to my parents, Mr. and Mrs. John Baskette. Their support and enthusiasm could never be adequately thanked.

Peter Mellini
Mill Valley, California
August 1977

The Earl of Cromer,
1907. (From *Modern
Egypt* by the Earl of
Cromer, by permission
of Macmillan, London)

The Khedive Abbas
Hilmi. (*Courtesy of
the Trustees of the
British Museum*)

Lady Jessica Sykes, *circa* 1890.
(Courtesy of Christopher Simon Sykes)

Romaine Stone
Turnure Monson,
circa 1900.
*(Courtesy of
Prudence de Lobiniere)*

Evelyn Rudd Gorst,
"Doll," *circa* 1903.
*(Courtesy of Mrs. K. R.
Thomas)*

The British Agency in Cairo,
circa 1908.

The summer British Agency, Ramleh,
near Alexandria, *circa* 1908.

The Khedive and Gorst, Opening Ceremonies, Esna Barrage, February 9, 1909. (*Courtesy of Mrs. K. R. Thomas*)

Gorst, the successful deer stalker.
(*Courtesy of Mrs. K. R. Thomas*)

Gorst and his wife on holiday in the
Egyptian desert, *circa* 1908. (*Courtesy
of Mrs. K. R. Thomas*)

Introduction

To many students of Anglo-Egyptian relations in the
early twentieth century, Sir Eldon Gorst's short term
from 1907 to 1911 as His Majesty's Agent and Consul-
General in Egypt remains an enigma. Sandwiched between
the two giant imperial proconsuls Cromer and Kitchener,
Gorst continues to be a shadowy figure, blamed by some
commentators for weakness, and commended by others for
shrewdness in handling the legacy of Lord Cromer's
twenty-four years as a just and benevolent autocrat in
Egypt. Cromer's reluctant departure in 1907 heralded
the end of an era. His handpicked successor, Gorst,
had to deal with economic problems and pressure for
political and social changes that had been repressed
under his stern and pragmatic predecessor.

Gorst initiated or accelerated changes in the
British administration of Egypt, and by doing so precipitated a degree of violence and turmoil among the
Egyptians that has not been adequately explained even
to this day. His motivations, actions, and policies
remain subjects of dispute. A Sudanese scholar, Jemal
Mohammed Ahmed, has commented: "Of all the characters
who played a part in the tumultuous drama of the first
decade of the twentieth century, Gorst is perhaps the
most difficult to understand."[1]

Still in office when he died of cancer in 1911,
Gorst enjoyed no leisurely retirement in which to com-
pose his memoirs and justify his career, and his policies were misunderstood by most observers of Egyptian
affairs. Robert Vansittart, a junior diplomat in the
British Agency in Cairo under Gorst, wrote in retrospect:

> Gorst had intellect enough to install new
> lamps . . . for old, and had he been in the
> Cabinet might have earned the laurels of
> innovation. Since he was only the execu-
> tant of thankless orders he was abused and
> forgotten instead of only being forgotten.

> He was a real loss to a country which
> treated him shabbily and got over it at
> once.[2]

In the last few years the voluminous correspondence of the Foreign Office—the ministry responsible for Anglo-Egyptian relations during this period—and various papers left by officials and private individuals concerned with Egypt and imperial affairs have become accessible to scholars. Gorst left two autobiographical notebooks and his private diaries,[3] which have never been published, as well as several volumes of clippings from periodicals. With these materials his entire career can now be reexamined.

This work, however, is not just an account of Gorst's life in England and in Egypt; it is also an examination of British imperial policy in an important stage of transition. I have sought first to discover the determinants of the policy Gorst tried to implement, then to evaluate the consequences of that policy, and finally to relate the events in Egypt to the larger process of imperial policymaking.

The illusions and false conclusions that British statesmen drew from Cromer's success and Gorst's experiment in conciliation in Egypt were part of the great failure of vision that bedeviled British relations with Egypt until very recently. Elizabeth Monroe accurately characterized these relations as "so manifest a failure that no Englishmen felt inclined to describe the heyday."[4]

Gorst assumed responsibility for British interests in Egypt at the tag end of this heyday, which had begun in 1882 when the British occupied Egypt "temporarily." Egypt lay astride the quickest and most convenient route to India and the Far East. Once the Suez Canal had been completed in 1876, it was judged imperative that no other foreign power be allowed to dominate Egypt. Alfred Milner, one of the major apostles of the imperial idea, put it succinctly to another proconsul, the Marquess of Curzon: "We want a strong foot-hold in Egypt as a vital link in the chain of Empire. That is the only reason why we ever went there. We could not let Egypt fall into other hands."[5]

Once the British occupied Egypt they found they could not withdraw. They had chosen to prop up a weak

dynasty and an administration in disorder. Either
would collapse without British support. They had sup-
pressed and discredited a nascent nationalist movement
that began largely in the Egyptian army and this army
had been disbanded. For the British to remain, they
had to assume responsibility for the country's administration. They might have ruled Egypt directly as
they did India. But for reasons that involved politics at home and the balance of power in Europe, they
chose to retain the fiction of Ottoman sovereignty and
the facade of Egyptian independence. The exceedingly
complicated and delicate task of "advising" the Egyptian government was entrusted in 1883 to Lord Cromer
(Evelyn Baring)[6] and a small group of British officials, drawn mostly from India.

Egypt prospered under Cromer's judicious guidance.
Though it never became a formal part of the British
Empire, Egypt swiftly became involved in the imperial
mystique that arose in the late nineteent century.
This meant that the British regarded themselves as
custodians for the interests of European civilization.
They asserted that they had saved Egypt from chaos,
but it was not enough to secure imperial communications. They somehow felt it necessary to assume the
task of physical and moral regeneration of the Egyptians as well.

Lord Cromer was the agent and prime example of
what his authorized biographer has called "a passion-
ate but sane Imperialism."[7] Cromer himself said of
the British mission in Egypt: "He [the British offi-
cial] came not as conquerer, but in the familiar garb
of a saviour of society." The British had a mission
thrust upon them by their nation's position as a world
power. That mission was to benefit the masses who had
been misgoverned and oppressed for sixty centuries.
The test of the Anglo-Saxon role would be how well
they fulfilled this mission and used their power for
the good of the people they ruled. Failure to make
good use of the imperial power would mean the inevitable downfall of the British Empire.[8] As long as the
British had the welfare of the Egyptians in hand, both
the British and the Egyptians as well as the world at
large would benefit morally and materially.

Many imperialists including Gorst assumed that
the Egyptians, though ungrateful at first, would come
to realize that the British had their best interests

in mind, and consequently that British interests were
Egyptian interests. Then and only then would the
Egyptians be fit for self-rule and autonomy. For the
foreseeable future, the British occupation had to continue to guarantee Egypt's security. While under
British tutelage, the diverse groups within Egypt
would be guided toward self-government. Cromer explained his program in *Modern Egypt*, published in 1908,
the year after his retirement:

> In the meanwhile, no effort should be spared
> to render the native Egyptians capable of
> eventually taking their share in the govern-
> ment of a really autonomous community. Much
> has already been done in this direction, and
> it may be confidently anticipated, now that
> the finances of the country are established
> on a sound footing and the most pressing de-
> mands necessary to ensure material prosperity
> have been met, that intellectual, and perhaps
> moral progress will proceed more rapidly dur-
> ing the next quarter of a century than during
> that which has now terminated.[9]

Modern Egypt not only served to explain Cromer's
efforts and define the British imperial mission in
Egypt, but also informed the public of the general
nature and special emphasis of the task which faced
his successor.

By 1907 some Egyptians had already shown clearly
that continued exclusion from control of their own
administration was intolerable. They were increasingly aware that the British, despite their pious
assertions of a civilizing mission, occupied Egypt
for reasons beyond Egyptian control and would continue to do so, whether the Egyptians liked it or
not, as long as Egypt remained essential to communications with the Indian Empire.[10]

Gorst had spent his career in the Egyptian service under Cromer, but he did not share his predecessor's illusions that the Egyptians, if lightly taxed
and efficiently governed, would submit to continued
exclusion from the management of their own destiny.
He knew, too, that British dependence on the European
communities and the native Christians in Egypt was un-
wise. Cromer had quickly lost what little faith he
had in the capacity of the Egyptians to better

themselves. Gorst at least was willing to experiment seriously with a more active involvement of the Egyptians in their own government. He also did not confuse the form of power with its substance, as did many of his official contemporaries.

Gorst replaced Cromer not long after the Liberal electoral landslide in 1906. The Liberals harbored something of a guilt complex about the Empire.[11] The Boer War and its aftermath, Curzon's rigidity and mistakes in India, and various critics of empire such as E. D. Morel and J. A. Hobson had made clear to many members of the Liberal Party the discrepancies between the old imperial vision and its recent applications.[12] Even Egypt, thought to be secure under the masterly influence of Cromer, showed signs of unrest in 1906 and 1907. The Liberal government, disquieted, sought remedies. Among other solutions, the British Cabinet and Gorst hoped that a judicious amount of self-rule might calm unrest, divert the energies of the Egyptian protestors, and—not least—placate the more radical members of the party at home. Gorst was dispatched in the spring of 1907 to apply this remedy to Egypt.

This then is a study of the failure of British imperial vision. It is also a study of a man who was too clever for his own good, who did not share many of his contemporaries' confusion about the realities of imperial power, and who was congenitally unable to mask his talents in an age when success in higher office depended to a great extent on both self-deception and hypocrisy. J. B. Priestley has written: "[In Britain] . . . there have always been the 'unsound' types, brilliant fellows no doubt but not to be depended upon to toe the line, not rock the boat, play the game, and these have almost always been brushed off by the establishment—except in wartime."[13] Gorst was one of these men, openly brilliant, ambitious, and devious. He was not a prewar precursor of the dismantlers of empire, as Professor P. M. Holt has alleged.[14] He was the victim of his own talents, and of the imperial failure of vision.

Chapter One

A PAINFUL CHILDHOOD

Sir Eldon Gorst's route to his short, tragic proconsulship began east of Suez in New Zealand where he was
born in 1861. His father was John Eldon Gorst, then
serving as a colonial official among the Maoris. One
of the more shadowy figures in late nineteenth century
British politics, John Gorst was descended from a line
of provincial gentlemen, mainly from Lancashire.[1] At
Cambridge in 1857 he earned a very good degree through
his cleverness: he was third wrangler in mathematics
without a profound knowledge of the subject. After
some European travel he found the study of law and
provincial life in Preston too dull. When his father
died in 1859, John Gorst opted for adventure in the
Antipodes.[2] He met his wife-to-be—Mary Elizabeth Moore,
the daughter of a retired Indian army officer—on the
voyage out. They were married in Australia, and
arrived in New Zealand in May 1860.

It was a time when racial strife again was brewing over the steady erosion of Maori culture and lands
by the more numerous and better organized white settlers. Maori grievances culminated in the late 1850s
in the protonationalist "King" or unity movement.
Open warfare erupted in 1860 due to a land dispute.[3]
The settlers, backed by the British government, were
superior in numbers and firepower. Sir George Grey,
who earlier had pacified the Maori, was recalled as
governor in 1861 in the hope that he could reach a
permanent resolution of the conflict. He appointed
John Gorst—who had made some friends among the Maori—
as an inspector of native and missionary schools, then
as Resident Magistrate, and finally as Civil Commissioner
of the Upper Waikato District on North Island. In
1863 the Maori in his district, provoked by settler
encroachments, violently revolted. Only the inter-
cession of one of their chiefs, Tamihana, enabled
Gorst and his family to escape.[4]

John Gorst had had enough adventure in the Antipodes, but the New Zealand fiasco did not lessen his
taste for public life. It stimulated a lifelong com-
mitment to the welfare of the underdog. The family—
now including Eldon and a baby daughter, Constance—
was settled in London, where he was called to the bar
in 1865, and swiftly established himself as an able
barrister. That same year he entered politics as a
Tory candidate for Parliament from Hastings. Unsuc-
cessful there, he subsequently won a seat for Cambridge in 1866, and impressed Disraeli with his
maiden speech. The latter selected Gorst to reorganize the party machinery after the Tory defeat in
1868. He served without pay as the first party agent,
and helped to create the Conservative Central Office.[5]
The details of his work and his subsequent career
remain cloudy, as his private papers have apparently
disappeared—the aftermath of a marriage to his house-
maid late in life. He was a prickly man, perceived by
some as a cynic.   John Gorst's younger son Harold
wrote that his father "always had something unconven-
tional to say that was generally too true to be palat-
able."[6]   John Gorst's difficult personality and his
comparative failure in Conservative Party politics
directly affected Eldon's career and attitudes. [7]

John Gorst's family grew rapidly in the next several years. He fathered six more children between
1865 and 1876: Violet, who died in 1871, Hylda, Harold,
Edith, Eva,and Gwen. Sir Eldon Gorst was his father's
namesake, but did not assume the name of Eldon— which
will be used here—until he was knighted in 1902.   In
public life he called himself John Lowndes Gorst to
distinguish himself from his father; to his family and
friends he was known as Jack. To this day some accounts confuse the two men, in part because the son
predeceased the father. During Eldon's childhood, the
growing family moved in and out of London. His earli-
est memories were of a suburban villa at Tooting,
south of the Thames beyond Clapham. In 1868 the family moved to Kensington where he attended the local
day school. The next summer they took a house on the
south coast at Worthing near Brighton where Eldon went
to a second school. His recollections of this area
were not pleasant:

> I was profoundly miserable at this school and
> was a good deal bullied by the other boys
> who were mostly bigger than I was. They

> used to wait for me after school hours and
> catch me as I was going home. I used to
> make all sorts of detours to try and avoid
> them, climbing over walls and returning
> across country to keep out of their way.
> On one occasion, when I was being rather
> more badly treated than normal, I appealed
> to a passer-by for assistance, and I still
> remember vividly my shame and discomfiture
> when he told me not to tell tales out of
> school and left me to the tender mercies
> of my persecutors.[8]

When he revisited Worthing years later this memory
was still fresh. The family returned to London and
young Eldon was sent to the private Kensington Grammar
School.

Not long before his tenth birthday a painful pel-
vic abscess was misdiagnosed as some sort of spinal
trouble. The mystified physicians confined him to his
bed. After a year the abscess festered, and several
operations failed to remove the diseased bone. Finally the bewildered doctors tried to burn it out with
acid. Eldon Gorst never forgot those pain-filled
years: "I suffered tortures (so it seemed to me) daily.
Every morning at 10 the acid was applied and I lay in
pain till 4 or 5 in the afternoon. It was a dreadful
time and I was not a patient invalid." Often he would
lie cursing at the frightful agony. "My poor mother
must have had a melancholy time of it, & I have no
doubt I was offensive & odious as it is possible to
be." After two and one-half years of this "wretched
existence" the thirteen-year-old had had enough. He
protested vehemently that he was no nearer recovery
than when the acid treatments had begun. "I pointed
out . . . that it was not the disease but the treatment that made life not worth living." His parents
agreed, and the therapy was abandoned. This pain-
racked period "overshadowed many years of my life and
. . . had a permanent influence on my physical and
moral development."[9]

Wearing an iron shield to protect his back, Eldon
was sent to Eton in January 1875 under the sponsorship
of his wealthy uncle, Edward Craddock Lowndes. He
later observed: "Seldom was any boy less fit to be
plunged into the little world of 900 boys of all sizes
and ages who made up Eton College." The tutoring

during the three years of confinement had been inadequate, but it took him less than a year to catch up
academically, despite his aching pelvis. "I made considerable progress in my studies and early earned the
unenviable reputation of being a 'sap'—a term of reproach, the awful import of which all good Etonians
will grasp."[10] It was not popular then—or even quite
recently, according to Cyril Connolly, the critic—to
be known at Eton as a worker and striver, a boy who
competes openly for the school prizes.[11]   Eldon Gorst's
intense drive, brains, and ambition never were masked
successfully.   The British upper classes tended to
distrust such men; they might use them, but only with
reluctance—out of necessity.[12]   In addition, Gorst's
enforced isolation and ordeal had left him emotionally
estranged from his schoolmates.   Initially he felt
he was perceived as "an unsociable and unsympathetic
outsider," and later recalled that "the four years
I had spent away from other boys had left me very
reserved, very sensitive and very old for my age.
I did not understand boys' ways, and it took me two
years before I learnt to get on with them."[13]

For the first two terms Gorst lived in a temporary house run by a man named Harry Tarver—a way station for a number of students waiting for permanent
houses.   Tarver reminded Eldon of Horace Skimpole in
Bleak House: half-French, kind, artistic, a "gentleman"
who had married below his station, he had gone bankrupt two or three times and knew nothing of normal
Public School discipline.   Gorst later was ashamed at
the tricks the boys played on "this poor, weak-minded,
gentle, inoffensive gentleman."   When they went too
far Tarver caned them, a punishment the young Gorst
avoided because of his back trouble.   In the autumn
of 1875 he moved into Evans House, run by the retired
drawing master and his family, and it was here that he
met Guy Oswald Smith—"[my] best and firmest friend
through life."   They were the same age, but at opposite poles in ability and looks.   Where Gorst excelled
in school work, Smith was thought to be stupid.   Later
Gorst commented:

It would be difficult to find two people more
entirely different, both in character and appearance. He was tall, fair, & good looking.
I, short, darkish, and ugly. He was of a
quiet, peaceable, retiring disposition; I,
restless, energetic, and much more sensitive

and warm-hearted. He was liked by his masters; I was disliked by mine, in spite of
their recognizing I did them credit.[14]

Gorst's sparse autobiographical notes rarely mention Smith
again though their friendship endured. Other friends
are only included by name. These notes give the impression that Gorst was a hardworking, intense, and
lonely boy at Eton. Until he was sixteen he was
excluded from team games and sports—a further cause
of isolation from his schoolmates—because of the back
trouble. A small bit of bone then fell off, the abscess healed itself and never troubled him again.[15]
From his limited description it would appear to have
been either a pilonidal sinus or osteomyelitis, an
infection of bone tissue usually caused by staphylo-
cocci.[16] Once it was healed he learned to swim and
to single scull, but did not distinguish himself. He
was delighted to be the first to win house colors at
football in the fall of 1878.

The first indication of an interest in women he
noted in an aside on the Evans House experience.
Three maids named Harriet, Kate, and Martha looked
after the boys' rooms, and "all three were thoroughly
unappetizing so as to be, like Caesar's wife, quite
above suspicion."[17] However else Eton may have shaped
him, it did not blunt an interest in women and he
never developed monkish tendencies, unlike some of
his contemporaries.

Even with physical recovery, Gorst was neither an
athletic nor a social success at Eton. He won some academic prizes, but was more amused when once he received
the divinity prize—an honor that might have startled
some of the prelates he encountered in later years.
The atmosphere and teaching at the school were not as
important to him as the desire for paternal approval.
John Gorst,

by well-timed severity, kept me up to mark.
Like most boys, I disliked work and I was
only made to exert myself by the fear of
my father's displeasure, when I went home
for the holidays. He never said much, but
when he was not pleased, he treated me in a
cold and distant manner which had far more
effect on me than anything else could have
had.[18]

Neither Gorst nor Eton seems to have been fond of one another. He was defensive yet skeptical about this famous public school:

> I cannot say that I learnt much in the way
> of studies while I was there. No doubt the
> public school life in England forms the
> character, making a man of one, & prevents
> one being a prig. But it is a pity that
> something cannot be taught at the same time.
> I was soon to find, when I went to the Uni-
> versity, how much my education had been
> neglected, especially in mathematics.[19]

He left to enter Cambridge University at the end of the summer term of 1879, when he had just turned eighteen.

Childhood experiences and the years of pain left him embittered and sensitive. In addition to the sep- aration from his peers at a crucial age, the unpleasant years at Eton contributed to a sense of emotional dis- tance that did not lessen as he grew older, and may have contributed—with his short physical stature—to the adoption of a cynical and tough manner as an adult.[20] Photographs and a diplomatic uniform circa 1907 (in the family's possession) show the adult Gorst to have been about 5'5" in height, shorter than aver- age for his social class and sex. A rare admirer, Lord Vansittart, the famous diplomat who served on Gorst's staff in 1909-1911, observed: "But an inch on Cleopatra's nose, six inches on Gorst's stature, might have affected the story of Egypt."[21]

The summer before he went up to Cambridge, John Gorst took him to tour the continent. It was not a holiday from studying, however, since the senior Gorst hoped to see a duplication of his own success in the mathematics honors examinations. In October Eldon moved into rooms between the chapel and the Master's Lodge in the Great Court of Trinity College, pleasant quarters that he kept during the three years spent at Cambridge. Under pressure from John Gorst, he worked very hard, beginning his studies "very far behind all my contemporaries in Mathematical knowledge." The tutor assigned him, a Mr. Ingram, was unsatisfactory, "an uninteresting man with snobbish proclivities," and Gorst resorted to private coaching. The most fashion- able mathematics coach, Routh, took no interest in his

work, so Eldon left him in the third year and was tu-
tored by a very clever young man, J. J. Thompson (later
professor of physics and a Nobel laureate). In the
final examinations, called mathematical tripos, Gorst
was twentieth—a solid second-class honors degree. It
was higher, he gloated, than "all my former colleagues
in the class of Routh's."[22] John Gorst's reaction has
not survived.

There is little indication that Eldon had any
special interest in mathematics. John Gorst had
excelled in it when at Cambridge; the son was expected
to do the same. Eldon thought that the intense, dis-
ciplined effort and concentration required were, in
retrospect, the most beneficial and useful aspects of
the three years at Cambridge, and later wrote:

> The knowledge of mathematics which I thus
> obtained has, of course, been of no direct
> practical use in my subsequent career. It
> has, however, been of the greatest possible
> service in enabling me to grasp clearly and
> easily any subject which it has since been
> necessary or useful for me to take up. In
> a word, my three years of college life were
> invaluable for me as an instrument of suc-
> cess, and not by filling me with any sort
> of useful knowledge. Indeed, as far as the
> latter was concerned, I left Cambridge en-
> tirely ignorant of all branches of know-
> ledge which could be of any practical use
> to me in real life.[23]

During these years the only recreation he mentioned
was acting. He joined the Amateur Dramatic Club,
played Crabtree in Sheridan's *School for Scandal*, Mrs.
Dangle in *The Critic*, and a number of minor parts. In
later years Gorst enjoyed a reputation as a highly
skilled amateur actor among the cosmopolitan social
set in Cairo. He also became an avid theatregoer.

There is a curiously diffuse quality about his
description of that childhood, school, and university
life. They were not on the whole happy memories, and
he may have found it painful to recall them. If he
made any friends at Cambridge, they are not recorded.
He was reduced to this conclusion: "The one great
thing I learned while at the university was how to
work."[24]

8

Eldon Gorst's life immediately after Cambridge resembled his father's exploratory years. He had dined at the Inner Temple while still at Trinity, but the law did not interest him; when he left with a degree in summer 1882 he was looking toward the home civil service. Mid-Victorian reforms had stiffened the examinations so that even a university graduate had to cram and spend time abroad learning German and French, and he lived that summer with a German family in Munich. He also met his first major love, "R. W." In the fall he moved into his father's house at number seventy-nine St. George's Square in Pimlico, part of a mid-Victorian set of row houses. According to David Piper, the architectural historian, the set "heavily encompasses with its insistent porticos and weight of window pediments a long rectangle of green and trees."[25] It was close to the Embankment and convenient to Parliament. Eldon enrolled at Scoones on Garrick Street, the most famous of the crammers for the civil service, and the next summer went to France to master that language.

He was called to the bar in 1885, but a political career momentarily turned him away from both the practice of law and the civil service. An upswing had taken place in the political fortunes of John Gorst which he imagined might work to his benefit. The father never managed to break into the largely aristocratic inner circle that dominated the Tory Party, despite a major contribution to its reorganization in the 1870s and his subsequent prominence in the House of Commons as one of the few conspicuous Tory activists known as the Fourth Party. In 1884 John Gorst persuaded the other members of the Fourth Party—Lord Randolph Churchill, Arthur Balfour, and Sir Henry Drummond Wolff—that the influence of their clique might be enhanced if they campaigned for control of the council of the National Union of Conservative Associations. This effort was designed especially to further the ambitions of Lord Randolph. John Gorst and Wolff were Churchill's strong supporters, while Balfour—whose political career was linked to the party leader, his uncle Lord Salisbury—acted as an intermediary between the factions.[26]

After a complicated set of maneuvers and negotiations, Lord Randolph and his insurgents won a narrow victory in the National Union council elections in July 1884. In the process, Churchill had offered

Eldon Gorst the honorary secretaryship of the National
Union in the spring. In spite of his father's warnings on the hazards of a career in Tory politics without the benefit of wealth, a potent family, and/or
powerful and influential friends, the young man
accepted. Churchill's victory at the annual confer-
ence in July was not sufficient to allow him to claim
the leadership of the party. Further negotiations
ensued with the "old gang," in Churchill's words, and
the settlement left the Gorsts out of the spoils.
Eldon Gorst's reflections on the incident were bitter:

> The future leadership of the Tory Party
> seemed within grasp, when Lord Randolph,
> by one of those fatal and unexplicable
> right-about-face movements which subse-
> quently earned him political and physical
> ruin, threw up the sponge, refused the
> chairmanship of the National Union and
> departed for India, leaving all his
> friends and supporters in dismay.[27]

Other less biased accounts of the situation argue
that Lord Randolph and his supporters made a sensible
compromise. In return for Churchill's agreement to
"act in harmony" with the established leadership—the
old gang—he would be allowed to join the inner circle
that controlled the Tory Party. Part of the price
paid was that the National Union would be relegated to
its early status of an advisory body. The Tory establishment kept its hold on the party through the agency
of its members in Parliament and the party whips.[28]
Direct appeals to the party membership such as the
Fourth Party had used, and the use of such opinion and
support as a basis for changes in the party, were not
regarded as seemly or practical and were certainly a
threat to the Tory inner circle. By including
Churchill they had stifled this threat.

Young Eldon Gorst, caught at the edge of this
minor political tornado, was blown about a bit and he
did not enjoy it. With a touch of self-pity he later
observed:

> The rather extravagant hopes I built on my
> new position were soon shattered . . . . Sir
> Michael Hicks-Beach [a trusted Tory war-
> horse] became chairman in place of Lord
> Randolph, and as I had nothing in particular

in view I continued to work for the
National Union . . . growing more and
more discontented, as I had perceived
that I had no chance of getting paid for
my work or of its leading to anything
better in the immediate future. I wrote
many useful and popular pamphlets for the
Party but I began to see clearly how right
my father had been when he had warned me
of the ingratitude and fickleness of party
chiefs. [29]

He remained at the National Union for the first three
months of 1885; meanwhile he looked for other more
fruitful opportunities for a career.

Whether it was insufficient influence, his
father's difficult personality, the vagaries of politics, or plain bad luck that thwarted the impatient
young Gorst's political ambitions in 1884-1885, he
nevertheless had the necessary wealth, influence, and
social standing to obtain a nomination to that bastion
of the Victorian establishment, the Diplomatic Service.
His sponsor was Sir Edmond Fitzmaurice, under secretary of state in the Foreign Office.

The Foreign Office and the Diplomatic Service had
reluctantly responded to informed public and political
pressure to open the selection of diplomats to people with
more concrete qualifications than sufficient wealth and membership in the English aristocracy. Competitive examinations for the Foreign Office were instituted in the
1850s. In 1880 a scheme of "limited" competition for
the Diplomatic Service was established by Lord Granville.
To enter either competition, the candidate had to secure the nomination of the foreign secretary, and men
from families unknown to that official or to his private secretary did not apply. It was "the weight carried by the position and interest of parents and spon-
sors, rather than the qualities of the candidates
themselves, which decided the chance of a nomination."
Furthermore, the nominee for the Diplomatic Service
had to be between the ages of eighteen and twenty-four
and have a private income. The examination involved
subjects such as Latin which only would have been
encountered at one of the public schools and a level
of accomplishment in French and German that normally
had to be obtained through a period of drill and residence in those countries. This combined system of

nomination and examination contrived to reserve the
Foreign Office and the Diplomatic Service to a limited
"caste" in Britain: the aristocracy, gentry, and some
few, like Gorst, from the professional middle class
who had   gone through the necessary rite of passage
at a great public school, usually Eton and sometimes
one of the ancient universities. Zara Steiner, in her
study of the Foreign Office during the period when
Gorst served there, concluded: "Few men who did not
conform to the generally accepted pattern applied and
fewer still slipped through the net."[30]

Just after Gorst made his decision to compete for
a place in the Diplomatic Service, Lord Randolph
Churchill asked him to be one of his private secretaries. In retrospect Gorst tartly observed: "He
doubtless felt himself in a certain degree responsible
for the unsatisfactory position in which I found myself at the National Union and thought in this way to
make amends." He now had a "wholesome distrust of
politics as a profession. Moreover, Lord R[andolph]'s
past career was not such as to encourage the idea
that he had in him the capacity for solid success; he
was, therefore, not a safe man to attach oneself to."[31]
Not wanting to offend Churchill by refusing his offer
outright, he offered to work without pay while preparing for the Diplomatic Service examinations. Lord
Randolph accepted. Gorst left the National Union in
April and went to work mornings at Churchill's London
house. The rest of the day he spent preparing for
the examinations.

Eldon Gorst's sense of discretion and timing was
excellent. Early the next month the Liberal government fell. The public was not aware that the elder
Gorst and Lord Randolph had fallen out over Churchill's
compromise with the Tory leaders the year before; had
John Gorst been left out of office, Lord Randolph
might have been blamed for deserting an influential
supporter. As a result Eldon Gorst found himself acting as an intermediary between his father and the Tory
inner circle, which now included his employer,
Churchill. John Gorst hoped to be given an important
legal post in the new government. His son observed:
"Lord Salisbury wished to buy him off with the Judge-
Advocate-Generalship, but he stuck out for being one
of the Law Officers of the crown, and after many ups
and downs succeeded finally in getting appointed
Solicitor General."[32]

Meanwhile, Lord Randolph was appointed secretary of state for India; the younger Gorst accompanied him at a salary of one hundred fifty pounds per year.   All this was excellent experience for a potential diplomat. Furthermore the National Union had voted him fifty pounds when he resigned, and in July he received fifty pounds more for a "legal mission" to Naples on behalf of a Prince Ibrahim, one of the sons of the deported khedive of Egypt, Ismail.   At twenty-four, Eldon Gorst had made a real start at earning his own living. Meanwhile he continued that summer and fall to prepare for the Diplomatic Service examinations.   With characteristic aplomb, he reported: "I was successful and came out an Easy first."[33]

At the end of October 1885 he was attached without pay, pending his overseas assignment, to the Eastern Department of the Foreign Office, where most honorary clerks were sent.   "Eastern" dealt with the political affairs of the Balkans, Russia, Turkey, Persia, Abyssinia, Somaliland, and Central Asia, and was headed by the "last great superclerk," Sir Thomas Sanderson.   A tall, slim man with pipestem legs, who wore thick glasses, his nickname was "Lamps."   His department was reputedly the most aristocratic in the Foreign Office; proper dress consisted of bowler, stiff collar, and morning suit.[34]   Other able and ambitious men found Sanderson's regimen constricting, but Gorst seems not to have chafed.   While learning the office routines, he found time to pass an examination in international law that qualified him for an allowance of one hundred pounds per year when he became third secretary.[35]

Eldon had watched John Gorst's political fortunes wax and wane in the aftermath of the breakup of the Liberal Party over Home Rule.   When the Tories, now gingerly allied to Chamberlain's Liberal Unionists, were returned to office in July 1886, the elder Gorst expected to be reappointed solicitor general, but his unpopularity with the Tory leadership—especially with Randolph Churchill—almost left him without a post. According to Eldon, only with great difficulty did he manage to obtain a lesser office: under secretary of state for India.[36]   For a period in 1886 there was talk of sending John Gorst to South Africa as governor-general of the Cape.   Had this happened, his son willingly would have gone with him as private secretary.

In his personal life, Eldon had revived a friendship in 1885 with the young German woman, R. W., whom
he had met a few years earlier. In London to pursue
a career as a concert pianist, she found herself
courted by young Gorst, who wanted to marry her. His
recollection of this episode is fatalistic:

> I have rarely met anybody with more genius,
> but her nature was too sensitive to go
> through the rough and tumble which must in
> this life preclude success. Her musical
> talents, the one art which has the power of
> taking me out of myself, her charming and
> sympathetic though essentially weak nature,
> exercised a powerful effect on my daily life
> during this year and the one following. . . .
> Had I at this time been in an independent
> position, there is no doubt that I should
> have married her, and I may add . . . I should
> have made a fatal mistake and regretted it all
> my life. Happily fate, often wiser than our-
> selves, ordered otherwise. Love's young
> dream—after passing through the burning noon-
> tide—faded away into the afterglow of pleas-
> ant memories, which, at all events as far as
> I am concerned, have no trace of bitterness
> in them.[37]

While the affair lasted in 1886, he made other efforts
to find a position with sufficient pay to support a
wife. He tried to join a new legal department in the
Foreign Office; then when the Conservatives returned
to office, he sought to become private secretary to
Lord Cross, the new secretary of state for India.
Happily for him none of these worked out.

The interest in R. W. was ephemeral, a pleasant
distraction. The year 1885-1886 was a crucial turning
point for Eldon Gorst. Not only had he begun to earn
his living, but after a false start in politics he had
found a career in diplomacy that was to lead almost
immediately into imperial administration in Egypt.
Though he obviously regretted that he could not capitalize significantly on John Gorst's erratic political
fortunes, he determinedly set out on his own. A few
years later he observed:

On looking back I am inclined to consider

the year 1885 as one of great importance
for my future prospects. After having
hesitated between various openings during
the past year or two, I definitely made
up my mind what I wanted to do and had
succeeded in going through all the steps
necessary to embark on the career I had
chosen. I had taken up an independent
line of my own and had decided to fight
my own battle and not to avoid the contest
by clinging to other people's coat-tails.
I have never regretted this decision since.[38]

From the time he entered the Diplomatic Service
as an honorary clerk in the Foreign Office, he sought
to persuade his superiors to assign him to the British
Consulate-General in Cairo where the stern, self-
righteous Sir Evelyn Baring, later the Earl of Cromer,
was shaping an unofficial imperial regime. Egypt in
the 1880s, when Cromer was establishing his proconsulship, held unusual opportunities for responsibility
and advancement for a few ambitious and talented young
English gentlemen. Gorst's friend from Eton, Vaux of
Harrowdon, was serving under Cromer and encouraged
Eldon to seek this choice post. The balmy climate,
relative proximity to England, and allowances for
housing and proficiency in Arabic of one hundred pounds
each, were additional attractions. Money was a strong
inducement to Gorst.[39]

In the autumn of 1886 the posting to Cairo was
made. He left England for Egypt in November. From
that moment his career was to focus on Anglo-Egyptian
affairs.

Chapter Two

AMBITIONS AND ASPIRATIONS

Gorst arrived in Egypt at a crucial period.   The
British had reluctantly invaded Egypt in 1882 in support of the collapsing Muhammad Ali dynasty, mainly to
protect their imperial lifeline through the Suez Canal
to India and the Far East.   Sir Evelyn Baring was dispatched by the British Cabinet as Agent and Consul-
General, supported by enough troops and the British
Navy to cow the populace,with the mission to try to
rectify Egyptian finances and stabilize the government so that the British could withdraw.   By 1886 the
pattern of control had not yet stabilized.

     Lord Cromer, as Baring was to become, came to
Egypt from a career as an army staff officer and imperial administrator in the Middle East and India.   A
member of an influential British banking family with
international connections, Cromer—with his autocratic
temperament, financial skills, pragmatic bent, and
experience in the empire—was well fitted to assume
direction of British imperial policy in Egypt.   He had
been a member of the Anglo-French Dual Control created
in 1876 by the powers concerned to administer the
finances of the bankrupt Egyptian state in the last
years of Khedive Ismail's reign, and thus was well
acquainted with the tangled finances and complex administration of the heirs of Muhammad Ali.   He became
one of the renowned proconsuls of the British Empire,
ruling Egypt indirectly for twenty-four years.

     Cromer's accomplishments for British rule in the
face of continuous frustrating restrictions on his
freedom of action cannot be deprecated.   The British
position in Egypt was anomalous: their occupation had
no legal foundation other than right of conquest.   Its
authority depended on the presence of the British army
and the willingness of the British to use force as a
last resort.   Juridically Egypt was a part of the

decaying Ottoman Empire, a situation which the British,
for reasons of policy and convenience, did not choose
to deny or change. Since the sixteenth century the
Ottomans had negotiated a series of treaties, known as
the Capitulations, granting certain privileges to foreign powers on Ottoman territory. Britain nominally
upheld Ottoman sovereignty until late 1914 when it uni-
laterally declared Egypt a British protectorate.

The British at first were determined only to
reform the administration of Egypt so that it would be
sympathetic and responsive to British interests; they
would then evacuate their occupation troops. Lord
Lloyd, one of Cromer's successors, clearly delineated
British policy: "to set up a Government working upon
honest and humane principles, and to withdraw from the
country as soon as we had made such a Government stable
and progressive, and therefore free from the danger of
foreign intervention which would menace our imperial
communications."[1] This policy proved impossible to
implement. Cromer and the British officials were
caught in the center of opposing forces and purposes.
They had to deal at first with a government in Britain
that was unable to make up its mind about whether to
withdraw or remain in Egypt. The balance of power in
Europe could have been disturbed dangerously—and at
times was—when two or three of the European powers
chose to meddle intensively in Egyptian affairs.[2]
Egypt's state of bankruptcy in 1882 meant that only
the most necessary reforms could be financed. "We had
to do the thing on the cheap," wrote Cromer.[3] Egypt's
southern borders were at that time threatened by the
revolt of the Mahdi in the Sudan. In Cromer's judgment, there were no Egyptians and few Englishmen capable of running the country.[4]

The Capitulations, originally granted as concessions of convenience forming part of a bargain between
the then powerful Ottoman Empire and various European
powers, had become an onerous restriction on the sovereign power of Egypt. Foreign residents of Egypt who
were covered by the capitulatory treaties had effective
immunity from Egyptian civil and commercial law. The
establishment of a special and privileged set of courts,
called the Mixed Tribunals, had been negotiated with
the Egyptian government by the Capitulatory Powers in
1876, six years before the British occupation of
Egypt.[5] Civil and commercial suits of all kinds, if
they involved a foreigner in Egypt, were tried before

these Mixed Tribunals, whose majority of judges were foreigners chosen by the Capitulatory Powers, and who could
not apply any new legislation of the Egyptian government without their consent.   The process of obtaining
agreement to any changes was tedious and confounded
by the necessity of trying to please all the Powers
concerned.

Furthermore, any accused who was a citizen of one
of the Capitulatory Powers could claim the right to be
tried under his own country's criminal laws by his
consular court.   Many criminals and their illicit bus-
inesses in Egypt sheltered behind their particular
consular courts and national laws.   The privilege of
inviolability of domicile for a citizen of one of the
Capitulatory Powers further complicated the Egyptian
government's task of controlling these illegal activities.   Perhaps the most important of the exemptions
granted to the foreign communities in Egypt under the
Capitulations was that no direct tax except that on
land could be levied on them by the Egyptian government without the consent of the Powers.   It meant that
the Egyptian government, under Cromer's veiled protectorate, dared not offend the masses of Egyptians by
imposing on them a tax that would not apply under the
Capitulations to many of the visibly wealthy sections
of the population.[6]

The Capitulations severely restricted Cromer's
freedom of action and policy.   To add to his problems,
the old "Turco-Circassian" ruling class hated the
British for usurping their control of a nation they
regarded as a lucrative private estate.[7]   In 1886
Cromer and a small group of British officials were
still attempting to work with the few malleable members
of this ruling class.   These men, largely descendants
of the various invaders who had dominated Egypt since
the Middle Ages, were allowed to administer Egypt as
long as their policies did not threaten British or
European interests.

Cromer's influence and prestige, later so seemingly overwhelming, were in the process of development
in the late 1880s.   By the time Gorst arrived, Cromer
would not much longer tolerate an independent line from the
Egyptians.   During these years he recruited a number
of able, young gentlemen such as Edgar Vincent, Alfred
Milner, and Gorst, gave them immediate responsibility,
and rewarded them with ample pay and lengthy leaves

when they performed well. The meteoric career of
Edgar Vincent (later Viscount D'Abernon) was the most
striking model for Eldon Gorst. He was appointed by
Cromer in 1883 as financial advisor to the Egyptian
government when only twenty-six. Vincent's British
political and social connections and his financial and
political skills, combined with the unimaginative
steadiness of Cromer—then at the height of his manage-
rial powers—reduced the chaos of Egyptian public finance. By 1886 Vincent was, after Cromer, the most
influential foreign official in Egypt.

Gorst arrived in the midst of what Alfred Milner
was to label the "race against bankruptcy."[8] The
British, under Cromer, had been working since 1882 to
establish the financial stability of the Egyptian government in the eyes of the major European powers and
private investors who had speculated in Egypt in the
profligate years before 1876. He was able to rise
swiftly by assisting Cromer, Vincent, and some other
officials to untangle and stabilize Egyptian finances;
in the process he contributed to the increasing European dominance of the Egyptian government. Vincent
subsequently resigned in 1889 to pursue a wide-ranging
career in international banking, finance, and diplomacy. After much struggle Gorst eventually became the
financial advisor in 1898. His success in that office
made him the most likely candidate to succeed Cromer.

The press of business meant there was ample opportunity for an ambitious, hardworking, well-educated,
relatively well connected young Englishman with an
ability in finance. Eldon Gorst knew something about
the Empire; when he arrived he seems to have known
little about Egypt. But he was a quick learner,
determined to make his own way as rapidly as possible.
He had had a taste of politics through his father and
Lord Randolph Churchill. His comparative youth—
twenty-five—might have been a barrier to swift advancement in England; it was not in Egypt.

Gorst spent the entire year of 1887 in Cairo
learning about Egypt, his new position, and most important, his superior, Lord Cromer. He reported later:
"The main feature of the year was my going to Cairo,
where after a comparatively short time, I was able to
get out of the ruck into a front place."[9] He got out
of the ruck by gaining Cromer's confidence as a man
with a talent for financial management. Though Gorst

had disparaged his education at Eton and Cambridge, the habits and skills he had developed stood him well, particularly the ability to concentrate his energies and master complex material. Cromer was impressed with his performance and allowed him a "prominent part" in the preparation of the *Annual Report of 1887 on Egyptian Finance*. Of Cromer's attention and encouragement during these first months in a strange and foreign city, he later wrote gratefully:

> He was the best chief I have ever served, and it is greatly to the interest and guidance which he bestowed upon me in the early days when I worked under him that I attribute whatever success I may have subsequently obtained in Egypt. He is one of the very few men to whom I consider that I really owe something, and he has without doubt aided me in my career far more than any other man.[10]

Gorst did not focus only on the tortuous complexities of Egyptian finance. He spent some of his leisure time acquiring "a sound knowledge of Arabic" and passed a proficiency examination in 1887 that entitled him to an allowance of one hundred pounds per year. He began to explore the Nile Valley. In January 1888 he made his first official visit up the Nile as far as the First Cataract with Colonel Schaefer, head of the Slave Trade Department and the secret police.[11] He was particularly pleased that by the end of his first year abroad he had no debts; until then he had been dependent for his entire livelihood on his family. In Cairo a house allowance of one hundred pounds plus the one-hundred-pound allowance each for Arabic and international law carried him until October 1887, when he was promoted to third secretary in the Diplomatic Service at a salary of two hundred fifty pounds per year. These were significant accomplishments.

When Gorst arrived, Egypt was fast becoming a mecca for wealthy winter sunseekers from the chillier northern Europe and even from the United States. Only a few years later Alfred Milner wrote to a friend: "Visitors are beginning to drop in, and in a month Cairo will be like Picadilly on a June afternoon. . . . It is a lovely climate. If only the inhabitants were English, and not Arabs, it would be earthly paradise."[12] The stability and security for Europeans brought about by the British occupation and administration

had enhanced the attractions of sun-drenched Egypt.
Thomas Cook's was busily organizing tours up the Nile,
and Cairo was in the middle of a substantial building
boom.   A European-style city now was taking shape and
stretching west to the Nile on the fringe of the teem-
ing maze that constituted late medieval Cairo, tucked
under the Muqattam Hills. Taller, more tightly spaced
buildings of a mixed architectural style and function
were replacing or supplementing the villas, small
apartment houses, and gardens built in the previous
decade or two.[13]   In *Baedeker's Guide* to Egypt for 1885
the European visitor was told: "Donkeys afford the
best and most rapid mode of locomotion in the narrow
and crowded streets of Cairo. . . . Donkey boys are
lively and humour-filled especially when well paid.
. . . Europeans will be astonished at the smallness of
their requirements and those of their beasts."[14]

        Cairo, especially the European sector, was soon
to outgrow these donkeys and their boys and replace
them with trams and horse-drawn cabs. The British
Agency (Cromer's headquarters) was located next to the
northwest corner of the Azbakiyah Gardens in a sector
of the city undergoing rapid commercial development.
The press of business and entertainment at the Agency
was increasing every year. Cromer, early in 1887,
appealed to the prime minister, Lord Salisbury, for
funds to build a new consulate and residence, as
befitted the growing British imperial presence. The
rush of visitors and the European social life, he told
Salisbury, called

        . . . for fairly suitable reception rooms.
        I doubt whether at any other diplomatic post
        so much entertaining is thrown on the Brit-
        ish representative as at Cairo. . ..there can-
        not be much under 1000 residents on my visit-
        ing lists, besides the swarms of visitors who
        now come out during the winter, all armed with
        semi-official or private introductions to me.[15]

Cromer strongly urged the British government to support the construction of a new and larger residence,
and in the early 1890s a new and more commodious
Agency was built on the banks of the Nile in the Garden City, the Qasr al Dubarah district.

        Eldon Gorst's initial welcome from the official
British community was cool. Vaux had overpraised him,

and Cromer did not highly value Vaux's judgment. The former connection of John Gorst with Sir Henry Drummond Wolff through the moribund Fourth Party also worked against him. The British Cabinet had sent Wolff as High Commissioner to Istanbul and then to Cairo in hopes that he could find a means of settling the Egyptian situation so that the British might be relieved of their troublesome occupation; but the mission had floundered on international jealousy, Cromer's opposition, and conflicting interests among the European powers. Wolff and his Ottoman opposite number, Ghazi Mukhtar, were suspected of possible intrigue against Cromer, and Wolff had been recalled a day or two before Eldon Gorst arrived. Gorst asserted that Wolff and Lord Randolph Churchill, then Chancellor of the Exchequer, had been maneuvering to replace Cromer with Wolff. For Eldon Gorst, neither the overpraise nor this intrigue was a helpful introduction to Cairo.

In the mid-1880s the official British community was quite small and close-knit. The staff consisted of Cromer, the consul-general; Portal, the first secretary; Clarke, Vaux, and Gorst on the diplomatic side; Boyle, the Oriental secretary (the interpreter and intelligence agent); and MacDonald, the military attaché. Lady Baring and her two boys were also included in the official household. Gorst wrote that the Cromers were "the most hospitable of people and expect the whole staff to lunch with them every day, besides inviting them constantly for dinner."[16]

Gorst took advantage of Wolff's departure to move into his large house, where several members of the British official community lived with their families. He managed to overcome the "bad press" he had received before arrival by his diligence at work. Any guilt by association through the familial connections to Randolph Churchill and Wolff was quickly dissipated by Lord Randolph's sudden and disastrous resignation as Chancellor of the Exchequer at the end of 1886—a foolish act which confirmed Gorst's earlier estimate of Lord Randolph as an essentially unstable personality. A few years later Gorst observed caustically: "This was an irreparable mistake from which his reputation never recovered. He went slowly downhill, physically and morally, and died in 1895 of drink and disappointment."[17]

Despite hard work it took a few years of seasoning before Gorst won the rapid promotion and higher

pay he sought. There were some opportunities along
the way, but luckily for him none materialized. In
1888 Cromer nominated him warmly to the new Indian
Viceroy, Lord Lansdowne, as a private secretary and
Sir John Gorst wrote to thank Cromer for the support
and encouragement given his eldest son.

> Nothing could have given stronger proof of
> the good opinion you have formed of my son,
> and I thank you most heartily for trying to
> secure for him so advantageous an opening in
> public life. You know how eagerly such a post
> is sought for and how many influences will
> be brought to bear on Lord Lansdowne in
> favor of various candidates and you will
> therefore not allow Jack to be too sanguine
> of success.[18]

Lansdowne decided that Eldon Gorst was too young for
the job. The next year, 1889, a post opened up in the
Egyptian ministry of finance, but it was soon abolished. When Edgar Vincent resigned as financial advisor later that year, the director general of accounts,
Sir Elwin Palmer, succeeded him, but Gorst's hopes to
be appointed to Palmer's vacated post were dashed when
the equally ambitious Alfred Milner was brought out
from England. Subsequently Cromer told Gorst he might
appoint him one of the commissioners of the Caisse de la
Dette Publique, the international agency designated by the
European powers to oversee Egyptian finances. The commissioners were supposed to supervise the use of the
Egyptian budget surplus, but they generally acted as
puppets for their respective European governments and
had increasingly little to do as Cromer solidified
British influence in Egypt and his own prestige in
England. The ambitious young Gorst realized that such
a sinecure, though very well paid, was undesirable for
his purposes.

The saying goes that all work and no play make
Jack a dull boy. Though he worked hard and kept his
eye on the main chance, Gorst did not neglect the
emotional and social side of his life. By the time he
arrived in Cairo late in 1886 his hopes for marriage
to the German "R. W." had faded, though his feelings
had not. He assuaged his regrets by developing new
friends in the cosmopolitan, wealthy, upper-class circles of Cairo and Alexandria. Unlike many of his
British contemporaries, he did not confine his social

activities to the growing British community.

Alfred Milner, who arrived in Cairo in 1889 to
join Cromer's small imperial elite, described the
British social life of that era. Work in the Agency
or the Egyptian ministries lasted no later than one
o'clock and afternoons were usually free. Friday was a day
of rest in this largely Muslim city, and the British
worked rather casually on Sunday. To a friend, Edith
Gell, he reported: "the gay world devotes themselves
to matches and race meetings." It was a "cardinal
offense" socially to choose, as did Gorst and Milner,
to cram Arabic rather than to involve themselves every
day in the whirl of the Cairo winter season. The
neurotic intensity of British social life in Cairo
which sought to ape the London Season drew Milner's
caustic comment:

> Indeed, rush is as I look upon it the charac-
> teristic of [the] English most deeply stamped
> upon my memory. It is its one great drawback.
>
> Now why is it? For it is a remarkable fact
> that even the English colony can't reproduce
> it here—though they may do their best, the
> idiots, with their endless social functions
> and tremendous demands of etiquette. But
> there must be something in this ancient land,
> which defeats their endeavor. You can't make
> Egyptian life into a rush of the English type,
> however you try.[19]

Many men, reported Milner, were doing excellent work,
"and the female society too is, I fancy, far above the
ordinary colonial or Indian station type, though it is
this side that the narrowness of one's world becomes
most noticeable. With *foreigners* one practically
doesn't mix." This exclusion of foreigners—which
meant both the wealthy upper-class minorities and the
foreign residents—was to him a "lost opportunity" and
a great political mistake, one that he hoped to rectify when he had acquired sufficient influence in
Egypt.[20] The Egyptians themselves went unmentioned.

Some members of the minority communities in
Egypt, especially the Jews and the Greeks, prospered
mightily under the security of British occupation.
And they created a cosmopolitan social milieu. Gorst
became a friend of Ambroise Sinadino, the Rothschilds'

agent in Egypt, who introduced him to "theatrical and
terpsichorean circles which helped enlarge the sphere
of my experience." By 1890 he had also become a
friend of one of the more unusual members of the
khedivial family, Princess Nazli Fazil. Unlike the
majority of her sex and status, she cultivated the
friendship of the British and maintained a colorful
political and social salon in a large palace immediately behind the khedive's Cairo residence, the Abdin
Palace, complete with family slaves and eunuchs. In
the early 1890s she encouraged Saad Zaghlul—a young
student from the Azhar, the ancient Muslim university—
to learn French, made him her lawyer, gave him part of
her Egyptian government pension, and helped to start
him on his career.[21] Zaghlul was to become the most
famous and influential Egyptian nationalist politician
in the early twentieth century. Gorst recognized his
talents and kept him neutralized.

When he was first establishing himself in Cairo
society, Gorst received a letter from R. W. that
severely distressed him, and he took refuge in work
and in new friends.[22] He mentioned a number of women
whom he met in those early years, but after R. W. none
were apparently of special importance until January 1889.
His autobiographical notes for that year end with the following:

> It was in January of this year that I first
> made the acquaintance of J. S., a woman who
> exercised a great influence over my life
> for the next two years and who undoubtedly
> contributed very largely to the formation
> of my character and general views of life
> during that period. Some years older than
> myself, she possessed great intelligence
> coupled with an extraordinary variety of
> knowledge and a force of character unusual
> in one of her sex. All these qualities
> made her in those days a most delightful
> and instructive companion. At the same
> time my intimacy with her completely cured
> me of my natural disposition which might
> have interfered with my future success:—
> viz. a certain want of confidence in my own
> powers and a consequent tendency not to aim
> high enough, and secondly a too humble appre-
> ciation of the position I had a right to oc-
> cupy among my fellow men. Since those days
> these are the last failings with which I

could be reproached and few would believe
that they had ever existed.[23]

Who was this J. S. who drew this remarkable trib-
ute from Eldon Gorst? She was Lady Jessica Christina
Sykes, or more informally, Jessica Sykes, a descendant
of one of the great Anglo-Irish aristocratic clans.
Her full name was Christina Anne Jessica Cavendish-
Bentinck Sykes. Since 1874 she had been the wife of
Sir Tatton Sykes, Bt., one of the great landowners of
Yorkshire. They had one son, Mark, the amateur diplo-
mat who would negotiate with France in 1916 the secret
Sykes-Picot agreement designed to dispose of the Otto-
man Empire's Arab domains after the 1914-1918 war.
Mark married Gorst's sister Edith in 1903.

Jessica Sykes was married at eighteen to Sir
Tatton, thirty years her senior, as the result of a
plot worked out by her domineering mother. A photo-
graph taken shortly after her marriage shows a young
woman of soft, pleasant features and a large firm jaw.
There are indications of strong character and determination in her posture and expression. In her prime
she was a striking woman, with dark hair and eyes and
a manner that her son's biographer, Professor Roger
Adelson, characterized as "rather overbearing." Mark
Sykes described his mother as "Napoleonic." She had
exceptional talents, including a facility for drawing
and languages, was very self-centered, and had the
character, money, and social standing to indulge her
interests and passions. Adelson characterized her
thus: "Her robust laughter and angry outbursts would
probably have been overlooked had she been a man,
but few men knew how to cope with such behaviour in
women, and to most she appeared imperious."[24]

Jessica's marriage was miserable and mutually
destructive. Quite early she and Tatton had established independent lives—except for money. They
shared few interests other than a passion for travel
and religious architecture. He rented a flat for her
on Portland Place where she cultivated a fuller life
than the one possible at her husband's estate at
Sledmere. Appearances were kept for a while; but
as her aging husband turned meaner and more reclusive,
Jessica became much more indiscreet—even careless—
socially and financially. In the late 1880s she persuaded Tatton to lease for her 46 Grosvenor Street, a
very grand townhouse in the heart of Mayfair. There

she entertained widely and lavishly and began to run
up large debts. She later dabbled in journalism and
wrote a set of revealing if unmemorable novels. She
also had extensive charitable interests in London and
Yorkshire. Disliked by her mother, a Victorian
battle-ax whose nickname was "Britannia," Jessica had
been close to her father. With him she had talked horses,
travel, and politics, and imbibed "a strong taste for
the old political order."[25]

     When Jessica Sykes met Gorst in Egypt in January
1889 she was thirty-two and he was twenty-seven.
Gorst did not leave any detailed chronicle of their
first encounter; his surviving diaries began in 1890.
The Sykeses spent that winter in Cairo, and Jessica
spent most of her time with Eldon. Cromer, in the
course of a review of Egyptian news with the departed
Edgar Vincent, observed: "As to Egypt generally, there
never was a time when we had less occasion to fear a
debate [in the House of Commons]. . . . Twinkle [Clarke,
the second secretary at the Agency] is growing steadily but surely fatter, and Gorst, when not occupied
with Lady Sykes' horse, continues to make pungent remarks on the whole human race."[26]

     Gorst's 1890 diary showed an intense round of
social events and activities with "J," "Lady S.," or
"J.S." Constantly in his company, particularly when
Tatton left for a journey up the Nile, she stayed on
in Egypt that spring without her husband. In his
diary Gorst recorded their many encounters and apparently kept track of the number of times they made love,
with a series of the marks "x" and "o." These entries
appeared regularly in association with Jessica, and
the next year with her and other women. At the end of
his diaries for 1890 and 1891 he totaled the scores:
in 1890 the sums were "x = 132, o = 18"; in 1891 the
totals were "x = 96, o = 21."[27]

     Eldon Gorst's absorption with Jessica and his
work was not diverted by the major social event of the
1890 Cairo "Season," the visit of Prince Albert Victor,
the Duke of Clarence, in April. Sir Philip Magnus
gently described "Prince Eddy" as a man "who possessed
attraction for women although he was mentally imma-
ture."[28] This unfortunate royal prince, who Milner
thought was "not quite an idiot," created a major stir
in the British social circles of Cairo.

> A scramble among the females for invites
> [*sic*] and places at dinners [to which] only
> Thackeray could do full justice. . . . at
> one race meeting one very pretty young
> woman, who has my fullest sympathy, for she
> is not one of the scrambling official pack,
> though a rare little flirt in other ways,
> completely collared the young man and marched
> him up and down in front of the grand stand
> where all the beauty and fashion sat glaring
> at her in dumb foundered jealousy, deepening
> to murderous hatred. A little beforehand
> you could have said that the stand was full
> of all sorts of bright colours, but when
> this performance had lasted a little while
> they all disappeared, and a universal shade
> of green eclipsed all cheerful tints.[29]

Gorst was more concerned with the impending departure of Jessica Sykes on April 12 than with the
visit of "Collars and Cuffs," as the prince was nicknamed. For him the most important event of the week
following her departure was a telegram from her from
Marseilles which said "success." This, he wrote, "took
a weight off my mind."[30] What that weight was remains
a mystery. He spent the rest of that spring working
productively, maneuvering for more income and a higher
post. When Sir Tatton Sykes returned from Syria, he
entertained him and made his travel arrangements.
Gorst left on his summer holidays toward the end of
June, and "J" met him on his arrival in London. Most
of his ten-week holiday was spent in Jessica's company.

It was a profitable period, financially and emotionally, for Eldon Gorst. His accounts were carefully kept at the end of each of his surviving diaries.
They show that while in the company of Jessica Sykes
he won over three hundred eighty pounds, mainly bet-
ting on the horses. During one interval at Goodwood
with her, he netted two hundred thirteen pounds, paid
one hundred to her, and noted that she still owed him
one hundred fifteen. In mid-August his diary shows:
"My present for Lady S.—a bracelet—arrived. Very
pretty diamonds and sapphires."[31] In September this
busy, seemingly blissful summer holiday came to an
abrupt end when Cromer informed Gorst that they would
have to leave immediately on a diplomatic mission to
Italy. It was, Gorst noted in his diary, "a dreadful

blow."[32] He assuaged his disappointment by another
profitable stay with the Sykeses, and won eighty-three
pounds at Doncaster. Lady Sykes accompanied him as
far as Paris on his trip out to Italy and Egypt.

     The diplomatic mission to Italy was unproductive.
Gorst toured parts of Italy, then returned to his
normal duties in Egypt. Jessica Sykes was not mentioned until November, when he met her with her husband in the
canal zone on a voyage going east of Suez. There is
no further mention of her until December, when she
wrote to inform him that she might not come to Egypt
the next winter. Other than the notation "Heard from
J." at odd intervals, his diaries reveal nothing more
about their affair. Gorst kept himself busy at his
new job in the finance ministry and at the hectic social
rounds of the 1891 Cairo Season. In February Jessica
telegraphed she was not coming to Egypt and his last
entry that day was, "Felt sad and melancholy." The
next day she had changed her mind (and, one hopes, Gorst's)
and arrived with her husband on March 24. Eldon and
Jessica kept constant company for the next month. However, when the Sykeses left on April 7 his diary
ceases to mention her. Late in July he closed the
day's entry with: "Heard from J & decided that our
liaison had better come to an end. Wrote acc'y."[33]

     From the surviving notes and diaries it is not
possible to determine whether this was the end of
Gorst's intimacy with Jessica Sykes. Nor is it possible to determine exactly why. As late as 1894, when
he had begun another significant love affair, from the
diary entries she appeared to be his companion again
for an interval, and he apparently loaned her a hundred
pounds in 1897.[34] What is clear is that Gorst, in his
late twenties and in the company of Jessica Sykes,
matured personally and professionally. Her companionship and support enabled him to shake off his self-
doubt and emerge as an independent individual.

     Of special importance was her help in his attain-
ment of financial independence. Again, explicit
details of her assistance are not clear, but his carefully kept accounts show the results. In 1891 they
had speculated in mining shares on the stock market
together. Until he went to Cairo he had been entirely
dependent on his family, especially his uncle Edward
Craddock Lowndes; by 1890 he had, by hard work and the
assistance of Lady Sykes, an annual income of fifteen

hundred pounds, and after that year he never received
further financial assistance from his uncle or family.

Jessica Sykes was an unique person and Eldon
Gorst appreciated her immensely. She appeared to have
a weakness for weak men,[35] but this time she chose a
strong personality. She hated the double standard of
behavior, so powerful in that era, and she often was
heard to say that if she had any vices they were only
those of a man. She liked to hear and to tell amusing
stories. When angry she could unleash a string of
almost Shakespearian invective. She never talked down
to anyone. People were important not for who they
were, but for what they did. Snobbery was stupid and
silly to her. All these admirable qualities affected
and shaped Eldon Gorst profoundly.

What is sad is that a woman of such talent, qualities, and independence could not control her self-
destructive tendencies. Her drinking and her promiscuity—one or both—appear to have caused Gorst, very
regretfully, to end their intimacy. That the affair
was important to her is indicated by the subsequent dramatic
increase in her profligate behavior. Professor
Adelson observed: "Her absence from the tours taken
by Tatton and Mark started with an affair she had in
the early 1890s [with Gorst]. When that came to an
end, Jessica's drinking seems to have become worse
and her promiscuity flagrant." Gossip transposed her
name from Lady (Tatton) Sykes to "Lady Satin Tights."
To her credit, she laughed at this. Understandably,
her son and Eldon Gorst never could. In the 1890s her
maid had to throw away her perfume for fear she might
drink it, and hide her stays to prevent Jessica from
getting dressed and going out to disgrace herself
haunting the bookmakers' shops in London's Henrietta
Street. Towards the end of the nineties her financial
extravagance and carelessness resulted in a demeaning
series of lawsuits that involved her husband and son
and resulted in her public humiliation.[36]

In mitigation, her marriage had been a disaster
from the beginning. She had the misfortune to live in an
age when many of her qualities and talents were disturbing to her associates. Eldon Gorst, however, profoundly
appreciated her, and she must have cared deeply for
him in view of her subsequent behavior. When he reluctantly dropped her, she never forgave him. Gorst's
tribute to Jessica Sykes was deeply felt and grateful:

During this same period, under her example,
accompanied simultaneously by a gradual
improvement in my material circumstances,
I gradually shook off and freed myself from
those sordid pecuniary cares which had ham-
pered the earlier years of my life. From
this date, I may say that I have never
lacked the means of living in the manner I
desired. For these reasons I shall always
feel that I owe her a debt of gratitude and
that the advantages I derived at this time
from her society outweigh the feelings of
pain which her conduct has since caused to
all her real friends. Though the terrible
failing, which has been the cause of the
termination of our friendship, was supposed
by popular rumour to exist long before our
acquaintance began, I saw no signs of it in
the first two years. It has only been very
slowly & reluctantly that I have been forced
to admit that, at all events latterly, popular rumour has been right. When once this
conviction was brought home to my mind, I
could not do otherwise than bring to a close
a friendship which could be productive of
nothing but sorrow.[37]

His words were prophetic. About two decades later she
was to contribute significantly to his downfall.

Chapter Three

A START ON THE LADDER

Eldon Gorst's personal maturation coincided with official and public recognition of his administrative and
financial talents. His career began to take a defini-
tive shape and direction in the early 1890s. Gorst's
memoranda on Egyptian finance and trade were published
as part of the Egyptian annual report for 1890, introduced by Cromer with some "very eulogistic remarks."
This work attracted public approbation in London. *The
Times* in April 1890, Gorst noted, "wrote a very complimentary article on my work, and altogether it became a recognized fact that I had especial talents for
finance."[1] Earlier that winter Joseph Chamberlain had
visited Cairo and consulted with Cromer on Egyptian
and imperial affairs. Cromer gave him some of Gorst's
work and Chamberlain was impressed. He told Cromer
that "Gorst's review is clear and good, and he has
certainly not exaggerated the results."[2]

Recognition for Gorst happened to coincide with
a period of official concern and informed public
attention focused on Egyptian affairs. Cromer, having
managed by 1888 to stabilize Egyptian public finances,
at the turn of the decade was widening British influence and control over Egypt. Gorst and several others,
including Alfred Milner, were his agents. The process
involved a calculated campaign of public relations and
propaganda in Britain and a steady increase of British
influence and interference in the administration of
Egypt.

Lord Zetland, who wrote the authorized life of
Cromer in the 1930s, mentioned the latter's strong
opposition early in the occupation to any "unnecessary
advertisement of what the British were doing in Egypt,
since he [Cromer] held the view that the less attention they attracted in England the better were their
chances of making real progress."[3] In the 1890s,

however, Cromer was neither secretive nor inactive in
presenting his case for the British occupation, or in
discrediting or preventing the publication of criticisms of his rule and the British role in Egypt. Some
lip service was given to evacuation, but in the light
of the political realities it was a very remote possibility.[4] The benefits of British rule to the Egyptians and the extension of this rule to the Sudan were
sedulously promoted in England.[5]

     There is evidence that Alfred Milner was appointed
to the ministry of finance in Cairo in 1889 principally in order to write a book publicizing British
rule in Egypt. *England in Egypt* was published in 1892,
and its picture of "a beneficent England, operating at
her most effective in Egypt" had an immediate and positive strong response from the British reading public.[6] As early as 1884 Milner informed his friend and
confidant Phillip Gell that he was thinking of
"chucking" the *Pall Mall Gazette* to help the banker
C. J. Goschen write his "German book" for a couple of
hours a day. Then Milner hoped "to spend the rest of
the time to myself concocting a work on England in
Egypt." It would be entitled "Ten Years of Recent
History, 1875-1885."[7] About a year after he arrived
in Egypt, Milner wrote to his patron, Goschen—financier and panjandrum of the Unionist Party:

     I am afraid I should never make a very good
     party man, but I hope I make a fairly decent
     Englishman. As England is doing some of her
     best work in the Valley of the Nile, I am
     glad to be of the company. The more I see
     of it, the more proud and convinced I become
     of the great services rendered to humanity
     in these regions.[8]

Cromer was assiduous in seeing that this viewpoint was
heard in the "correct circles."

     In late 1889 Cromer had suggested to Reeves, edi-
tor of the *Edinburgh Review*, that Gorst write an article on Egypt. Entitled "England in Egypt," it was
published in January 1890. In the autumn of that
year—before Milner wrote his book—Gorst was appointed
secretly by *The Times* as its correspondent in Egypt.
Cromer had been carrying on a regular correspondence
with the paper's managing editor, C. F. Moberley Bell,
who had represented *The Times* in Cairo until he returned

to London to help pick up the pieces of the paper's
reputation after the disgraceful episode of Parnell
and the forger Piggot. Cromer and Bell were conspira-
tors for the good, as they saw it, of greater Britain.

In April, a month before Gorst initially sought
the appointment as a reporter, Cromer wrote a long
letter at Bell's request on "Why I read *The Times*" in
which he delineated his views on the role the responsible press should play and some of his political
prejudices. Its importance lay in Cromer's notion of
how the news should be managed. Ever practical, he
suggested that Bell might explore the possibility of
lowering the price of the paper from 3d. to 1d.; he
assumed the readers would remain the same—"in social
life the 'respectable classes' and in political life,
Whigs." The expansion of the vote and the appearance
of a cheap press may have lowered the power and influence of "The Thunderer" in the last quarter-century by
about twenty-five percent. Nevertheless, these "Whigs"
were defined by Cromer not as the party or faction of
the early part of that century, but as groups and individuals who unknowingly are "Whigs" because, he
wrote,

> they are not violent political partisans,
> not stupidly conservative or wildly radi-
> cal. . . . This is the class which, I con-
> ceive, *The Times* has always sought to rep-
> resent. It is, of course, much more diffi-
> cult to do so now than formerly—for now
> instead of English society being divided
> into Whigs and Tories, it is divided into
> the party of order and disorder. Hence
> *The Times* must adapt itself to circum-
> stances & become more a party than was
> formerly the case. [9]

However, Cromer was not optimistic about the state of
British politics at the end of the 1880s. The crux
of his letter to Bell was that its editorial stance
had been uncertain and the staff had listened to and
printed one-sided, unreliable opinions and reports.
Cromer advised Bell not always to trust the paper's
correspondents. Instead, it should seek out "responsible opinion" more consistently. He admonished:
"Don't mind being a bit dull—respectability is always
dull & *The Times* must be respectable." [10]

When Gorst proposed that he become *The Times*'s man
in Cairo in May 1890, Cromer lobbied the Foreign
Office and Bell in his support. In another letter to
Bell, marked "very private," he amplified his concern
that the news about Egypt in the respectable English
press, particularly *The Times*, be controlled and written by someone who was both responsible and reliable.
He told Bell: "It is from every point of view extremely
desirable that you should have a good man. But the
good man is very difficult to find—your own position
here was quite exceptional. I know of no other non-
official who would do." Both the situation and Gorst's
special talents and experience warranted overlooking
the disadvantages and objections of appointing a member of Cromer's diplomatic staff as the correspondent
in Egypt. Gorst's position in the Agency gave him the
advantage of access to the thinking of the senior
British officials. Gorst also wrote "very well"; as
evidence Cromer reminded Bell of Gorst's recent article on Egypt in the *Edinburgh Review*, which he had
inspired. He cited Gorst's political connections and
Egyptian experience as points in favor of the idea:
"Moreover besides knowing Egypt he has been a good
deal mixed up in English political life & English public opinion to a degree not always found in an official. Hence so far as his personal attitude is concerned I have no hesitation in recommending him to you
very strongly."[11]

However, the appointment, if made by *The Times*,
had to be kept secret. As the premier British official
in Egypt, Cromer could never condone such an act. "It
would be, officially speaking, quite too shocking for
me to do so. But could I not turn my head staunchly
in the opposite direction & know nothing about it! I
think if I tried hard & if I knew that the F.O. would
be prepared to adopt a similar course." They were,
and he did. Cromer went on to describe what Gorst's
position would be to Bell and to himself:

> Your relations with Gorst would be simply
> those of any other correspondent. My rela-
> tions would be that I would rely on him to
> make a discreet use of any information not
> available to the general public, & also I
> should expect him not to send anything which
> would be seriously embarrassing to me or the
> English Gov't.[12]

Otherwise Cromer did not intend to censor or even be
consulted on the articles or letters Gorst might write
"except perhaps on some great occasions when it might
be a question of the sort of line to suggest to *The
Times*." To preserve secrecy, Cromer proposed not to
tell the Agency staff and suggested that the paper's
current representative be kept on as a cover to send
the dispatches.[13] Two weeks later, at the end of May,
Cromer informed Bell that the Foreign Office would not
object to the scheme and that Gorst would do it for
five or six hundred pounds "including a dummy" (i.e.,
the present correspondent, Carey).[14]

Gorst completed the arrangements with Bell and
The Times in London that summer; all was settled early
in August. During the fall of 1890 the paper published at least five articles by Gorst, by-lined "Our
own correspondent," and a few letters as well.[15] This
mutually advantageous arrangement ended when Gorst was
promoted to a post in the Egyptian finance ministry. His
new duties, a higher salary, and much more work made
it imperative to give up the secret assignment.[16]
Cromer agreed.

However, the persistent proconsul continued in a
variety of ways to influence and, where possible, control the news about Egypt that flowed to Britain. One
of the most effective vehicles was the annual report.
In the 1890s he insisted that this report, which was
compiled from notes sent in from the departments, be
ready soon after the close of the year so that it
would reach London in the spring. Egypt was, according to C. E. Coles Pasha, the prison chief during the
Cromer and Gorst eras, "at one time the most adver-
tised country in the world. . . . Lord Cromer held
that if he waited until the autumn, when full and more
correct statistics would be available, the report
would have lost a good deal of interest." Coles criticized this practice:

> This was undoubtedly true, but at the same
> time, although Lord Cromer's reports could
> not be surpassed as literary efforts, I
> think there can be no question but that the
> Annual Reviews of Departmental Reports issued
> by the Government of India are more reliable
> for reference, based as they are on statis-
> tics and tables which give information *in the*

same form [his italics] year after year.[17]

Cromer was fully aware of the propaganda value of his reports. They were structured and styled not to inform objectively but to convince the reader of the necessity of continued British control and guidance in Egypt, for the good of the British Empire, and only secondarily for the good of the Egyptians.[18]

Not only did Cromer manipulate public opinion on Egyptian affairs through his annual reports, but he also sought to control the flow and content of news in and out of Egypt, particularly outside. News management, despite frequent and fervent claims for freedom of the press, became the established practice of his administration in the 1890s.[19] Cromer's assurances on press freedom appeased the dogmatic Liberal opinion in Great Britain, but he used a combination of pressures, favors, and secret subventions for some of the major British and Arabic papers. When necessary he imposed censorship and suppression on books, magazines, papers, or articles which he considered subversive or seditious. He did not resort to the old Press Law of 1881 or to politics to enact a new, more stringent control.

Egyptian writers who offended the British could be prosecuted by a decree of the minister of the interior, but under the Capitulations a foreign journalist was immune from this kind of threat.[20] In the early days of the occupation the Arabic press was not felt to be much of a threat to the British; the impact of a vitriolic anti-British and nationalist Arabic press on the illiterate masses in Egypt was judged to be minor. When a new generation of nationalists began to seek a means of expression for their aims and policies in the 1890s they were allowed to publish what they liked, except when they offended certain unwritten canons established by the Agency.[21] Otherwise their writings were largely ignored by the British officials. This particular policy of "freedom of the press" had adverse effects on British influence and control in the years just before the 1914-1918 war.

Cromer was assiduous in his efforts to insure that the flow of news and information from Egypt to Britain would be partial to his administration. When his own men did not write the dispatches for *The Times* and some of the other London newspapers, their correspondents in Egypt submitted their material to be censored by the staff at the Agency. William Willcocks, a hydrological engineer who served as an irrigation inspector in the ministry of public works, wrote:

> Not only did the British Agency do everything it liked through the English officials, but the great London dailies and the telegraphic agencies used to have their letters and telegrams corrected and edited by the staff of the Agency, so that Lord Cromer was not only the real actor of the Egyptian stage, but also the critic of his own actions.[22]

Indeed in the 1890s Cromer threatened Willcocks with immediate dismissal if the latter published some "comic writings" about Cromer's regime in Egypt. Willcocks resisted this threat and insisted that Cromer should abide by rules which did not forbid such amusements. "I had my way, but the rules were changed the next day. After that I experienced the bright side of Lord Cromer's character, for like Archbishop Temple, though a brute, he was a just brute."[23]

Reuters, the major British news service, received a regular subsidy from the Agency that apparently went on at least three years after Cromer left Egypt. In answer to a question in the House of Commons in 1910, Gorst informed Sir Edward Grey that "Reuters Agency has had for *a great number of years* [my italics] quite a considerable subvention from the Egyptian government."[24] In the Sudan, Wingate, with Cromer's permission, even acted as Reuters' correspondent.[25] *Al-Muqattam*, one of the most prominent Arabic dailies, received a subvention from the Agency at least until Cromer's departure.[26] In return one of its proprietors, Faris Nimr, a graduate of the Syrian Protestant College, used his newspaper as the "mouthpiece" of the British policy in Egypt.[27] It was alleged that Cromer provided guidance and hints of the official line to *The Egyptian Gazette*, the major English-language paper in Alexandria and Cairo.[28]

The Agency staff, of course, worked constantly to influence journalists and visitors to Egypt and to give them the "correct" view of Egyptian policy and events. Harry Boyle, Cromer's closest confidant and, as Oriental Secretary, the intelligence officer at the Agency, wrote home at the end of the crisis-ridden

year 1906 that he had been having trouble with British
journalists out to see Egypt and its problems.   "But
it is an important matter to let them know the *truth*
[his italics] so I don't grunt much." [29]   All in all,
the British public's impression of British rule in
Egypt, created by this combination of public relations
and news management, was distorted and misinformed.
When Gorst succeeded Cromer, he was to suffer from
this legacy.

        Gorst's venture into journalism and news manage-
ment was only part of his official advancement in
1890.   In hopes of a better opportunity in Egypt, he
refused an offer from the East Africa Company early in
the year.   Cromer's efforts to expand British influence in the Egyptian administration led to a post in
the financial ministry and the opportunity for Gorst
to emerge as one of the "coming men" in Egypt and the
Empire.   In 1890 the second post in the ministry, that
of the under secretary, was vacated by Julius Blum
Pasha, an Austro-Hungarian Jew who decided to return
to his family's bank, the *Credit Anstalt*.   Cromer decided that Milner would be promoted to succeed Blum,
and Gorst would succeed Milner once the position had
been redefined.

        "Blum Pasha" was a noteworthy figure in the poly-
glot gang of European bankers, financiers, speculators,
promoters, and confidence men who descended on Egypt
in the 1860s in hopes of profiting from its rapid and
chaotic economic growth.   Born in 1843 in Budapest,
Blum went to Egypt in the 1860s as the representative of
his bank.   Its office was liquidated by the Egyptian
bankruptcy of 1876, and Blum joined the Egyptian ministry of finance in January 1877.   From available accounts an adroit and honest man, he survived the ban-
ishment of Ismail, the Urabi Revolt, and the first
years of the British occupation.   We have only a
sketchy view of what Blum accomplished, but he left
things in such order that his successor, Milner, had
plenty of time to begin to learn Arabic and start his
influential book, *England in Egypt*. [30]   The "race
against bankruptcy"—Milner's label—had been "won" in
1888, largely as a result of the work of Vincent,
Palmer, and Blum under Cromer's guidance.   When Blum
retired in 1890 Cromer was moving to increase British
influence in this crucial ministry.

        In June Cromer instructed Salisbury's private

secretary at the Foreign Office, Eric Barrington, that
Milner would become under secretary. He was determined to have an Englishman to replace Milner as financial advisor and hoped the foreign secretary would
agree.

> I want to get Gorst named. He would do the
> work capitally. He has a special aptitude
> for finance. He speaks Arabic. The ques-
> tion is, could he remain on the list of the
> Diplomatic Service whilst his services were
> lent? Of course, he would not draw English
> pay and I presume that, whilst he was in
> Egyptian Service, the time would not count
> towards English pension. On the other hand,
> looking to the general uncertainty—as re-
> gards the future of Egypt, Gorst—and indeed
> all the English officials—are naturally re-
> luctant to abandon their places in the English
> services. . . . I want to be in a position to
> act promptly, when the moment arrives. . . .
> P. S. Gorst has written a line to his father
> on the subject.[31]

The Foreign Office gave its approval by July, but
there was resistance from the Turco-Circassian ruling
class, especially old Riaz, then the prime minister,
who recognized Gorst's appointment as another sign of
increased British interference and the decline in the
power of the pashas. They could only delay the inevitable and shift the terms slightly. Early in November
Gorst was appointed controller of direct taxes at a
salary of one thousand Egyptian pounds per year.[32]

Eldon Gorst found a challenge in his first major
administrative appointment. At twenty-nine he had to
manage a section of the ministry where no European had
worked, and to do it in Arabic. His first comment in
his diary on the new job was: "Hercules & the Augean
stable nothing to it."[33] He wrote later:

> This department, which superintended the
> collection of half the revenue of the
> country, having . . . been left entirely
> in native hands, was in a state of chaos
> and disorder. No better task could have
> been given me than that of bringing it
> into order, or one more calculated to
> form and strengthen my character and

bring out any administrative qualities I
might possess.[34]

The effort to learn Arabic paid off. Without it he
might not have been able to cope effectively in his
new post. "As it was, all I wanted was practice, and
in a month's time I had enough of that to make me feel
quite at home in the language. In fact I have never
used an interpreter during the whole time I have been
in the Egyptian Service."[35] Late in November he
appeared in a *tarboush*—a fez—for the first time.
Since he was a small man, this sign of Egyptian offi-
cialdom probably did not dignify his appearance.

From now on his career was to be focused almost
exclusively on the expansion and maintenance of the
British "veiled protectorate" in Egypt. Eighteen-
ninety was a year of accomplishment for Eldon Gorst.
He managed to attain a comfortable income, to mature
through a love affair, to plunge successfully into
journalism, and to practice diplomacy in Italy. The
year was capped by his appointment to the ministry of
finance, a noteworthy progress for so young a man.
Jessica Sykes fully deserved the diamond and sapphire
bracelet he gave her in August. Her companionship,
support, and advice had certainly helped him, but he
never looked back. His talents matched his ambition.

A hard worker, Gorst invested all of 1891 in
learning his new job and the complexities of Egyptian
administration. He made several inspection trips to
various Egyptian provinces, including a second visit
up the Nile as far as Wady Halfa. On this trip he
encountered Miss Margot Tennant in an officers' mess
in Edfou. He found this lady—soon to marry H. H.
Asquith—"very amusing."[36] By this time, December
1891, his skill in the language had increased: "I had
become quite at home in the Arabic language, and was
able to transact business in it without any inconvenience."[37]

Meanwhile, Cromer continued to maneuver in order
to pressure the old guard Turco-Circassian politicians to expand direct British influence on the Egyptian administration. Riaz was too independent. Up
to this time, Riaz—and Nubar before him—had been
able to forestall British control over the ministries
of justice and the interior. However, in March 1891
Cromer told Bell he thought Riaz would be resigning

soon. "He is a complete savage but he has his advantages. I always like to keep behind rather than be in
front of my English officials in a matter of this
sort."[38]   By May of that year Cromer had maneuvered
Riaz into resignation. It was tricky, as the khedive,
the pashas, and the French all had to be convinced
that this change of ministries did not diminish their
prerogatives.[39]   The new prime minister, Mustafa Fahmi,
was honest. That was about all. Cromer had earlier
described him as "a dummy" who was willing to do what the
the British told him from then on.[40]   As a result, he
was prime minister—with the exception of two years,
1893-95—until Gorst had him "retired" in 1908.

British intentions to evacuate Egypt were increasingly just a pretense. Cromer, using as his agents
such men as Milner, Palmer, Garstin, Kitchener,
Dawkins, and Gorst at the top, inserted increasing
numbers of British officials into the Egyptian administration, determined to forge what they perceived as
a new and "reformed" Egypt. Milner put it bluntly to
his patron Goschen in 1890:

> We have got beyond solvency, but we are going
> far beyond that in the next ten years, if we
> keep the flag flying in the Citadel of Cairo.
> Take it away, and all will be chaos, for Egyp-
> tian progress has one key-stone. Only the
> unobtrusive but absolute dictatorship of
> Baring. And that depends on the presence of
> a handful of Tommy Atkinses! Without them
> I don't believe even his great prestige could
> maintain that dictatorship and there is noth-
> ing here between one man government and chaos.
> Neither is there another man.[41]

As a consequence, during the 1890s more and more
British officials took over the senior posts in the
Egyptian government. The result, as far as Gorst was
concerned, was that his scope for advancement was
widened. In Egypt, rule by foreigners was nothing
new. But the nature of the changes wrought by the
Europeans was to generate more than one generation
of frustrated and resentful Egyptians.

Chapter Four

A RISING MAN IN EGYPT: 1891-1897

Among the most frustrated and resentful Egyptians who
were to trouble Gorst and his mentor Cromer was
Khedive Abbas Hilmi. He succeeded his docile father
Taufiq early in 1892. His father died, it seems,
largely as a result of carelessness or incompetence on
the part of his Egyptian physicians. Cromer carefully
insured that this information did not become public
knowledge and also concealed allegations that Taufiq had
suffered from venereal disease.[1] He informed Bell of
The Times: "The poor Khedive was killed by Salem and
Issa Hamedi who did everything they ought not to have
done." Had European doctors reached Taufiq earlier
they might have saved him. "Here they call it murder
and say rather suicide." He was grateful when Bell
later altered Taufiq's obituary notice to preserve the
dead khedive's reputation.[2]

    Cromer's concern did not extend to his personal
relations with Taufiq or his son Abbas. One of the
more unfortunate aspects of the sixty years of British
predominance in Egypt was the insensitivity they accorded to their puppets, the Muhammad Ali dynasty.
Gorst seems to have been the only British Agent and Consul-
General, High Commissioner (as he later became), or
ambassador who had decent, humane relations with the
Egyptian rulers under his influence. Indeed Gorst
and Abbas became friends—a notable accomplishment
since Gorst was involved directly in the process of
Abbas's repression.

    As for Cromer, his overbearing manner affected
his relations with the young Khedive Abbas. Whereas
Taufiq by temperament and experience had known that
to oppose the British meant his downfall, his son in
the first years of his reign—he did not rule—would
not accept the subordinate role that Cromer and the
British expected of him. The facade of power and the

trappings were not enough, and Abbas, surrounded
mainly by incompetent advisors, overtly challenged
Cromer and covertly supported the growing Egyptian
nationalist movement.[3] These challenges failed.
Cromer and the British were too strong for the young,
ill-advised, and wayward khedive. But Abbas's resistance reinforced Cromer's scorn for the old Egyptian
ruling classes. Cromer's prejudice was not confined
to this class, most of whom were incompetent, but
extended—with some rare exceptions—to all Egyptians
who were, he judged, corrupted by their religion,
selfish, and incapable of responsible self-rule in the
foreseeable future.[4] Cromer's brusqueness had little
appeal to a monarch somewhat more secure on his throne
than Abbas, Edward VII.[5] Despite Cromer's claim that
he was "never wanting in that outward deference which
constituted a legitimate prerogative of his high position,"[6] he failed to recognize that a more gentle
handling of the young and sensitive khedive might have
reduced Abbas's resentment and his subsequent meddling
and plotting against his British protectors. The dissatisfaction of the khedive and his capacity for
trouble-making, a persistent difficulty for Cromer,
were to be among the main problems Gorst had to face
as his successor.

Cromer's utter scorn for Abbas Hilmi II and the
rest of the Muhammad Ali dynasty was conveyed in a
letter to Lansdowne, the foreign secretary, in 1900.
Di Martino Pasha, the khedive's private secretary,
acting apparently as an informer, told Cromer that
Abbas's behavior indicated the khedive might possibly
be insane. The khedive's family, asserted Cromer, was
mostly degenerate. Ibrahim, his great grandfather,
was "almost a homicidal maniac," as was Abbas I, his
great granduncle; Saïd, another great granduncle, and
Ismail, his grandfather, were, in Cromer's words, "to
say the least eccentric." Furthermore, "Tewfik, the
father, [was] a mass of disease . . . and a blood
relative of his own wife [the khedive's mother]. The
Khedive's brother has epileptic fits, his eldest child
was born dumb and deformed, and his cousin was recently confined to an English lunatic asylum."[7] If
this was all true, the maintenance of this incapable
clan as the reigning family is a sad comment on the
British in Egypt. It certainly belied their oft-
stated intention to "reform" Egypt.

Of greater significance was Cromer's tendency to

blame Abbas for causing much of the anti-British and
Egyptian nationalist feeling that grew in the 1890s.
Abbas helped to feed the plant but he did not germinate
it. By blaming Abbas, Cromer and his advisors often
tended to misinterpret the thrust and misjudge the
genuineness of nationalist feelings. Abbas early in
his reign had applied his talents and influence to
making money to finance the nationalist movements.
Discouraged by his failure to assert himself against
Cromer and the British, he began to divert his energies and influence to increasing his wealth, in part
from frustration, but more likely as insurance against
his eventual deposition by the British. His alleged
venality and his opposition to certain reforms and to
a constitution for Egypt dismayed and alienated the
liberal nationalists.[8]

The successful campaign to retake the Sudan, coupled with the setback to France at Fashoda, thoroughly
disillusioned the khedive. The Anglo-French Entente
of 1904 removed the French as the most significant
foreign threat to the British veiled protectorate in
Egypt. It was clear to all, including Abbas, that the
British intended to stay in control of the Nile Valley
for an indeterminate length of time. Reluctantly and
bitterly, in 1904 Abbas made gestures to the British
that indicated he had accepted their conception of his
role in the Cromerian protectorate.[9] This act estranged
Abbas from Mustafa Kamil, the nationalist leader, whom
he had encouraged and supported for a time; eventually
they made a secret reconciliation.[10] Cromer's prejudices and perceptions of Abbas and the nationalist
movement were not altered as Abbas's venality apparently did not cease.[11]

Gorst first mentioned Abbas in 1892 in his autobiographical notes:

> Towards the latter part of the year, it began
> to be evident that the young Khedive was go-
> ing to give a good deal of trouble. The prin-
> cipal causes of the hostile frame of mind
> into which H[is] H[ighness] Abbas had been
> drifting during the summer and autumn were
> the foolish counsels of Tigrane Pasha, the
> Minister of Foreign Affairs, the injudicious
> treatment of Sir E[lwin] Palmer, and the long
> absence through illness of Sir E.Baring and
> consequent rumours of his departure from Egypt.[12]

Records of his relations with Abbas are sparse, but they indicate that Gorst had a more subtle touch in the management of His Highness than Cromer and most of the rest of the senior Anglo-Egyptian officials. It is to Gorst's credit that he was willing to cater to Abbas's sensitivity. Had the majority of British proconsuls been more considerate and willing to tolerate a wider range of initiative and talent on the part of the Muhammad Ali dynasty, the modern history of Egypt might well have been happier. At the least, British relations with Egypt might have been less a failure.

Gorst's relations with Butrus Ghali, a Copt who became minister of finance in the Riaz ministry of 1893, are illustrative of his more subtle treatment of Khedive Abbas and the other Egyptian officials. Gorst had solidified his reputation as a financial expert as controller of direct taxes, and when Milner resigned from finance to return to England in July 1892, he was appointed to succeed him as under secretary—the second highest British official in the ministry. As such, he was nominally Ghali's subordinate when the supple Copt became finance minister. The Riaz cabinet was, asserted Gorst, a hostile and obstructive body that made changes and reforms desired by the British very difficult, but he had little trouble with his minister. "Our tacit understanding was that he might do everything himself, so long as he did what I wanted."[13] One of Gorst's characteristics was that he was more concerned with substance of power than the form.

In a letter to his predecessor in finance, Milner, now in London, he cynically observed:

> You ask me about Butros. That gentleman's policy may be summed up in a very few words:— having after many years succeeded in becoming a minister, he is going to do his very utmost to remain one. At present he is in a very unhappy state as he is not sure which side will win. Don't imagine either he, Tigrane or Mazloum will have any influence over Riaz. They used brave words and then capitulated during [the] first meeting in front of "that violent little old Man."[14]

Gorst not only used tact to handle the touchy

Egyptian ministers, but he sought with minimal success
to persuade Cromer and the other senior British officials that there was an alternative to the open bullying
and threats that they had been using increasingly on
the khedive in 1893-1894. In November 1893 he wrote
Milner:

> My own view is that we ought to decline to
> incur the responsibility of recommending to
> the Khedive this or that minister. I should
> leave the choice to him absolutely, at the
> same time warning him that he would be held
> more or less responsible for the selections,
> and that the only thing we must insist on
> would be that the man chosen would work cor-
> dially with us. If we took up this line, the
> Khedive would I fancy be pleased at the idea
> of appointing his own ministers, and at the
> same time his influence would be on the side
> of trying to make them go along with us:—and
> there is no doubt that if Effendim [Abbas]
> wishes it, any minister will get along with us.
> I think you will easily see the advantages of
> the system. You must bear in mind that the
> Khedive personally has no objections to reform
> and that his general ideas are more or less
> European. [15]

Gorst left a description of a risible encounter with
Riaz, then prime minister, at an Egyptian Cabinet
meeting during the summer of 1893. Riaz was complaining strongly about one Hooker in particular and the
interference of Europeans in general. In the same
letter he wrote:

> I smiled very unobtrusively to myself. The
> little man (Riaz) turned savagely at me and
> said: "Pourquois riez-vous mon Gorst?" I
> was so taken aback by this sudden onslaught
> that I could only reply by a bald statement
> of the real reason. "Parceque votre excel-
> lence exaggère tellement." Riaz nearly ex-
> ploded with wrath and the Khedive burst out
> laughing. The rest sat with open mouths
> expecting the earth to swallow me up. [16]

Despite the tension between the British officials
and the Turco-Egyptian pasha class, Gorst's salary was
raised toward the end of the year. He was able to

manage the touchy Egyptian officials and please his
mentor as well. Cromer praised him highly to Rosebery,
the prime minister, on the occasion of Gorst's long
annual holiday in 1893:

> Gorst is gone home by Constantinople and
> Vienna. I hope you will see him when he
> arrives. He is far and away the most able
> of the English officials here—very clear
> and very steady. I found him during the
> crisis [with Abbas], and on other occasions,
> one of the few who could take a non-local
> view of matters.[17]

His success as under secretary at the finance ministry
came despite his having to serve under Sir Elwin Palmer,
the advisor to finance. Gorst considered him to be
"a man of very inferior capacity, who preferred, like
all inferior people, to do everything badly himself."[18]
Gorst's successor at finance, Clinton Dawkins, also
complained of Palmer's behavior, especially his
"inconsiderate jack-in-office kind of ways of treating
his subordinates."[19]

    Second place in finance was not enough for Eldon
Gorst. By the end of 1893 he sensed that he had gained
enough experience and began to look for a more challenging position. His ambitions reeked of the puritan
ethic. He sought more responsibility, "not to mention
the moral good for myself which I anticipated from
some such stimulus."[20] Moral improvement or not, Gorst
set out to become the advisor to the interior ministry,
which had not yet been effectively controlled or
"reformed" by the British. Some attempts had been
made in the 1880s, but financial reform and agricultural improvements had priority. The old Turco-
Egyptian ruling class stubbornly resisted, and British
efforts were limited by Cromer's reluctance to meddle,
except where absolutely crucial, in the day-to-day
affairs of the Egyptians. Gorst calculated that
interior "was a field worthy of anyone's energies."[21]
He spoke Arabic, and his nine years of experience in
Egypt had made him familiar enough with local life to
think his remedies might work.

    Gorst supported the appointment of Nubar as prime
minister in 1894 as a means to his ends. He laid the
groundwork, then waited out the summer without pressing a claim for the post. A few years earlier his

mentor, Cromer, had complained to Bell of *The Times*
that the impatience of the British officials was one
of his major difficulties. Timing, said Cromer, was
crucial. They needed to learn "to sit tight and not
to be in too great a hurry. It is sufficient to make
some of them see that the main thing in Egypt is not
what you do, but when you do it, and how you do it."[22]
Gorst understood this tactic, and it enabled him to
further his plan to attain the advisorship.

Cromer informed the Foreign Office in April 1894
that he intended to increase British influence in the
interior ministry. Gorst assisted by drawing up a reorganization scheme that both Cromer and Nubar, the
prime minister, thought was sound; part of Gorst's plot
to attain the interior advisorship involved the removal
of British military influence in the interior ministry.
Finally in the fall, a reluctant khedive and a support-
ive Nubar yielded to Cromer's pressure and Gorst's maneuvering. Gorst alleged that his selection was inevitable:

> On one point all were unanimous. If an
> English Advisor was to be appointed . . .
> I was the only possible man for the post.
> Therefore when the scheme was accepted, the
> personal side of the question caused abso-
> lutely no discussion. Indeed one of the
> principal arguments of the opponents of the
> measure, was that I might die or resign and
> who could answer for my successor. Without
> vanity I may honestly say that no appoint-
> ment was ever more a man's own doing than
> was this in my case. Whether the results
> were success or failure, I had deliberately
> entered upon the business of my own freewill
> and at my own initiative.[23]

Eldon Gorst was appointed advisor to the interior
ministry in November 1894. Within a month he had sufficiently impressed Cromer that the Consul-General
praised Gorst's work to the foreign secretary, Lord
Kimberley: "We are having a tolerably quiet time here.
A good deal of this is due to the tact and judgment
displayed by Gorst, who has, so far, been a great success. I no longer hear anything of the affairs of the
interior."[24]

For more than a year Gorst flourished. A relatively young man, just thirty-three, he had largely

on his own reached a challenging and highly responsible post in the British Empire. Cromer, for a period, depended on him for advice. Gorst was one of a select few who were ruling Egypt under his imperious guidance. Another member of that band, Sir William Garstin, advisor to the ministry of public works, told Milner in a letter that he thought Gorst would be a success. "He is very determined, very clever, and has lots of tact."[25]

Change and reform were indeed long overdue at the interior ministry. Financial and agricultural prosperity had not brought local stability; rather, they may well have contributed to the weakening of the formal and informal bonds that held village society in Egypt together. During the reign of Ismail Egypt had been unusually secure, even by European standards.[26] But Ismail's rule was, to say the least, draconian, and not feasible for the British protectors of Egypt to institute on their own. Attempts had been made by Cromer in the middle 1880s to bring British methods and men into the affairs of justice and the interior, but financial and agricultural problems took priority. Cromer's successes in these areas and the death of Taufiq led to more direct British interference in the day-to-day affairs of their veiled protectorate. Early in the 1890s efforts had been made to reform the police, under the guidance of officers from the British army. Gorst was not impressed: "The police, run on stiff military lines by a series of incapable chiefs, was the one English failure. The rest of the local administration was hardly touched at all."[27]

The removal of military control from the police was the first step in Gorst's reform of the interior. In 1895 he embarked on a campaign to tighten up local administration and extend Egyptian government and British influence into the numerous villages of Egypt, using his experience with land taxation. An English inspectorate was created at the ministry with the responsibility for supervising security and administration at the village level. Though it was only advisory, the ability of these inspectors to appeal to Gorst gave them considerable impact and produced—inevitably—a hostile reaction from the local notables whose prerogatives they tended to usurp. Furthermore, their knowledge of the language, customs, and practices of the countryside and their technical skills were not up to the high standard of those of their counterparts from the

ministry of public works. As a result there was considerable local opposition.[28]

        The British inspectors at the provincial level
did not replace the Egyptian administrators, as Gorst
did not replace his technical superior, the Egyptian
interior minister. They only gave "advice," but that
advice was not often ignored. The tension and resentment that resulted from this arrangement was considerable. Adding to this tension was the general exclusion of qualified Egyptians from the top posts in
their own administration. In a study of Cromer's
regime, Robert Tignor put it aptly: "There can be no
question, however, that Egyptians were discriminated
against in top administrative positions. Few Egyptians were given opportunities to work at levels commensurate with their educational attainments where
they possessed them."[29]

        The deliberate increase of the British into Egyptian
administration in the middle 1890s further distorted
Anglo-Egyptian relations. Prior British recruitment
for the Egyptian Service had been numerically small,
and for special jobs. In the 1880s many of the officials came on loan from India, particularly in the
ministry of public works. Cromer himself had had
Indian administrative experience. On the financial
side he selected men of talent such as Vincent, Milner,
and Gorst; but the mid-nineties expansion diluted
this talent, and Cromer did not and could not exercise the close supervision he had earlier.

        In the early and middle 1890s the recruitment
was never systematic. The top posts were personally
filled by Cromer and the technical services recruited
on their own. The major route for Englishmen into
the Egyptian Service was a haphazard sort of appren-
ticeship in the education department. It had low
prestige, low funds, and was supervised by an unimaginative Scot, Douglas Dunlop. Cromer had a political
reason for increasing the number of British in this
department; they might help to counteract French
influence among the educated in Egypt. He informed
Bell in 1892: "My way is to compete [with the French]
through Dunlap and English schoolmasters, whose numbers have been quietly but steadily increased."[30]
Despite the deliberate reduction of French influence,
the language continued as the official departmental
tongue. The Anglo-Egyptian officials, while on duty,

conversed and corresponded with one another in it,
often with laughable results.[31]

Most men served in education for as short a time
as possible and then had themselves transferred to
higher paying and more prestigious posts in the other
departments, especially finance and the interior. The
majority of these candidates were selected from recent
graduates of the ancient universities: Oxford, Cambridge, and Trinity College, Dublin. There were no
examinations. After their backgrounds had been
checked, the candidates were interviewed in England
by an *ad hoc* committee of British serving in Egypt.
The "old boy net" and family connections were important, if not crucial, in this process. Gorst, for
instance, found a post for his sister Constance's
first husband. His sister Hylda married an officer,
George Hunter, who was the head of the Egyptian coast
guard, one of the departments under Gorst's supervision when he was advisor to the interior ministry.
George Hunter's son Archibald recalled that in those
days recruitment to the Egyptian Service hinged to a
large extent on one's social and familial connections.[32]

Gorst's performance in his first year as advisor
was not inhibited by recruitment problems. He rapidly
mastered both the difficulties and personalities of
the ministry. A testimony to his accomplishment appeared in the 1902 edition of Milner's apologia for
Cromer's regime, *England in Egypt*. In an appendix
entitled "Egypt in 1898," written by Clinton Dawkins,
Gorst's leadership at the interior is praised. Dawkins,
a protégé of Milner's, had replaced Gorst as under secretary of finance in 1894. His calm and positive
assessment seems credible. Of the interior in 1894,
Dawkins wrote, "It was decided to remove the English
hands and rely upon the directing brain." The brain
was Gorst. The new inspectorate created by Gorst
based on Cairo, "has borne good results upon the
whole." All depended though, Dawkins warned, on the
tact and reputation of the inspectors and "the general
tone and character imparted to their work by the
Advisor." He commended Gorst's strengthening of the
umdahs (the head *shaikhs* in the villages), the establishment of reformatories, and the more effective use
of prison labor under the guidance of Coles Pasha.
The one lunatic asylum had been modernized and the
sanitary department had done much more effective work,
particularly in controlling the cholera epidemic of

1896.   Gorst's direction of the interior was "a bright page to the story of British occupation."[33]

Eldon Gorst's successes as a young "thrusting" imperial administrator began to attract attention in the British, European, and even American press. As early as the spring of 1889, *The Times* complimented him on his memorandum on Egyptian finances for its "fullness [and] lucidity." *Le Figaro* called Gorst one of Egypt's "coming men" in August 1892, and *The New York Herald* noted his growing reputation as a financial expert in the spring of 1893. *Le Temps, The Times,* and *The Home News* all approved his appointment as advisor to the interior minister. Faris Nimr, the Lebanese-born proprietor of the pro-British Arabic paper in Cairo, *al-Muqattam,* was quoted in *The Pall Mall Gazette* as saying that the proposed reforms in the ministry did not go far enough, but that Gorst was the official best suited to the post. *The African Review* and *The Globe* praised Gorst's regime in the interior ministry.[34]

From a painfully unhappy childhood, Gorst had developed by his mid-thirties into an intense, abrasive, and cynical official, controlled and driven by his ambition—a realistic, calculating ambition to attain high office in Britain or the Empire. In his autobiographical notes for 1896 he recorded with some self-pity that his father's comparative failure in Conservative Party politics forced him to depend on his own talents and on the chance that the British government would need a capable man. Unable to look to his family for patronage and influence, he was forced to remain in Egypt and wait for an opportunity. Yet few men at his age had done as well. "All this sounds rather common sense, but they are unwelcome truths, learnt slowly and with difficulty by an ambitious mind that must suffer to see others, more favorably situated as regards external circumstances but with perhaps inferior talents, passing it in the race."[35]

Gorst's relations with his fellow Englishmen were never good or easy. For the average range of British officials he was too intelligent—and aware of it—and too pushy and calculating. The historian Richard Hill has described the British imperial attitude that excluded men as different as Eldon Gorst or Ronald Storrs as "outsiders."

The precise significance of the word [out-
sider] is elusive. Soldiers, though not
usually eminent soldiers, were given to
using the word in their private letters
when describing men whom they disliked.
Social origin was not the first criterion.
The great Cromer was indubitably and overwhelmingly a gentleman, yet he came not too
many generations back from quite unpreten-
tious German stock. It was something more
subtle. You were an outsider if your way
of life or your thoughts differed percep-
tibly from those of the men and women who
were looking at you. Though they were the
ruling institution of an empire, the English
upper and middle classes were culturally provincial and, like provincials the world over,
they disliked deviations from the rigid pattern of their cloistered orthodoxy. Anybody
who looked un-English, who did un-English
things, who lacked English social inhibitions
and restraints, above all who was too clever
by half and added to his offence by demonstrating it, was liable to be referred to as
an outsider, or a Jew. In London the camp
followers of the previous Establishment
smirked at the distressing colours of young
Disraeli's waistcoats; in Cairo their grand-
sons accepted Sir Ernest Cassel in the Gezira
Club but showed repugnance to the "Orientals"
in his retinue.[36]

Gorst was aware of his inability to be accepted
by the British officials and the community he worked
with, and alert also to the fact that his abrasiveness could
affect his chances for further advancement. In 1899
he wrote: "In the last two years I had been making
great efforts to cure those defects of character and
manner which prevented my being popular with the
Anglo Egyptians—a most difficult class to concili-
ate."[37] He could not dissimulate as could other men,
sometimes of lesser abilities. Sir Ronald Storrs,
Gorst's Oriental secretary, described the man: "He was
fiercely capable, and achingly ambitious. He could
not bear fools gladly: he could hardly bear them at
all . . . for he lacked stature, and he lacked the
personality which sometimes outweighs that advantage."[38] Lord Rennell of Rodd, head of chancery in

the Cairo Agency from 1894 to 1901, described Gorst
during the 1890s in a passage censored by the Foreign
Office from the Milner Mission report. Cromer, during
a meeting with Gorst and Rodd, looked down from his
six feet at Gorst in a Stambouli coat with a *tarboush* on
the back of his head and chaffingly remarked, "Why
Jack, you look just like a corrupt Oriental official."
Rodd then asserted: "the lack of presence inspiring a
sense of authority in a country like Egypt is not com-
pensated by the most brilliant ability. The Egyptians
are very clever and quick themselves."[39]

          Gorst could not say "no" without sounding cyni-
cal.[40] Robert Vansittart, who served under him in the
Agency, observed that Gorst "gave umbrage moreover by
having the most powerful brain that I have ever encountered in the public service or in politics . . .
too clever by half; he could not help it, but it never
pays."[41] Beset by his ambition, congenitally unable
to relax, lacking the small talk that soothes, Gorst
remained—despite all his efforts or perhaps because
of them—a prisoner of his talents and an outsider
until his death. His aspirations had already assumed
specific form in 1896. At that time his major rival
in the Egyptian Service, Clinton Dawkins, wrote
to Alfred Milner about Gorst's ambitions:

          My own relations with this self-centered
          little cynic are quite pleasant . . . the
          little man has an extraordinary and rather
          impudent programme of his own. He believes
          that Cromer must go soon; and that Cromer's
          successor must inevitably make a mess of the
          job, and that he, if he has gone elsewhere
          meanwhile and distinguished himself, he must
          be brought back to put things straight.[42]

          Gorst's hopes that Cromer might leave Egypt soon
were frustrated by the latter's increasing belief in
his own indispensability. Dawkins, who conspired to
promote Milner as Cromer's successor, also was stymied
by his reluctance to leave. In 1896 he wrote Milner
that Cromer would never leave Egypt until there was a
more decided British policy at the Bosporus toward the
decaying Ottoman Empire. Besides, most of Cromer's
family life had been forged in Egypt. An impatient
Dawkins wrote:

Many personal ties bind him to Egypt. I
don't suppose two people live so exclusively
for themselves, on themselves and in their
children as do Cromer and Lady Cromer. Their
children were born here. All the associations nearly of their married life are here.
They have built their own house and made
their garden here after their own fancy—a
very ugly and uncomfortable house I think.
Cromer exults in his strength and success
here.[43]

Gorst, like Dawkins, recognized that Cromer was
not leaving Egypt and he sought opportunities elsewhere from 1895 on. His father's appointment as vice-
president of the council—the minister for education—
in the Unionist government in 1895 gave him a momentary hope "that the time was ripe for making an effort
to change my sphere of action from Egypt to England."[44]
However, the time was not ripe. Not long after he was
appointed education minister John Gorst quarrelled
with all his political colleagues and, in his son's
words, "took up the position of a sulky and discontented outcast."[45]

Before his illusions about finding some new
sphere of activity outside Egypt through his father's
influence were shattered, Gorst explored some other
possibilities. He began to learn Turkish: "I see that
Constantinople is likely to be the centre of attention
and it may be useful to know the language."[46] While
on his summer holiday in 1895 he sounded out with one
of the directors the possibility of being appointed a
government director of the Suez Canal. Also, Cromer
questioned him about becoming a financial advisor to
the government of Siam, but Gorst swiftly declined.[47]
In 1896 Gorst found himself out of favor with Cromer.
Dawkins informed Milner in August that Cromer tended
to be dependent on one man and that it was no longer
Gorst:

Big as he [Cromer] is it seems he must be
under the domination of someone. The tendency will increase. It is very convenient
to him, and suits an odd vein of laziness
which is combined with great energy to work
through some one agent and to hear everything

> through him alone. It used to be Gorst.
> The little man has fallen into disfavour.
> He mounted too quickly and then showed
> faults of temper and manner. Now it is
> Palmer [the financial advisor].[48]

Moreover, Gorst had a disagreement with another
rising and more powerful man in Egypt, the Sirdar
(commanding officer of the Egyptian army), General
Sir Herbert Kitchener, which resulted in his losing
further ground with Cromer. The matter itself was
apparently trivial, but Kitchener quite typically
used the episode to malign him, claiming that it was
Gorst's aggressiveness that had caused the dispute.
Gorst was furious, for he had always prided himself on
his ability to get along with everyone "whether English
or native" and get his work done efficiently. He defended himself for a time "with undue vigour." Eventually he put his pride in his pocket and accepted the
undeserved blame. He wrote bitterly:

> At last I reluctantly perceived that Lord C.
> could not or would not appreciate the real
> facts of the case, whether because he was
> too indolent to really go into the matter or
> whether it was more convenient to put me in
> the wrong than the Sirdar on the eve of the
> Dongola expedition, I cannot pretend to say.[49]

From then on Gorst and Kitchener were enemies. Gorst's
sense of justice and pride had been hurt and his position with Cromer worsened. Kitchener, "to whose
duplicity and falseness I owe this unmerited censure,"
would never be a friend again. This episode could be
a symptom of why Gorst lost Cromer's favor. His rapid
rise seems to have gone to his head and he lost his
political sense, temporarily.

Gorst was bitter and even self-pitying about his
troubles. Eighteen ninety-six was "a year of disillu-
sions and of having to swallow several bitter pills."
He assessed his situation thus:

> With no powerful friends at home to support
> me, and no means of making my capabilities
> directly known to those who pull the strings,
> my only chance must be to depend on the gov-
> ernment of the day being in difficulties about
> filling up some post in which the appointment

of a really capable man of my experience
and knowledge is imposed by the force of circumstances. Until such a contingency occurs,
I shall have to stay where I am, and all I
can do is to prepare myself to be ready to
seize the opportunity whenever it comes.
. . . The great mind puts all these considerations of mutual rivalry on one side and moves
straight to the goal. But we are all human
and it takes a good deal of training to arrive
at the proper pitch of philosophic calm. For
myself, I am only half-way there at present
if even that.[50]

Gorst remained as advisor to the interior ministry for the rest of 1896 and 1897. Cromer gave further signs of waning confidence in him, which, he
wrote, "caused me no little anxiety." By his own
admission Gorst was unpopular with his fellowcountry-
men. Accused—unjustly, he felt—of being rough,
arbitrary, and ill-mannered, he responded: "I know that
the principal foreigners looked upon me as one of the
most courteous, if decided and resolute, of my compa-
triots."[51]

Meanwhile he continued to seek a new and better
job. At the end of 1897 he lost out to his major
rival, Dawkins, for the post of financial minister in
India. His spirits fell further. He wrote sadly:
"I seemed to have got into an impasse at the Interior
from which there was no prospect of escaping." Earlier
he had been left off the Honors List of the Queen's
Jubilee. After an Agency reception, he wrote in his
diary, "Felt rather disappointed at not having received one of the numerous K.C.M.G's flitting about on
this occasion."[52] There were other reasons for his
depression. The great love of his life unexpectedly
hurt him deeply and, it appears, permanently.

Chapter Five

AN AMERICAN ROMANCE: 1894-1899

My affections were wounded in their tenderest
spot in an absolutely unexpected manner, and
I had to endure the harshest treatment from
the quarter from which I had least expected it.

Sir Eldon Gorst, 1899[1]

Gorst's autobiographical notes for 1897 began: "This
was another year of trials and disappointments which,
while perhaps helping to form one's character, did not
certainly tend to increase the enjoyment of existence."[2] On top of the frustrations at work, a love
affair that had enlivened his life since 1894 suddenly
began to go sour.

    Once he had broken off his intense relationship
with Jessica Sykes in 1891, Eldon Gorst did not pause
to mope. He obviously relished women's company and
made and kept a number of female friends. In the summer of 1891 he alluded in his autobiographical notes
to a new friend, "M. R." She was probably Mattie Rees,
a half-American, half-Armenian woman, who later married a Colonel Bird.[3] His diaries indicate that for
the next two years she was a steady companion in his
spare time in Cairo. He treasured their "warm and
durable friendship." During this period she had to
endure some personal misfortune and public criticism,
and Gorst admired her fortitude. He later wrote:

    In spite of many sufferings and much ill
    treatment at the hands of destiny, she has
    stood out against all her misfortunes with
    a courage and lightheartedness which has
    secured the admiration of her friends— few
    in number but very devoted. I know of no
    woman who has had more reasons to complain
    of the hasty and ill-formed judgements passed
    by the general public on actions which they
    could not appreciate.[4]

Unfortunately, Gorst gave no more information on what
trials and tribulations "M. R." had to suffer; she
remained a loyal friend and helped him years later
when his marriage was in difficulties.

There were other women besides "M. R." that Gorst
cultivated in the next few years. Most often mentioned
were Madame Camille Petit, who remained a lifelong
friend, a Miss Kourtam, and Lady Alice Portal. However he did not confine his attentions to ladies of
his social class. In the spring of 1893 he traveled
to London by way of Athens, the Greek islands,
Constantinople, and then via the Orient Express to
Vienna. There, in the *Prater*, he was introduced to a
Frau Felix. This lady was a madam; in his words, "a
küplerein, as her profession is delicately named."
(The word is a sexual pun on the German verb to couple
or to join.) The next afternoon, "the excellent Frau
Felix . . . provided me with light and agreeable amusement." The following day Felix catered to a happy
Gorst with "a pleasant lady" for a drive in the *Prater*;
after dinner he spent the night under "Frau Felix's
hospitable roof."[5] Spare though the description is of
this encounter with Frau Felix and her *ménage*, the
mood conveyed there and in other mentions of women is
that Gorst did not share the guilt or fear of female
companionship of many of his male contemporaries. He
was a normally sexed civilized man who genuinely liked
women. He apparently made no secret of his inclina-
tions, and this behavior harmed him in this hypocritical and repressive era.

After he returned to Egypt in the fall of 1893,
M. R. and he "decided to be friends in the future and
nothing more." Not long after, at a New Year's dance
at the home of the commanding officer of the British
army in Egypt, General Walker, he was introduced to an
American, Mrs. Turnure. By the last week of January
1894, his diary indicated that this acquaintance was
swiftly ripening. On the 24th he attended a ball at
the British Agency which was "a great success." He
closed his entry for that day with: "Supped and danced
cotillion with Mrs. Turnure. To 'bed' [his quotation
marks] at 4 a.m."[6]

His new companion was Romaine Madeline Stone
Turnure, the daughter of General Roy Stone of Mendham,
New Jersey. She was married to the son of a New York
banker of Huguenot descent, Lawrence J. Turnure, Junior.

The elder Turnure, who died in 1899, was described in
his obituary in *The New York Times* as "one of the best
known bankers in New York" and as a prominent figure
in that city's social circles for many years. Lawrence
Turnure, Junior, had not joined the family business in
New York City. A consumptive, he moved to Cairo for
the winter "Season." He and his beautiful young wife
became part of the *haut monde* in Europe and spent their
lives traveling from one fashionable spa to another.
They were part of the late-nineteenth-century equivalent of the current jet set. The photos of Romaine
that have survived reveal a stunning beauty. She had
delicate features and complexion, the kind one tends
to see on cameos, beautiful eyes, and a very pretty
face.

She became, with her husband Lawrence, a constant
figure in Gorst's diary for the next month and a half.
Late in March they all went for a camp-out on the
desert. Gorst recorded enigmatically: "Had a very bad
piece of luck in the evening." Eight days later,
Romaine was described as "very seedy with an attack of
fever, due probably to nerves."[7]

Meanwhile Gorst had decided to take an early
annual leave. The Turnures, who left Egypt the second
week in April 1894, invited him to join them in southern France and he met them in Monte Carlo, leaving his
new dog "Bacht" in the care of M. R. in Cairo. On
arrival, to his surprise and chagrin, he encountered
Jessica Sykes, just returned from a visit to the
United States; she departed—probably in a huff—almost
immediately, leaving Gorst and his sister Hylda to
enjoy the Turnures' company. On this visit Eldon and
Romaine apparently drew closer.[8] Gorst was lucky to
have five younger sisters—Constance, Hylda, Edith,
Eva (known as Dolly), and Gwen. Each of the last three
often came to Egypt in the 1890s as his guest, acting
as his hostess and as a convenient chaperone or cover
for her bachelor brother. Hylda married an English
officer in the Egyptian coast guard and lived in Egypt
during the working year.

After a few days' idyll on the Cote d'Azur, they
all entrained together for Paris. On the journey, for
some reason, Lawrence Turnure lost his temper.[9] While
it may have been just the doldrums of travel, it might
well have been caused by unhappiness over Eldon and
Romaine's emerging romance. Whatever the reasons, his

temper had cooled by their arrival in Paris. A round
of shopping, walks, rides, and dining out at fashionable restaurants followed. On May 8 Gorst went on to
London where he bedded down at his club, the St. James,
and consulted a physician about a painful foot. The
doctor informed him he had a touch of "rheumatic gout."
Gorst's recent diet, judging by the restaurants named
in his diary, must have been rich; perhaps rich enough
to cause gout in so young a man. His ailing foot did
not slow his social life significantly. He plunged
into a round of visits, parties, theatre, recitals,
opera, and dinners out. He visited his family, discussed Egyptian affairs with Milner over dinner at
Willis's— a famous restaurant— and spent parts of four
days with Jessica Sykes. Romaine was not forgotten.
On May 11 a letter arrived, "Not a very kind one," he
observed. A few days later she wired him to come to
see her in Paris.[10] He left immediately.

On arrival in Paris he took an apartment at the
Hotel Terminus and dined with his friend Camille
Petit. The next morning he met Romaine and they were
inseparable for the next two weeks. They embarked on
a round of lunches, dinners, and evenings together,
without her husband,who had apparently gone to Aix.
Gorst's gout must have been in remission, for they ate
at such fasionable gourmet haunts as Laperouse,
Gaillon's, and Vefours. Romaine often came to his
rooms at the Terminus. When her husband asked her to
join him in Aix she became depressed. But he changed
his mind and wired permission for her to go instead
to London with Gorst.[11]

They arrived in London May 23 and began a further
round of parties, dinners out, the opera, and theatre.
At intervals Gorst spent time with others, including
Jessika Sykes. Business was not neglected. He met
with Valentine Chirol of *The Times*, Vincent Corbett,
and Ambroise Sinadino. On May 28, Gorst went shopping
and "then to the [Inner] Temple Library to look up
American divorce laws." At the end of that week,
Romaine returned to France and Gorst accompanied her
as far as Boulogne. When he returned he "felt very low
and miserable."[12]

It was a transitory mood. He plunged into a
month of varied activities, rearranged his financial
affairs, visited his family at Lawford and Castle
Combe, and indulged his love of the opera. He mentioned

meeting a Radical member of Parliament who was an
"enthusiastic Wagnerite." In London he often attended
repeat performances of an opera—the sure sign of a
genuine "buff." His concentration on Romaine did not
lessen his friendships with other women. He enjoyed
the hospitality of Jessica Sykes again, escorted several ladies, including the actress Gertrude Silver,
"J. K." (possibly Jennie Kourtam), and Mrs. Sassoon.
His last night in London was spent with "J. K." at his
hotel; it was, he wrote, "a very pleasant evening—
until 1 a.m." Early in July he met the Turnures in
La Bourboule, a town in the Massif Central near Cler-
mont-Ferrand, and spent several pleasant days with
them. When he boarded the boat for Egypt in Marseilles,
he wrote letters to Romaine, J. K., and Lady Sykes.
Apparently he was "keeping his options open."[13]

Gorst returned to a pleasant summer in Cairo and
Alexandria. Bacht had become a "delightful dog."[14]
In late August this animal leaped off an express train
while he and his master were en route to Alexandria;
when the train slowed for a bridge Gorst went in pur-
suit and found the wanderer in a nearby village.
Aside from chasing Bacht, Gorst sought other amusements such as learning to bicycle and house hunting
for the Turnures. They arrived in Egypt late in September and settled "comfortably and contentedly" into
the house Gorst had found for them. By late fall
Eldon and Romaine were seeing each other nearly every
day, but their relationship apparently had its ups and
downs and Gorst resumed seeing his friend M. R. in the
intervals.

Eldon Gorst had a good year in 1894. At thirty-
three he had been appointed to a challenging post
in the Egyptian Service at a substantial increase in
salary, and he had begun a love affair that obviously
gave him much satisfaction. The affair continued
for the next two years, and Gorst and the Turnures
were inseparable whenever the latter were in Egypt.
They had apparently established a *ménage à trois*,
though Gorst usually kept one of his sisters in tow
as a chaperone.

A momentary disturbance in this idyll came in the
form of an unexpected visit by Lady Sykes in March
1895. Gorst noted that on the night of Jessica's arrival Romaine visited him at his home and was "rather
disagreeable without reason." It sounds like jealousy.

Gorst spent the next few days with Jessica, but eventually had to shake her off in order to see Romaine.
Finally he deliberately snubbed Jessica when she came
to call one day after lunch. He wrote: "I received
her very coldly and soon got rid of her. It appears
that she was disgracefully drunk last night at the
Gezireh Palace when dining with Lady Charles."[15] Three
days later, to his relief, she left Cairo. The following summer one of her relatives, Miss Leslie, asked
Gorst to help his profligate ex-companion. Gorst
coldly refused to intervene "about Lady S. whose conduct has been deplorable. I told her [Miss Leslie]
that it was no business of mine and that, besides, I
had done all that I could two years earlier without
any success."[16]

In May 1895 Romaine Turnure left Egypt for the
continent. Gorst did not languish; much of his free
time was spent with his old friend M. R. That summer
he saw Romaine in England and in France. It was at
the height of the bicycle rage and Eldon and his sister Hylda went to Battersea Park in mid-July "to see
the rank and fashion on bicycles—the latest craze,"
he noted in his diary. Indeed the eminent Milner had
injured his leg bicycling when Gorst visited him to
discuss Egyptian affairs that summer. At the end of
August Gorst and the Turnures went to Fontainebleau
and bicycled while there; but shortly afterwards there
were hints of trouble between Eldon and Romaine. He
felt "low and miserable" after accompanying her to a
matinee performance in Paris by Yvette Guilbert.
When he went to say good-by before leaving on a bicycle
tour in Normandy with his father and sister Dolly
(Eva), the visit was cut off short as "T [Lawrence
Turnure] had been very offensive as regards me."
Gorst ate alone that evening and went to bed "in an
unhappy frame of mind."[17]

After the bicycle tour, which lasted about two
weeks, he rejoined the Turnures in Paris. However
"T," he noted sourly, "got most inconveniently well
again." Gorst then went back to London where his
diary entries indicated he was troubled about Romaine.
On September 21 he noted: "Felt low & uneasy in my
mind all day. No letter from R." Five days later
he wrote: "Felt worried about R. all day. Had a wire
telling me not to come to Paris, but decided to tomor-
row *quand même* [nevertheless]."[18] She met him on arrival, but the pages for the next two days in the

diary have been deliberately excised. Whatever happened in Paris, the Turnures and Gorst traveled back
to Egypt together that fall. The rest of the year
passed without any further sign of trouble or conflict.
Any recorded details of their romance in 1896 have not
survived. His diary has vanished, and nothing personal was mentioned in his autobiographical notes. We
know it was not a good year professionally.

    The year 1897 was worse. To his surprise and
shock Romaine contrived nearly to wreck their affair.
Two years later he wrote bitterly: "By patience and
perseverance I won in the end, but the effort soured
my character and removed much of the pleasure of living. The crisis caused me to make a serious but futile effort to put matters on a more satisfactory
basis."[19] Difficulty with Romaine erupted early in
the year. After a ten-day trip up the Nile the two
had a serious quarrel, apparently over another man.
Lunching together in Cairo, "We had," he wrote, "a
very necessary and painful explanation." There was
a temporary reconciliation but more trouble ensued.
Romaine came for supper on February 20 and "I talked
to her seriously about a certain person." There are
no clues as to who this was. A week later she
remained in "an impossible mood," but they continued
to meet until she left Egypt in April. There was no
further mention of her for more than a month, until
Gorst noted her birthday on June 5. The next day he
received a letter she sent from New York City.[20]

    Meanwhile Gorst busied himself with official
duties, with a newly formed racing stable, and with
M. R. He justified the stable's expenses by asserting that galloping the horses gave him useful exercise. He left Egypt for England on annual leave on
July 11, traveling on the same train as Cromer from
Marseilles, and took the opportunity to discuss with
his boss his future professional desires. Cromer
promised to help.[21]

    Two days after his arrival in London, the
Turnures wrote inviting him to visit them in the
United States. He accepted immediately and embarked
from Liverpool on a Cunarder, the *SS Etruria*, after
a week spent visiting with friends and family. Typically, Gorst won fourteen pounds playing piquet on
the swiftest Atlantic crossing ever of the ship;[22] the
other players were undoubtedly glad the voyage was

short—or unhappy it was not long enough to recover
their losses.   On his arrival in New York City, Gorst
lunched at the Waldorf and caught the afternoon train
for Bar Harbor, which he reached on Sunday, August 8,
to find the Turnures "all flourishing."

His holiday on the east coast of America seems to
have been pleasant, if rather banal.   He spent the
first three weeks relaxing at Bar Harbor and environs—
sailing, swimming, and visiting.   Lawrence Turnure's
fever forced them to cancel a tour of the Maine woods;
otherwise nothing marred the occasion.   At the end of
August the ménage à trois embarked on an extensive
trip.   They visited Boston and Harvard—where Gorst
dined at the Somerset Club—and Lawrence's brother
George in Lennox, Massachusetts; then they entrained
for Montreal, went by boat up the St. Lawrence to
Toronto, across to Niagara Falls, and on to Cleveland,
where they stayed with a Mrs. Hickox.   Gorst left no
description of the sights, smells, and sounds of this
journey other than an expression of relief at the comfort of the Hickox house after a string of hotels.
Eventually they returned to George Turnure's home in
Lennox.   While staying there Eldon and Lawrence were
presented to President McKinley, who was visiting nearby.[23] In late September the three went to New York City
where they plunged into an intense social round.   Various Turnure relatives and friends entertained them;
there were dinners at Delmonico's and the Waldorf,
and an oyster lunch at Dolan's, and they attended a
play or two.   He left on September 29.

Two years later he recalled this interlude: "I
spent a happy holiday in America, but nevertheless left
with a feeling of insecurity, which has for long cast
a shadow over my hopes for the future."[24]   The autobiographical notes indicate that he was depressed. His
hopes for something more settled with Romaine had been
dashed, and his career prospects seemed blocked.   He
returned to Egypt swiftly, only pausing overnight in
London and Paris.   In the fall he occupied himself with
his official duties, his racing stable, and a new lady
named Hawkes—although he sat for his portrait by an
artist named Ralli and sent it to Romaine in January 1898.
Lawrence arrived without Romaine late in November.[25]

He was sufficiently frustrated to suggest a semi-
demotion to his mentor Lord Cromer.   "In my despair,"
he wrote, "I asked Lord C. to let me go back to the

Finance as Under Sec.[retary] if Dawkins went to
India." Gorst had his critics in Egypt, and he
acknowledged that they could have perceived this
change, had it occurred, as a sign of failure. He
later recalled:

> I was really getting discouraged and soured.
> Other reasons [the state of his affair with
> Romaine] also tended to make my life during
> these years an unhappy one. I am distinctly
> of the class that are improved by prosperity.
> Though so far I have never allowed my natu-
> rally despondent temperament and excessive
> sensitiveness to interfere with my constant
> struggle to improve, outwardly and inwardly,
> still a much longer continuance in unfavour-
> able circumstances might have damped my
> energy and thrown me into a lower plane.[26]

Another cause of his frustration and pessimism
early in the year was the apparent failure of his
lengthy campaign to better his relations with his
fellow countrymen. He wrote bitterly: "It was an
uphill task, and I often felt, when I perceived what
progress I was making, that it was a case of giving
a dog a bad name." Encouraged by some of his best
friends, he persevered; by the end of 1898 he sensed
that he had begun to live down his past reputation.[27]

However, in mid-year he felt his prospects were
at their lowest. Romaine was absent, his professional
advancement was stalled, his relations with his fellow
countrymen were unhappy, and even his racing stable
was "as unlucky as usual." The previous January he
had been left off the New Year's Honors list for the
second year in a row. His reaction is revealing: "The
year before I had felt badly when I was apparently
passed over in the annual distribution of honours.
This year I was absolutely indifferent."[28]

In 1898 the second mention of Romaine in his
diary came in late May. She wired to announce her
arrival in England. Gorst left on summer leave
shortly after and met the Turnures in Paris on June 9,
and they spent the next ten days together. It was
not a happy visit. His only direct comment followed
a drive and walk alone with Romaine in the Bois de
Boulogne: "Sad afternoon," he noted tersely. He went
on alone to London, and later recalled: "In the month

of June my prospects seemed at their lowest ebb, but when things are at their worst they begin to mend, and so it was in this case."[29]

In London early in July, Gorst learned that Sir Elwin Palmer, the financial advisor in Egypt, was considering resignation in order to accept a more lucrative and less demanding post as governor of the private National Bank of Egypt. A few days later Palmer confirmed his decision to resign and wrote to Gorst "as if I were certain to succeed him."[30] Ironically, these brightened prospects were dimmed by more difficulty with Romaine. While awaiting word on the desirable post he returned to Paris to attempt to smooth over another crisis with her. Thus—pehaps luckily—he was not able to lobby for himself in London. On July 15 Eldon Gorst learned from his rival Dawkins that the post was his. Buoyed up by this news, he negotiated with Romaine: "Walked with R. Peace restored," he noted in his diary the next day.

He returned to London, and in a few days Cromer officially informed him that the appointment was his. The diary on July 21 showed: "Saw Lord C. and heard that my app't as F.[inancial] A.[dvisor] has been approved by H. M. G." He wryly recorded the occasion about a year later:

> On my nomination as F. A. Lord Cromer seized
> the opportunity to read me a little homily on
> my future conduct. The two points which he
> criticized were my relations with the fair
> sex, which were apparently too conciliatory,
> and those with my own sex, which were apparently not conciliatory enough. The former
> defect—if it is a defect—is not, I fear,
> to be changed. The latter I had already
> taken in hand, and at last I begin to feel
> that I have really effected good progress.[31]

This appointment was one of the most significant in his life. Gorst's professional career, in the doldrums for two years, now had immediate challenges and rewards; success would put him, still in his thirties, in the first rank of imperial administrators. When the aging Cromer finally retired, Gorst would be one of the top candidates for the post of British Agent and Consul-General. He could now face with some equanimity the imminent collapse of his

affair with Romaine. His autobiographical notes for
that year, 1889, ended bittersweetly:

> As regards my more private affairs, I again
> went through a crisis in the summer which
> caused me great anxiety and perturbation of
> mind. By the exercise of infinite pains
> coupled with great tact, I averted—I hope
> removed altogether—the danger of a catas-
> trophe which would have wrecked my happi-
> ness for years, and I won again for the sec-
> ond time affections which were on the point
> of concentrating themselves elsewhere. At
> the same time, since that moment, I have
> realized on how frail foundations my hopes
> for the future were founded and what a seri-
> ous danger I am running that one day they
> will be dashed to the ground. *"Souvent femme
> varie, bien fol qui s'y fie."* [Woman is
> fickle, he who relies on her is very fool-
> ish.] It is rash to stake so much upon a
> single issue, but in such matters the wis-
> est of us are ruled by the heart and not the
> head.[32]

Someone else was to add to the difficulties that
Eldon and Romaine were having. That fall she returned
to Cairo with an infant. This was Gorst's first mention of his godchild Marga (Margaret) Turnure. Her
mother stayed on in Egypt throughout the winter and
early spring of 1899, leaving for the continent on
April 15. Until they met in Paris early in July there
were no indications of further problems. However, he
then wrote: "After lunch drove with the T's and had
the usual unsatisfactory interview with R." Three
days later he noted: "Walked with R. in the Bois and
came to a decision about the future." He skipped dinner that evening and took a long walk.[33] From then on
that summer neither Romaine nor her husband nor Gorst's
godchild is mentioned. It is clear from his diary and
autobiographical notes that the affair had finally
ended. In June 1900 he recalled: "The long-threatened
catastrophe, upsetting the dearest hopes of many years,
at last occurred, and this time without even a faint
prospect of saving anything from the wreck."[34]

We know it happened, but we do not know just what
happened. Apparently Romaine had found another man.
Despite his foreknowledge, Gorst's feelings were badly

hurt.   A year later he recalled:

> After this lapse of time I am able to con-
> template it with resignation and philosophy,
> though not with satisfaction, but at the
> moment the blow was the hardest I have had to
> support.   By force of will and by taking my-
> self most seriously in hand, by constant move-
> ment & change of scene during my wasted holi-
> day, and by application to work when I
> returned to Egypt, I managed to pull myself
> out of the slough of despond and emerged
> from the struggle unsoured if somewhat chas-
> tened.   The homopathic [*sic*] method, which
> I also tried, did not at all events in that
> year, produce any successful results, and
> my present feeling is that a certain portion
> of me is dead and cannot be revived.   Per-
> haps time will change this, *Nous verrons*.
> [We shall see.][35]

The affair was over, though Gorst continued to hope
she might change her mind.   The Turnures remained his
friends; they met off and on in Egypt and Europe until
Lawrence Turnure died in 1902.   His wishful thinking
may explain why his homeopathic methods—attempts to
treat his hurt by having other love affairs—failed.

Chapter Six

HEALING OLD WOUNDS: 1898-1904

Before returning to Egypt to assume his new post,
Gorst spent some time with his family and friends and
made a number of official contacts in London with such
people as Valentine Chirol of *The Times*. Then he rejoined the Turnures and Mattie Bird for a strenuous
bicycle tour of Normandy. They were joined early in
August by Max Müller, the famous German Orientalist.
Gorst left for Egypt the last week in August 1898.

Since Cromer had to delay his return due to his
first wife's fatal illness, Gorst had little time to
reflect on his new responsibility or his troubles with
Romaine. He shared the management of Egyptian affairs
with the counselor at the British Agency, J. Rennell
Rodd, while Cromer remained in England. Three days
after his return, news of the defeat of the Khalifah
at Omdurman reached Cairo.[1] This meant an extension
of British influence way up the Nile. He appears to
have taken the news all in hand and plunged into the
new tasks eagerly, rearranging the business of the
ministry of finance with marked efficiency and success.
By the end of the fall, Gorst felt that he was again
trusted by his bereaved mentor, who by now had returned
to Egypt: "Within three months . . . I may say without
boasting that I had quite regained all the confidence
he [Cromer] formerly reprised in me when I worked directly under his orders and which, not altogether by my
own fault, had been oosing [*sic*] away during the last
few years."[2]

As financial advisor he had daily contact with
Cromer, which he put to effective use. He abolished
a series of undesirable and dubious financial arrangements that his predecessor Palmer had made to feather
his personal nest. He negotiated effectively with the
Caisse de la dette for the advance of a large sum for
public works and railways, and wrote a detailed note

on the Egyptian budget for the annual report. At the
end of the year he accompanied Cromer on the Consul-
General's first visit to the newly conquered Sudan.
The budget note and the visit to Khartum gave Gorst
the kind of publicity he had longed for; what he termed
"useful advertisement in the English press."[3]

In addition to Gorst, Cromer's party to the Sudan
was made up of his two sons, Rowland and Evelyn,
Arthur Stanley from the Agency, and Harry Boyle, the
Oriental secretary, interpreter, and intelligence
agent. They visited Luxor, toured the Valley of the
Dead, sighted crocodiles in the Nile, and made a series of ceremonial visits "showing the flag" to the
locals on the way. In Khartum and Omdurman they visited the Mahdi's tomb and the Khalifah's house and inspected
the troops, and Cromer made a series of speeches to
the British officials, soldiers, and Sudanese dignitar-
ies. One wonders what sense the latter made of
Cromer's self-righteous pomposities translated into
Arabic by Boyle.

Back in Cairo in mid-January 1899, Gorst had a
busy and rewarding winter. He met for both business
and pleasure such notables as Winston Churchill and
the financial magnates Cecil Rhodes and Ernest Cassel
who had considerable investments in Egypt. Gorst's
partnership in the Desert Stables broke up; for the
first time, on his own, he had a successful year in
racing. Khedive Abbas sold him an Egyptian-born
English thoroughbred named Cedar for one hundred
pounds. This horse performed well and won several
stakes that year and the next. During that period
racing was his "chief amusement."[4]

Aside from entertaining Churchill, Rhodes, Cassel,
and other luminaries, Gorst, with the help of sister
"Dolly" (Eva), made further efforts to increase his
popularity among his fellow Anglo-Egyptian officials.
He later observed cynically:

> With Dolly's help I endeavoured to entertain
> the people of the place [Cairo] on a larger
> scale than heretofore. This, though often
> tiresome, and always expensive, I consider a
> very necessary way of what is vulgarly called
> "keeping up one's position," and impressing
> the vulgar herd with a due sense of one's
> importance.[5]

By the end of 1898 he had convinced himself that
his lengthy and expensive efforts had succeeded.
There seems to be an element of wishful thinking or
self-delusion in this estimate. Once he had been appointed financial advisor, Gorst ostensibly found himself treated with "due respect" arising from his new
position rather than from any efforts on his part.
For most English men or women in the imperial service,
a personality such as Gorst—brainy, worldly, driven,
cynical, and energetic—would have been difficult to
tolerate. Despite their situation, they were more
often than not rather narrow in their viewpoints.
That he was so clever and able did not matter so much
as that he did not care who knew it. That he also ignored some of the social mores of his class did not
help him either.

By June of 1900 Gorst had made himself master of
the two most important matters that preoccupied the
Egyptian government and Lord Cromer. The first was
the conversion of the Egyptian debt and the consequent
suppression of the Caisse de la dette. The second was
the development of the Sudan. He noted:

> The Financial Advisor can be practically the
> Prime Minister of the country with Lord Cromer
> as a very easy going sovereign when once his
> confidence is attained. . . .
>
> Nothing is done without my approval, and with-
> out boasting I may say that subject to the
> influence rather than the direction from Lord
> Cromer (which I do not in the least wish to
> minimize), I practically run the internal gov-
> ernment of the country [Egypt]—I trust
> wisely. . . .
>
> I think that he [Cromer] would agree that
> nobody but myself understands or could carry
> out his ideas on these subjects.[6]

Not only did he establish a close working relationship
with his boss, but he developed amicable relationships
with the native Egyptian officials and further cultivated the friendship of the wayward and neglected
khedive. Ronald Storrs asserted: "Alone of the higher
British officials, he [Gorst] had succeeded in winning
the confidence of the Khedive, hitherto assumed irrec-
oncilable with that of Lord Cromer."[7] Gorst was to

use this friendship to further his own policies when
he succeeded Cromer.

The last two years of intensive work had their
reward when Gorst learned during the summer of 1900
that Cromer was thinking of him as his successor. The
proconsul let him know too that the selection would be
left to Cromer by the British government. As a result,
Gorst was patient, letting Cromer refer to the future
at his own discretion, while Gorst concentrated on
making himself even more useful to Cromer and the
Egyptian government. Egyptian affairs were becoming
more complicated; the British government would have to
appoint a good man, not a mediocrity, and Gorst declared with self-assurance that he had "the pretension
of being included in the former category." Formal
recognition of his accomplishments came early in 1900
with the award, on Cromer's recommendation, of a Companion of the Order of the Bath—"a C.B." Looking
ahead, Gorst was pleased by this honor: "The main
attraction of this distinction for me was that it removed the possibility of my being made a K.C.M.G. to
which I have a great objection, as it is usually conferred on nonentities and failures." [8]

With the advice of Lord Cromer, on the urging of
his friends, and as part of his program to make himself more respectable to the British community in
Egypt and thus eligible for further promotion, Gorst
set out in the summer of 1900 "to find a suitable
object" —in short, a wife. He hoped to satisfy "the
sentimental and romantic side of my nature, and at my
age with my past experience this is no easy task." [9]
That year his search was complicated by continued contact with Romaine. In the spring the Turnures were in
Egypt, and he met them in France that summer. The
object of his attentions, a lady named Alice or "A,"
was courted while he visited them in Paris. Eventually Alice stood him up in London; for Gorst this was
"the last straw." Back in Cairo he dismissed her
tersely: "Heard from A. and wrote her an answer." He
judged her unsuitable "in spite of many charms and
other inducements. . . . The attempt, however, helped
to heal some old wounds." [10]

Meanwhile, Cromer confirmed that he was seriously
considering Gorst as his successor. In December 1901
he told Gorst that he thought it necessary that Gorst
should leave Egypt in order to gain wider experience

and stature in the British official world, and Cromer
consequently made inquiries to London about a suitable
posting.[11] Further official and public honors came when
Gorst was promoted to secretary of the legation in
1901 and gazetted Knight Companion of the Bath at the
coronation of Edward VII in 1902. The new king subsequently invested him with the knighthood in a private
ceremony at Balmoral, and Gorst took the opportunity
to cultivate the king's friendship over some rubbers
of bridge. Until that meeting His Majesty, wrote
Gorst, "had been somewhat prejudiced against me"; he
did not say why. When Edward's close friend, Mrs.
George Keppel, visited Cairo the following fall Gorst
entertained her and sought her friendship, hoping to
please the king.[12]

    Apparently Gorst had better luck at pleasing the
king and his mistress than in appealing to prospective
brides. His autobiographical notes for 1901 began:
"During this year no event of importance took place
either in my public or in my private life." The last
entry dismissed an attempt to get married during the
summer as a "failure." A year later he asserted that
he was relieved that nothing had come of the affair,[13]
but his diary for 1901 belied his lack of concern.

    His usual intense social life continued that
winter, and among many women he mentioned was one
"Lady B." After several encounters in Cairo they
met again in the summer in London. Gorst, with part
of his family, spent most of August and part of September in the Scottish Highlands. Lady Beatrix joined
the party on August 24. Four days later Gorst wrote
in his diary: "Took Lady B. up the woods opposite the
house & asked her to be my wife. She will if her
mother gives her consent. Today for the first time
in my life I feel really happy." He then composed a
letter to the Marchioness of Headfort, Lady Beatrix's
mother. That night he lay awake for hours, and the
next day the couple went walking in the woods. He
wrote afterwards: "I feel happier every moment & more
certain I have done the right thing." Later that day
he and an apprehensive Beatrix bicycled to the station
where she left to confront her family.

    The next day brought bad news to the euphoric
Gorst. "The bubble has soon burst," he wrote. "At
9 a.m. received a wire from B. to say that she had
yielded to her mother's objection." Downcast he went

for a walk and returned to find a letter from Beatrix:
"Her mother and Aunt have bullied her into giving me
up.   Wrote to her to encourage her & to cheer her
up." He made a futile appeal to the determined mother;
when that failed he was ill for more than a week.
Clearly this rejection hurt more than he cared to
admit.   Beatrix wrote "a nice letter" as he was recov-
ering from his illness.[14] The last mention in his diary
of this unfortunate affair appeared in December of
that year.   Cromer had apparently spoken to Dolly Gorst
about "the lady question" while at a dance at the
Agency in Cairo.   The next day Gorst went "To Agency
& talked to Lord C. about the lady question and told
him the Lady B. story." More than likely his pride
hurt more than his heart, as he obviously had been
deemed unsuitable by Beatrix's family.

      Two glimpses of Gorst have survived from this
period when he was actively seeking a wife. An anonymous writer in *The Candid Friend* in 1901 described him
as "very small and very slender." The writer asserted
that Gorst was "an extraordinarily good amateur actor"
who, when the late Lady Cromer was alive, organized
dramatic entertainments for her many charities. Now
he had ceased acting in public, as it did not befit
his station. The writer gossiped on:

      Mr. Gorst is still unmarried, but he is the
      best and kindest of brothers, and every win-
      ter one or other of his handsome sisters
      goes out to Egypt and stays with him in his
      charming little villa which he has built
      himself near the British Legation, where she
      acts as hostess. It is whispered that, al-
      though he is apparently a confirmed bachelor,
      he is not entirely indifferent to the charms
      of the fair sex, with most of whom he is a
      great favorite.[15]

      His brother Harold recalled an episode from the
same era. Gorst had been deputized to get presents
for the men who were to attend a ball for the German
kaiser in Cairo. He obtained fifty pair of ladies'
garters, and then the ball was cancelled. Soon after,
the second Lady Cromer organized a charity ball and
Gorst set up a stall. On a sign over this stall he
announced: "Ladies' Garters: Personally Fitted by Sir
Eldon Gorst." Lady Cromer is alleged to have "blush-
ingly consented" to be first; from then on business

was brisk, and all the garters were sold.[16]

Whatever his true feelings about Beatrix, his
quest for a suitable wife continued throughout the
year. However, most of the women whom he squired
either in Egypt or England or on the continent were
married. This was, I suspect, a matter of preference
and necessity in that more hypocritical period. Moreover, it is clear that he had some hope of a reconciliation with Romaine. This expectation was finally
crushed when Lawrence, her husband, died suddenly in
Cairo in April 1902. Romaine had returned to Cairo
the previous January with Gorst's godchild, Margaret,
and he had seen the Turnures often that winter.
Margaret came to lunch and stayed with Gorst on the
day Turnure died. Gorst was ill and depressed while
Turnure was dying. Two days after the funeral Romaine
and her child left Egypt for Paris and New York where
Lawrence was to be buried.

A month later their mutual friend, Mattie Bird,
who had accompanied Romaine as far as Paris, told
Gorst that his old love planned to remain in Europe
for a while. Late in May he heard from Romaine directly and sent her a birthday greeting. In June she
wrote to tell him not to come to France to see her on
his way home on summer leave, and toward the end of
July again brushed him off. "Heard from R. that she
does not want to see me before her departure."[17] Gorst
was stubborn and hoped she might change her mind. A
half-year later he wrote in his diary: "Heard from R.
after many months—a very cold and uncompromising
letter." This finally prompted him to resolve the
issue. The next day he "wrote fully and plainly to
R. with view to bringing matter to a head. Felt more
comfortable when this was done." Two weeks later he
recorded: "Had a definite answer from R. which closed
that chapter of my existence."[18]

This answer may well have been the news of
Romaine's impending marriage on July 1, 1903 to Sir
August Debonnaire John ("Jocko") Monson, thirteenth
Baronet and ninth Baron Monson of Burton, County of
Lincoln. "Jocko" Monson served as an attaché and
private secretary to his uncle, Sir Edmond Monson,
ambassador to France from 1896 to 1900, and Romaine
may have met him in Paris or in Cairo on a visit in
the late 1890s. Lawrence Turnure's ill health was
known, and according to family lore Romaine had a

number of suitors other than Eldon Gorst waiting in
the wings for her to be free to marry.[19]

Two days before the "uncompromising letter" from
Romaine, and not entirely by coincidence, Eldon Gorst
was introduced by Mrs. Satow in Cairo to his future
wife, Evelyn Rudd, the daughter of Charles D. Rudd, a
wealthy financier and associate of Cecil Rhodes in
South Africa. "Doll," as she was nicknamed, was
twenty-two years old and must have been attracted to
Eldon Gorst, now the second most powerful man in
Egypt. Once he determined that Romaine would not
change her mind, he courted Doll intensely and during
the next six weeks they met almost daily. On March 7
he noted in his diary: "After dinner spoke to D. on
the balcony. Had a very disturbed night"; three days
later, "D. was somewhat out of spirits." Finally, on
March 15, he went to see her on the big island, al
Jazirah, and "got a definite answer out of her." It
was "yes," and to celebrate they drove that evening
to dine at the Mena House near the Pyramids and to
look at the Sphinx by moonlight.[20] Gorst felt very
happy.

Family, friends, and officials such as Cromer were
immediately informed, and their engagement was formally announced on April 1. They decided to be married in London on June 25, Gorst's forty-second birthday, and the khedive promised to attend if he could
arrange it. In an ironic gesture of continuity the
couple planned to move into the former Turnure house
in Cairo after their marriage. In early April Doll
left for England to prepare for the wedding. Gorst
remained in Egypt, and at the end of May took possession of the house from Carton de Wiart, a Belgian financier. On May 26 his diary reads: "Slept for the
first time in Turnure house." Some might have disputed the precision of the statement.

On his arrival in London a week before the wedding, Gorst was met by Eva "Dolly" Gorst and Evelyn
"Doll" Rudd, his fiancée. He busied himself in prep-
arations, met his father-in-law, and shopped for a
wedding ring and an automobile, among other things.
In a bit of bad luck, his opal stud was stolen from
his rooms at the St. James. Wedding presents flooded
in; he noted greedily, "I have over 100 and between us
over 300." The night before the wedding he did not
neglect his semiofficial duties: he visited the king's

friend, Mrs. Keppel, and met the khedive at Charing
Cross. Unfortunately the latter's audience with
Edward VII was scheduled for the same time as the
wedding. [21]

The couple was married on June 25 in the mid-
afternoon at Christ Church, Lancaster Gate. The best
man was Captain Percy Machell, Gorst's selection to
succeed himself as advisor to the interior ministry
in 1898.[22] A reception followed at the Rudd home in
Hyde Park Gardens, attended by the khedive, and their
honeymoon began at Castle Combe. They then returned
to London and stayed next door to Doll's father until
mid-July, when they went to her family's estate in the
Scottish highlands at Sheilbridge. Late in July on
Doll's twenty-third birthday the estate's tenants
gathered to give presents to the newlyweds and Gorst
made a short speech. The couple went fishing and
deerstalking; early in August he noted: "Killed one
young stag & hind & her calf. Shot them all dead.
Very pleased." Aside from a quick business trip to
London in August, the Gorsts remained in Scotland
until the last week in September. They were apparently quite happy, and on the way to Egypt they bought
another automobile in London and arranged for its
shipment to Cairo. [23]

In 1902 Gorst had successfully negotiated a commercial treaty between Egypt and France which he
claimed was "a very considerable diplomatic triumph
as indicating a great change on the part of the French
as regards the Egyptian question."[24] As a result,
barely had the Gorsts settled into the Turnure house
before he was recalled to act as Cromer's agent in
negotiations that culminated in the Anglo-French
Entente of 1904. They took up temporary residence in
London's Coburg Hotel and Gorst plunged into the complicated discussions. By the end of the year he had
enhanced his reputation. He made a good impression at
the Foreign Office during a briefing session in December. Lord Lansdowne, the foreign secretary, wrote
to Cromer: "Gorst came here last week and gave Austen
Chamberlain and myself an excellent review of the
Egyptian situation."[25]

The personnel of the Foreign Office did not
impress the critical Gorst. Though pleased with the
progress of the French negotiations, he wrote Cromer:
"When we have finished with the French, I almost think

I had better superintend the Foreign Office proceedings as regards the other powers. It is rather tiresome hanging about in a hotel, but they are all very
helpless in the Foreign Office, and we must not leave
anything to chance."[26] His successful work with the
French impressed both Lansdowne and Cromer,[27]and resulted in the offer of a position at the Foreign
Office as one of the assistant under secretaries to
replace the diplomat Charles Hardinge, who was moving
up to permanent under secretary. Gorst readily
accepted. This significant professional success was
somewhat marred by a personal loss, his wife's miscarriage.

This did not slow Gorst down. Once the negotiations were completed in the winter of 1904, he went
immediately to Cairo to conclude the remaining business, pack, and take leave of the khedive and his
friends. Cromer had depended heavily on Gorst, and
he found it difficult to find an acceptable replacement. "Gorst's departure will cause a small convul-
sion here. I had thought of Mitchell Innes, but I
find both native ministers and the high English officials strongly opposed, though they all like him personally. So I have dropped the idea. I think Corbett
will do."[28] As it turned out, Vincent Corbett was
appointed but ultimately did "not do" for Gorst, who
forced his resignation when he replaced Cromer in
1907.

Cromer gave Gorst a farewell dinner in Cairo on
April 22. He used the occasion to laud Gorst and also
to deliver a lengthy, elaborate, and somewhat defensive explanation to the assembled officials and notables about the difficult task of implementing his
policies in Egypt. Gorst was honored for his ability
to reconcile Egyptian needs with the maintenance of
British control and interests. However, Cromer did
not choose to specify Gorst's contributions, and
instead relied on slogans such as "Egypt for the
Egyptians." The following passage was typical of the
speech:

> I have had very explicit opportunity of
> appreciating the value of the services ren-
> dered by Sir Eldon Gorst to this country.
> Sir Eldon is one of the principals of that
> small band of Europeans who, for many years
> past have been engaged in carrying out a

policy of "Egypt for the Egyptians." . . .
It is a policy that does imply that the
touchstone to be applied to every Egyptian
question is to inquire how far this or that
proposal is in the true interests of the
dwellers in Egypt, of whatsoever nation-
ality or creed they may be . . . In my opinion, Sir Eldon Gorst's chief claim to be considered a successful reformer in this country
is that he fully recognized that "East is
East and West is West."[29]

Cromer's approval of Gorst's accomplishments in Egypt
was accompanied by an annual pension of five hundred
pounds Egyptian from the Egyptian government, an
unusual award since the normal practice had been to
give a departing official an indemnity not amounting
to more than nineteen months' salary.[30]

Chapter Seven

AMBITION FULFILLED

While the Anglo-French negotiations were going on, the
Gorsts lived first in the Coburg Hotel and then in
a flat in Whitehall Court. After he had accepted the
post at the Foreign Office, they began to look for a
more suitable, convenient house, and leased Number 36
in Queen Anne's Gate. This handsome enclave is ide-
ally located for someone working in Whitehall, just a
minute or two's walk from St. James's Park in Westminster. It was and is one of the most elegant sets of
townhouses in central London. The architectural historian David Piper labeled it "a remarkably preserved remnant, the best in London of early eighteenth
century domestic architecture."[1] The specific house
that Eldon and Doll leased from 1904 to 1907 apparently was pulled down about 1909 and has been replaced
by a building in the French baroque style.

His marriage enabled Gorst to live very well. As
part of the marriage settlement, his father-in-law
gave him three thousand pounds per year. That first
year the rent, rates, and utilities alone came to
eight hundred sixty-one pounds, and their food, servants, and upkeep brought the annual cost to almost
twenty-two hundred pounds. Furnishing and refurbish-
ing came to another twenty-one hundred eighty-three
pounds.[2] The bulk of this sum was paid by Doll's
father. They bought a Steinway and another automobile,
hired a chauffeur, and had the entire house redecorated.

For most of 1904 they lived relatively quietly,
mainly to forestall Doll's having a second miscarriage.
They acquired a new dog, a wire-haired terrier, that
fall. Doll's portrait was painted by a Mr. Herkomer,
who had painted her father. Tours in their electric
car became one of their main amusements. Eldon Gorst
relished high-speed driving. One day he borrowed his
father-in-law's Mercedes and drove to Hatfield

and back; "She went like the wind," he exulted. He
took up two other sports: real tennis, which he had
not played for years, and ice skating. Christmas Day
1904 he noted: "Skated in the morning and was able to
do an 8 comfortably." The Gorsts had the time and
money for grouse shooting and deer stalking. The ever
competitive Gorst asserted his prowess at the latter
during the summer of 1904. "During my stay in Scotland I continued my deer stalking exploits with success and shot two royals—one of the best in the whole
of Scotland." Their relatively calm life had the desired result. Doll gave birth to a girl without complications in May 1905. She was christened Katherine
Rachel. Gorst was relieved: "Felt glad that this anxious time was over," he noted in his diary.[3] "Kitty,"
as she was nicknamed, was the Gorsts' only child.

     Meanwhile Gorst kept in touch with his godchild
Margaret Turnure. In February 1905 he arranged with
Romaine to take "MR" (Margaret) to the zoo the next
month and in June he sent the child a birthday present. Throughout 1906 and into 1907 he entertained her
regularly; she came to tea and/or to dine and he took her
for drives and to the zoo. At less regular intervals
the Gorsts visited or were visited by Romaine with and
without her second husband, Lord Monson. Late in 1906
Gorst noted cryptically in his diary, "To tea with M.
[Margaret] T. [Turnure]. Lady M. [Monson] evidently
to present M. with an olive branch soon." Perhaps the
"olive branch" was a stepbrother of Margaret Turnure,
born to the Monsons in February 1907. Gorst visited
them in March in Lincolnshire, and Margaret showed him
the new baby.[4] His daughter Kitty, still a baby, is
hardly mentioned during this period.

     When not at work in the Foreign Office, he and
Doll often went driving in their car and Gorst kept
careful track of the time, speed, and mileage. Toward
the end of 1905 they ordered a Fiat 16-24 for four
hundred twenty-five pounds. Continuing his deerstalking exploits, at Sheilbridge in 1906 Gorst shot
nine stags in fifteen outings, lost two, and missed
two. Late that year he went ballooning with a friend
near London; they had a rough descent near Ilford, and
the ladies who were watching were "badly shaken."[5]

     Gorst's social life in London from 1905 to 1907
involved a number of diplomatic parties and other
upper-class social affairs. On occasion he played

bridge with such luminaries of Edwardian aristocracy as the Duke of Devonshire, Mrs. George Keppel, and Mr. Cavendish-Bentinck. He attended symphonies, operas, and the theatre regularly. He saw most of Shaw's plays and judged *The Doctor's Dilemma* "clever but disagreeable."[6]

The tone of his autobiographical notes and diaries indicates that Eldon Gorst kept his attention focused, in and out of work, on the main objective—to succeed Cromer in Egypt. In December 1906 he recorded a meeting he had had with Cromer and Lansdowne the previous summer concerning Egyptian business—"thereby emphasizing my position as *the* [his italics] Egyptian expert after Lord C., and the idea that I am eventually to succeed him seems to be gaining ground."[7]

Gorst's area of responsibility at the Foreign Office included Egypt and the Sudan, the commercial department, Abyssinia and Morocco, and some "unimportant European countries." When Sir T. H. "Lamps" Sanderson, the permanent under secretary, fell ill the summer of 1904, Gorst took charge of the consular department, Persia and Central Asia.[8] Egyptian affairs remained, however, his major concern and responsibility.

Gorst plunged into the new position with his usual intensity. Important negotiations were in process in several of the areas under his authority; with no false modesty he observed: "so that I had a certain amount of opportunity of showing the value of my work."[9] His manner disturbed some of his co-workers, but his performance was highly creditable. Always finished with his work early in the day, he could not collect enough work from others to keep him occupied, Storrs reported.[10] His initial reactions to the new position were mixed: "Considering how irksome all change is after a certain time of life, I am satisfied with the way in which I have grappled with many new and unforeseen difficulties and I feel that my energy and spirit of enterprise are so far not on the wane."[11] Zara Steiner lauded Gorst's work in her study of the Foreign Office during the years 1898 to 1914. She wrote of him: "As supervising undersecretary of the Eastern Department, he quickly mastered many of the details needed during the course of the Anglo-Russian negotiations, and his minutes suggest that here was a first-class mind at work."[12]

In general he was not impressed with the workings
of the Foreign Office. He wrote: "I found the bureaucratic atmosphere and want of responsibility—as well
as the dead-weight obstacles to any real reform—dis-
heartening and dreary beyond words."[13] This post, important as it was, was just a stepping-stone for Gorst
in his path back to Egypt. Thus he seems to have
avoided involvement in the Foreign Office internal
politics that led to certain reforms during his tenure
there. His single-mindedness and scorn for polite
forms and procedures did not endear him to some of
his co-workers. His "pushiness" bothered a senior
Foreign Office official, Louis Mallet, who wrote to
Sir Francis Bertie, the ambassador in Paris: "Gorst
continues to give dissatisfaction and I hear that the
boys will not go to his room now because he is so
infernally rude."[14]

Gorst, however, gave enough satisfaction to
others, both in and out of the Foreign Office, that
Mallet warned Bertie in 1905 that if Hardinge did
not accept Lansdowne's offer to succeed the retiring
Sanderson, Gorst might obtain the post when the Liberal Party came into office.[15] Cromer, who might have
been foreign secretary himself in the Liberal government, and Grey, the new foreign secretary, were
pleased with Gorst's performance. In a postscript to
a letter to Grey, Cromer wrote: "I quite agree that
Gorst has covered himself with glory over the Bahr-el-
Ghazal arrangement."[16] This was a delicate and complicated series of negotiations with King Leopold and
the Belgian government over a disputed area that
involved Nile River control on the border of the Belgian Congo and the Sudan.

Meanwhile Gorst kept his attention on the opportunity to succeed Cromer. In 1905 he dismissed the
threat of "a certain clique among the English" in
Cairo, which included Wingate and Brunyate. Their
candidate was Sir Rennell Rodd, who had been Cromer's
counselor at the Agency in Cairo from 1894 to 1901.
"I do not fancy they are dangerous," he estimated, but
he noted a year later that Kitchener, then in India,
was making efforts to succeed Cromer. Earlier, in
1904, Eldon Gorst had refused an offer to serve as
financial member of the council in India.[17]

In the summer of 1906 he persuaded his wayward
brother Harold not to write a book about Egypt, "the

idea wh' [which] would have greatly injured my prospects in Egypt." That same year he also refused an
offer from Cassel to use the financier's influence
with the king to appoint Gorst ambassador to the
United States. "The idea," Gorst observed, "would
not have been congenial—principally pouring butter
on the Americans, and it would have been too far from
my natural destination—Egypt." Cassel, even earlier, had sought without success to recruit Gorst to
succeed Sir Elwin Palmer as governor of the Egyptian
National Bank.[18]

During these years of intense, calculating struggle for advancement, Gorst exhibited few signs of
ideological development or thoughts about a political
theory of or a justification for the British Empire.
Unlike Cromer, he died too soon to have the leisure
to discuss and explain his career at length, or to
work out, even after the act, a rationale for his
imperialist "philosophy." However, up to 1907 Gorst
had published a few articles in Britain that gave
some insight into his attitudes toward the peoples
over whom he ruled, some hints of what his own Egyptian policies were to be, and his own view of the role
of the British Empire. These articles, like Milner's
book *England in Egypt* or Wingate's propaganda against
the Sudanese Mahdi,[19] were primarily designed to promote favorable British opinion toward policies the
Cromerian-veiled protectorate wanted to implement, and
were not explanations of Gorst's career.

Gorst shared with Cromer and most of his countrymen the assumption that Europeans, particularly the
British—"the Anglo-Saxons"—were specially fitted
through experience and through their superior cultural
and moral system to rule over Oriental races. He did
attempt to analyze the differences between the races
and the reasons for "Anglo-Saxon" superiority; his
writing revealed more about the prejudices of Sir
Eldon Gorst than about the Oriental character.
Gorst's experience with "Orientals" was limited to
Egypt, yet he presumed like Cromer and most of his
contemporaries to judge the rest of the Asian peoples
then under imperial rule.

In 1899 he delineated the characteristics of the
Oriental races in an article for the *Anglo-Saxon
Review*.[20] Orientals (which should be translated as
Egyptians and Sudanese) were passive and accepting,

but possessed great physical endurance. No better
"material" existed to be used for soldiers or to be
misgoverned. The British officers in Egypt were,
by their example and training, helping the men in
the Egyptian army to regain their physical courage,
lost in the misrule of the century. Class distinc-
tions did not exist for Orientals; because they had
no sense of inferiority, they made the best servants
in the world. They still possessed the "barbaric
virtue of hospitality," although changing social conditions were undermining this custom; they were also
charitable to the poor.

However, the extreme "conservatism" that per-
meated their family structure made social relations
between Europeans and Orientals very difficult. Here
Gorst was in part alluding to the Egyptian sensitivity to any changes in the Islamic social structure,
especially those initiated by non-Muslim Europeans.
"It is this peculiarity [conservatism] that renders
the task of improving the condition of oriental peoples an especially delicate one. The zeal of an
earnest reformer may do far more harm than good unless
it be directed with abundance of tact." He cautioned
against dogmatizing on this trait by noting that although it might be very difficult to persuade an Egyptian clerk that he would be more efficient at the
office if he ceased his age-old practice of sitting
cross-legged and writing on his palm, Egyptians of all
classes rapidly accepted and learned to use the railroad and telegraph.

The Oriental, unlike the European, kept his women
in bondage. "It is difficult to see that any permanent regeneration of these races can be expected so
long as one-half the population remains in a state of
perpetual servitude." The impulse for change must
come from within. The degenerate Oriental family that
resulted from this servitude was the cause of much of
their troubles, and Gorst warned cynically against
changes in the Western family that might cause similar
decay. "It may be doubted whether the conversion of
women, now in so many ways man's better half, into an
inferior man would be a sufficient compensation."

Social relations with the Orientals were complicated not only by the absence of women, but by the
fact that they were "singularly devoid of any capacity
for enjoyment." Orientals were rarely amused and

tended to be vindictive in personal and family matters.
They were "in general extremely humane, only their
humanity is mitigated by great ignorance, which frequently produces effects the reverse of what is
intended." Their judgment was defective and focused
on detail to the exclusion of the main point. They
were not logical thinkers, but apt special pleaders,
and were extraordinarily clever and persistent in
their own individual interests. "As an official the
main character of the oriental is his extreme dread
of responsibility." They were very unwilling to criticize their superiors.

The religion of Islam had different effects on
the Oriental races in certain areas. In Egypt the
Muslims were very sensitive to any attempt at Christian proselytism. Yet they were not intolerant toward
Christian rule and had a specific preference for imperial rulers. "The Egyptian Mohammadan [*sic*] . . . is
like the Indian Mohammadan perfectly satisfied to be
ruled by a Christian power."[21] In another article,
Gorst amplified this idea:

> Curiously enough, the Eastern races have gen-
> erally exhibited a marked preference for
> Anglo-Saxon masters as compared with those
> of other nationalities. The reason perhaps
> is that though we are very slow at under-
> standing them, they easily understand us, and
> quickly acquire the comfortable feeling of
> knowing exactly where they are.[22]

Gorst, like his mentor Cromer, admitted that even
after many years, a European could never hope to
understand the Oriental races. Their thought processes, their ways of life, were too different. Lack of
understanding did not preclude imperial rule, for the
"logical West," which had succeeded in civilizing itself, should—in the best interests of "the illogical
and picturesque East"—provide the guidance and experience that might in the future promote civilized
self-rule in the Orient.[23] "Successful states should
lend them a helping hand, even if that hand cannot be
withdrawn, and should give them the opportunity of
sharing in the material blessings which the peoples
of Europe have earned by the labour and suffering of
many centuries."[24] Gorst, a realist, was pessimistic
about the immediate effects of the British efforts.

> In spite of the unquestionable talent of
> the Anglo-Saxons in ruling Oriental peoples,
> the two races are at the opposite poles of
> humanity. No dominant race can expect to
> inspire affection in the peoples over whom
> it rules but the Englishman has, as a rule,
> succeeded in inspiring the next best feel-
> ings—respect and fear.[25]

In the "long run," a time span left unspecified, Gorst
believed that the small British efforts might successfully "instill a public spirit in the hearts of a subject race."[26]

   In three articles written while working at the
Foreign Office, Gorst hinted at the future emphases
of Britain's Egyptian policy. Although intended to
promote support for the Cromer regime, they do indicate that some changes in policy—changes mainly of
degree—were being considered. Gorst gave Cromer's
practical genius for administration full credit, in
the face of the absurdities and paradoxes of the
Egyptian situation, for the transformation of Egypt
internally and externally since 1882. Like other
Anglo-Egyptian officials, he emphasized the personal
character of the administration, the "benevolent despotism" that Cromer created. The business of government was carried on by personal communication,
eliminating the delays and misunderstandings of
departmental paperwork. It was a system that demanded
efficiency, tact, and talent from the men involved,
and when the men changed, the administrative system
worked erratically. Under "an unskilled hand" disaster could quickly result. "Consequently there is at
times a want of continuity in the methods adopted,
owing to the fact that the personal factor has a tendency to overshadow tradition and precedent."[27] Gorst
was fully aware of the dangers and difficulties of
such a personal system as Cromer had created, and by
implication was somewhat critical of it.

   Some British efforts at reform, especially in the
ministries of justice and the interior, had been frustrated by "the inherent deficiencies of a population
that has been oppressed for centuries." Gorst thought
that the only permanent and true remedy for the elevation of moral standards among the masses in Egypt was
a "statesmanlike educational policy." The Egyptian
government would continue to expand its efforts to

create an adequate educational system, but, Gorst
cautioned, it would take time and money. Local self-
government was a second area where future efforts at
reform should be concentrated. Here it was better
to aim at increasing public spirit than to impose complicated and sophisticated European governmental
institutions like elective legislatures "unsuited to
the genius of the oriental character."[28] Gorst suggested that self-governing municipalities would provide a suitable outlet for the classes that were
pushing for autonomy, and would prepare them for more
responsible positions when the British felt willing
to grant them.

A third reform that Gorst proposed would be to
increase diplomatic efforts to remove the restrictions
of the Capitulations, especially where they affected
municipal government. In January 1907, after a year
of increased nationalist pressures in Egypt, Gorst—
still in the Foreign Office—hinted at some "minor
changes" in the constitution of the moribund Legislative Council. "There might be advantages in adopting some such method of conciliating native opinion."[29]
This last vague suggestion to increase the Egyptians'
participation in their own government came just four
months before Gorst was selected to succeed Cromer.

Gorst, as Cromer's agent in London, obviously
eager to succeed him, could hardly be expected to
criticize Cromer's policies openly, much less to repu-
diate them. Still, hints of his own future policies
were evident in these articles. He believed, unlike
Cromer, that the Egyptians deserved a chance to prove
they were capable of limited self-rule, and he therefore advocated increased employment of Egyptians in
government offices. He was willing to experiment with
self-rule, especially at the local level and even in
the Legislative Council,which had been almost totally
ignored under Cromer. As a senior official in Egypt,
Gorst had gained the friendship of the khedive and
helped to make him more comfortable under British
rule.

Gorst's attitude toward criticism of the British
by Egyptians was affected by his notion of the imperial role. He apparently genuinely believed that the
British had the Egyptians' welfare at heart, and while
it might be impossible under the conditions of the
occupation to gain more than their respect and fear,

British guidance was beneficial and necessary. He
regretted that a reliable and sympathetic public opinion had not arisen in Egypt that would make this necessary process of rule easier and more beneficial for
both sides:

> In England we suffer from a plethora of dis-
> cussion combined with a poverty of results.
> The reverse is the case in the land of the
> Pharaohs. Neither in the institutions of the
> country nor in the Press can there be heard
> at present the voice of an honest and well
> informed public opinion. The want of local
> restraining influence of this kind is much
> felt by those who have at heart the welfare
> of the Egyptians, and who would only be too
> thankful for some trustworthy barometer of
> the wishes and feelings of the people. Time
> alone can repair this deficiency by the grad-
> ual spread of education and by the regular
> evolution of some simple system of local self-
> government which will help the people to a
> more complete understanding of public affairs.[30]

The assumption that education and increased responsibility in local government might be conducive to Egyptian understanding as to the necessities of British
rule seems from this distance naive for a man of
Gorst's experience. But it does demonstrate the British imperialistic conviction that rationality coupled
with the reality of British power would uphold British
rule. This was a conviction not easily shaken, as the
Egyptians and others were to discover.

These general ideas about Oriental races, Egyptian policy, Britain's imperial role, and her fitness
to rule were put to the test of reality not long after
Gorst's last article appeared. Published in January
1907, it attempted to explain the unrest and turmoil
that had unexpectedly arisen in Egypt in 1906 and continued into the following year. As a consequence of
the strain, Cromer's health collapsed quite suddenly
during the late winter of 1907. Gorst was the most
available and logical candidate to succeed him. He
had lengthy experience in the Egyptian Service and in
the Foreign Office as well as adequate political connections, and had married into a wealthy family. His
lack of public renown was the only significant mark
against him. His most important rivals had eliminated

themselves. Kitchener was out of the running, since
he had committed himself to two more years in India.
Milner, in the political wilderness after his South
African proconsulship, was a prominent member of the
opposition party. The Liberals were also more inclined than the Conservatives to select candidates
for important jobs by merit.[31]

Wilfrid Blunt reported hearing on March 7 from
George Wyndham, a prominent Conservative politician,
that Gorst was "inevitable" as Cromer's successor.[32]
Inevitable or not, Gorst's own intense preparation
and the circumstances combined to produce the result
that he had so long desired. Harry Boyle, Cromer's
Oriental secretary, wrote to his mother on March 27:

> The Lord [Cromer] is going to urge the
> appointment of Gorst, and I sincerely hope
> they will send him, as he is the only man
> I know at all capable of taking it on. Of
> course the Lord's retirement will cause an
> enormous sensation, and very possibly some-
> thing in the nature of a financial and
> social crisis here, but the announcement will
> have to be carefully made. It will be a tri-
> umph for the Khedive and the Nationalists,
> but that can not be helped, and I hope the
> event will show that their exultation was
> misplaced.[33]

Cromer wrote the same day to Grey firmly recommending
Gorst: "If, as I hope will be the case, Gorst succeeds
me, you could lay stress on the fact that, inasmuch as
he may be almost called a pupil of mine, his nomination is of itself an adequate guarantee that no change
of policy is in contemplation."[34] Grey agreed with
Cromer's recommendation, but had to consult the prime
minister, Sir Henry Campbell-Bannerman, before offer-
ing the post to Gorst. The prime minister concurred,
slightly reluctantly, the next day:

> It seems to point straight to Gorst. The
> outside world will not be impressed, but it
> would be difficult to set aside Cromer's
> strong advice, and obviously his acquain-
> tance with the past history, atmosphere and
> present position of Egypt is a qualifica-
> tion possessed by no other possible
> candidate.[35]

Gorst, well aware that Cromer was retiring, had
to wait a few days before the post was his. On Tues-
day, April 9, he wrote in his diary, "F.O. [Foreign
Office]. Sir E. [Grey] sent for me to say that the
Gov't and King wished to appoint me Lord Cromer's successor. As the cabinet were to be asked, the matter
was to be kept secret until Thursday. He spoke most
nicely about me & I replied appropriately. Told D.
[Doll] at lunch." His appointment as His Majesty's
Agent, Consul-General and Minister Plenipotentiary in
Egypt was formally announced by Grey to the House of
Commons on April 11, 1907. His salary would be sixty-
five hundred pounds per year. Gorst recorded his reactions to the news of the long-hoped-for appointment:

> After a few anxious days, caused by the ne-
> cessity of consulting H.M. The King and the
> Prime Minister, who were both abroad, Sir E.
> Grey offered me the place in flattering lan-
> guage, saying that if I had not been available
> neither he nor the Gov't would have known
> which way to turn to find a successor to Lord
> Cromer. The fact that no other name was seri-
> ously considered in connx'n with the appmt. . .
> reflects credit upon the thoroughness with
> which I had been for some years qualifying
> for this post.[36]

Reactions of the press to the Gorst appointment
were mixed. *The Egyptian Gazette,* generally acknowledged to be the voice of the British community in
Egypt, called his appointment unexpected. Two days
earlier it had speculated that if Cromer retired soon,
Alfred Mitchell Innes, the under secretary of finance,
might succeed him. It advised its readers to "react
with the utmost skepticism to all reports relative to
changes in Ministries or among the advisors."[37] In
England, press reaction was generally favorable. *The
Saturday Review* wrote: "No better choice of successor
to Lord Cromer could have been found than Sir Eldon
Gorst." *The Sketch* was pleased because Cromer had
interfered with the speculators in Egypt, and Gorst,
they asserted, would not. *The Methodist Times* had
hoped for a stronger appointment, and *The Bystander*
wondered if he was the right man socially: Why, it
asked, was not Milner selected for the post? *The
Morning Post* foresaw difficulties for Britain in Egypt
when Cromer departed. Gorst would not be able to
remain content with Cromer's record, the military

establishment would have to be strengthened, and reforms and improvements would have to be made in education and sanitary conditions to fit the Egyptian peasants for parliamentary government and increase their
life expectancy. Female emancipation should be encouraged and crime prevention increased. A European
legislative council should be instituted in Egypt to
replace the Capitulations. Gorst would be a strong
replacement and would be able to cope with the changed
conditions.[38]

In Egypt, the Anglican missionaries were distinctly unhappy about Gorst's selection. Cromer had
represented stability to them. The secretary of the
Church Missionary Society in Cairo, the Reverend
Rennie MacInnes, deplored the choice in letters to
his London headquarters.

> The great topic of the hour, as you can imag-
> ine, is Lord Cromer's resignation, and now
> that it has come we are wishing that he might
> have stayed on for years rather than give
> place to a man like Sir Eldon Gorst, who is
> popularly supposed to have neither religion
> nor morals, and in favour of whose appoint-
> ment one has never heard a word in all past
> speculations. However, we ought not to cry
> out before we are hurt, and I feel sure that
> Lord Cromer will speak to him about his treat-
> ment of the native Christians and of the mis-
> sionary societies, and show him that it may be
> to his gain not to spurn them. . . .
>
> We can only trust that the first disappoint-
> ment on hearing of this appointment may not
> be justified, and that Sir Eldon Gorst, at
> least while he is in office, will act towards
> the Christians of Egypt, both native and for-
> eign, as an Englishman ought to act, and that
> none of the reports that we have heard in re-
> cent years of what we might have to expect if
> ever he got hold of the reins may be justi-
> fied either.[39]

MacInnes then wrote to Cromer expressing his disappointment at the resignation and his concern for its
effect on the Missionary Society and its activities:
"I can hardly hope that we may be fortunate enough to
find in any of your Lordship's successors such kindness

and courtesy as we have experienced at your hands."
Cromer replied assuring the worried missionary leader
that he would not fail to speak to Gorst about their
work and that he had no doubt that relations would
continue as before. Reverend MacInnes commented hope-
fully to his superior in London that "for a man who
says so little, the letter was a remarkable one, and
we feel that his good offices on our behalf with Sir
Eldon Gorst are no small gain for the future."[40]

If the Church Missionary Society had qualms about
the appointment, many British officials did not.
Ronald Storrs, then very junior at the Agency, wrote
home: "The people here are relieved that Gorst is coming: They were in a (mild) terror that it should be
K. [Kitchener] or Milner."[41]   Sir John Gorst was very
proud that Cromer had recommended his eldest son as
his replacement. He sent his thanks to the retiring
autocrat: "His [Eldon's] public character has been
almost entirely of your making, and I trust he may be
able to follow in your footsteps, and justify the confidence which has induced you to commend him as a fit
person to carry on your work."[42]

Gorst of course was immensely pleased, for the
post for which he had worked so long and fiercely was
now his:

> Throughout the British Empire there is no
> place of which the occupant enjoys greater
> freedom of action than that of British Agent
> & Consul General in Egypt. The C-G is the
> *de facto* ruler of the country, without being
> hampered by a Parliament or by a net-work of
> Councils like the Viceroy of India and the
> interference of the home Govt has hitherto
> been limited to such matters as are likely to
> arouse interest or criticism in the British
> H. of C. Otherwise H.M. Rep've can practi-
> cally run the government of the country on
> whatever lines he thinks right—a great re-
> sponsibility involving the welfare of some
> 11 millions of human beings—productive of
> effects, not easy to forecast, on the desti-
> nies of the British Empire itself. I embarked
> on this great trust at the age of 46, with my
> mental & bodily powers unimpaired & full of
> vigour, and with the feeling that my past
> training and experience of affairs had been

exactly what was necessary to prepare me to
fill the position worthily.[43]

On April 12 he sent his thanks to Cromer: "The only
way I can show my gratitude is by promising you that
the rest of my working life shall . . . be devoted to
continuing the great work which you originated and
brought so far on the way." His appointment had been
received with favor because he was "a member of the
Cromer school." Gorst promised to continue as well
as he could Cromer's policy.[44]

Chapter Eight

THE AUTOCRAT'S LEGACY

*Egypt has always been the home of
improvisation and of its first
cousin, bluff.*

Sir Ronald Storrs[1]

The dilemmas and difficulties that faced Sir Eldon
Gorst when he returned to Egypt in 1907 were largely
the legacy of his predecessor. Perhaps it is incor-
rect to attribute the total British effort to Lord
Cromer, but for almost a quarter of a century he represented Britain in Egypt. Whatever one's viewpoint
on the merits of Cromer's policies, it was his impress
that best defined the British rule from 1882 to 1907.

Through a morass of intrigue, local and international legal restrictions, legal and political machinations of the European powers, and the threat of
financial chaos, Cromer in twenty-four years—always
backed by the presence of the British army of occupation and the availability of the British fleet—gave
Egypt a viable European-style administration. The
American Consul-General to Egypt from 1893 to 1897
described the omnipresent British soldiers in Cairo
during that era:

> No picture of Cairo that does not include
> the soldier can be considered complete, for
> the military aspect is in almost aggressive
> evidence. . . . By company or regiment, sol-
> diers are so frequently marched through the
> streets that the visitor might believe Cairo
> to be a vast military camp. Martial music is
> the adjunct of every function, and every anni-
> versary, religious and festive. . . . It is
> part of the scheme of administration to keep
> the soldier in evidence, impressing the simple
> native with the importance of the army.[2]

Backed by this threat of force, Cromer ruled through
a system of skilled British advisors to the khedive's
government. Each Egyptian minister had at his elbow
a British official who took orders from the Consul-
General and then "advised" the minister. If his
advice was not followed, the Egyptian minister or
other officeholder usually ceased to hold office.[3]

Cromer, in the process of accomplishing his program of reforms and implementing his policies, chose
occasionally—if infrequently—to humiliate Khedive
Abbas Hilmi publicly. Indeed, his general policy was
to bypass the lawful ruler of Egypt. In the first
nine years of British occupation the necessity to
override the khedive had not arisen, as Abbas's father,
Taufiq, well aware that British backing had preserved
his position and his dynasty, had been docile and
cooperative.[4] Cromer's treatment of Abbas, however,
served to weaken further an already discredited dynasty and encouraged Abbas's tendency toward intrigue
and self-aggrandizement. In the 1890s and early
1900s he intrigued with the Ottoman sultan, with the other
foreign powers—especially the French—and with a reviving nationalist movement to block British efforts
at significant reform.[5] Just a month before his sudden resignation Cromer wrote scornfully and cynically
about Abbas to one of his sons.

> I do not in the least want to get rid of him.
> He is what your outspoken brother in South
> America would call a "hopeless swine," but
> at the same time, unless some cataclysm oc-
> curs which enables the whole Egyptian ques-
> tion to be put on a different footing, he had
> better remain where he is.[6]

In spite of the khedive, the meddling of foreign
powers, and the restrictions imposed by the Capitulations, Cromer effected several major reforms. The
judicious use of talented British advisors and administrators in the Egyptian government—among them Sir
Edgar Vincent (later Viscount D'Abernon), Alfred
Milner (later Viscount Milner), and Sir Eldon Gorst—
enabled Cromer and the British to regularize Egyptian
financial affairs. The country quite rapidly became
solvent and prosperous. During the first decade of
this century Egyptian per capita income was probably
higher than at any time in modern Egyptian history

except the early 1920s. Vital agricultural reforms
were effected. British engineers, drawing on the
experience they had gained in India and Britain, re-
paired the Nile Barrage, neglected since the reign of
Muhammad Ali, improved the irrigation system in the
Delta, and in 1902 finished construction of the first
stage of the Aswan Dam. This completed a system of
summer storage of water that permitted extensive
expansion of land under perennial irrigation.[7] The
new high dam at Aswan is an elaboration of the vast
and effective system inaugurated in that period.
Since Egypt's prosperity depended on the products of
her soil, this reform of the agricultural system by
the British was the most important of the Cromerian
era.

Cromer also supervised the reconstitution of the
Egyptian army, under the close control of British
officers and noncommissioned officers.[8] To prevent
another Urabi-like revolt this army was kept on garrison duty on the frontiers and in the Sudan, once that
region had been reconquered by an Anglo-Egyptian army
in 1898. Cromer created the Anglo-Egyptian condominium that ensured British control in the Sudan—and
avoided the diplomatic, political, and legal problems
that had made British efforts to reform Egypt so complicated. He participated in the delicate diplomacy
that resulted in the Anglo-French Entente of 1904. As
it affected Egypt, the Entente recognized the special
position of the British there, removed some onerous
financial limitations on the Egyptian government, and
lessened the chance that an Egyptian dispute would
poison relations between the British and the French.
Robert Vansittart, then a junior diplomat in the
Agency in Cairo, observed that the Entente was

> no more than a bit of common sense. . . . it
> ended a bicker about Newfoundland fisheries
> dating back to the Treaty of Utrecht at the
> beginning of the 18th century, a record of
> trivial ill-humour. . . . For our part we
> gained French acquiescence in our special
> position in Egypt [in return for giving the
> French a free hand in Morocco] so that we
> no longer needed the support of the Germans.[9]

The Entente of 1904 seemed a fitting capstone to the
edifice that Cromer had been building in Egypt. It

appeared to settle the Egyptian question internation-
ally, and to allow Cromer to proceed with further
internal reforms. [10] Triumphant and in firm control in
1904, Cromer nevertheless resigned in 1907 in ill
health, overwhelmed by the pressures of his position,
leaving to Sir Eldon Gorst an administration in confusion and the country in a state of unrest. The future
of British hegemony in Egypt was far from clear.

By 1904 the administration that Cromer had created to cope with the complexities of Egyptian rule
had hardened into a pattern of personal government
that was not sufficiently responsive to the political
and social problems of Egypt in the first decade of
this century. Its success depended on Cromer's own
sense of the possible, and his ability to maintain a
delicate balance of power between the British advisors
and officials, the khedive, and the British government
in London. The Egyptian government itself, in Cromer's
words, "is no government at all. . . . The Khedive is
deprived by the Egyptian constitutional charter of all
rights of external sovereignty which are inherent in
the rulers of all independent, and even of some semi-
independent states."[11]   These rights of external sovereignty legally belonged to the Ottoman sultan in
Constantinople, but Great Britain had in fact assumed
them when she occupied Egypt in 1882. Cromer as the
British Agent and Consul-General was deputized to keep
Egypt safe from foreign interference or internal sub-
version that might threaten the lifeline of the British Empire, the Suez Canal.

The character of Cromer's rule grew increasingly
autocratic and overdependent on his prestige as the
years passed. Harry Boyle, Cromer's fervently loyal
Oriental secretary, wrote to a friend in England in
1899 that "Egypt, . . . a country of ten million people" was administered on a personal basis: "In all
this, the most important part of the whole work, no
writing passes, all is by word of mouth."[12] In 1904 he
described Cromer's rule as "a most amazing business,
this one-man government of an immense territory. It
has never had its parallel anywhere except perhaps
John Lawrence's administration of the Punjab and he
had no beastly foreign powers' complications to deal
with."[13] Sir J. Rennell Rodd, counselor in the British
Agency from 1894 to 1901, the golden years of Cromer's
rule, recalled:

> Circumstances developed the autocratic char-
> acter to which he [Cromer] was temperamen-
> tally predisposed. The success which attended
> his efforts to produce order from chaos, and
> the eventual elimination of all the inter-
> ference from home, increased his sense of
> absolute self-dependence, and made an auth-
> ority which became too exclusively personal
> tend to diminish the sense of responsibility
> in those who had worked under him. It was
> curious, when he had adopted a suggestion
> made to him which proved successful in its
> effects, in how short a time he convinced
> himself that the measure was due to his own
> initiative.[14]

Though he had working under him over the years a
number of distinguished and capable individuals,
Cromer overwhelmed them all. He well deserved his
nicknames: "The Vice-Viceroy" (acquired during his
relatively short career in India),[15] "Overbearing," and
"The Lord" (earned during his long rule in Egypt).[16]
Even strong men such as Kitchener and Sir Leslie Rundle
admitted they always approached an interview with
Cromer with some trepidation.[17]   Sir William Willcocks,
a prominent irrigation engineer and designer of various major hydrologic projects in the Middle East and
India, served in Egypt as an irrigation inspector in
the ministry of public works in the early days of the
British occupation. Another strong and independent
man who was not afraid of controversy, he clashed with
Cromer several times: "I used to imagine that Lord
Cromer was never so happy ordering officials to march
to right or left as when ordering them to think to
right or left. He was a thorough autocrat."
Willcocks's successful resistance, however, was an
exception, for the habits of autocracy grew more rigid
as Cromer grew older. Such independent men were not
encouraged to stay in the Cromerian administration.
Willcocks observed: "He [Cromer] did a great work for
Egypt, but I do not regret not having been able to get
along with him, as all the officials who enjoyed working under him seemed to lose their backbones."[18] P. G.
Elgood, an inspector in the ministry of the interior
in Egypt, testified that "it was not his [Cromer's]
practice to retain Lieutenants whose view ran counter
to his own."[19] Edgar Vincent, who as the financial
advisor was one of Cromer's most influential and talented young officials in the early and crucial years

of the occupation, wrote of Cromer: "Being rightly
convinced that no one could state a case more clearly
than himself, he accepted emendation with definite
reluctance."[20]

If Cromer was unwilling to tolerate independent
behavior from his colleagues or from the khedive, he
naturally allowed little or none to the major Egyptian
ministers or senior officials in the government. By
the mid-1890s he had given up trying to find any capable Egyptians who could work with his administration
and he followed a deliberate policy of increasing the
numbers of British in the service of the Egyptian
government. The result was that the Egyptian ministers were "ciphers," with rare exceptions, and were
regarded with scorn by their knowledgeable countrymen
and the British officials. Gorst referred to these
men in private as "dummies."[21] Thus when Cromer,
under pressure of events in the last full year of his
proconsulship, began to look for capable Egyptians
there were few available. Twenty-three years of tutelage and reform by the British had not produced, it
appeared, enough able and responsible native administrators. Cromer had ignored or discredited many of
them, especially men like Mustafa Kamil, so that they
would not be acceptable to the British administration.

Cromer did not believe that the Islamic modern-
ists such as Muhammad Abduh or Ahmad Lutfi al-Sayyid
could provide much more than political support for
the British policies. Islam, he held, was degenerate,
and until the Egyptians had somehow on their own attained a level of sophistication and morality that
implied acceptance of British values and practices
and a denial of their Islamic heritage, they would
not be fit for full collaboration with the British
in ruling Egypt. Consequently, by 1905 the higher
posts of the Egyptian civil service were dominated
by the British in numbers as well as by influence.
They held 42 percent of all posts, other Europeans
and Syrian or Armenian Christians held 30 percent, and
the Egyptians held only 28 percent.[22] Cromer's published figures in his annual reports of 1906 and 1907
documented an increase in Egyptians in the administration, but neglected to make a breakdown according to
rank.

Cromer may well have given the Egyptians their
first concerted experience of ordered administration

in the modern era, but the heavy influx of British in
the top positions in the Egyptian civil service after
1895 did not increase the efficiency of the system.
By the end of his rule, the Cromerian organization may
well have decreased in efficiency from the standards
it had set earlier. Cromer's autocratic habits, his
imperious and personal style which worked through an
organization—the British consulate—designed for
nineteenth-century diplomacy and not for the efficient
and just administration of what amounted in fact to
a Crown colony, meant that the increasingly complex
and subtle business of the Agency and its relations
with the various Egyptian departments were conducted generally on an *ad hoc* basis.[23]   In the early
years of the occupation Cromer kept in touch with his
officials and through them with the Egyptian government, and he kept a closer watch on Egyptian affairs.
But with old age, success, and the growth of various
bureaucracies, he lost much of his sensitivity to the
Egyptian administration he had created. His indiffer-
ence to the nuances of Egyptian public opinion and
Egyptian needs had unfortunate consequences for both
the Egyptians and the British.

During the last years of Cromer's proconsulship
nothing concerted was done to reform the administrative machinery of the British Agency. Ronald Storrs,
a 1904 recruit to the Egyptian civil service, found
himself moved from department to department as no one
knew quite what to do with a recent graduate of Cambridge who had no particularly needed skill. Not only
was personnel placement haphazard, but the processes of
communication between the Agency and the various departments of the Egyptian government were inefficient.
Already complicated by international restrictions and
by the necessity of having to maintain the facade of
Egyptian control, the business of the Egyptian government struck a bottleneck in the Agency. Work was
never allocated systematically. "This was sometimes
trying for the Residency [the British Agency], for the
administrations it was maddening." Even the most
patient of British and Egyptian officials found themselves paralyzed at times by the consequent lack of
continuity in their work.[24]

Gorst's familiarity with the vagaries of day-to-
day administration in Egypt, acquired during his
eighteen years of service there (1886-1904), did not
preclude difficulties in planning and organization

when he returned in 1907. Many departments of the
Egyptian government did not keep systematic records.
Only the public works and prisons departments published annual reports;[25]the other individual departments were not subject to a systematic scrutiny, and
the records necessary for guidance when problems arose
were not immediately available. C. E. Coles Pasha, a
police and prisons official under Cromer, Gorst, and
Kitchener, was critical of the voluminous oracular
annual reports and accused Cromer of boasting that
they would be the only official record left for his
successor. Sir J. Rennell Rodd, second in command at
the Agency from 1894 to 1901, observed: "Cromer had
all the threads in his hands; his methods were largely
personal, and there was little to be gleaned from the
consultation of records."[26]

At the time of Gorst's appointment as Cromer's
successor, the British public's impression of its
government's rule in Egypt was distorted and misinformed. The British government itself, relying heavily on Cromer, did not have enough accurate information to assess the situation. The care of Egypt had
been left in the hands of one man for too long, and
that man was old, autocratic, and eager to discredit
and discourage those who might have criticized or
acted as a "loyal opposition."[27] Although "loyal"
opposition was a pipe dream, responsible opposition
was not. In the government in Britain, Cromer had
established himself as the reigning expert on Egyptian
affairs. His word was not to be disputed, nor his
prestige threatened, or,as he warned so often, chaos
would result.

Over the years Cromer had been careful to refer
to London only those questions that affected interests external to Egypt.[28] Neither his administration
nor the British government was much interested in the
Egyptians' own affairs unless they impinged on British
imperial interests. Cromer won the confidence of
every secretary of state for foreign affairs and prime
minister under whom he served. He was even offered
the foreign secretaryship by Sir Henry Campbell-
Bannerman when the latter was forming his Liberal
Cabinet in 1905.[29] Cromer refused, but the offer
shows how highly his prestige and abilities were regarded. Virtually all the initiative and responsibility for Egyptian policies were left to Cromer and his
officials. Whitehall was in an awkward position: if

confronted by an internal Egyptian question, it lacked
the requisite knowledge and experience to make a sensible decision. Cromer, despite his disclaimers, had
created a curious form of Oriental despotism by the
end of his rule; administrative and financial efficiency had been increased, but contact with the people
had been lost.[30] Many British officials were too
inexperienced to make decisions in a balanced and sensible manner.

At least part of the blame for the semihysterical
behavior of the British in Egypt during the first half
of 1906, and particularly the tragic Dinshawai affair,
can be laid on Cromer. He had stayed in Egypt too
long; he and his administrative system needed to be
revitalized. The retrogressive quality of Cromer's
final years was underlined in his administration's
handling of this unrest. It had been brewing since
the mid-1890s as Egyptian nationalism of various
sorts, in shock for a decade after the debacle of
1882, began to revive. Two crises in particular led
to the accession of Sir Eldon Gorst as Cromer's successor in the spring of 1907. The first, a border
dispute with the Ottomans over the frontier in Sinai—
the so-called Tabah crisis—nearly brought the Ottoman
Empire and Great Britain to war. More significant
still, it aroused in Egypt latent anti-foreign feelings and demonstrations that surprised and thoroughly
frightened the British administration and the other
foreign communities resident in Egypt. A second crisis was precipitated when some British officers were
beaten by Egyptians from the Delta village of Dinshawai in June 1906, and one died as a result. The
frightened Cromer administration inflicted on the villagers a hasty and extremely harsh punishment.

Reaction in Great Britain to these two indirectly
related events, particularly to the Dinshawai incident, led to increased questioning in the newly elected
Liberal-dominated House of Commons and in the newspapers. There was embarrassment for the British government and more intense interest, particularly in
Parliament, in Egyptian affairs. In Egypt a small but
vocal group of nationalists was able to capitalize on
the shock and horror generated among almost all classes of Egyptians by the Dinshawai trial and punishments, making it increasingly difficult for Cromer and
his administration to continue to rule in their autocratic and narrow pattern, ignoring Egyptian needs.

The combination of these two pressure groups led to
some changes in policy within Egypt, a further rapid
deterioration of Cromer's health, his surprise resignation, and the selection of Sir Eldon Gorst as his
successor. [31]

Many of Cromer's claims about reform in Egypt and
his concern for its long-misgoverned masses were
belied by the reactions of the British government and
the Cromer administration to the events of the first
seven months of 1906. These crises brought into a
harsh light, for the Egyptians especially, the reality
of British imperial interests. Above all, the British
government was concerned with the security of the Suez
Canal, and regarded any external or internal threat to
British control of this waterway as inimical to its
interests. Egyptian needs would always be judged in
the light of British imperial concerns, particularly
the security of British passage to the Indian Empire.
The British claim or hope to be in Egypt to assist
the Egyptians until they were capable of self-government
could not be reconciled with the the British obsession with the security of the canal.

In the climate of opinion about the Empire in the
governing circles of Britain and Egypt in the first
decade of this century, it should not be surprising
that Cromer and the British government felt so strongly
or reacted firmly when they sensed their major interests threatened. What is interesting is that they
felt obligated to give more than just lip service to
eventual self-government for the Egyptians. The imperial policy resembled that denizen of Dr. Doolittle's
fictional world, the "pushme-pullyou"— an animal with
one head at each end: the head that represented imperial interests continued to dominate, but the head
that represented Egyptian self-government wanted quite
naturally to go in a different direction. It has
taken a number of decades for this improbable crea-
ture finally to remove one head and grow a more sensible body. British imperial policy in Egypt was a
confused story; the results in conditions of crisis
were sometimes comical—but more often tragic—for
the people involved.

The Tabah crisis illustrated some aspects of
Cromer's attitude toward internal unrest or the threat
of it. Despite his unparalleled successes and claims
of reform, he felt the British position in Egypt was

uncertain. In the past he had generally resorted to
force and demanded an increase in the garrison to
quiet what he called the "pan-Islamic" threat. So
again, in the Tabah crisis, he used the warning of
possible chaos and revolt to badger the British Cabinet into making a show of force in Egypt.[32] This was
a serious misreading of the meaning of current Egyptian unrest. His analysis and consequent overreaction,
an almost Pavlovian response to what he viewed as a
danger of pan-Islamic revolt, was later repudiated in
practice by Sir Eldon Gorst. Gorst, unlike Cromer,
had some limited appreciation of the real strength and
direction of the forces of unrest in Egypt.

A short recapitulation of the Tabah crisis is
necessary to comprehend the sensitivity of the British
to any other nation's incursion into this desolate
area of the Sinai Peninsula. Before the opening of
the Suez Canal in 1869 the peninsula, almost waterless
and inhabited only by a few Bedouin tribes and dessi-
cated monks, had little commercial or political significance. It was crossed by the pilgrim camel track,
the *Darb al-Hajj* from Egypt to Mecca via Aqabah, and
policing of this route was recognized by the Ottoman
government as the responsibility of the khedive's government, although it ran across Ottoman territory.[33]
Once the Canal had been opened, the Sinai Peninsula
became essential, as it remains today, for any power
that controlled the Suez Canal. Should it be occupied
by an enemy of Egypt or Britain, operation of the
canal would be made extremely difficult, if not
impossible.

In 1892, upon the accession of the new Khedive
Abbas, the sultan attempted to reassert the right to
station Ottoman troops through the greater part of the
Sinai Peninsula. This would of course pose a threat
to the Suez Canal, particularly the southern exit.
Cromer and the British government emphatically opposed
the plan and after a series of heated diplomatic ex-
changes between Cairo, London, and Constantinople, a
compromise favorable to British interests resulted.
It left the frontier in the Sinai at a line drawn from
al-Arish on the Mediterranean to the head of the Gulf
of Aqabah. Ottoman jurisdiction thus was excluded
from the Sinai and a buffer zone created between the
Suez Canal and the Ottoman domains in Palestine, although no frontier was legally delimited at that
time.[34]

This arrangement between the British, Egyptian, and Ottoman governments was challenged in January 1906 by the Ottomans, who sent troops to occupy the old fort of Tabah at the head of the Gulf of Aqabah. Cromer detected in this move "another and more determined threat to occupy the Sinai Peninsula."[35] British officials in Cairo thought the action reflected German meddling, but they also realized that the area had recently become important to the Ottomans as a result of their plan to extend the Hijaz railway—with German assistance—from Maan to Aqabah. On receiving intelligence reports of Ottoman troop activity in Sinai and rumors of German support, the British caused the Egyptian government to send a small detachment of the Egyptian army under a British official to the Aqabah area to assess the situation, and when the Ottoman government complained, an Egyptian coast guard vessel was dispatched to support the Egyptian detachment.[36] Another diplomatic crisis resulted, involving the British, Egyptian, and Ottoman governments.

The response of the Egyptians to this conflict of interest and power in the Sinai was very disquieting. The sultan's cause elicited considerable and fervent support from large numbers of Egyptians. Cromer claimed that the Egyptian nationalist papers, especially those of Mustafa Kamil and his followers, used the episode to stir up dormant pan-Islamic feelings among the ignorant but prejudiced Muslim peoples. Cromer and his officials, with few exceptions, became increasingly disturbed by what they called Muslim fanaticism. There were disturbances, organized demonstrations, and individual hostility against the British in Egypt. In February 1906 the students of the Khedivial Law School went on strike against certain policies and regulations allegedly inspired by the British. This was the first strong indication that the nationalists had captured student support (by 1908 student strikes for nationalist causes were a significant factor in Egyptian politics), and Cromer had to intervene. "It would be fatal," he wrote to Grey in March, "for us to let the Turks get the best of this controversy." He strongly urged armed coercion to demonstrate British determination.[37]

The Egyptian nationalist press, Mustafa Kamil's *al-Liwa* in particular, capitalized on the Islamic sympathies and anti-Christian prejudices of the Egyptian people to elicit support for the Ottoman sultan-

caliph. British officials interpreted this appeal as
an incitement to open revolt. Fearful that soldiers
of the Egyptian army would refuse to fight their own
countrymen, Cromer, in his usual fashion, pressed the
British government for an increase in the army of occupation. Shortly before the Ottoman capitulation
early in May,[38] he strongly urged Grey to hurry the
dispatch of reinforcements, for the prestige of the
British in Egypt was at stake:

> It is most disappointing, after all the
> enormous benefits conferred on this country,
> that the Egyptian public should allow them-
> selves to be guided by a number of newspaper
> agitators and fanatical sheiks, but I am not
> altogether surprised. The hatred of the Mos-
> lem for the Christian is so intense that it
> dominates over all other sentiments. As to
> fanaticism, I am not really sure that the
> Ulema of the El-Azhar mosque are much more
> fanatical in their way than Hugh Cecil.[39]

The apprehension that distorted British judgment
that winter and spring appeared in the journal of
Humphrey Bowman, a junior British official in the
Egyptian education department, and more clearly in
dispatches from Charles de Mansfeld Findlay, the counselor at the Agency who replaced Cromer when the great
man went on holiday. Bowman wrote on May 1 that the
Tabah "incident" had caused worry in the British community and the dispatch of a British ship to the area
and the "considerable addition to the Army of occupation here" might lessen the tension and the possibility of unrest. "Let us hope that this [the reinforce-
ments] will be eno' to quench the smouldering flame
of discontent which is still lying dormant in Egypt."[40]
Findlay, writing from Cairo to Hardinge, the permanent
under secretary at the Foreign Office, was convinced
that the Tabah border dispute was part of a larger
German conspiracy against the British position in the
Middle East. He was relieved to hear that the army of
occupation would be reinforced. One had to live in
Egypt, he declared, to comprehend "the phenomenal
weight of Lord Cromer's prestige." His absence
amounted to a "withdrawal of force impossible to estimate." And Findlay concluded the dispatch ominously:

> I may tell you in confidence that I do not
> look forward to running the country for four

months this year with the present small
garrison. There is too much inflammable
material lying about loose, and an incident—such as possible complications on
the Aqaba or Tripoli frontier—might have
caused a blaze which we should have been
powerless to smother as promptly as to prevent it spreading.[41]

Findlay's fears may have been exaggerated, but
the British imperial officials in countries with large
Muslim populations took seriously the possibility of
some kind of pan-Islamic revolt.[42]   Another European
power such as Germany could use Islamic sympathies to
stir up trouble in Egypt. During the Tabah crisis,
Cromer was encouraged slightly when the other European
communities, usually so selfish and fractious, rallied
to the British side. He thought their recognition
that the successful assertion by the British of their
right to interfere with the Ottoman government in all
matters concerning Egypt might make those European
groups in Egypt more amenable to entrusting their
rights under the Capitulations to British protection
and might hasten the removal of these onerous restrictions on the sovereignty of the Egyptian government.[43]

In Egypt the cause of pan-Islam alone never seriously threatened British control, except in the minds
of some officials. But various influential foreign
communities in Egypt, insecure despite their wealth
and privileges, were subject to periodic fits of panic
at the alleged threat of Muslim fanaticism, and it
appears that Agency officials such as Findlay had suc-
cumbed to similar hysteria over the Tabah crisis that
spring.

Considering that the British garrison in Egypt
numbered barely 4,000 officers and men in April 1906,
and after reinforcement only 5,400, there was some
reason for concern on the part of the officials at the
Agency.[44]   The Egyptian army, numbering about 16,000,
was kept under strict control by its British officers.[45]
Aside from a palace guard for the khedive, it was
stationed in lower Egypt and in the Sudan, far from
the major centers of population, and any efforts to
subvert it were vigorously repressed. Memories of the
Urabi Revolt were still vibrant enough to discourage
the British from relying on the Egyptian army in case
of a serious uprising; in fact it was kept deliberately

weak to reduce the possibility that it might threaten the
British hegemony. Cromer wrote in a private letter to
the Sirdar, General Sir Reginald Wingate, British
commander of the Egyptian army:

> They [the British Government] have to recog-
> nize that we are on the horns of a dilemma—
> the Egyptian Army has to be kept efficient
> for service against our enemies. At the same
> time, we want to keep it inefficient in order
> that it shall not be a danger to ourselves.
> . . . the cleverest of statesmen have not yet
> arrived at any method under which a pudding
> may be preserved and also consumed. [46]

Certainly some credence must be given to the
power of British prestige. Throughout this period,
despite crises and unrest, the British army of occupation—bolstered when necessary by ships of the British
Mediterranean fleet—never numbered more than about
5,000 "effectives."[47] This small force insured British
control over a population of ten million people. In
the spring of 1906, despite the fact that Cromer early
in the crisis had obtained the British Cabinet's permission to reinforce the garrison in Egypt if he
judged it necessary, the arrival of the reinforcements
themselves was delayed long enough to heighten the
tension in Egypt. Cromer formally requested the reinforcements on April 16, but they did not leave England
until May 15 and reached Alexandria May 24, about ten
days after the Ottoman sultan had acceded to British
demands. During this period the Egyptian government
had had to suppress an agitation that might have led
to serious disturbances which, Cromer believed, the
unreinforced garrison would have been inadequate to
control. [48]

Cromer and the British knew that as long as they
controlled the Egyptian army and had the respect and
acquiescence of the Egyptian peasants—the *fellahin*—
it would be relatively simple to maintain British
influence. Control of the major cities and the Suez
Canal could be guaranteed by relatively small garri-
sons of British soldiers. The British had visibly
improved the life of the *fellahin* since 1882 and a
new generation experienced an improvement in its
living standard, but modern European-style education
had had little effect in the Egyptian villages. The
growing nationalistic fervor had barely begun to make

its impression on the mind of the *fellah*. Threats to
his religion were far more likely to stir him to
unrest.

Cromer and most of the knowledgeable British knew
how flimsy was popular support for the reviving nationalist movement in the early 1900s, and how disorga-
nized were the nationalist groups in the urban centers.
Yet the British reaction to what can objectively be
described as a minor misunderstanding over the right
to shoot domestic pigeons in the Nile Delta village of
Dinshawai was so violent, cruel, and extreme that more
than twenty years of efforts to succor the downtrodden
fellahin were undermined. Egyptians of all classes
now had strong cause to realize that the British, for
all their moral tone and significant accomplishments,
would react harshly under pressure in order to protect
their interests and their prestige, without much care
for Egyptian interests and rights, and would continue
to do so until they were forced out of Egypt.

The details of the Dinshawai incident are relatively simple. On June 13, 1906, five British officers
of the mounted infantry on a march with their troops
from Cairo to Alexandria left their encampment on the
bank of the Baguria Canal for some afternoon recreation. Major Pine Coffin, the senior officer, had shot
pigeons at Dinshawai in previous years and thought he
had obtained permission of the local notables for
another shoot. The villagers, however, resented the
intrusion of the British hunting party, because for
them the pigeons were a means of livelihood. The
officers, who did not speak Arabic, arrived and began
to shoot pigeons in the fields adjacent to the village, though they failed to find the village headman.
A small fire broke out in a barn, and the angry villagers apparently blamed the hunters and attempted to
disarm them. In the ensuing struggle one of the officers' shotguns went off and wounded four men and a
woman. Enraged, the villagers beat the officers severely. Two of the officers, Captains Bull and
Bostock, managed to escape and ran for help. The
fierce heat of the afternoon sun and the beating overcame Bull, and he collapsed in the marketplace of the
nearby village of Sersena. Bostock reached the British troops, and a rescue patrol was immediately sent
out. On their way the patrol shot at some villagers
who looked threatening, and clubbed to death a *fellah*
who had sought to aid the stricken Bull in Sersena.

Bull died that evening of sunstroke and head wounds.
Local police meanwhile reached Dinshawai and freed the
three remaining British from the ungentle care of the
villagers. The authorities in Cairo were informed and
an immediate investigation was set in motion. Cromer
laconically telegraphed the Foreign Office about the incident and informed them that General Bullock, the commander of the occupying army, had requested that the
accused villagers be tried by special tribunal.[49]

In the first years of the occupation, cases of
individual assault by Egyptians against the occupying
military forces, particularly against officers, had
been quickly and firmly dealt with by the Cromer administration. Agency influence had been brought to bear
on the Egyptian courts in each case to insure that the
Egyptians involved were rapidly punished, even if the
British officers had been irresponsible or provocative.
The punishments were not especially severe by the
standards of the time; immediate flogging and prison
sentences up to ten years in length were normal.[50]
Cromer's prestige and the inviolability of the British
forces in Egypt were accepted by the British government as absolutely essential for the maintenance of
British interests and the progress of the Egyptians.
In 1895 Cromer and the other British officials in
Egypt decided that they needed formal legal sanction
from the Egyptian government to inflict extraordinary
punishment without delay in cases of offenses committed by Egyptians against the occupying forces. A
khedivial decree was obtained authorizing the immediate convocation of a special tribunal, with a British
majority, at the request of the Consul-General of
Great Britain and the general commanding the occupying
army. This tribunal, not restricted by existing Egyptian judicial codes, was allowed to inflict any punishments it considered necessary; its sentences were
not subject to formal appeal processes, and they were
to be carried out immediately.[51] It had been convened
only once (in 1897) before the Dinshawai incident in
June 1906.

The unrest in Egypt during the first five months
of 1906 had so unsettled British officials that when
news of the assault on the five officers reached them
they apparently decided to teach the Egyptians a lesson. The merits of the case were largely ignored in
the rush to make a punitive example of it. A. P. B.
Weigall, inspector general of antiquities to the

Egyptian government, later recalled the emotional climate of the period:

> The Anglophobe sentiments of a certain class
> of Egyptians were now at their height, and
> there was a very grave danger of an anti-
> English uprising in favour of the Ottoman
> Sultan. . . . I recall personally many weeks
> of great anxiety when the massacre of all
> Christians was openly advocated in everyone's
> presence, and the lonely days in remote dis-
> tricts were shadowed by the hourly expecta-
> tion of disaster. Then came the news that
> some British officers in uniform had been
> attacked at the village of Deneshwai . . .
> and it was generally felt that a rising was
> imminent. [52]

Harry Boyle, Cromer's confidant, wrote in some
annoyance to his mother on June 18 "that we are very
much bothered with this confounded attack on the officers. . . . It is a tiresome business, and shows what
creatures our Egyptian friends are. It is to be hoped
that the Court finds sufficient grounds to hang a few
of them or they may do it again." [53] Cromer the next day
informed Grey at the Foreign Office that "everything
however leads us to conclude the attack was prepared
beforehand." He asserted that the officers' behavior
had been exemplary under extreme provocation, expressed
no doubt that the incident came under the jurisdiction
of the special tribunal,[54] and the same day—satisfied
with the management of the investigation and the arrangements for the trial—left Cairo for his annual
summer leave accompanied by his wife and the judicial
advisor, Sir Malcolm MacIlwraith. *The Egyptian
Gazette*, unofficial voice of the British community in
Egypt, reported that the Cromer party was seen off at
the Cairo train station by Butrus Ghali, the Copt who
was foreign minister and, as acting minister of justice, president of the special tribunal.[55]

Five days later, on June 23, the special tribunal
formally sat to try the fifty-nine accused villagers.
Of the five judges, only two understood enough Arabic
to comprehend the testimony of the defendants and
their lawyers: Butrus Ghali and Ahmad Fathi Zaghlul,
a president of the Egyptian court of the first instance
and the only Muslim on the tribunal. The rest of the
judges were British: W. C. Hayter, acting judicial

advisor, W. G. Bond, vice-president of the Egyptian
court of appeal, and a Lt. Colonel Ludlow, acting
judge advocate general of the army of occupation. The
trial lasted only three days and the procedure
and the harsh sentences deserve to be described— as
they were by an Egyptian historian— as a "gross miscarriage of justice."[56]

The special tribunal established premeditation on
very flimsy evidence and condemned four villagers to
death, two to life sentences, one to fifteen years in
prison, six to seven years in prison, three to one
year and fifty lashes, and five to fifty lashes. Allowed no appeal under the rules of the special tribunal,
the condemned men were taken to Dinshawai the very
next day accompanied by a heavy military and police
escort. The gallows had already been erected in antic-
ipation of the judgment. Dinshawai residents were
confined within the village by a cordon of police, but
neighboring *fellahin* "in immense groups" witnessed the
arrival of the prisoners and the executions and floggings, which were carried out on the site of the attack. *The Egyptian Gazette*'s special correspondent
wrote from the scene of the executions: "Every now and
then a loud wail from the women came from the village
[Dinshawai] but save for this all was strangely
quiet."[57]

All did not remain quiet in Egypt or Britain once
the details became known of the hasty investigation and
trial, and the harsh sentences carried out without
pause for an appeal. Except for the foreign communities, the reaction among all classes in Egypt was
strongly adverse— from the lowliest *fellahin* to the
educated nationalists. They were shocked and angered
at the injustices of a court exempt from Egyptian laws
and imposed by a Christian occupying power that
claimed to be there to save the Egyptians from barbar-
ism and lawlessness. Cromer and the British had
boasted of abolishing *curbash*—flogging as a punishment—but then had reimposed it when their position
seemed threatened. Widespread resentment among all
classes of Egyptians against the occupation increased
rather than decreased as Cromer and his officials had
apparently hoped.

Reaction against the Dinshawai punishments gal-
vanized various groups opposed to the British hegemony
in Egypt, stimulated their political action, and

widened the base of their support. Mustafa Kamil was able to capitalize on the feelings of outrage, the national humiliation, and the shock among students and the growing educated classes; he overcame some of the antipathies of Muslim versus Copt and of city versus village, and channeled growing Egyptian resentment into further demonstrations of opposition on the streets and in the schools, and into formal political organization. The Egyptian press invoked the memory of Dinshawai to focus attention on the iniquities of British rule. More moderate nationalists like Lutfi al-Sayyid, a follower of the Muslim reformer Muhammad Abduh, in the year following Dinshawai founded a newspaper, *al-Jaridah,* to combat the more radical nationalists and to promulgate a gradualist approach to independence from Britain.

June 1906 marked a turning point in Anglo-Egyptian relations. The Egyptian sense of national humiliation, nourished by twenty years of British occupation, had a focus that all classes and groups could understand. One of Cromer's successors, Lord Lloyd, a staunch imperialist himself, admitted it was "the kind of barbarity which is generally dictated by panic."[58] Dinshawai has never been forgotten in Egypt.[59]

During the imperialist heyday in Britain before the Boer war, there had been too few individuals or groups that could speak out with any significant influence in Britain against harsh and repressive acts by the proconsuls of the British Empire and their subordinates. Cromer's successes in restoring Egypt's stability and finances had rendered him particularly immune from criticism. Voices like Wilfrid Scawen Blunt's were in the political wilderness and generally not even listened to. Few members of the Conservative or Liberal Cabinets in the 1890s and the influential back-benchers in the House of Commons had any real knowledge of the civil rights of Egyptians or interest in defending them.[60] The Conservatives controlled the government throughout most of the 1890s; the influence of such Liberals as Morley and William Harcourt was not enough to change Cromer's policies in Egypt.

The experience of the Boer war damped the jingoism of the public and the enthusiasn of many politicians for the "imperial idea," and attitudes toward the conduct of imperial affairs shifted significantly. Criticism increased. Curzon in India, Milner in South Africa,

and Cromer in Egypt were no longer free to govern des-
potically. The details of imperial rule began to be
examined in the House of Commons.[61] Moreover, the
1904 Entente with France shifted the power alliances
in Europe; even though it sanctioned British hegemony
in Egypt, it also helped to change the nature of local
pressures and demands on Cromer's position there. By
then Cromer was an old man who had become rigid and
unresponsive to suggestions for change, particularly
if they came from Egyptians he considered unreliable.
His regime and policies seemed vaguely anachronistic
to the Liberal Party's radical wing, the Labour Party
members, and the Irish members who were elected in
large numbers to the House of Commons in the 1906 elec-
tion. Milner's dictum—that the prestige of the British Agent and the British garrison in back of him were
absolutely essential conditions for the maintenance
of British imperial interests and Egyptian regeneration—was challenged in the House of Commons, in certain sectors of the British press, and by the increasingly active and noisy Egyptian nationalist groups.

When news reached England of the Dinshawai incident, the harsh sentences, and the swift public hanging and floggings, it was not enough for Cromer to
assert with his usual oracular firmness: "I consider
that the sentences, though severe, were just and necessary. I can see nothing reprehensible in the manner
in which they were executed."[62] While not all concerned
parties in Britain accepted the acerbic and pungent
criticisms of the incident in George Bernard Shaw's
preface to *John Bull's Other Island*,[63] Cromer, with Sir
Edward Grey representing him in the House of Commons,
was forced reluctantly to answer questions about the
incident.   Persistent demands were made that the
Dinshawai prisoners be pardoned.[64] There was increased
attention in the House of Commons to the details of
Egyptian affairs. During the winter and spring of
1906 only twenty questions regarding Egypt were laid
before the House. Seventeen dealt with some aspect of
the Tabah border dispute with the Ottoman government;
the other three ranged over the rumored sale of a Nile
mailboat to a German firm, the progress of negotiations to end the Capitulations, and the disposal of
the Egyptian tribute to the Ottomans. During the remainder of the year seventy-four questions were asked
about Egyptian matters, fifty-two of them concerning
the Dinshawai incident.

Of the Dinshawai questions, twenty-eight were
laid before the House between June 18 and July 5, when
Grey attempted to suppress discussion of the incident
by solemnly warning the members that the situation in
Egypt was very dangerous: "by debate and language used
in this case you the House of Commons may set in
motion forces, always near the surface, which if they
once break forth will lead to consequences which I
know the House will deplore." He hinted that further
questioning and debate could cause the whole of India
and North Africa to explode in revolt.[65] Even this
strong warning, a backhanded and exaggerated compli-
ment on the effects of debates in the House of Commons,
did not quiet the questioners. After July 5 the
Dinshawai issue was raised twenty-four times and the
conduct of Egyptian affairs questioned twenty-two
times. Seventy-three percent of the questions asked
in 1906 about Egyptian affairs specifically dealt
with the border dispute at Tabah and the Dinshawai
incident and fifty-five percent of all questions about
Egypt dealt with Dinshawai, whereas in 1905 roughly
fifty questions about all Egyptian affairs including
the Sudan had been asked in the House, and in 1904—
the year of the Anglo-French Entente—there had been
about sixty. In 1906 more than a hundred fifty questions were laid on Egyptian affairs, and members began
to ask for details. The outcry over Dinshawai in
Britain continued to bedevil the Foreign Office through
much of the summer and fall, and it became more and
more difficult and embarrassing in private for Grey to
defend the handling of the incident in the House of
Commons as the facts became known.[66]

Grey and Cromer began moves during the fall of
1906 to prevent any further incidents like Dinshawai.
Cromer continued to declare publicly that the sentences
were justified: "I concur generally in Mr. Findlay's
remarks; and that, had I remained in Egypt, I should
in every respect have adopted the same course as that
which he pursued."[67] But his private correspondence
with Grey and others through the fall of 1906 and up
to his resignation indicates that he too felt a serious error had been made. Not that Cromer was much
concerned about the Egyptians involved, but the handling of the affair he felt had created a distorted
picture of his administration in Egypt. He would have
preferred to do nothing, to let the incident be forgotten in Britain as well as Egypt, but the pressures—

especially in the House of Commons—did not abate that
year.

Cromer wrote Gorst shortly after his return to
Egypt in October 1906 that he proposed to abolish the
special tribunal, and admitted to Grey about a week
later that the procedures of the tribunal were in
error for it had had no clear-cut definition of the
sentences or an appeal process.[68] The British judges
who served on the special tribunal were "furious at
the accusations which had been made [by Blunt and
others] against them of being political agents" for
the British, and these judges had to be prevented
from bringing action against their accusers; moreover,
they refused to sit on any other special tribunals.
Since Cromer's return to Cairo there had been an attack on a couple of British soldiers, but it did not,
in his judgment, justify resort to such a court.[69] Despite urgings from Grey, Cromer delayed acting on the
matter, writing to the foreign secretary on December
15, "Pray let us try and leave the subject of Denshawai
alone—at least until the next autumn." Pressure from
his officials and the army of occupation apparently
contributed to his unwillingness to act. In January
1907 Grey wrote privately to Cromer: "The one tender
and weak spot for debate is Denshawai . . . but it
will hardly be as acute as last year."[70]

In March, Grey gently prodded Cromer again toward
remission of the sentences. "The effect of the trial
has really been, not wholesome but mischievous, in
Egypt itself." Grey urged clemency and an appointment
or promotion for Fathi Zaghul, the one Muslim on the
special tribunal; this course of action would be proper
provided it was understood to have come from Cromer
rather than "pressure from home or pressure in the
House of Commons." However, Grey then left it up to
Cromer to decide the issue.[71] Cromer was ill, about to
resign, and refused to grant clemency at least for
two to three years. Although he admitted privately
to Grey his agreement that "the sentences were unduly
severe," he pointed out that the whole of the Egyptian official world was against him, any clemency
would appear due to outside pressures, and the British
position must be made clear on future offenses of this
nature. In Egypt:

the state of the case is that everyone
thought a severe lesson should be dealt;

> the effect of that lesson, as it is, has
> been good; that it would have been very
> much better if it had not been for the
> English agitation; but on the other hand,
> that most people consider that severity,
> though necessary, was carried too far.[72]

Under continued party pressure on the issue Grey
finally ordered Cromer to abolish the special tribunal
a week later, and Cromer acquiesced reluctantly.[73]
Both admitted that an injustice had been done, Grey
explicitly and Cromer implicitly; both were concerned
above all to preserve the prestige of the British
officials involved. The "face" of Cromer's administration was more important than making amends for a
gross miscarriage of justice.[74] Cromer's resignation
late in March left the final settlement of the matter
to Gorst, his successor; it was one of the first issues
he dealt with once he had established himself in the
Agency in the fall of 1907. Even after his resignation, however, Cromer was consulted and kept informed
by Grey on the necessity for concessions and clemency
over Dinshawai, and Cromer argued against such a decision for fear it would permanently weaken the British
position in Egypt and shake the confidence of the
officials.[75]

The policy of the Foreign Office seems to have
been to defend in public the actions of the officials,
and to punish them as it deemed fit in private. Findlay,
left in charge of the Agency when Cromer went on holiday in June 1906, took three months' leave when Cromer
returned to Egypt that fall and was shifted to a new
post in Dresden the following winter. It was his
early dispatches on the Dinshawai incident that Grey
relied on to support the necessary severity of the
sentences, and it seems likely he was relieved of his
position in Cairo for having acted, under pressure,
with too little restraint.[76] Eventually, when Gorst
succeeded Cromer, the British government attempted
quietly to rectify the injustice done to the imprisoned villagers and to lessen the damage inflicted on
Egyptian feelings and sensitivity.

Chapter Nine

THE LORD RESIGNS

Despite the warning conveyed by the Dinshawai punishments, the increase of the garrison, and Grey's firm
declarations of support in Parliament for Cromer's
policies, Findlay in Egypt that summer viewed the
political climate as potentially very stormy. The
absence of Cromer, he thought, was equivalent to the
loss of a brigade of British troops.[1] Religious fanaticism was "artificially" aroused, disrespect for the
law had increased that year, and sadly— reported the
alarmed Findlay— the Dinshawai incident had been manipulated by Mustafa Kamil to fan the hatred of foreigners. Native attacks on Europeans had increased,
though Findley gave no statistics to support this assertion. Agitation among law students— "They are
quite the most despicable class in the country"— had
continued, and the khedive was involved in a scanda-
lous abuse of his prerogative by selling titles and
decorations.

Only Lord Cromer could deal with the threatening
situation, wrote the unhappy Findlay. In July 1906
he requested that a warship, preferably a cruiser, be
sent to Alexandria or Port Said and the Admiralty
granted the request. Shortly afterwards, upset by
further Turkish troop movements out of the Yemen, he
sent an "urgent" telegram that the ship be sent "at
once."[2] When Cromer returned to Egypt that fall a decision had been made to keep one of the British warships
in Egyptian waters as long as it was necessary to damp
down the threat of internal unrest. It appears that
the aftermath of Tabah and Dinshawai, despite the additional military forces and the harsh punishments,
only stimulated further discontent in Egypt.[3]

Harry Boyle reported to Cromer early in September
that Mustafa Kamil was now the "tribune of the people"
and had abused *al-Muqattam*, the influential Arabic

newspaper sympathetic to the British occupation.[4]   A
proposal to give Kamil a reception on his return in
October from Europe might help the British in Egypt
to assess the strength of his movement and see who was
in it. Boyle, who was fluent in Arabic, was Cromer's
major source of information on the feelings of the
Egyptians, yet he appeared to be poorly informed and
confused about Egyptian sentiments toward foreigners.
Aware that the nationalists were few in number and
poorly organized, Boyle could not comprehend their
ability to stir up such a vast amount of turmoil after
all the obvious material benefits and stability created and ensured by British occupation.[5]

     Mustafa Kamil was allowed to hold a meeting in
Alexandria, but indoors, to avoid the possibility of
a disturbance. British troops in Cairo were kept in
readiness for trouble.[6] An entry in Humphrey Bowman's
journal for September 27, 1906, confirmed that while
the summer had been "uneventful, . . . there was a
growing feeling of unrest in Egypt, chiefly displayed
among the educated classes, but also no doubt to a
certain extent among the *fellahin* themselves, who have
been acted upon by the native papers and by the agency
of men like Mustafa Pasha Kamil." Since the riot at
Alexandria in the fall of 1905, the Tabah crisis and
Dinshawai had heightened internal tensions:

     It now remains to be seen what will be the
     result of all this unrest during the coming
     year; and no one looks forward to the out-
     come more keenly than I do. I feel very
     strongly that what we want here is a firmer
     rule, but a more sympathetic one: and I be-
     lieve that this can only be procured by
     obtaining full suzerainty over the country.[7]

     Neither Cromer nor the British government was
ready to take such a drastic step as to assume legal
responsibility for Egyptian rule; but Cromer did ini-
tiate some changes designed to lessen the unrest,
restore confidence in British indirect rule, and propitiate the moderate nationalists and the foreign communities. His understanding of the reasons for the
unrest was clouded by his prejudices about the nature
of Islam, and of what he called "orientals," the
Egyptians. That he did not bother to learn Arabic
during his twenty-four years in Egypt (although he had
taught himself to read Greek and some Turkish) is an

indication of his attitude toward Egyptians and his
sense of priorities. In a memo to the Foreign Office
he was very pessimistic about the future, and about
the "edifice" he and the British had erected in Egypt
to run the country. He marveled that it had been possible to produce beneficial results of any kind, and
doubted that the system could endure much longer. The
only effective remedy would be for the British government actually to assume control and abandon the fiction that the British representative was a mere diplomatic agent; but he rejected this solution, "failing
some cataclysm."[8] Rejection of the assumption of outright control meant that Cromer's response was only a
palliative and that he did not intend to deal with the
real difficulties that had arisen in Egypt after 1904.

His judgment was obscured by a misunderstanding
of the nature of the nationalist movement, particularly his confusion, amounting almost to an obsession,
about the pan-Islamic aspect of this movement. Cromer
thought most of the nationalist movement was tied to
pan-Islamic goals, and he reasoned that this dependence on what he called decadent Islamic principles and
the Ottoman sultan provided no real hope for Egyptian
regeneration. He therefore scornfully dismissed most
of the nationalists as worthless rabble-rousers,
blamed the venal khedive for backing them, and finally
in his last years turned to the European communities
as the only hope for establishing some sort of limited
self-government for Egypt.[9]

As discussed earlier, the major legal and political obstacles to Egyptian autonomy were the strictures
placed directly on Egypt and indirectly on the British
by the Capitulations. Cromer, in his annual report
for 1905, proposed that the British be responsible for
protecting the interests of the foreign communities as
assured under the Capitulations, and then create a new
legislative body composed entirely of members of the
foreign communities. Certain matters such as the Suez
Canal and the khedivial debt would be excluded from
consideration by this new body, and the Egyptian government would be forbidden to deviate from any existing or future treaties dealing with free trade or the
customs duties. New courts were to be created by the
proposed council of the foreign residents; the consular courts and the mixed courts were to be abolished.
The languages to be used in the new legislative body
for foreigners would be French, English, and Italian![10]

This proposal indicated that the aging Cromer had given up what faint hopes he had ever entertained that the Muslim majority in Egypt could be trusted to govern themselves in the foreseeable future.

Under the Egyptian Organic Law of 1883, the Legislative Council and General Assembly had been created to serve as the basis for future legislative bodies in the Egyptian government. After twenty-four years of British tutelage and supervision, Cromer wrote: "The future of the Legislative Council and the General Assembly depends very largely on the action taken by members of these bodies."[11] They were completely under the control of the Egyptian government, and that meant of course indirect control by the British. The yearly budget and accounts had to be submitted to the Legislative Council, and administrative laws had to be submitted to the Council before they were promulgated by the Egyptian government. The Council was permitted to express its opinions and wishes, but the Egyptian government had no obligation to do anything but listen and give reasons for not adopting any proposals offered. The General Assembly met only once every two years and its only real power was to give assent to the imposition of direct taxes, land taxes, or personal taxes. No new taxes of this nature had been proposed under the British occupation. The proposals for constitutional reform and self-government that were made during its four-day meeting in March 1907 were scornfully dismissed by Cromer as unrepresentative and entirely premature. He yielded only on a request that reporters be admitted to the sessions of the Legislative Council and General Assembly. This, Cromer conceded, might be possible.[12]

In his last annual report, written in 1907, he hinted that after careful further study he had decided that the provincial councils might be allowed a small extension of their responsibilities in local affairs, such as schools. The whole matter of local jurisdiction was under study, but no change in the government of the towns or cities was possible without the alteration or abolition of the Capitulations. Cromer strongly discouraged any rush toward self-government that could damage progress in Egypt, cause instability, and bring back a less benevolent autocratic personal government such as had harmed Egypt in the past. By 1907, if not considerably earlier, Cromer had given up hope that there would be a significant native Egyptian contribution to

the system he had created, and he continuously deprecated any attempt to wield authority by the British
government in London. The powers of his position were
difficult to define; any attempt toward a precise definition might be detrimental to British influence in
Egypt.[13] In his plans for further reform, however, he
tried not only to enlist the support of the foreign
communities but also to use the native Christian minorities, especially the influential Copts, for British
ends.

One of the standard justifications for the occupation of Egypt was that the British presence protected
the Copts and other native Christians from possible
massacre by the Muslim majority.[14] The Copts had long
been the clerks of Egypt, but their influence and numbers had diminished until the last half of the nineteenth century, when the Coptic community underwent a considerable "modernization," responding to the presence,
stimulus, and protection of Europeans in Egypt. By
reforming their church and community organizations
they rapidly became relatively prosperous and educated
by comparison with the Muslims. They welcomed the
British occupation, and the secular leaders of the
Coptic reform movement— apparently despairing in the face
of the entrenched conservatism of their old clergy—
began to look to the Egyptian government and behind it
to the British for protection and support for their
reforms. This action tended to weaken the old Millet
system by sacrificing its traditional internal liberty.
(The Ottomans had recognized certain confessional
groups—the Millets—and ruled through them.) The
Copts entered into a "golden age after 1882. . . . a
dwindling minority in the mid-nineteenth century
swelled into an entrenched one of about a million in
1914."[15]

The Coptic reform movement underwent several
phases, one of which occurred about 1905, roughly
coinciding with changes in the British position after
the 1904 Entente. The reform leaders in the Coptic
community again appealed for support to the British
Church Missionary Society (CMS), which had assisted
them at an earlier phase of the reform movement.[16] They
also could depend on Butrus Ghali Pasha for influence
with the khedive and the British. Ghali was a prominent Coptic community leader—the first Copt to be
made pasha in Egypt—and a clever, supple careerist in
the Egyptian civil service who rose to be one of the

most important figurehead ministers in the Egyptian
Cabinets of the 1890s and early 1900s. As minister
for foreign affairs he signed the Anglo-Egyptian condominium on the Sudan for the Egyptian government, and
as acting minister for justice sat on the Dinshawai
special tribunal and became the "go-between and the
consummate mediator between the British and the Egyptians."[17] Cromer himself was under no illusions as to
the ultimate loyalties of the Coptic community, but
his scorn for the inept old ruling classes and the
various nationalists left him little choice but to try
subtly to use religious tensions in Egypt to further
British interests and dissipate the fervor for self-
government.[18]

     Cromer not only began to seek support among the
Copts, but shortly before his sudden resignation
attempted to enlist the assistance of the Church
Missionary Society in Cairo to combat the pressure
coming from Britain to force changes in his regime.
Missionaries in the recent past had been more an annoyance than a help to the British occupation, since their
efforts to convert Muslims might have inflamed the religious sensitivities of the traditional and conservative Islamic majority in Egypt; these and other related
activities had to be restrained. In the winter of
1907, however, Cromer granted a long interview to the
Reverend Rennie MacInnes, secretary of the CMS branch
in Cairo.[19] Through him and the CMS in London Cromer
hoped to reach influential church organizations in
England that could help counter the Egyptian nationalist claims of British misrule, the rumors of disquiet in Egypt, and the continuing detailed criticisms
of Egyptian affairs in the House of Commons.

     MacInnes was astonished by Cromer's frankness and
convinced that he was not afraid that the missionaries
might misconstrue his words. More than once Cromer
urged the Reverend MacInnes to write his superiors in
London that Egypt was quiet, despite the claims of the
nationalist papers and the parliamentary critics.
Cromer himself could not make such a statement, but
this information coming from the representative of the
Church Missionary Society would lend it credence and
authority. MacInnes quoted Cromer as saying,

     "What is required for Egypt is a steady con-
     tinuance of the old policy, and of the pres-
     ent regime [the khedive's government], and

no Westminster fussing. This is the most
extraordinary government one has ever had
to deal with." "But," I [MacInnes] asked,
"surely Sir Edward Grey is all right?"
"Oh, he's all right, but he has that Liberal
majority to appease," Cromer replied.[20]

Not only did Cromer deny any significant discontent in Egypt, but he emphasized his conviction that
the nationalist movement was a sham and that its supporters in Parliament were ill-informed and bigoted,
especially the Radical and Liberal member of Parliament John Mackinnon Robertson, who had just visited
Egypt that winter. Robertson, in an interview with
Cromer, had shown himself "to be the most narrow-
minded man he [Cromer] had ever met. He [Robertson]
had swallowed everything he was told by the Nationalists, and since his departure they [the Nationalists]
had been saying that they had never believed anyone
could be so gullible." Cromer attempted to use the
threat of pan-Islamic inspired fanaticism which lay,
he claimed, at the root of the national movement in
Egypt. MacInnes quoted him directly as saying:

> The plea for a national parliament is merely
> an attractive bait for the people of England,
> who may be gulled into giving national insti-
> tutions to a struggling little state, and
> the talk of pan-Islam merely conceals what is
> the real issue . . . not "Egypt for Egyp-
> tians" but "Mohammedanism versus Christian-
> ity," and the exclusion of Christians from
> any share in the administration of the country.[21]

MacInnes was impressed by Cromer's arguments.
First, however, he took the opportunity to present
some grievances that the missionaries and native
Christians had voiced. He told Cromer that the Egyptian government appeared to be favoring Muslims over
Christians at the national as well as the local level,
and complained of the difficulty of observing Christian
worship on Sunday since it was not a holiday in Egypt.
He urged on Cromer the necessity to teach the Bible in
the schools.[22]

MacInnes spent some days reflecting on the interview, but decided against writing a formal letter to
his headquarters as Cromer had suggested. He felt it
would be impolitic to involve the CMS in a public

denunciation of the Egyptian nationalists while at the same time criticizing what he called Cromer's policy of support for the Muslim majority. To avoid offending the Muslims Cromer had resisted considerable pressure, particularly from the missionaries, to declare Sunday a holiday for Christians; but he did tell MacInnes he would support Bible study in schools where there were at least fifteen Christian boys. Although clearly still unhappy about Cromer's stand on the Sunday matter, MacInnes finally decided to consult with his co-workers and the London headquarters, and to present a draft statement of CMS policy in Egypt for Cromer's reaction. Before this first interview it appeared that the missionaries had not had regular access to Lord Cromer, despite the latter's claims that he was accessible to all.[23]

The initiative for a second interview came rather speedily from Cromer, who sent MacInnes a note on April 23, a little more than a week before the proconsul was to leave Egypt. The message contained a clipping of some critical statements made by J. M. Robertson in the House of Commons about missionary activities in the southern Sudan, and said, "I don't know whether you noticed this [the Robertson statements]. It is really monstrous that a European—I believe that one can hardly call Mr. Robertson a Christian—should endeavour to excite Moslem fanaticism in this manner."[24] Though MacInnes and the CMS in Cairo were still reluctant to come out openly in support of the Cromerian administration, they were eager to take advantage of the opportunity to exert influence on British policy in Egypt. MacInnes wrote to his society headquarters that this "message . . . and its obvious intent to remind us of the possibility of writing something which will be of use to at least a wide circle of people at home, made me feel it was an opening that ought not to be lost."[25]

MacInnes obtained an interview with the ailing Cromer two days later, and was shocked at Cromer's deterioration since the first interview a little more than a month previously. During this second interview, Cromer strongly urged MacInnes and the CMS in Cairo to suggest that the member who spoke for them in the House of Commons, Sir John Kennaway, allude in the House to the danger of listening to any of the foolish and irresponsible criticisms of a man like Robertson. MacInnes reported:

> The point upon which he laid stress was
> that any attention given to the agitation
> in Parliament against the British regime
> in Egypt would have a most prejudicial ef-
> fect upon the conduct of affairs here
> (because as usual, all the natives think
> that Robertson's influence is practically
> equal to that of the Prime Minister and
> that therefore very shortly the British
> policy will be changed) and thus sooner
> or later upon our work. [26]

MacInnes again brought up the CMS grievances against
a British policy that had tended to elevate the Muslims by "its steady adherence to the idea that the
country is a Mohammedan country" and asked Cromer to
alert Gorst to the dangers they saw in the policy. He
warned Cromer that the Copts were alarmed over Gorst's
being pro-Muslim, but Cromer "entirely pooh-poohed the
idea and said there was nothing in it."[27]

These maneuvers during Cromer's last year indicate an increased willingness to use religious tensions
to further the ends of British rule in Egypt. It may
not have been a conscious systematic effort to "divide
and rule," but it is clear that Cromer, for all his
pious declarations about preparation for self-rule, had
little faith in the Egyptians. Consequently he sought
support where he could find it, and at the same time—
quite reluctantly—made carefully limited changes in
response to the pressures brought on him in Britain
and Egypt for increased Egyptian participation in the
management of their own country. These few changes in
educational policy and support for some moderate Egyptian nationalists did not indicate any significant
shift in British policy. They were simply designed to
defuse the nationalist movement and to lessen the criticism in Britain, particularly in the House of Commons.

Early in the fall of 1906 Cromer announced the
upgrading of the Egyptian department of education,
which was made into a separate ministry. Since the
British occupation it had been part of the ministry
of public works. The elderly Armenian Yacoub Artin
Pasha, who had occupied the post of under secretary
for public instruction almost continuously since 1884,
was "retired," and Cromer prevailed on the khedive to
appoint Saad Zaghlul as the minister of education with
a considerably expanded budget.[28]   However, to counter

any tendency Zaghlul might have had to promulgate policies inimical to British interests, Douglas Dunlop,
a dour, rule-following Scot, was elevated to the position of advisor to the ministry of education. Cromer
was appreciative of Zaghlul's abilities.

> The new man [Zaghlul] is not likely to be a
> cypher. It remains to be seen whether he
> will be wise enough to cooperate, or whether
> he will adapt the foolish advice given him
> by the opposition press, to resist English
> opinions merely in order to show that he is
> not a dummy. To put the matter in a form
> which you [Grey] will readily understand, I
> have brought an English John Burns into the
> Cabinet.[29]

Cromer admitted that the Egyptians who occupied cabinet posts in their own government were ineffectual
and inept, but only a very cautious change in personnel could be allowed.

> Of course, it is anticipated we shall go
> further in the direction of pushing on the
> natives. I am quite prepared to do so, but
> I shall not be in too great a hurry. I
> want to see how the present experiment [the
> Zaghlul appointment] succeeds. What I want
> from the natives in the higher positions is
> by no means absolute submission to English
> advice, but intelligent cooperation. By
> force of circumstances, rather than from
> any definite design or intention, the pres-
> ent ministers have unquestionably drifted
> rather into the position of cyphers.[30]

For the moment the appointment of Zaghlul, accompanied
by the promotion of the rigid and reliable Dunlop, was
about as far as Cromer was willing to go to meet the
nationalist demands for increased participation by
Egyptians in their own government. There is no indication that Cromer contemplated any large-scale replacement of ministers or cabinet reorganization.

At the time of Zaghlul's appointment, which was
made largely with the hope that Zaghlul could calm the
increasingly rowdy pro-nationalist students, Cromer cautioned
that the "utmost care" had to be exercised in the selection of Egyptians as officials in their own government. He

rejected the nationalists as incapable and irresponsible,

> and I have no hesitation in saying that the
> men required are not to be found in the
> ranks of the agitators, or those who pro-
> claim most loudly their own fitness for
> places of political trust. The number fit
> at the moment who could with safety of the
> true public interest be invited to occupy
> important positions is very limited.[31]

Cromer also informed the Foreign Office that, according to information he had received from "responsible
Egyptians," the appointment of Zaghlul had obliterated
the recollection of the Dinshawai incident.[32]   This
was a delusion.

     In his annual report for 1905 Cromer vigorously
defended his Egyptian educational policy. Expenditures on education had had the lowest priority in the
early years of the occupation, and when the immediate
financial problems had been solved after 1890 there
was a very slow increase in the moneys allotted to
this field in the Egyptian budget; they grew from
81,000 in 1890 to 276,000 pounds Egyptian in 1906.
However, it was Cromer's policy to raise much of this
money by charging fees to the students; in 1905 student fees amounted to 90,000 pounds Egyptian, about
thirty percent of the budget allowance. Total revenue
that year was 14,813,000, with a surplus of 2,688,000
pounds Egyptian; yet with the inclusion of student
fees expenditure on education amounted to barely two
percent of Egyptian revenue. Dunlop, the advisor in
the ministry, had requested 400,000 pounds Egyptian
for education in 1906, but Cromer alleged it was not
feasible to allot that much money and maintain Egyptian financial equilibrium: "Moreover, even if it were
granted, I very much doubt whether it would be possible, if proper supervision is to be exercised, to
spend so large an amount of money very rapidly."[33]

     The next year the budget allotment for education
was raised to 374,000 pounds Egyptian. Ways were
found to spend the sum properly, and no public mention
was made of threats to the financial equilibrium; but
Cromer was concerned in private that the pressures for
rapid reform, especially in education, could result in
such a large increase in expenditure and shift of priorities that Egypt's financial health might be

disturbed. He told Gorst in February 1907:

> We must next year, if possible, spend a
> further large sum on education, both be-
> cause the demand here is universal and
> very legitimate, and because it is the
> chief point of attack of Robertson and
> his friends. . . .
>
> To my mind it is very necessary to sit
> tight, and not to yield to pressure in
> the way of carrying out reforms which
> can be postponed. What we have to look
> to is not the intrinsic merits of any
> proposal but its relative importance as
> compared to other proposals. This is the
> system, which as you know, has been per-
> sistently adopted for years past.[34]

It appears doubtful that the budget for education
would have been significantly increased at that time,
or the department of public instruction elevated to a
ministry, or such a capable Egyptian as Zaghlul appointed had there not been considerable "pressure,"
particularly from the House of Commons. The 1904
Entente with France had removed the major international
restrictions on British influence in Egypt, but it
does not appear from the records that Cromer anticipated any major changes in the direction of Egyptian
self-rule. In fact, as has been shown, he intended to
move in the opposite direction, depending on the minorities and foreign communities to support British
rule.

In January 1907 he appointed Sidney H. Wells, an
Englishman whom he described as an "expert," as director general of the administration of agricultural and
industrial education, with the "warm approval of
Zaghlul."[35] He also created a higher council for public instruction. Members of the Legislative Council
were added to this second board to placate them, since
the council had been asking for the right to approve
educational policy, and Cromer wanted to diffuse their
interference in this area. Dunlop was also appointed
to this higher council along with the Copt Murqus
Simaika Bey. The Scotsman would help to frustrate any
ideas inimical to British interests, and the Coptic
notable, Cromer hoped, would propitiate the sensitive
Coptic community.[36]

Although Cromer had totally written off the more virulent nationalists, he did give grudging support to what he called the moderates of the school of the late Muhammad Abduh. Through Zaghlul and his brother Fathi, he was in touch with the founders of *al-Jaridah*, a newspaper that first appeared in March 1907.[37] Its backers were wealthy and influential Egyptians who disapproved of the virulent tone and pan-Islamic, pro-Ottoman tendencies of the nationalists led by Mustafa Kamil. They had been appalled by the Egyptian reaction to the Tabah crisis and the repressive British reactions at Dinshawai in 1906, and had decided to publish a newspaper that would represent more moderate and realistic Egyptian nationalistic views. The first editor was Ahmad Lutfi al-Sayyid; under his editorship the policy of *al-Jaridah* was to campaign and educate for social reform, arguing that with social reform under way in Egypt, the British occupation would naturally cease to be necessary. After Cromer's retirement in September 1907, the stockholders of *al-Jaridah* formed a political party, *Hizb al-Ummah*, the People's Party. Neither the paper's circulation nor the party's membership was ever large, but their influence on the development of political consciousness in Egypt was considerable.[38]

Whatever hopes the moderate nationalists behind *al-Jaridah* and the nascent People's Party had for practical support from Cromer were quickly disappointed by the publication of his annual report for 1906 the following April, shortly after his resignation, and by his farewell address delivered in May. Although Cromer wrote favorably about these more moderate nationalists in his report, declaring they were the main hopes of Egyptian nationalism, his proposal for an international legislative council indicated that he had little concern for the development of genuine Egyptian self-rule.[38]

During the fall of 1906 and winter of 1907 Cromer repeatedly pressed Grey and the British Cabinet for permission to issue a statement affirming the permanence of the British occupation of Egypt. Grey indicated in a private letter that he as foreign secretary might say something in Parliament, "but some people probably will object to making a declaration of something which is taken for granted and not challenged." The French might be vexed since they were in trouble at that period in Morocco and would not appreciate

having their concession on the status of Britain in
Egypt rubbed in. The British Cabinet and the prime
minister were not satisfied with the necessity of such
a declaration. Grey suggested that Cromer might say
something on the issue in his annual report for 1906,
or perhaps appeal to Grey officially about the uncertainty of the British position. [39]

     Cromer immediately responded in an official let-
ter reaffirming the necessity for a statement on the
permanence of the British occupation. He told the
Foreign Office that apprehension from the British business community in Egypt about its status had so increased that it opposed any change in the Capitulations unless the British supremacy in Egypt was affirmed to be permanent.[40] Cromer continued to badger
Grey and the British Cabinet on the issue throughout
December and January. Cromer's plans for the reform
of the Capitulations were being delayed by the uncertainty of the British position in Egypt. The Italians
in Egypt, like the British businessmen, were disturbed;
pressure from J. M. Robertson and other members of
Parliament for Egyptian home rule and immediate reform
of the Capitulations was hurting Cromer's own plans
for reforms in these areas.[41] At the end of January the
issue was submitted to the Cabinet which, although
it objected to the inclusion of the words "perpetual"
or "permanent" in any statement on the duration of the
occupation, authorized Cromer to make formal, public
assurances that "His Majesty's Government recognize
that the maintenance and development of such reforms
as have hitherto been effected in Egypt depend upon
the British occupation."[42]

     It was clear from the ideas and plans expressed
in the last two annual reports that Cromer was groping
for some sort of new direction and policy in Egypt;[43]
this direction would not be towards Egyptian self-rule,
but towards increased British participation, and the
actual enlistment of the foreign colonies in the process of Egyptian rule.   Cromer was aware of the growing hostility between Egyptians and the British which
was caused, in part, by the sharply increased numbers
of British officials in the Egyptian government since
1895. Although he admitted his unhappiness over the
situation, he justified it by alluding to the complex-
ity of the government machinery. Only Englishmen, or
Europeans perhaps, could be relied on to handle the
complicated tasks of governing Egypt. The European

staff, in some cases, would even have to be enlarged.

> After thirty-five years' experience of
> Oriental administration, I am unable to
> define with any degree of precision what
> qualities should be possessed or what be-
> haviour should be adopted to command the
> confidence and to acquire the good will of
> the Eastern, but I am none the less certain
> that generally that confidence can be com-
> manded and that good will can be acquired.[44]

Whatever confidence Cromer expected to generate
by his actions and his policy among the moderate
nationalists in the last year of his proconsulship was
largely dissipated by his scornful rejection of the
nationalist cause in his farewell address at the Cairo
Opera House. Cromer commended Zaghlul—"he should go
far"—as well as Butrus Ghali, and the ancient and
cooperative prime minister, Mustafa Fahmi, as the kind
of men who could be responsible for Egyptian affairs.
Egyptian reform and self-rule were matters of generations, worthy ideals, but not possible except at a
"dog trot."

> I shall deprecate any brisk change, any vio-
> lent departure; more especially, if neces-
> sary, I shall urge [back in Britain] this
> wholly spurious manufactured movement in
> favour of the rapid development of parlia-
> mentary institutions be treated for what it
> is worth, and let me add, it is worth very
> little. It does not really represent the
> voices of the intelligent dwellers in Egypt,
> European or Egyptian.[45]

In his speech he described his policy in a few words
as "to tell the truth." The truth in this case forci-
bly confirmed his scornful misunderstanding of the
nationalist cause, and perhaps unwittingly helped to
push the more moderate nationalists into opposition
to the British. Cromer had an ample supply of that
characteristic quality of the English ruling class,
a benevolent impenetrability. His successes had confirmed his opinions; his age had sanctified them. It
is doubtful that he was ever aware of the negative
impact of his words on those very Egyptians who might
have lightened the British task in Egypt.[46]

Cromer's resignation, when it came in March 1907, seems to have been unexpected. Contrary to his reports home that the changes instituted since his return from holiday in October 1906 had lessened the opposition to British rule in Egypt, it appears that Cromer was under increasing pressure in Egypt—but even more at home—to effect further reforms. His health, which had been somewhat fragile since 1905, suddenly deteriorated in the middle of the winter of 1907. Early in February he went up the Nile to rest from the strain of his work, but the rest did not suffice; on March 22 he was confined to his room, and on March 28 he informed the foreign secretary that he could no longer remain at his post without sacrificing his health completely. His letter of resignation to Grey pointedly denied that outside pressures had determined him to resign or undermined his health. He alluded to a "domestic cause," the loss of his first wife, age (sixty-six years), and overwork, due to his having had to accept too much responsibility in the years since 1904.

> Moreover in spite of all my efforts to decentralize the tendency is to throw work and responsibility more and more on my shoulders. Gorst's departure in 1904 made a great difference to me. I now have absolutely no one here except Garstin who is not departmental in the somewhat narrow sense of the term.[47]

Cromer was worried that an early leak of his resignation might look like a victory for Mustafa Kamil's extreme nationalists in Egypt and for Robertson's parliamentary pressure group at home; but what he feared most was a loss in confidence of the international business community which might precipitate a heavy slump in land and in the value of Egyptian currency. He predicted that no political consequences of a serious nature would result, but to avoid both dangers, he suggested that Grey announce his resignation in the House of Commons. There the foreign secretary should emphasize that Cromer had resigned for reasons of health, and that a change in the British representatives in Egypt did not mean a change in policy.[48]

In the letter of resignation Cromer recommended Sir Eldon Gorst as his successor. Two days later

Findlay, Cromer's second in command at the British
Agency, affirmed that Cromer's health had collapsed,
and that "he ought to leave Egypt at once . . . he is
simply not fit for work," and seconded the recommendation of Gorst: "Gorst has greater knowledge and experience of this country than anyone else and with his
undoubted ability he ought to succeed if anyone can.
But the situation has changed since he left and his
task . . . will be one of enormous difficulty." The
situation in Egypt was dangerous, wrote Findlay: "the
result of the combined campaign of Robertson in England
and the nationalists in Egypt has been disastrous."
The Arabic press had attacked anyone supporting the
British, and Findlay found that practically the whole
pasha and *effendi* class, including the government officials, were anti-British. The nationalists, the
khedive, and Robertson were all working against British rule. The *fellahin* had not yet joined nationalist
agitation but Findlay felt a religious issue could
provide a spark to set them off.

> I believe Egyptian nationalism has come to
> stay. It is extremely lucrative to its pro-
> moters, and it will provide a permanent
> source of mischief in the country. At the
> same time I do not apprehend any immediate
> danger from its present adherents. They are
> the most cowardly class in the country and
> will only be dangerous when joined by the
> Army, the fellahin, or both.[49]

He reported a heavy fall of Egyptian securities and
said this emphasized the need for a prompt appointment
of Cromer's successor, an emphatic affirmation of
British control in Egypt, and perhaps an increase of
the garrison. Politically Findlay sensed a pause in
activity to assess Cromer's successor.[50]

The fall in Egyptian securities was coincidental
with Cromer's resignation. A decline in the American
stock market in March 1907 transmitted itself quickly
to Europe, and leading bankers in London and Paris,
disturbed by the frenetic speculation in Egypt, tight-
ened credit and forced a sharp decline in the invest-
ment boom in Egypt which had begun in 1893. Local
conditions created an economic crisis whose effects
were not ameliorated until the start of the First
World War.[51]

Findlay and the ill Cromer himself were disturbed
by the reactions to the latter's resignation. The
Agency sent the Foreign Office a report of the most
notorious nationalist leader's reaction: Mustafa
Kamil was pleased, but cautioned his readers in *The
Egyptian Standard* (English edition) that it was only
"a formal satisfaction . . . and only fundamental when
English policy changes." Kamil asked his readers to
withhold their judgment on Gorst whom he respected
for his personal dignity and independence. "If Sir
Eldon Gorst continues the autocratic regime it will at
any rate be tinged with a different color."[52] Findlay
believed the situation so dangerous that he recommended
an increase of the garrison in support of Gorst when
he arrived, but Findlay had been known to exaggerate
before. Thomas Russell, then a junior official in
Egypt and later Cairo's police chief, wrote to his
father on April 19 that things were very unsettled.
"Gorst though not particularly agreeable personally
is the best man to succeed him [Cromer] but I don't
envy him his job."[53]

In a letter to Grey the same day Cromer noted the
threatening political conditions and, apparently piqued
by criticism, reaffirmed his policy and said he was
"not at all averse to Liberal measures, but the trouble with orientals was that they feared to govern."
He strongly urged Grey to take every opportunity to
assert in public that there would be no change of
British policy in Egypt, and he asked that the prime
minister say something to support that policy: only a
few words would dash the hopes of the Egyptian nationalists. He accused the Irishmen who ran *The Egyptian
Standard* for Mustafa Kamil of being better liars than
the Orientals;[54] later he reported that the situation
had worsened by April 22 and that Europeans in Egypt
were becoming exasperated. He continued to press Grey
and the British government to make a public statement
in support of British policy in Egypt.[55] Grey finally
responded on May 1 that the "Prime Minister will, when
the opportunity presents itself, say something reas-
suring about Egypt in the sense you desire."[56]

Meanwhile Cromer paid his farewell visit to the
khedive, making his final admonitions "of a purely
political character" to the much younger man he had
so thoroughly dominated since 1892. He warned Abbas
that the present situation was serious, hinted that

the British held him responsible, and cautioned that
"circumstances might arise which would endanger his
own position and that of his dynasty" if the British
garrison had to be called in.   As certain as ever of
his own rectitude, Cromer wrote to Grey that "generally I endeavoured to impress upon His Highness the
serious risk he would run if he did not entirely change
his attitude and line of conduct."   All of this, Cromer
reported, was delivered in "a friendly tone . . . without use of the phrases which would have tended to personally irritate the Khedive."   The effect, he noted,
might not last very long.[57]   Abbas undoubtedly had
little choice but to listen quietly.   Cromer was not
the last of the British Agents or High Commissioners
or ambassadors to dominate and threaten their puppet
rulers in Egypt and to delude themselves that these
rulers somehow were not deeply offended and embittered.

Careful precautions were taken by the Agency in
Cairo to prevent any anti-Cromer outbreaks during his
last weeks in Egypt.[58] After delivering his farewell
address in the Opera House to the assembled leaders
of the foreign communities and some senior Egyptian
officials—but not the khedive—Cromer left Egypt.
He had ruled but not reigned for twenty-four years.
Ronald Graham, then in the Agency and in charge of
the security for Cromer's departure, wrote some years
later:

> In spite of Lord Cromer's immense claims
> upon Egyptian gratitude, the Khedive suc-
> ceeded in alienating public sympathies from
> him to such an extent that when he left the
> country in the Spring of 1907, it was be-
> tween rows of British soldiers and an atmos-
> phere of native mistrust and hostility which
> has never since been equaled.[59]

Graham's analysis was too simple—Egyptians have
had further reason to hate the British—but Cromer's
legacy to Sir Eldon Gorst, his handpicked successor,
seemed unclear and very troubling.   Sir Edward Grey,
who had relied on Cromer to manage Egypt, had been
shocked when the old man resigned; but he accepted
Cromer's choice of a successor, and indicated he
wanted to keep Cromer for assistance on Egyptian matters if he could: "I hope it will not be bad for you
to give advice privately when you are at home."   In
the same letter Grey observed presciently:

I am sure Gorst is the best choice . . . but
he will have great difficulties at first.
Soon or later the Khedive etc., will try to
take advantage of your absence, and Gorst
may have difficulties, which you have not had
in recent years, because he will not have the
same ascendancy over the British element and
the officials. . . . I am satisfied in sending Gorst we are doing the best we can.[60]

Chapter Ten

THE NEW POLICY INITIATED: 1907

One of the most difficult things here . . . is
keeping the English in order.

Sir Eldon Gorst, 1893[1]

Conditions in Egypt, according to information received
at the Foreign Office, appeared to be deteriorating at
the time of Cromer's resignation. Stirred up in the
aftermath of Tabah and Dinshawai and bolstered by radical and Irish support in the House of Commons, the
nationalist movements had intensified their anti-
foreign and anti-British campaign in the Egyptian
press and on the streets.[2] The European minorities
were having one of their periodic fits of near hysteria over Egyptian threats to their position and privileges, the economy was shaky, and a financial depression had set in. The Anglo-Egyptian administration
was beset by internal squabbles as well as financial
and political uncertainties. The stability that
Cromer had worked so long to attain seemed vulnerable.
Cromer admitted to Grey that he had become the focus
of discontent among the Egyptians: "I shall be very
glad, when Gorst has taken over the reins, and I am
able to go, and I shall be rather relieved if, before
I go away, there are not some broken heads. . . . my
name is beginning to be used as a sort of war cry in
a racial battle."[3]

Upon his appointment Gorst left immediately for
Egypt to assess and, if possible, alleviate the danger
to British control and influences. Grey, meanwhile,
affirmed in the House of Commons that Gorst's status
and powers as Consul-General would be identical to
Cromer's.[4] Gorst and his wife arrived in Cairo on
April 24 and stayed at the Agency as the guests of the
Cromers. He was shocked at Cromer's deterioration:
"He is greatly changed since last autumn both physically and morally, and there can be no doubt that, had
he endeavoured to struggle on here any longer, he

The Consul-General.

would very soon have entirely broken down. . . . according to doctors there is nothing organically
wrong."[5] The strain on Cromer's health was eased
with Gorst's assumption of responsibility.

In a letter to Grey soon after his arrival, Gorst
sounded eager and self-confident about his ability to
manage the complicated affairs of Egypt, yet he found
the situation quite menacing: "At the moment of my
arrival political unrest & excitement, which had
been simmering throughout the winter, boiled up again
with the news of Lord Cromer's departure and threw the
press, the authorities and even the Agency into a
state bordering on hysteria."[6] Thomas Russell wrote
of nationalist strikes and the overturning of electric
trams in Cairo leading to British troop demonstrations. "It is the result of the so-called nationalist
campaign who tell lies and are believed. I hope Gorst
will adopt the policy of 'scorpions' if they consider
Cromer's was a whip, which it wasn't."[7] Measures were
taken by the British administration to assure there
were no embarrassing outbreaks before or during Cromer's
departure. Gorst informed the Foreign Office that the
police were kept "as inconspicuous as possible, to
avoid anything to make the British look ridiculous."[8]
Storrs, then in the finance ministry, wrote home:

> We are straining every nerve . . . to try
> and prevent the L'ds [Cromer's] demonstra-
> tion from being a fiasco: Europeans are
> right— to a Dago: but the fact of Gorst's
> having been a friend of the Kh[edive] is being
> pushed among the natives for all it's worth—
> and they, typically, think to gain favour w.
> Gorst by neglecting Cromer.[9]

After reaping another harvest of bitterness from
the nationalist groups with his farewell address,
Cromer left the country. Gorst wrote the Foreign
Office that Cairo was full of rumors but that no trouble occurred during the week preceding Cromer's departure. "Indeed both Lord Cromer's meeting and his
send-off at the station were altogether worthy of the
services he has rendered to this country."[10] Storrs
judged that the meeting was "an immense success,"[11]
but noted that troops were to line Cromer's departure
route to the station to forestall any possibility of
an incident. The need to station two ranks of
Inskilling Dragoons on Cromer's departure route

indicated that the Egyptian public's view of his long
reign was highly unfavorable if not openly hostile.[12]
The pro-British *Egyptian Gazette* reported that "the
native populace clapped as Lord Cromer's carriage arrived at the station. The police arrangements were
excellent and not a single unpleasant incident occurred
to mar the proceedings."[13]

With Cromer out of the country, Gorst expected
that there would be a temporary lull in nationalist
activity, especially as the khedive was leaving for
a summer holiday.[14] The threat of outbreaks that might
embarrass the British had been only a symptom of the
difficulties he had to resolve. The immediate problems were divided by Gorst into categories: financial,
administrative, and political policy, all of which
interacted with each other. Gorst judged that his
successor as financial advisor in 1904, Sir Vincent
Corbett, was "incapable and disloyal." Instead of
supporting and restraining Cromer—"an old man in a
hurry"—where necessary, Corbett, in less than four
years, had permitted the financial reserves of the
Egyptian government to be nearly used up. Planning
necessary to sustain even ongoing projects had not
been done. The Egyptian economy, after several years
of prosperity and uncontrolled speculation, was upset
in the spring of 1907 by the unexpected outbreak of a
severe financial crisis that undermined public confidence. Secondly, Cromer's decline and concurrent illness had caused, Gorst wrote, "administrative anarchy."[15]

> As I had anticipated, things had for some
> time been steadily going from bad to worse.
> And it was high time they sh. [should] be
> seriously taken in hand. The whole machine
> of govt absolutely depended on one man, and
> that man had been going to pieces, physically
> and morally. Lord C. had lost his nerve and
> was no longer able to keep his team in hand.[16]

Not only had the administrative system degener-
ated, but the British had rapidly increased their
"invasion" of Egypt in the last few years, especially
by taking over Egyptian government positions. The
Egyptians saw themselves being ousted from the posts
that had up to that time remained open to them in the
government service. Among the departments, Gorst
thought that education in particular had been over-
anglicized. Too many British teachers were imported

annually and Arabic had been supplanted by English in
"far too many directions." The results were extensive
insecurity, backbiting, intrigue, and inefficiency in
the Egyptian government administration.

The recent British influx complicated the political and administrative problems facing Gorst in 1907.
Cromer gradually had drifted into an anti-Egyptian
attitude in the last few years, and the growth of the
nationalist spirit had pushed him into "an attitude of
antagonism to the Egyptian Moslems generally." To
counterbalance their influence Cromer had begun to
lean towards the European communities and the native
Christians for political support. Gorst, who dis-
counted their political significance, disagreed with
Cromer's policy: "The latter, however, formed such a
small proportion of the total population that they
made a frail reed to lean upon." The growing anglophobia among the Egyptians had been strengthened by
the British intrusion and by "the acute personal hostility which existed between himself [Cromer] and the
Khedive." Newer British officials tended to become
anti-Egyptian, and the natural result was an increase
in "racial antipathy and caste prejudice." One rash
British act in 1906 had distinctly poisoned the political atmosphere. Gorst commented tartly: "First and
foremost was the Denshawai affair—our most mismanaged
piece of work since the beginning of the occupation.
Our ill-timed severity gave a tremendous fillip to the
nationalist party and alienated the middle-class Egyptian Moslems."

Gorst's immediate task was to damp down the forces
that tended toward internal disruption—from the
khedive to the nationalist groups to the nervous British officials to the hysterical European minorities and
on to the impending financial chaos. The individuals
and groups involved had to be placated, diverted, or
firmly dealt with without compromising Gorst's prestige and the British position in the country. He deliberately did nothing of a polemical or radical
nature that spring, and publicly maintained that no
change of policy was envisioned.[17] In quiet he set about
calming the Egyptian political atmosphere. No drastic
measures were taken against the nationalist press;
Grey wrote that opinion at home was not favorable to
censorship of the press, which should be instituted
only after violence had occurred. He suggested that
Gorst seriously consider ways to increase the British

forces in Egypt unless conditions improved, but after
consultation with those in his administration in touch
with Egyptian opinion, Gorst decided that there was no
immediate necessity for this.[18]   Reinforcement of the
occupying army had been a favorite Cromerian response
to the threat of Egyptian unrest.

An example of the pressure from British official
circles on the Foreign Office to take military steps
to lessen the state of unrest in Egypt was a mid-May,
1907, memo from the Duke of Connaught, a royal duke and
a senior officer in the British army. An inspection
trip earlier that year had convinced him that the
British and Egyptian troops were not sufficiently prepared to meet internal and external threats, particularly from Ottoman Turkey. He found the state of affairs during that spring in Egypt and the Sudan "very
unsatisfactory" due to an "unfortunate incident"—
Dinshawai—Cromer's resignation, and Turkish schemes
abetted by foreign advisors. All these factors, in
his judgment— added to the possibility of the recru-
descence of the Eastern question in an acute form in
the event of the death of either the Austrian emperor
or the sultan of Turkey, the present condition of
European politics, and the unsatisfactory state of the
British and Egyptian military forces—posed a serious
threat to British control in Egypt. The worried royal
duke recommended considerable strengthening of the
composition, mobility, and training of the military
forces in Egypt. This document was sent to Gorst for
his appraisal, and he responded: "His Royal Highness
was there [in Egypt] when recent agitation was in full
swing and he attaches more importance than the situation warrants. The rapidity with which the so-called
unrest is subsiding confirms me in my opinion that it
has not penetrated very far down."[19]

Gorst quietly dealt with one important cause of
the unrest, the disaffected khedive, taking advantage
of their old friendship and his new position of influence to deflect, if not completely detach, the khedive
from his mischievous and disturbing contacts with the
nationalist groups. He "speedily and easily attained"
their former relationship.[20]   Gorst continued in the
next few years to use their renewed friendship to influence the khedive towards British interests and policies. Conveniently, the khedive and Mustafa Kamil,
still the most influential nationalist leader, chose
to leave Egypt for the summer.

Education, long neglected by Cromer, received
immediate attention from Gorst. He saw the present
lull in Egypt and the parliamentary recess in England
as a time "to put right any weak places in our armour
and make feasible concessions to satisfy the more reasonable sections of the Egyptians."[21] Zaghlul, the education minister, and Dunlop, the inflexible British
advisor to the ministry, he found troublesome. In
Gorst's opinion, Zaghlul had wild notions of his
countrymen's capability, while Dunlop thought only of
administrative efficiency.

Gorst's reforms would make Egyptian education
"rather more Arabic." The examination for a secondary
school certificate could now be taken in Arabic, and
starting in October 1907 the first year of mathematics
in secondary schools would be taught in Arabic. Gorst
proposed to enlarge the training center for Egyptian
teachers, and to send a certain number of young Egyptians to training colleges in England for a two-year
course; one or two would also be sent to a technical
school in England to qualify them to become teachers
in their specialty. These were all small measures,
he noted, merely developments of Lord Cromer's plans.
He had intended to make the changes in October, as a
"pleasant surprise" for the Egyptians. Zaghlul, however, had been talking in public that spring, and
Mustafa Kamil had become aware of the proposals.[22]

A minor financial and social reform long resisted
by Cromer was instituted immediately by Gorst. He allocated the *rachat militaire*—exemption payments made
by wealthy Egyptians to avoid military conscription—
to a fund to go to poor recruits as a form of mustering-
out fee. During the Cromer era, this fee had been a
means of taxing the rich Egyptian families who managed
to avoid most other forms of taxation. A considerable
amount was raised each year when the Egyptian army
called for far more recruits than were needed, and
then allowed those who could afford it to buy their
exemption. Using the fund as a mustering-out fee
helped to make military service more attractive to the
poor—most of the Egyptian army recruits.[23]

Gorst proposed a more significant change in policy for the next fall: the expansion of the functions
and authority of provincial councils as a means of
developing responsible local government. Cromer had
supported the idea on paper, but had never implemented

it. A hint of Gorst's diversionary political tactics
comes from the comment he made to Grey after announc-
ing this plan to the Foreign Office. "In any case
even if the measure meets the fate which often attends
any moderate and reasonable schemes of pleasing nobody,
it will have served the useful purpose of directing
the journalistic energies of the opposition into a
comparatively harmless channel." Grey fully approved
this proposal: "This seems to be all in the right lines
of gradual progress, selecting each year one or two
reforms which are practical."[24] The details will be
discussed when the new policy of Gorst is described.

The measures taken to bring the Egyptian governments's finances to order led to the resignation that
spring of the financial advisor, Sir Vincent Corbett.
It was, wrote Gorst, "a most fortunate circumstance
for the success of my future work here." During the
summer he obtained the services of Sir Paul Harvey,
"a very promising recruit," for this crucial post— after that of Consul-General the most important position
in the Egyptian government. Despite a considerable
amount of private and public pressure, Gorst refused
to allow the Egyptian government to intervene in the
public financial crisis. "My object was to let the
disaster burn [?] itself out as quickly as possible
and to prevent the Govt from being foolish in deference to the universal clamour that 'something must be
done.'"[25] Certain foreign financial interests, together
with Egyptian speculators suffering from the spring
1907 "crash," put intense pressure on Gorst to secure
a loan of two million pounds from the Egyptian government to ease the pressure on the staggering Egyptian
market. Just who these specific interest groups were
is not clear from available evidence, but Gorst's firm
refusal to intervene incurred their bitter and lasting
resentment. Part of the unfavorable press he received
until his death and even after is due to their resulting loss of confidence in his policies. He refused
because the money was needed for capital expenditures
by the Egyptian government, because the government had
no business helping speculators, and because the amount
was not enough in any case to help the situation.[26]

At the end of May, Grey congratulated Gorst on
how well Egyptian affairs seemed to be going. Gorst's
quiet and conciliatory moves had succeeded for the
moment. But there was still parliamentary pressure—
especially from the radical M.P. John Mackinnon

Robertson— on Egyptian educational policy, and Grey was
happy to hear that Gorst would be making some "alterations in education" soon. Grey wrote that he now
wished the Egyptian government to announce its own decisions, which would seem to indicate that Gorst had
the full confidence of the foreign minister.[27]

Gorst was confident enough in the results of his
initial handling of the Egyptian scene to take the
usual long summer holiday in England that Cromer had
enjoyed. Indeed, it might have been an admission of
failure both at home and in Egypt to have remained. It
was then that he recruited his new financial advisor and
made his long-term plans for Egypt.[28] He conferred with
the convalescing Cromer, who wrote to Grey from Scotland:
"You may like to have a line from me after my talks
with Gorst. He is most sensible. I wholly agree with
all he is doing." [29]

Egypt did calm down during the summer of 1907.
Humphrey Bowman wrote in his journal in July:

> A great deal has happened since I last
> wrote. Lord Cromer's resignation in April
> & Sir E. Gorst's appointment in his place
> created no little stir: but things appear
> to be settling down in Egypt, & everyone is
> beginning to realize that we have got a
> really strong man in the position, which
> after all is what we wanted.[30]

Gorst, he noted, had asked all the department heads to
return early from vacation that year. Ronald Graham,
the new counselor at the British Agency, who was in charge
in Gorst's absence, wrote to the Foreign Office in
August that Egypt was quiet. Various factions of the
nationalist party were too busy abusing their rival
leaders to have time to attack the Egyptian government. Although the Egyptian Arabic press had devoted
some time to the Commons debates over the Cromer grant,
Graham reported that the Egyptian general public remained absorbed in the acute financial crisis.[31]

Gorst returned to Egypt October 9, 1907, two days
after Mustafa Kamil had arrived from his summer holiday. It is safe to assume both men came prepared with
plans for Egypt's future, plans that doubtless did not
agree, and both men died before their respective policies could reach fruition. Gorst was welcomed at the

railroad station in Cairo by senior British officials
in the Egyptian and Sudanese services. Mustafa Kamil's
Egyptian Standard listed Ronald Graham, the counselor
at the embassy; Harry Boyle, the Oriental secretary;
Sir Reginald Wingate, the Sirdar of the Egyptian army
and governor-general of the Sudan; Sir Rudolph von
Slatin, inspector general of the Sudan; Edgar Bernard,
financial secretary of the Sudan; Lord Edward Cecil of
the finance ministry; Vincent Corbett, the departing
financial advisor; Douglas Dunlop, the educational
advisor; Alfred Mitchell Innes, the under secretary
of finance; Captain Percy Machell, the advisor to the
interior minister; and Dr. Faris Nimr, the Lebanese
proprietor of *al-Muqattam*. *The Standard* remarked that
there were only three prominent Egyptians present, the
minister of education, Saad Zaghlul, and two others;
the editor felt this indicated the lack of Egyptian
support for the British.[32]

Political and social tensions in Egypt were not as
acute as they had been during Cromer's final year. Gorst had
managed to ease the pressures, mainly by acting firmly
and discreetly that spring. He had taken advantage of
the lull that often accompanies a sudden change in
leadership, when conflicting sides usually pause to
see what the results of the changes may be. The
nationalists were not well led or well organized, and
the combination of Cromer's abrupt resignation and
departure, the distracting financial crisis, and
Gorst's quiet but successful efforts to detach the
khedive may have confused them. Mustafa Kamil had
chosen to solicit support in Europe that summer, rather
than spread "sedition" in Egypt.[33]

Despite his frequent public statements that no
changes in British policy were contemplated, Gorst came
to Egypt with instructions from the Foreign Office
that would mean significant alterations from the policies of the Cromerian era. He did not, however, bring
detailed or written instructions. Grey dined at Gorst's
two days before Gorst left for Egypt in April, and "we
had a long talk on Egyptian matters."[34] Since 1904 Gorst
had been responsible for Egyptian affairs at the Foreign Office, and he had had frequent opportunity to discuss policy with the foreign secretaries and other high
officials. In fact, the specific implementation was
left for him to develop, and the Foreign Office and the
Cabinet were no longer either interested or able to
advise on the day-to-day administration of Egypt.

For twenty-four years Egyptian internal policy
had been left almost entirely to Cromer. The Foreign
Office had become concerned only when some action or reaction from Egypt affected wider questions of foreign
policy, or attracted attention from certain influential sections of the British public. The Liberal government, more than the Conservatives, was sensitive to
questions from the House of Commons. Since 1906 certain Radical and Irish members of the House had taken
an increasing interest in the affairs of Egypt, and
their questions tended to be an embarrassment and a
distraction to the government; as a result, Gorst had
been sent to change the Cromerian pattern of rule from
a personal autocracy dependent on the character and
prestige of one man to a more rational *system* of administration that would bring the Egyptians into the
process of governance. It was to be an experiment to
see if Egyptians could be given some limited responsibility for their own internal affairs. It was hoped
this new policy would ease pressure on the British
government at home and make Egypt more easily and
cheaply controlled. A similar policy for India would
be initiated under John Morley at the India office
during this same period. [35]

Certain officials then employed in the British
Agency have remarked on the shift in policy. Robert
Vansittart, then a second secretary in Cairo, wrote:

> Indeed change was the purpose of the Gorst
> appointment. . . . The Liberal Government
> had sent him out with a woolly mandate to
> liberalize the administration. . . . no one
> knew what that meant. . . . It was widely
> interpreted as a sign of weakness which might
> affect many jobs. Reforms were taken as a
> reflection on Cromer who was suddenly
> faultless. [36]

Ronald Storrs, soon to be appointed Gorst's Oriental
Secretary, commented on the new policy:

> The British Government had decided to use
> the occasion of the great change of persons
> to introduce an equally great change of
> method, and had given strong if not very
> precise instructions in this sense. The
> Liberal Cabinet entrusted Gorst with a pol-
> icy of steadily increasing Egyptian self-

government; essential if Great Britain was
ever to redeem her promise of ultimate Evacuation and (in the opinion of some of us) no
less essential even if we were to remain in
Egypt for ever.   Lord Cromer created Egypt:
his successor has to produce good Egyptians. [37]

In a short monograph written in 1915 mainly to
discredit the deposed Khedive Abbas II, Cromer very
grudgingly, critically, and ironically admitted—after
Gorst's death—that a shift in the political climate
in Great Britain, combined with certain events in
Egypt, had created conditions in 1907 that made a
change in policy necessary.

Many circumstances contributed to render an
experiment in this direction inevitable in
Egypt.   The idea that Egyptian institutions
required remodeling in a Liberal sense, that
insufficient attention had been paid to Egyptian education, and that the Egyptians should
be allowed a greater and more effective share
in the government of their own country, had
been sedulously fostered both by influential
politicians, who had derived their knowledge
of the state of affairs from a rapid visit
to Egypt, and by a section of the British
press. . . .

Sir Eldon Gorst made a thoroughly honest and
very courageous attempt to carry out the pro-
gramme which, if it had not been dictated to
him from the Foreign Office—a point as to
which I am not in possession of sufficient
information to justify any expression of opinion—was certainly prescribed for him by the
circumstances with which he had to deal. [38]

One of Gorst's successors in Egypt, Lord Lloyd, who
had access to Foreign Office correspondence, did not
discover any written instructions to Gorst.   Still he
blamed the Liberal Cabinet for sending Gorst out with
a specific mandate for changes; changes that Lloyd,
unlike Cromer, did not feel were inevitable.

For it seems clear that the Liberal Government then in power had expressly selected
him for the purpose of introducing a new
spirit and a new practice in Egypt, and

that he had received definite instructions
to this end from the Secretary of State, Sir
Edward Grey . . . There was undoubtedly considerable need for administrative reform in
Egypt at this time, but it can scarcely be
denied that the political reforms which
Gorst introduced responded much more to the
demand of Liberal opinion in England than
to any need inherent in the circumstances of
Egypt.[39]

In the fall of 1907 Gorst began to act on his
general instructions. He had effectively dealt with
the immediate tensions consequent to Cromer's departure the previous spring, and he had had the opportunity
and time to assess changes in the Egyptian administration and political climate since 1904. In his autobiographical notes he outlined his specific policy
lines, a policy of "conciliation" and of "moderation":

1. While outwardly proclaiming that Lord Cromer's
    policy was unchanged, to apply the precepts
    laid down in his annual reports rather than
    to follow the actual practice of recent years
    — in a word to carry into execution the many
    excellent practical and statesmanlike maxims
    which abound in Lord C's [Cromer's] writings
    but which remained in the stage of "pious
    opinions."

2. To avoid stirring up contentious questions
    or providing new points of attack for the
    nationalist party in Egypt or hostile critics
    in the House of Commons.

3. To render our rule more sympathetic to the
    Egyptians in general, and to the Mohammedans
    in particular, by restoring good feelings
    between the Anglo-Egyptian officials and the
    natives of the country, and preventing the
    British element riding roughshod over the
    Egyptian, by putting a check on the annual
    British invasion of new recruits, by giving
    greater encouragement to the Egyptian offi-
    cial class, and last but not least, by giv-
    ing a more national characteristic to the
    educational system.

4. To resume Lord Cromer's original attitude

of hostility to European privilege and to
try & unite English & Egyptian interests by
the policy of one and the same law for all
denizens of Egypt.

5. To cultivate good relations with the Khedive
so that his influence & prestige—whatever
they may be worth—may be an asset on our side
of the account. My trump card for this purpose was to hold out to H. H. the prospect of
reconciliation with the King and the British
Royal Family provided he behaved well in local
matters.

6. To settle quickly & definitely various questions regarding the pay & pensions of officers
& officials which had been allowed to remain
open for the last year or two, thereby creating much perturbation and discomfort among
those classes.

7. [numbered 5] As regards the Soudan, to supervise its administration on the sound lines
laid down & practiced by Lord Cromer, namely
to push on its material development as funds
permitted, to keep a tight hand over the expenditure, but to interfere with the man on
the spot as little as possible with regard
to matters of detail.[40]

The failure or success of Gorst's new policy depended largely on his gaining the support of the British
officials in the Egyptian administration. Fourteen
years earlier, in a letter to Milner, Gorst had delineated the difficulties of dealing with the Anglo-
Egyptian officials.

One of the most difficult things here, and
in my opinion the thing at which Lord Cromer
shines most, is keeping the English in order.
They are a difficult team to drive. . . . I
do not think anyone could possibly keep them
in hand who did not know the ropes thoroughly.
If ever Lord Cromer goes and an ordinary diplomatist comes here who does not understand
the details of the situation, you will see
that this element will bring him to grief and
upset the whole Egyptian coach. (Please ex-
cuse the rather mixed metaphors.)[41]

Soon after he returned that fall, he set about
"wheeling the English into line."[42]   About two hundred
of the senior officials were called to the Agency on
November 2 to listen to a confidential summary of the
new policy and Gorst's practical suggestions for implementing it. He clearly affirmed that Great Britain
had no intention of leaving; but her present position,
supported by the British army of occupation, meant
that the British "were morally bound to see that an
enlightened and just administration is maintained."[43]
The British could not escape responsibility for abuses
of this trust. Neither anglicization, nor protection,
nor annexation was British policy. Instead there was
a double task: first, to educate the Egyptians to rule
themselves and, second, to maintain British interests
and control. The British government was responsible
for the formulation of this policy, not the Consul-
General. Many of his listeners apparently missed this
latter point and blamed Gorst for the new policy.

Cromer's policy of "English heads and Egyptian
hands" had gone too far in the direction of English
heads. From now on a strong effort had to be made to
find and train Egyptians, particularly in the technical areas. "Our business here is to train Egyptians
beforehand for any posts for which they may possibly
be eligible, and wherever possible, preference must
be given to the natives of the country, even at some
loss of efficiency." Gorst outlined a few "practical
maxims" as guidelines for implementing the new policy.
There was to be no reform unless the people understood
it. "A reform . . . which causes general disagreement
is to my mind self-condemned." The British were to
beware of over-government and to stay in the background. Any changes in the existing condition which
required European assistance were "inadvisable." Simplicity rather than perfection had the greatest merit
in the East. Moreover Gorst advised: "Simplicity fa-
cilitates control—the branch of administration that
is more peculiarly our province."[44]

In every administration he alluded to a boundary
or limit for Egyptian accomplishments: "If the policy
which the British Government has prescribed is being
properly carried out, that high water mark ought gradually to get higher; and it is a confession of failure, if it is necessary to bring Englishmen into this
country to perform duties for which Egyptians might
have been trained." The sole justification of the

British presence in Egypt was moral and intellectual
superiority. This should be shown by setting a good
example, not by giving themselves airs. Incompetent
or unsatisfactory fellow countrymen must not be brought
in.

> It is not our fault if the moral standard of
> the Egyptian is low, nor can we altogether
> hope to avoid the evil consequences which
> must naturally follow from this fact. . . .
> No doubt the more vexatious sides of the
> Egyptian character demand infinite patience,
> but we must try to remember that these are
> not due to any extra dose of original sin,
> but are the natural inheritance of the past,
> and indeed, if they did not exist there would
> be no reason for our presence here. We should
> therefore deal with them in sorrow, not in
> anger.[45]

The qualities necessary for the British officials in
Egypt were kindness, sympathy, and understanding for
the Egyptian ways of thought and prejudices, and a thorough knowledge of Arabic. Constant tact was essential, the tact that can guide without the appearance
of guiding.

> Above all we must be constantly on our guard
> against doing or saying anything which might
> imply social superiority. There is no point
> in regard to which people of all nationali-
> ties are more sensitive, and unless we are
> prepared to treat the Egyptian as man and a
> brother, we had better remain at home. More-
> over, the Anglo-Egyptian official receives
> his salary from the people of this country,
> and if he is too proud to associate with them,
> he should be too proud to take their money.[46]

Public spirit and a zeal for the common cause should
characterize the Anglo-Egyptian administrator. Unity
and cooperation must be increased and backbiting and
criticism must be considerably reduced.

The day after the speech Gorst informed Grey he
had:

> preached them a sermon upon the objects of
> the British occupation. My text was that

>our business here is not to rule Egyptians,
>but to teach them to rule themselves and I
>added various suggestions as to the best
>method of carrying out this policy. They
>seem to have been impressed and I hope that
>the meeting will have done good. [47]

However, this speech did not elicit the sympathy or
the support of a majority of the British officials in
Egypt, although the policy changes outlined were neither new nor revolutionary. In fact, as Gorst wrote
to Cromer shortly after the speech, they were largely
Cromer's ideas: "I think everything I said has been
laid down in your Annual Reports, but I thought it
wise to drum it in once again, and I am told that the
effect has been beneficial."[48]

Gorst's information that the speech was beneficial was mistaken. Many of the British officials in
Egypt had come to regard Egypt as a British imperial
possession, to be managed and guided by them. Their
careers were threatened by a change in policy that
seemed to close the doors of promotion. Their comfortable and often luxurious life-styles were threatened by the more dynamic policy articulated by Gorst.
Most work days in Cairo among the officials rarely
exceeded five hours; according to one member of the
diplomatic community, nearly every week there was some
kind of holiday. Pay was good to excellent, and there
were abundant cheap servants. The senior officials
automatically received three months' holiday with pay,
the ordinary officials received two months on full pay
and one more month on half pay. They had neither sympathy for nor confidence in a policy that was going to
train Egyptians to replace them. Reactions among the
officials ranged from mild disappointment to a "storm
of indignation." The next day Storrs wrote home:

>Last night at six Gorst gave a resume of his
>policy to about 200 of the British Officials
>here: it was plain and, though of necessity
>containing nothing new, instructive, and made
>one feel what folly it was for England to
>pledge herself never to make the place a pro-
>tectorate. Our life here is one long post-
>ponement. [49]

P. G. Elgood, another Anglo-Egyptian official, recalled
it only as "a gentle reminder of Great Britain's

early pledges on the subject of the occupation."
Thomas Russell was uncertain what the new policy of
"Egypt for Egyptians" meant, and Gorst's cynical manner added to his uncertainty: "The interesting thing
will be to see if possible from his face whether he
believes in it himself." C. E. Coles Pasha, inspector
general of the Egyptian prison system during the Gorst
era, blamed the speech for causing a significant loss
of sympathy for Gorst and his policy among the British
officials:

> It has always appeared to me an irony of
> fate that Sir Eldon Gorst, as H.B.M. repre-
> sentative should have assembled us all at
> the Agency to tell us (amongst us a number
> of young men who he had himself been instru-
> mental in bringing out to Egypt) that a new
> policy was about to be introduced. 'Egypt
> for the Egyptians and no English need apply'
> was practically the purport of the discus-
> sion he gave us. . . . No one likes to be
> told their career prospects are blighted
> and no fault of his. Perhaps this is not
> altogether what Gorst meant . . . but judg-
> ing from the conversations that night at the
> Turf Club, this was the general interpreta-
> tion given to the speech.[50]

Under Cromer's direction Gorst had been responsible for revamping the entrance requirements and for
expanding the Egyptian civil service, a body of
officials that had proliferated as necessity and occasion demanded, especially since the 1890s. When the
British first occupied Egypt a civil service was not
planned, as the occupation was thought to be temporary; officers, officials, and engineers were seconded
for five years. Various British professionals and
soldiers were brought in to change the character of
the police forces and the department of public works
began to import engineers, who eventually became permanent members of the department. In the nineties,
when the grants for higher schools were increased, the
education department brought in English masters to
teach English and higher mathematics. Coles was not
impressed with the qualities of these men and wrote
sarcastically: "Not a few of the education experts
passed on to other administrative posts as soon as
they had acquired a knowledge of Arabic, and became,
if I may say so, social successes."[51]

In 1901 Gorst and Sir Reginald Wingate, the governor-general of the Sudan, had completed a revision of the requirements and procedures for appointment to the Egyptian and Sudanese civil services.[52] The officials appointed under the old systems, or the officials newly recruited by the processes developed by Gorst and Wingate, were not likely to be sympathetic to a policy that effectively appeared to end their chances for advancement or shorten their careers. Even more than officials in the Indian civil service, they had become rapidly conservative in philosophy and practice, committed to the status quo, to a narrow and somewhat selfish concern with their careers, and to a vision of the British Empire that did not admit that the "natives" could soon be capable of self-rule.

Earlier in the Agency speech, Gorst had reminded the assembled officials that:

> It is not always easy to insist upon a high standard of administration, and at the same time to foster a development of the native element in the departments of government . . . to endeavour to steer a middle course between the Scylla of administrative inefficiency and the Charybdis of Anglicization.[53]

This was to be Sir Eldon Gorst's chosen course in the few years left to him, and he would have little support or sympathy from those most essential to the implementation of his policies, the British members of the Egyptian civil service.

Chapter Eleven

THE NEW POLICY IN ACTION: 1908-1909

*. . . the system of pulling strings in the background
and letting others do the shouting, provided I had my
own way, was so thoroughly and successfully carried
out that it deceived even those who should have known
better.*
                              Sir Eldon Gorst, 1908[1]

To implement the "new policy" that he had outlined to
senior British officials at the Agency that November
evening in 1907, Gorst needed to minimize criticism in
Britain, particularly in the House of Commons, and to
appease any residual Egyptian hostility from the Cromer
era. One very troublesome matter, the disposition of
the Dinshawaï prisoners, had deliberately been left
unsettled by Gorst in the wake of Cromer's departure.
Cromer had been adamant in his opposition to any public rectification of the harsh sentences. Such action
would, he feared, endanger British prestige and undermine the confidence of the British officials and army
officers serving in Egypt. Grey had reluctantly but
characteristically acquiesced, hoping that after a
year or two of inaction the interested members of the
House of Commons might transfer their attentions to
more immediate matters. Gorst was more realistic than
Cromer or Grey about the consequences of further delay.
He wanted to bury the issue as quickly as possible so
that it would neither serve as a pretext for further
nationalist disturbances nor hinder the new policy of
conciliation.

     Meanwhile Grey's hopes that the prisoners' plight
would be forgotten and that discussion of Egyptian affairs in Britain would decrease were not fulfilled.
It was unusual for foreign policy matters to be examined so closely in Parliament. The Front Benches of
both parties had sought for a long period of time in
the nineteenth century to withdraw discussion of foreign policy from the sphere of party politics.[2]

Gorst and
the porter.

Egypt meets
Gorst.

Naturally, foreign secretaries tended to discourage
debate on the details of foreign policy or the day-to-
day administration of the Empire. Routine business
was left to the "man on the spot," and the foreign
secretary was neither interested in nor prepared to
respond to persistent questions on the internal affairs
of Egypt. However, the Tabah crisis and the Dinshawai
punishments focused considerable attention in the House
of Commons on British policy and administration in
Egypt, attention that did not abate in the spring,
summer, and fall of 1907.[3]

Neither Cromer's retirement in May 1907 nor Grey's
warnings in late June that further debate might endanger the stability of the British Empire managed to
damp the interest of certain House members. Despite
the apparent easing of internal tensions in Egypt as
a result of Gorst's arrival and maneuvers, an unhappy
Grey informed Cromer in August: "Denshawai is far the
most troublesome thing in the House of Commons and
does more harm there than anything else."[4] The persistent questions in the House and some private pressures
finally convinced the foreign secretary (who was uncomfortable about the sentences) that it was necessary
to review the case. He had the Foreign Office send
the papers on the incident and trial to the Lord
Chancellor, Lord Loreburn, for his legal opinion. He
explained the situation to Cromer: "I think, myself,
that the two men now imprisoned would have got sentences of two years in England, but I am sure they
would not have got the very long sentences which they
now have." Grey told Cromer he wanted to arrange with
Gorst to revise the sentences "if things are still
quiet a few months hence," but the foreign secretary
did not want to appear to be under parliamentary pressure. Cromer was displeased. He acknowledged the
difficulty of defending such severe sentences, but
pleaded with Grey: "I hope you will not go too far in
the way of concessions."[5] The Lord Chancellor meanwhile reviewed the evidence and informed Grey privately that none of the accused should have received
a sentence of more than eighteen months. Loreburn's reaction was quite strong: "So clearly do I hold this
opinion that I would say it would be a reproach to the
cause of justice if their punishment was protracted
beyond the period I have named."[6]

This firm declaration from the Lord Chancellor
finally prompted Grey to grant Gorst permission to

arrange the release of the prisoners. In a letter to
Cromer in September Grey blamed the petitioners for
delaying remission. It would never do for the British
or the Egyptian puppet government to appear to yield
to pressure on the issue.[7] Now Grey deluded himself
that enough time had passed for British prestige and
self-esteem to be salvaged. Gorst was more realistic
about the importance of burying the issue so that it
would not stir up further nationalistic disturbances
in Egypt. "I quite agree with you," wrote Gorst to
Grey, "that the sentences were too severe and that the
effect on native opinion has not been good, and the
sooner we put an end to this undesirable state of affairs the better." Gorst also assured Grey he would
give his opinion privately to any British officials
who were dissatisfied. The new proconsul refused
Grey's offer to assume the fullest responsibility for
the decision to release the prisoners; it would, he
told Grey, undermine his own prestige in Egypt to take
shelter under the Foreign Office or the Lord Chancellor.
Gorst had arranged that the khedive would pardon the
prisoners if the British government acquiesced.[8] Until
the date of the release, he intended to keep the matter quiet so that the Egyptian nationalist press would
not be able to claim credit.

        Final arrangements for the prisoners' release
were made in mid-November, apparently hastened by continued pressure from House members and certain influential sectors of the British public.[9] Ronald Storrs
noted with irritation a petition that had been circulated in London; in an October letter to his mother he
voiced his disappointment that George Meredith's name
was "amongst the crapulous signatories for the release
of the Dinshawai prisoners."[10] Grey was amazed and then
annoyed that the agitation in England for the release
of the prisoners had been renewed. Gorst's plan—that
the khedive pardon the prisoners on the khedive's birthday early in January—was approved in the Cabinet.
Grey said he would try to prevent any leakages of the
plans, "but a great deal of pressure has been brought."
The khedive would be allowed to claim credit for the
act of clemency, "as long as he is acting well."[11]

        Crediting the khedive with the pardon would salve
the pride of the members of the special tribunal. The
British military in Egypt and the khedive would be
informed only at the last minute to prevent damaging
leaks. The still sensitive issue of the special

tribunal would be settled by following Cromer's proposal to let it lapse from disuse. The British military in Egypt would have been upset if the special
court had been officially and publicly abrogated.[12]
Any future cases would, if possible, be tried in the
ordinary Egyptian criminal courts. This negative recognition by the British of the jurisdiction of the
Egyptian courts in cases where their self-interest
was involved was a small but significant step in le-
gitimizing these courts for all the residents of Egypt.
When Butrus Ghali was assassinated in 1910, Gorst was
able to resist great pressure from certain groups in
Britain to transfer the case to the jurisdiction of another
special tribunal. Instead, the Egyptian courts assumed
jurisdiction.

     Despite Gorst's and Grey's precautions against
leakages, Mustafa Kamil's paper *al-Liwa* announced the
plan for the release of the prisoners on December 31.
Ronald Graham, the new counselor at the Agency, blamed
the leakage on a correspondent from London called
William Robertson, whom he identified as a Jew on the
staff of *The Tribune*, connected with the so-called
Egyptian Committee in Parliament. Although the khedive had not yet been officially informed when the
news of the release was published, he told Gorst that
he was much pleased, and British officials including
the military appeared to accept the decision as a matter of course. In January Grey discovered that the
information had been released to the press through a
Cabinet indiscretion.[13]

     To avoid hostile nationalist demonstrations and
a reception organized by Kamil's followers in Cairo,
the British released the prisoners a day earlier than
announced. Grey wrote to Gorst: "With the Denshawai
business out of the way, I hope to have an easier time
as regards Egypt in Parliament than I have had for the
last two years." Graham informed the Foreign Office
that any other form of demonstration by the nationalists would fall "rather flat," thanks to the early
release: "Such a demonstration would be objectionable
to the British but I don't suppose it could be stopped
in this free country. At times the freedom enjoyed
here seems almost excessive."[14]

     Gorst was not convinced that there was excessive
freedom in Egypt. After settling the Dinshawai affair
late in 1907, he began to implement the other aspects

of his policy of conciliation. He concentrated first
on bringing more Egyptians into the internal administration of their country. Under Cromer, Egyptian
political and administrative responsibility had remained
insignificant.[15]   Gorst enlarged the powers of the
existing provincial councils, principally in the area
of local education. Although the franchise for the
provincial councils was not altered, their size was
increased.[16]   More important, they were given the
right to increase the land tax as much as five percent, and with the approval of the ministry of interior they could apply that increase to certain local
projects.

        Like many other officials, Gorst was influenced
by the British experience in India, and as the advisor
to the interior ministry in the 1890s, he had initiated
in Egypt some efforts to vitalize provincial and municipal government. Now as proconsul, over the objections of some of his staff, Gorst slowly evolved a
scheme to give the Egyptians increasing responsibility
and channel some of the growing nationalist fervor
into productive action. The specific changes that
Gorst devised with his staff are detailed in his
annual report for 1909, and the new provincial council
legislation went into effect in June of that year.[17]
Especially significant was Gorst's attempt to involve
the existing Egyptian officials in the process of
strengthening the functions of provincial councils and
local government in general. Where Cromer had generally ignored Egyptian Cabinet members and scorned
the khedive, the Legislative Council, and General
Assembly, Gorst carefully sought their assistance and
support. The khedive, Butrus Ghali, the newly appointed prime minister, and the khedive's uncle,
Prince Husayn Kamil—who was president of the Legislative Council—all worked behind the scenes to promote the proposed changes among members of the Legislative Council and Assembly.[18]

        Gorst meanwhile set aside time to reacquaint him-
self with the provinces whose governments he sought to
reform. In the autumn of 1907 he explored the Nile
Delta and appraised the mood of the local officials
and notables. He himself said that his knowledge of
Arabic enabled him to "talk freely" with the Egyptians
without an interpreter, a distinct change from the
imperious Cromer. In 1907 Gorst visited the Sudan
after Christmas, where he noted, "I was received with

the customary Wingate pomp and circumstance," and in
1908 he inspected all the provinces of Upper Egypt.[19]
The purpose of these travels was not only to solicit
opinions but also to prepare the way for further
changes in the personnel and responsibilities of the
Egyptian Cabinet and the British or European advisors.

By the end of 1908 Gorst had effected major
changes—changes that were long overdue. Under Cromer
most senior Egyptian officials had been nonentities or
"dummies" as Gorst aptly described them. Initiative
and responsibility for policy had been concentrated
among the British advisors, some of whose imaginations
and practices had ossified during the Cromerian era.
After a suitable waiting period so that the changes
did not appear to be a rejection of Cromer's men or policies, Gorst arranged for the retirement of the aging
Egyptian prime minister, Mustafa Fahmi Pasha, and his
entire "Cabinet of dummies." They were replaced by
"a team selected for efficiency and able to exercise
some influence over their countrymen." To head this
team Gorst, in consultation with the khedive, selected
the prominent Copt Butrus Ghali Pasha for the post
of Egyptian prime minister. "We decided to appoint
Butrus and introduce new blood into the ministry."
Gorst had first thought of Fakhri Pasha, then the minister of public works, as a replacement for the waning
Fahmi, who had been a willing tool of the British; but
eventually Fakhri declined to serve and Gorst was much
relieved. Gorst wanted Egyptians who could keep the
British in touch with the people and who possessed
some ideas of their own while still remaining useful
to the British.[20]

When Gorst settled on Butrus Ghali for prime minister he admitted to Grey that the appointment of a
Christian was a risk, but a risk he was willing to
assume to gain the services of a capable man. He had
few illusions about Ghali, since this elastic leader
of his community had been an important and influential
Egyptian civil servant since the 1860s. Ghali was an
excellent linguist with a knowledge of Arabic, Turkish,
English, French, Italian, Persian, German, and Coptic.
He had begun his career in the Alexandria Commercial
Council, and had held positions in the mixed courts,
the commission of public debt, and the ministry of justice before being appointed minister of finance in 1893.
Gorst was then under secretary of state for finance
and recorded his reaction to Ghali in his autobiographical

notes: "The Minister of Finance was Butrus, a Copt,
an arch trimmer with whom I managed to get on very
well."[21]

A recent assessment of Ghali's career by an historian of the Copts states that he made himself nearly
indispensable as go-between and mediator between the
British and the Egyptian ruling classes.[22] After serving as finance minister, he was appointed foreign minister in 1895 and in that capacity signed the Anglo-
Egyptian Conventions for the condominium over the
Sudan in 1899. Ghali used his influence with the
khedive and Cromer to ease their bitter relations. He
presided over the Dinshawai special tribunal as acting
minister of justice in June 1906. Cromer singled Ghali
out, along with Mustafa Fahmi and Saad Zaghlul, for
marked praise in his May 1907 farewell address in the
Cairo Opera House.[23] Ghali was apparently the "willing
instrument" for measures unpopular with the majority
of the politically sensitive Egyptians: partly because
he had developed a keen affection for political sur-
vival and for office, but also because he had helped to
lead his prospering community into an alliance of interests with the British and Khedive Abbas.[24] Ghali's
good relations and influence with the khedive appear
to have been crucial factors in his selection as the
new Egyptian prime minister. Since a reconciliation
with the khedive was a major objective of the "new
policy," Gorst decided to risk the religious conflict
or dissatisfaction that might result from the appointment of a Christian to govern a Muslim majority.

Gorst himself was a very clever and devious man,
and it appears that he may also have hoped that the
appointment of Ghali would detach the Coptic community
from anti-British activity in Egypt, especially from
the noisy nationalist movement that had emerged under
the leadership of Mustafa Kamil. Before his untimely
death in February 1908 at the age of thirty-two, Kamil
had managed to forge a tenuous alliance between his
Egyptian Muslim followers and some of the Coptic leaders. This alliance was generated in part by the shock
of many Egyptians at the Dinshawai punishments, and as
a reaction against solidification of British influence
after the Anglo-French Entente of 1904. In the wake
of the Tabah crisis, the Dinshawai incident, increased
nationalist agitation, Cromer's resignation, and Gorst's
return to Egypt as Cromer's successor, formally organized Egyptian political parties appeared in the fall

of 1907. Kamil's Nationalist Party (*al-Hizb al-Watani*)
was the only organized political group that commanded
any significant popular support, and its original
ten-point program invited the Copts to join with the
Egyptian Muslims to further the nationalist cause and
promote unity and harmony between the two major communities of Egypt. Kamil's death meant the loss of
his dynamic and unifying leadership.[25]

By July 1908 very serious differences had arisen
within the National Party over policies and tactics.
One of the differences was over the place of the Copts
in the movement, and the appointment of Ghali came
just as relations between Copts and Muslims in the
Nationalist Party had become seriously strained.[26]
Gorst hoped that the choice of a Copt might further
split the nationalist movement, besides pleasing the
Coptic community and the khedive, whom Gorst had already
detached from his intermittent support of the nationalists. Moreover Ghali was efficient and reliable,
experienced in the delicate and complicated administration of the Egyptian government. His appointment
would be received with sympathy in Britain in all but
a few unimportant Radical and anti-imperialist circles,
since Ghali was a native Egyptian Christian. The
Christian missionary groups in Egypt would also be
pleased. Some Egyptians, however, expressed their
distress to Ronald Storrs, who wrote home that his
Muslim friends were "as sick as the devil at the appointment of a Copt as Prime Minister. . . . you must
remember that here religion takes the place of nation-
ality, which is non-existent."[27]

Ghali and Zaghlul were the only carry-overs from
the old ineffective cabinet. Besides assuming the
prime minister's post, Ghali kept the largely ceremonial post of minister of foreign affairs he had held
since 1894. The other carry-over, Zaghlul, was appointed to the new cabinet despite the opposition of
Ghali and the khedive, who did not like the independence of the man or the interests and ideas he represented. Gorst convinced them that it was important
for Egyptian political stability to keep Zaghlul in
the government in a responsible position. He informed
Grey:

> He [Zaghlul] has many defects,—but he is
> honest— and always ends by yielding when
> matters come to a crisis. . . . the argument

by which I finally prevailed was that he'd
be a great danger if left outside the government and might be able to place himself
at the head of all the hostile elements in
the country. [28]

Zaghlul was appointed to both cabinets formed during
the Gorst era, and was an active member. He resigned
in 1913 when he judged that Gorst's successor,
Kitchener, was promulgating social and political
policies that he could not support. [29]   Zaghlul's
open opposition to the British in Egypt was to prove
formidable, as Gorst predicted.

The other ministers, new to the Cabinet, were all
pashas: Muhammad Said at interior, Ahmad Hishmat at
finance, Hussain Rushdi at justice, and Ismail Sirri
at public works and war. The British had decided they
would be allowed increased responsibility along with
their elevation to the Cabinet. In the final years of
Cromer's proconsulship the influence on the Egyptian
government of British officials and advisors and minority communities had grown and even, as has been seen,
received official encouragement. Gorst had now initiated changes in this pattern of influence and control.
He proposed that the new Cabinet members attend meetings of the Legislative Council more frequently and
defend government measures with the council members.
Gorst told Grey that this conception of the Cabinet's
more responsible role in the government of Egypt might
cause some inconvenience and trouble for the British,
but the difficulties were worth it if the new, more
liberal system was to work. [30]   Gorst's motives in
strengthening the provincial councils and in appointing Ghali and the rest of the new Cabinet were complex.
On one hand he sought to divert the growing nationalist pressures for self-rule and reinforce British influence. On the other hand, there is evidence that
he was genuinely interested in participation by Egyptians in their own government.

C. E. Coles Pasha, the police and prison official,
knew Gorst quite well. In his memoirs Coles recalled
a dinner conversation during the Cromer era, in which
Gorst "was all for Home Rule, and at that time I was
all for government by some disinterested outside authority, such as Lord Cromer or the Government of India."
As early evidence of interest in bringing Egyptians
into their own government, Coles cited Gorst's

pioneering work with the local commissions and the
mixed municipalities when Sir Eldon was advisor to
the ministry of the interior in 1893. According to
Coles, Gorst made "radical" changes in the organization of provincial and national government after
Cromer retired: "In Egypt Sir Eldon Gorst was undoubtedly the pioneer of Home Rule, both urban and rural."[31]
Ronald Storrs pointed out how quiescent and powerless
the Egyptian ministers had become under Cromer's influence. "The Ministers had larger salaries, little
work beyond an occasional signature, scarcely any
responsibility and no constituents." It was the policy of Gorst and the British government to reverse
this trend, to see that responsible Egyptians gradually took, as Gorst put it to Grey, "as large a share
as is possible in the government of their country."[32]

Among the new ministers, Zaghlul was the most
active in asserting the prerogatives and responsibilities of his post. His appointment, and the elevation
of education to a separate ministry, was the consequence of considerable political pressure on Cromer
from England and Egypt. Almost from the moment of his
arrival as Cromer's replacement, Gorst was subject to
similar pressure to reform and upgrade Egyptian education. Liberal Radicals such as J. M. Robertson, combined with the Irish Nationalists such as John Dillon
in the House of Commons, pressed the foreign secretary
to provide evidence of significant progress in the reform of the long neglected Egyptian educational system.[33]
In Egypt, Mustafa Kamil's followers campaigned for
reform in their newspapers, and agitated in the schools
against the British occupation. Furthermore the more
moderate nationalists, former followers of the late
Muhammad Abduh—men who sponsored the influential
newspaper, *al-Jaridah*, and who founded *al-Ummah*—were
deeply committed to educational reform as the major
means of creating a politically healthy and independent Egypt. These ideas and opinions on educational
policy were increasingly influential in the seven years
before the First World War. Zaghlul never joined
al-Ummah; instead he chose during the Gorst proconsulship to exercise his considerable experience and talents within the framework of the Egyptian administration. Zaghlul had been in the inner circle of
Muhammad Abduh's disciples and was therefore committed,
like the group that organized *al-Ummah*, to remoulding
the laws and institutions of Egypt toward the goals
of self-government and independence.[34]

Zaghlul's ideas for reform, his intelligence, independence, and continual efforts to assert his authority over the British officials in his ministry brought him into direct conflict with the advisor to education, the unimaginative Scot, Douglas Dunlop. This meant, of course, indirect conflict with Gorst. The agitation for educational reform in the national- ist press was often coupled with demands that Dunlop be replaced, so Gorst delayed some changes and the dismissal of Dunlop until such furor had died down.[35] In April 1910 Gorst wrote to Grey that he wished to discuss Egyptian educational reform with the foreign secretary in England that summer. He had long been concerned that the system as it existed, like that of India, was doing more harm than good. Most of the high British officials in Egypt agreed on one neces- sary change, that the advisor, Dunlop, be fired. His department was "really a matter of political impor- tance from the point of view of our work out here," Gorst wrote emphatically, and emphasized that the lull in political hostility toward Dunlop offered a "good opportunity for dispensing with his services without the appearance of yielding to popular clamour."[36] It is to Gorst's credit that he sought the removal from Egyptian service of this rigid bureaucrat.

Gorst's successors, too concerned with other mat- ters, let Dunlop remain in his post; his removal and many other needed reforms were thus postponed until it was too late, and a whole generation of students was neglected. While it is doubtful that the Egyptians growing up in the first two decades of this century would have been much more content with the British occupation had they been the beneficiaries of an ex- panded and more enlightened educational system, they might have acquired far more technical and administra- tive skills. Political instability in Egypt during the first forty years of this century was due partly to the neglect that the British lavished on Egyptian education.[37]

Gorst was concerned about signs of disquiet in the schools and the students' potential for causing seri- ous trouble for the British, but during his short term as Consul-General he was unable, largely for political reasons, to change significantly the long neglected system.[38] He did, however, make a start. Cromer had effectively prevented the creation of an Egyptian uni- versity. Gorst allowed a private university to open

in 1908, despite British fears that it would provide
another forum for the nationalists. A group of prominent Egyptians, led by Prince Ahmad Fuad (later King
Fuad I) and a few British and European supporters collected the necessary funds. During its first three
years the Egyptian University offered only a limited
number of courses in the humanities: for example,
English, Arabic literature, and the history of
Mohammedan nations. The faculty grew from two Egyptian and three European professors to four Egyptian
and seven European professors by 1910. A ladies' section was added with a course on French literature and
lectures in Arabic on hygiene and infant care.[39]

Attendance at university lectures was never substantial. Even an annual subsidy of 2,000 pounds
Egyptian from the Egyptian government, beginning in
1910, and the addition of departments of social and
economic science and chairs for political economy and
rural economy (general and Egyptian), did not produce
an institution which would have a significant impact
on Egyptian education. Only after World War I was a
truly viable national university created in Egypt.[40]
Gorst was exaggerating when he wrote Grey in March 1911
that the Egyptian University had made good progress.
In 1911 he asked for some assistance from the department of education. British authorities in Whitehall
were skeptical of the quality of the Egyptian University, and reluctant to grant the books and periodicals
he had requested. Lord Kitchener, Gorst's successor
in the fall of 1911, described the Egyptian University
as misconceived. He noted it was "not easy to see,
how on the present basis, improvements can be introduced."[41]

The Egyptian University did sponsor advanced students in Europe who would be expected, once they had
completed their training, to return to professorships
in the university. They joined a group of Egyptian
students who had been selected and sent to Europe and
Britain to be trained as teachers for secondary and
technical training schools. This too was a departure
from the policy of Cromer, who had acted to prevent
Egyptians from going to study in Europe. Cromer feared
that the experience abroad would subvert these young
students, and that they would return to Egypt prepared
to act against British interests there. In 1912 he
told Kitchener: "When I was in Egypt I did whatever I
could to discourage young Egyptians being sent to

England at all, the true solution being to improve
higher and technical education in Egypt to such an extent as to render the dispatch of young Egyptians to
Europe unnecessary."[42]   Zaghlul was actively in favor
of the project to send students abroad for their final
training. Beginning in 1908 twenty students per year
were sent abroad, mainly to England, under close supervision of a one-man office called the Egyptian
educational mission. Supervision of the students included police surveillance by Scotland Yard. Still,
complaints were received during the next few years
in Egypt and at the Foreign Office that a number of
these students returned to Egypt more hostile than
before to the British occupation. Gorst remained
firmly in support of the program, but attempted to
tighten up the selection process and expand the services of the mission to include both students supported
by the Egyptian government and those who went on their
own. He asserted to Grey that a tight rein in Britain
would stamp out the "Anglophobe tendencies" that in
the past had frequently accompanied the acquisition of
greater knowledge.[43]

The reforms and changes that Gorst initiated in
Egyptian education during his four-year term as proconsul were not enough to enliven a system whose development had been stunted by neglect and misdirection
during Cromer's twenty-four years. From 1907 on there
were a number of student disturbances and strikes, encouraged and sometimes started by the nationalists.
The Khedivial Law School, the engineering school, and
al-Azhar, the ancient Muslim university, were impeded
by student and faculty protests. At al-Azhar in 1909
Gorst reluctantly sent Egyptian police in to break up
a student strike, again postponing long-needed changes.
He informed Grey that time was not ripe yet for the
Egyptian government to force the reform of al-Azhar:

> The attempt to reform al-Azhar and thus to
> modify or interfere with the time-honored
> traditions of a religious institution is
> generally regarded by the Egyptians as an
> offense against the Mohammedan religion and
> the introduction of police within the pre-
> cincts of the mosque has aroused very bit-
> ter resentment.[44]

Official inertia, and in some cases deliberate obstruction, helped to frustrate some of Gorst's plans. Both

the nationalists and Gorst wanted to remove Dunlop,
but with different ends in mind. Dunlop was not alone
among the British officials who had acquired a habit
of inertia and bureaucratic obstructionism during the
Cromer era; he was just one of the most obvious.

Gorst was not able to get rid of Dunlop, but in
other less visible and controversial cases he sought
to appoint qualified Egyptians or British who were
sympathetic to the Egyptians and self-effacing enough
to apply Gorst's method of indirect control. When he
set out to reduce the numbers, visibility, and power
of the British officials, Gorst was consciously attempting to change a set pattern of behavior. Cromer
had created an administration dependent on his prestige, and on the loyalty and skills of a rapidly growing body of Englishmen whose behavior increasingly
antagonized the Egyptians. Gorst, as early as 1893,
in a letter to Milner, warned of the problems of
"keeping the English in order" after Cromer left. [45]
Ironically, one of his last completed projects before
he left Egypt in 1904 had been a reorganization of the selection process for the Anglo-Egyptian and Sudanese
civil services. Thus Gorst was himself responsible
for the presence of some of the officials whose jobs
he sought to end.

Too few of the British officials in Egypt, junior
or senior, were sympathetic to the policy Gorst had
been instructed to implement. After a quarter-century
of ruling Egypt, many had come to feel and act as if
Egypt were a British possession in fact if not in name.
Grey at the Foreign Office was aware of the dangers
that faced Gorst in his attempt to change the habits
and attitudes of British officials in Egypt. After
the resignation of financial advisor Vincent Corbett
in the spring of 1907, Grey warned the just-retired
Cromer that summer that Gorst would have to struggle
to gain the loyalty of the British officials:

> In Egypt itself, what I am most afraid
> of is want of public support on the
> part of some of the British officials
> and their making things difficult for
> Gorst. If there be one or two, they
> can be got rid of, and can resign as
> Corbett has done. But should there be
> several, matters might be very much
> disorganized. [46]

Although Gorst moved relatively slowly, uncertainty about their positions and misunderstandings about the policy snowballed among Anglo-Egyptian officials. Part of Gorst's difficulty was the impossibility of living up to the reputation of his predecessor. The turmoil that had preceded Cromer's sudden resignation was rapidly forgotten as Gorst's self-effacing style emerged, and a void of leadership was felt. Many of the most experienced and sensitive officials from the Cromerian period had already retired; the resignations of Corbett and Sir William Garstin, the highly respected advisor to the department of public works, and the transfer of Findlay almost immediately after Gorst's return accelerated the sense of insecurity among many British officials. Gorst's confidential speech to assembled senior British administrators in November 1907 apparently increased their confusion about his intentions and their fears for their futures.

During the fall of 1907 Gorst also "sought to revive the departed glories of the British Agency, as in the reign of the first Lady Cromer." Doll and Eldon spent more than three thousand pounds to brighten and refurnish the building. "As a sort of housewarming" they hosted a reception for nearly six hundred guests—"mostly Britons" noted Gorst—on November 9, the official birthday celebration of the king. "The buffet arrangements were rather in confusion but otherwise the affair was a success," he wrote in his diary. In December they gave a ball for about four hundred and fifty; aside from a "sticky" dance floor, Gorst judged that the occasion went well. Throughout their first full season in Cairo (1907-1908) the Gorsts gave regular dinner parties, usually hosting about thirty guests seated at three round tables.[47]

This intensive and expensive social activity was intended by Gorst to remedy the neglect of such matters by Cromer in his final years in office. Yet it had a negative effect on the British community in Egypt. Ronald Storrs, soon to become Gorst's intelligence officer as Oriental secretary at the Agency, asserted that Gorst's manner, his hospitality and informality—a contrast to Cromer's brusqueness, isolation and formality—were met by scorn, derision, and jealousy. Storrs wrote:

> Sir Eldon Gorst . . . assisted by a young
> and charming wife, with the means to and
> the desire to show a large hospitality, was
> at great pains to give pleasure by taking
> the utmost trouble with the numbers, the fre-
> quency, and the arrangement of his luncheon
> and dinner parties, which indeed could not
> have been improved upon materially, or in
> the choice and placing of guests. As a
> reward for this solicitude the same critics
> [who had criticized Cromer for not enter-
> taining much] pronounced that it was really
> no compliment to be asked to the Agency now:
> You seemed to meet everybody there. And
> his endeavours to stem the rising flood of
> insularity by a judicious mingling of ele-
> ments served but to evoke the classic dia-
> logue "Were you at the Agency last night?"
> "No, but then you see I'm not a foreigner;
> I'm only British." [48]

Gorst went on reshuffling the top officials. By
the close of 1908 he had obtained the resignation of Percy
Machell, advisor to the ministry of the interior and
Gorst's best man, whose work Gorst judged to have been
a failure; he replaced him with Sir Arthur Chitty.
Eustace Corbett, the procuror general, was replaced
by Sarawat, "an active and capable Egyptian." These
personnel changes were part of a larger scheme Gorst
had thought out to give Egypt "a proper degree of
public security."[49] Gorst also reduced the powers
and responsibility of Cromer's long-time advisor and
confidant, the eccentric Harry Boyle, who was given
another post in the consular service and was replaced
in 1909 as Oriental secretary by the clever young
Ronald Storrs. Aside from the fact that Boyle was
Cromer's man, Gorst blamed him for blocking reforms
when Gorst had been advisor to the ministry of the
interior. In his autobiographical notes Gorst wrote:

> My effort to improve the public security of
> the country and the establishment of a more
> satisfactory system between the parquet and
> the police failed due to Lord Cromer's in-
> ability to shake himself clear from personal
> considerations and to his unfortunate sub-
> servience to the influence of Boyle.[50]

According to Gorst, Boyle had lost his perspective on
the Egyptians. His contacts and his sympathies lay
with the decaying Turco-Circassian class, and the Syrians like the Nimrs. Boyle himself admitted he had
been in Egypt too long, and even refused posts in Beirut
and Crete because he had lost his taste for Middle
Eastern affairs. When offered Crete, he responded, in
a letter home: "I declined as I simply don't want any
more orientals of any kind." He expressed his disil-
lusion in a letter to his revered ex-master, Lord Cromer,
addressed "Develetu Effendim": "I understand I am to
come away as soon as may be. There is nothing to keep me
here. . . .it is hard and sad to think of leaving.[51]

In 1908 Gorst was forced to use all his powers
of diplomacy to prevent the "Kamlin Affair" from becoming another Dinshawai. Sudanese officials, usually
calmer than their Anglo-Egyptian counterparts, lost
their heads when a British military officer was killed
by some tribesmen in the Southern Sudan. Apparently
the spectre of the appearance of a new Mahdi in the
Sudan threw the officials into a panic, and Gorst had
to intervene very firmly to prevent the authorities
from hanging twenty-three Sudanese in retaliation.
The Foreign Office supported the proconsul fully, not
wanting to revive questions and agitations from "sen-
timentalists in Parliament." Gorst was disquieted by
the "violent and unreasonable spirit" displayed by the
Sudanese officials, who in contrast to most of the
Anglo-Egyptian officials he had found to be "a fine
lot of fellows from Wingate downwards. If in time I
can infuse the Cairo English into as good a spirit as
prevails here [in the Sudan] among all the officials,
civil and military, I shall be very pleased."[52]

As early as the spring of 1908, Gorst's policy
had greatly disturbed the British community in Egypt.
Harry Boyle wrote home of the impending changes in
personnel and recorded Gorst's blasé attitude:

> so you see the indomitable sportsman [Gorst]
> is bringing down the birds right and left.
> The other day he asked me: "Frankly, do you
> think there is any section or subsection of
> society here, British or foreign or Egyptian,
> which has a good word for me and my policy?"
> and I frankly answered, "Not one," at which
> he grinned cheerfully. He certainly has the
> pluck of the very devil and we are all in

> admiration, though how it will all end,
> goodness knows. Anyway it is not courage
> or brains that are lacking.[53]

Discontent among the officials in the next year increased, as Gorst continued quietly to implement the
policy of liberalization and conciliation.[54]   This
discontent had reached the eyes and ears of Cromer in
England, now fully recovered from his tension-inspired
illness.   In February of 1909 he closed a letter to
his son: "I do not altogether like the state of things
in Egypt.   From what I hear, and also from indications
in the *Egyptian Gazette* I am afraid the English are
getting very discontented.   Gorst is going on the right
lines, and must be supported, even if he makes certain
mistakes in detail." By July his disquiet had increased.   In another letter to his son he noted unhap-
pily, "Things in Egypt are certainly not going very
well.   It is not easy to say what should be done to
improve them.   If Grey asks me I will of course give
him the best advice I can."[55]

In January 1909, in a private letter, Hardinge
affirmed the support of the Foreign Office for Gorst's
policy:

> It may interest you to hear that Runciman
> [President of the Board of Education] came
> to see me the other evening, and gave me a
> long account of his impressions in Egypt.
> I am glad they were most favourable.   The
> only thing he seemed to criticise was the
> capabilities of some of the English members
> of the administration.   I told him I thought
> you appreciated this fully as he does, but
> that it would be impolitic to make a clean
> sweep at once.   Things must go slowly, and
> we have plenty of time.[56]

The changes did not seem slow to the British officials
in Egypt.

Gorst not only continued a reduction in the apparent influence of the British authorities, but affirmed his working relationship with the khedive and
the Egyptian Cabinet.   He also set in motion an effort
to improve the quality and efficiency of the complex
Egyptian judicial system.   The process was a very complicated one, involving delicate negotiations with the

Capitulatory Powers, the incumbent judges, and the
Egyptian secular and religious authorities. Gorst
sought to set limits on the terms of the European
judges, to toughen their selection process, to ensure
the choice of better men, and to clarify the jurisdiction of the mixed courts and the Shariah courts. Much
of this ambitious and intricate program was successfully accomplished by the end of Gorst's term in
Egypt. [57]   These reforms, however, were unpopular among
the British and other foreign judges in Egypt and
among business interests accustomed to sheltering
themselves under the various and confused jurisdic-
tions of the Egyptian courts.[58]   These successful efforts to reform the Egyptian courts may well have contributed to the hostility already directed against
Gorst and his policies.

     The financial crisis of 1907 threatened the in-
vestments and profits of various individuals and companies in Egypt, and accusing fingers were pointed at
Gorst. He refused to allow the Egyptian government to
provide a substantial loan to prop up some of the wavering speculators. Their bitterness and fears were
compounded in April 1908 when the mixed courts ruled
that a joint-stock company formed with the sole object
of exploiting an enterprise in Egypt had to be considered Egyptian. Many companies had registered abroad
to avoid Egyptian regulation; as a result of this
mixed-court decision, a large number, nearly fifty,
with a paid-up capital of 222,000 pounds Egyptian,
were forced into liquidation between 1907 and 1914
because they were unable or unwilling to reorganize
themselves under the Egyptian commercial and financial
regulations. [59]   Egypt had been a ripe and succulent
source of profits. The British presence provided stability and security, and the capitulatory privileges
gave exemption from certain kinds of financial regulation and taxes. The complex Egyptian judicial system
was also a form of protection. Gorst's program for
judicial reform endangered those financial interests
who depended on the status quo for their freedom to
maneuver within the Egyptian economy.

     Gorst's attempt to toughen the selection process
for the judges in the Egyptian courts also disturbed
the British officials. Cromer's correspondence with
Grey hinted that the quality and performance of the
British judges in Egypt were poor. Consequently
Cromer supported Gorst's innovations so that

more able lawyers might be appointed in the future and
the dead wood among the judges be cleared out. When
Gorst refused in 1909 to allow the Egyptian government
to renew the contract of J. S. Willmore, a British
judge on the native tribunals, proposing a Belgian
lawyer instead, the Foreign Office received many complaints. Questions on the issue were asked in the
House of Commons, in the major English language newspaper of Egypt, and in the London press. Willmore
brought suit to retain his judgeship in the mixed
courts.[60] Gorst was accused not only of being prejudiced against his own people, but of appointing an un-
qualified man and of interfering with the independence
of the Egyptian judiciary.

Through 1908 and on into 1909 discontent with
Gorst's policies mounted on several fronts: the Egyptian nationalists, the European communities resident
in Egypt, and many British officials. But since these
were not united, they did not represent a serious
threat. Many of the "vested interest groups" had contacts in London who maneuvered in private or complained
in public to force Gorst to shift from his policy.
According to this private and public clamor, he was
weakening Britain's position in Egypt. Gorst evalu-
ated this view acidly: "The one administrative quality
which the man in the street is capable of admiring is
the adoption of what he considers 'strong measures,'
and he is too stupid to understand that patience and
conciliation are not incompatible with firmness and
decision."[61] As long as he had the backing of the
Foreign Office and the Cabinet and as long as Egypt
remained in a manageable state of calm and economic
stability, the complaints did no more than damage
Gorst's public image. He himself remained free to
continue his work. In the spring of 1909 Gorst reminded Grey that, although the last two years in Egypt
had been relatively quiet, any wavering of support
from the Foreign Office would endanger his influence
in Egypt and the policies he had been sent out to implement. Concern and frustration were evident in this
letter, in contrast to the more ebullient tone of the
correspondence of his first months as British Agent:

> Although I endeavor to worry you and the
> Foreign Office as little as possible about
> our affairs, you must not imagine from my
> silence that I lie on a bed of roses. The
> difficulties of running the complicated

and illogical system under which we rule
Egypt are quite as great, though perhaps
of a different order, as was the case in
Lord Cromer's time, and the number of
Englishmen here who are of real use to me
can be counted on the fingers of one hand.[62]

The year 1908 had been one of retrenchment, on
the whole successful. Gorst had concentrated on conciliating the nationalists, reorganizing the provincial
councils and the Egyptian Cabinet, and replacing several Anglo-Egyptian officials. The relative tranquility of the political climate and British control were
maintained, and in 1909 Gorst initiated two new measures: the reimposition of the Press Law of 1881 and
the Criminal Deportation Act. The persistent nationalist press attacks against the British, which had begun during the Cromer era, had resumed under Gorst
after a brief honeymoon period. At the same time the
incidence of violent crime in the provinces had grown
dramatically. Gorst now sought to give the Egyptian
government the means to deal quickly and summarily
with the major perpetrators of these disturbances and
crimes. Neither of these measures could be called
liberal. For Gorst, however, they were an integral
part of his program to pacify and control Egypt. Looking back on 1908, he wrote:

During the latter part of the year a certain amount of demonstrating and speechi-
fying went on; especially amongst the
students in favour of a constitution, but
beyond irritating the Khedive and causing
trouble to the Cairo police, no evil results ensued and public order was not
disturbed.[63]

Gorst utilized a "carrot-and-stick" policy of timely
repression. To lessen tensions he sought first to
liberalize the Cromerian autocracy and expand Egyptian
self-rule. Then, once the country's political climate
was less stormy, he developed a specific program to
secure British control and to increase "public
security."

Gorst sent the first proposals to revive the
Press Law to the Foreign Office in March 1908. He
told the foreign secretary that he needed help in controlling the nationalist press, particularly the Arabic

newspapers.   Some Cabinet members reacted negatively.
Lord Ripon wrote: "To meddle with the press is a serious thing, indeed I doubt the expediency."   John Morley
pointed out that Cromer had always resisted the temp-
tation to impose a press law.[64] There was more correspondence that spring on the matter.   Then the Egyptian
government failed to obtain a court verdict against
the most offensive nationalist writer and agitator,
Shaikh Shawish, whose articles in *al-Liwa* in June 1908
especially upset the Agency.[65] When Shawish accused the
British in the Sudan of perpetrating a "new Dinshawai"
over the Kamlin Affair, he struck a very tender spot.
The Agency judged it necessary to silence the fiery
Tunisian, but the suit brought against Shawish only
made him more of a hero to students and other nationalist sympathizers.[66]   Other papers increased their
campaign against the hated British.

News of the unexpected success of the Young Turk
revolution added urgency to Gorst's desire to revive
the Press Law of 1881.   The Ottoman Empire held a
nominal sovereignty over Egypt.   Establishment of a
constitutional regime in Turkey might have led to considerable embarrassment for the British in Egypt unless Gorst had by that summer asserted British control
over the Egyptian administration and politics.   Plagued
by difficulties at home and elsewhere, the British
government now was receptive to Gorst's advocacy of
such expedients as the Press Law, even if it violated
the liberal sensibility and the Cromerian precedent.
In September 1908 Gorst submitted a long memorandum to
the Cabinet requesting permission to revive the Press
Law which, since he could not trust the Egyptian courts,
would provide an administrative remedy for the virulent nationalist press.[67] In November the Cabinet consented, but cautioned him against arousing the suspi-
cions of the Young Turks in Constantinople.   Gorst
after some consultation decided to postpone the imposition of the Press Law until the following spring.
In the interval he would prepare to move against the
offending papers and individuals, and to answer the
questions that would inevitably arise in the British
liberal press and in the House of Commons.[68]   He instructed the Foreign Office to be evasive if they were
questioned on the issue.

By August 1909 the Agency became concerned about
the threat of violence if the nationalist press were
not effectively bridled.   Ronald Graham, acting for

Gorst in Egypt that summer, informed the Foreign Office
of the increasing tone of violence in the nationalist
press:

> [The] danger is they [the nationalists]
> . . . might inspire some overstrung stu-
> dent, ignorant peasant, or bemused "hashasi"
> to emulate Dhinga in the hope of acquiring
> similar fame at the expense of one of the
> Egyptian Ministers or officials. Butros
> Pasha holds this opinion. [69]

The Egyptian government invoked the Press Law: *al-Liwa*
was warned, and Shawish was imprisoned. [70]

The success of the Press Law was debatable. It
was too easy for the nationalists to find a foreigner
willing to lend them his immunity under the Capitulations. And the cooperation of the Powers was as usual
difficult to obtain. The French in particular used
their right to intervene as a means of extracting concessions and backing for their interests inside and
outside Egypt. [71]

The more moderate nationalists also objected to
the imposition of the Press Law. Lutfi al-Sayyid of
al-Ummah and the editor of *al-Jaridah* visited the
Foreign Office in the early summer of 1909 and warned
Louis Mallet that the Press Law measure would be
ineffective and divisive. The Germans in fact had
made many overtures to him, which were refused. But
Gorst, who was not interested in working with the moderates and had advised the Foreign Office not to receive Lutfi, ignored this gesture. [72]

After a year in power, Gorst had in fact resigned
himself to a "bad press." His autobiographical notes
for 1907, drafted in July 1908, end with a cynical
assessment of the public's reaction to his new policy.
He wrote that after the traditional honeymoon period
for a new man in power, "the inevitable reaction followed as soon as it became clear that miracles were
not forthcoming." By the end of that year Gorst felt
that whatever the Egyptian government did under his
tutelage, it "could always rely on a 'bad press' all
round, coupled with injurious reflections on my conduct of affairs as compared with my predecessor."[73] A
cartoon preserved from the *Cairo Punch* in Gorst's
papers showed him lying on a couch, whiskey and

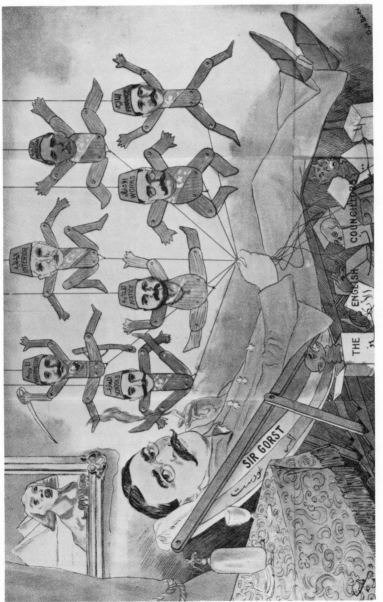

Gorst and his toys.   By A. H. Baki,
The Cairo Punch

siphon at his side, cigar in hand, pulling the
strings of puppets who were the Egyptian cabinet ministers; British advisors were portrayed as jacks-in-
the-box lying on the floor, and the Sphinx observed
this scene through the window. It was captioned:

> Sir Eldon Gorst - "The toys dance well, but
> they need somebody to make them move. The
> manufacturer said they could dance by them-
> selves alone without string, and receive
> wireless signals; he showed me, moreover,
> fixed above the trademark of the Lord [Cromer],
> which proves them to be excellent toys for
> the New Year."

> The Toys - "Do not trouble to pull; we will
> dance alone, to any movement you require
> without any effort on your part, his 'Lord-
> ship' has foreseen the case."[74]

By January 1908 this unknown cartoonist in Cairo had
accurately sensed the nature of Gorst's new policy.
The Egyptian Gazette, the unofficial English voice for
Cairo and Alexandria, was not so perceptive. In an
article in April 1908 Gorst was compared to Hamlet—
sinking beneath his burdens, unable to make up his
mind; the reporter thought Gorst might even be planning to be transferred to Constantinople.[75]

The cartoon had grasped the essence of Gorst's
policy. Self-effacing, he worked behind the scenes,
endeavoring to maneuver the various players on the
Egyptian scene into the patterns he deemed appropri-
ate. When the students and others demonstrated for a
real constitution in 1908, he took careful steps to
see that unwarranted force was not used.

> My main difficulty throughout was to pre-
> vent the employment of measures of exces-
> sive rigour which would have created
> martyrs and given encouragement to the
> [nationalist] movement. As it was I felt
> sure that the wise policy was to employ
> patience and passive resistance until the
> psychological moment came when firm mea-
> sures of repression would be generally
> approved and welcomed. [76]

He cultivated some of the English newspaper correspondents

and writers who came to Cairo, but they generally
missed the point of his policy.[77] The bullying style that
had characterized Cromer's regime was simpler to comprehend. And, I would guess, Gorst's manner, especially his cynicism, did not aid matters. It was a
period that placed a high value on hypocrisy. Gorst
was devious but he was not a hypocrite. In an attempt
to scotch some of the rumors about British intentions,
he drafted an interview for *al-Muqattam* in the fall of
1908. He then "sent for Faris Nimr & gave him the
'interview' which I am supposed to have had with his
correspondent."[78] This article apparently did not help
much. To the end of his career and life he received
a bad press.

The need to reduce the incidence of violent provincial crime and improve public security in general
gave rise to Gorst's second repressive measure, the
Criminal Deportation Act. After consultation with
Sir Arthur Chitty, whom Gorst had chosen to take over
as advisor of the ministry of the interior, the act
was promulgated in July 1909. Gorst warned the Foreign Office that the provisions for the detention of
criminals by an administrative act might provoke radical opposition in Britain. The Foreign Office opposed
the measure, and asked Graham to delay the promulgation of the act, but it was too late, for the act was
already in force. Foreign Office officials were disturbed at what looked like a provision for punishment
without conviction. Radicals and others might well
criticize the government for this kind of legislation.
Louis Mallet, who had never liked Gorst, was particularly critical. He felt that the situation could have
been met by an efficient police force rather than by
such extreme measures. In his minute on Gorst's dispatch, he wrote to Grey:

> You will no doubt talk the whole situa-
> tion over with Sir E. Gorst. It would
> be well to ask him to record his views
> on the results of the policy which we
> are now pursuing in Egypt, whether he
> considers that there is any truth in the
> statements so widely made and recorded
> in the *Saturday Review* article, whether
> it is safe to continue on the same lines
> or whether it would be prudent to revert
> quietly to an increased British control
> and supervision.[79]

Mallet had a private discussion with J. F. Kershaw,
a judge in Egypt, who was highly critical of Gorst
and his policies and condemned the deportation law.
Kershaw asserted that there was "social dissolution"
in Egypt, and that the withdrawal of British control
under Gorst's influence was leading to administrative
chaos. Englishmen in Egypt were wondering why Gorst
was there.[80]

Gorst and his officials in Egypt sent the Foreign
Office supporting evidence for the Criminal Deportation Act. This evidence eventually was presented to
the Cabinet. The foreign secretary supported Gorst in
his note on the memorandum: "We have in recent years
been trying to govern Egypt more and more through the
Egyptians themselves, and when they ask for a measure
of this kind on the ground that it is essential for
the repression of crime, it is very difficult to refuse our consent."[81] Grey assured the Cabinet that the
implementation of the act would be carefully watched
by Gorst and the Agency officials. In the fall of
1909 the ministry of the interior, from an initial
list of about 12,000 names, put 281 men under some
form of police supervision. By the time of the writing of the annual report for 1909, 272 men were deported to the Dakhla oasis. Gorst reported that as
a result the number of violent crimes fell off.[82]

The departments of the ministry of the interior
were also extensively reorganized in 1909. A special
branch was created to deal with the provincial municipalities and local commissions, designed to help those
bodies manage their own affairs. Permission for a
major scheme to provide a modern drainage system for
Cairo was negotiated in 1907 with the fifteen Powers
who agreed (with one exception) to raise the city's
house taxes from eight to ten percent. In 1909 Gorst
sought to do the same at Port Said. A Land Registra-
tion Law was also promulgated in June 1908, the fruit
of negotiations begun in 1904.[83]

What should be clear is that through 1909 Gorst
was generally successful in implementing his policy:
a judicious liberalization of the creaking and autocratic administration he had inherited from Cromer.
He maintained his amicable relationship with the
khedive. His diaries from 1907 to 1909 indicate that a
regular, friendly process of consultation went on between Gorst and Abbas Hilmi. Late in 1908 he "soothed"

the khedive, who was "rather upset" at a demonstration
for a constitution. Their relations went beyond the
formal and official level. The khedive was interested
in Gorst's new racing stable. In March 1908 Abbas
entertained many of the proconsul's family for lunch.
Gorst wrote: "We had a great family lunch with the
Khedive at Koubbeh [Palace]." It included Sir Eldon
and Lady Gorst, his mother and father, and three of
his sisters and their husbands then living in Egypt.[84]

  In general he consulted with the Egyptian Cabinet
and the Legislative Council over many matters, including the Press Law and the Criminal Deportation Act.
He encouraged members of these bodies to involve themselves, as Cromer would never have done, in the administration of their country. Butrus Ghali, the Copt
whom he appointed prime minister, became his "chief
standby." Gorst told the Foreign Office that the June
1909 session of the Legislative Council displayed "an
activity quite unexampled throughout the history of
the institution." No less than sixteen draft laws
were discussed. "This display of energy . . . and the
reasonable attitude they have in general taken up in
their discussions with the Ministers . . . are also of
good augury as regards future cooperation between the
Council and the Ministers."[85] It also indicated, he
felt, that though the council did not possess powers
as extensive as some of its members wished, it would
prove to the outside world that Egyptians could advise
and legislate sensibly.

  Throughout this period Gorst had had to resist
pressure, particularly from the extreme nationalists,
for a constitutional regime. Some members of the
Legislative Council also campaigned for more self-rule.
If Gorst had wished to accelerate the process—and
there were many in Egypt, and some in London, who
thought he had gone too far in his "Egyptianization"
policies—he was stymied, like his predecessor, by the
necessity to revise or get rid of the Capitulations.
In order to do so, Gorst and the British had to negotiate with the Powers. The major obstruction had always been France. Provisions for revision of the Capitulations were written into the secret articles of
the Anglo-French Entente of 1904, but the French were
having some difficulties in their gradual takeover of
Morocco and were disinclined to involve themselves in
any scheme for Egypt that might endanger what bargain-
ing power they had with the British. As a result,

Gorst had to postpone serious efforts to revise or
abolish the Capitulations.[86]   Without such a revision,
other reforms and real self-rule in Egypt, however defined, were impossible.

While engaged in his official duties and the implementation of his "new policy," Gorst also set a
less formal style than his imperious predecessor. He
had reviewed his Arabic on his way to Egypt to take
over for Cromer and was pleased with his recall of
this difficult tongue: "Read Willmore's Arabic grammar
& found that I remembered the language very well."
From the beginning of his tenure, he sought to reac-
quaint himself with the various parts and peoples in
Egypt and the Sudan.   Late in 1907 when his Delta-
bound steamer tied up for the night at Ramala, and
Gorst and his official party went for a stroll by the
Nile, he noted: "As we walked along we had amusing
conversation with *gaffirs* on the bank as to the iden-
tity of the 'Pasha' whom they were housing."[87]   He and
Doll continued their intensive entertaining throughout
1908 and 1909.   They also imported at least one of
their cars, a Fiat with black and green stripes. Gorst
apparently disturbed some of the Anglo-Egyptian community by driving the car himself in Cairo and the countryside.   This relatively informal style, his considerable hospitality, and his deliberate policy of self-
effacement confused many of the Anglo-Egyptian community and some observers at home.   They were neither
the first nor the last set of imperialists to confuse
the form of power with its reality.

Unfortunately, Eldon's and Doll's personal lives
were not all "wine and roses" in 1908 and 1909.   Their
daughter Kitty was too young to be included in their
busy lives.   In the fall of 1907 her mother reported
in a diary she kept about her daughter that Kitty,
then just over two years old, loved Cairo.   Gorst's
diaries rarely mention Kitty, except to note at the
odd interval her health— usually good— and that she
had gone to the Cairo zoo again.   Kitty had her own
small menagerie at the Agency.[88] The hustle and bustle
of the official residence must have been fascinating
for her.   As for his godchild, Margaret Turnure, before he departed for Cairo as Consul-General in 1907
Gorst had kept in regular touch with her; but once he
had returned to Egypt he saw neither Margaret nor her
mother, Romaine, for two years.   Finally, in the summer of 1909, he visited Romaine in London and later

at her husband's home, Burton Hall near Lincoln, and
was pleased with Margaret's development. He wrote:
"My godchild, Margaret, whom I have not seen for two
years [is] much grown and greatly improved."[89]

In the diary Doll kept about Kitty, she rarely
mentioned her husband, and never by name. He was
"Kitty's daddy." Doll apparently found life with
Eldon and the demands of official life in Egypt full
of stress. So much so, in fact, that she suffered
what Eldon labeled a "species of melancholia" serious
enough that she almost did not return with him to
Egypt in the fall of 1908. There are hints of trouble
in his diary before her breakdown that summer. On the
train to the Mediterranean in April of 1907 Gorst
noted: "D [Doll] much happier in her mind that her
apprehensions for the immediate future are turning out
unfounded."[90] Not one word of praise or endearment about
his wife ever appeared in his private diaries or autobiographical notes after 1907. The major events of
their lives were recorded, but little else.

From the surviving evidence it is difficult to
determine when her "melancholia" began. The first
mention came when a London physician was consulted
about Doll's condition in July 1908. A few days later
Gorst noted: "D. far from well & very depressed." The
next day he wired a friend, Mrs. Playfair, to come to
take care of his wife. No further notes about her
condition appeared until the end of August; then he
remarked grimly: "Walked with D. in the afternoon.
Matters go from bad to worse and I begin to fear it
will be impossible for her to come out to Cairo this
winter." Two days later he told her that unless things
changed considerably she could not return to Egypt
with him in the autumn. Her condition seemed to improve after that, and a few days later they resolved
to make another trial. Shortly before they left
England in September, Eldon took Doll to consult
Victor Horsley, a prominent "nerve specialist." The
outcome, Gorst noted, was "fairly satisfactory." There
was no further mention of her difficulties until almost
a year later. They appeared to have had a normal season in Cairo in 1908-1909. Then, while on holiday at
her father's highland Scottish estate, Gorst reported:
"Returned to Shielbridge where I found D. in more impossible mood than ever." A day later he abruptly cut
short his stay: "In view of recent worries decided to
leave here on Monday and arranged to stay with the Sykes.

Explained the situation to C. D. R. [Charles Rudd, his
father-in-law], who was very sympathetic." He left
without his wife. Subsequently she appeared to have
recovered. [91]

The scanty available evidence indicates that
their marriage was one of convenience. She was a
wealthy young heiress, he was a successful, experienced man, attractive to women. When they met, his
great love, Romaine, had just rejected him. Refer-
ences to each other in their surviving papers are
usually impersonal. After Gorst's rapid decline and
death in 1911 his widow rarely, if ever, talked to
their only child about him. Apparently her memories
were too painful or unhappy. At the least, it was
not a happy marriage. [92]

Almost immediately after Doll's "melancholia"
appeared to have subsided for the first time, Gorst
contracted a very unpleasant fever that turned out
to be a mild attack of typhoid which the doctors
failed to diagnose until after he had embarked on
an inspection trip up the Nile in January 1909. Once
the disease was recognized he was sent back to Cairo
to recover and within a month the fever had abated,
but he found himself plagued by boils for the rest of
the year, causing him "a good deal of pain and inconvenience." Late that winter he and his sister Dolly
took a week's holiday in Brummanah, a Lebanese moun-
tain village. Doll was not with them. By the end of
the year 1909 he appeared to have fully recovered, and
Doll's melancholia was not noted again. He went on a
rigorous inspection trip up the Nile accompanied by
Robert Vansittart, the second secretary at the Cairo
Agency. The usual visits to local notables, official
receptions, and inspections were supplemented by shooting at crocodiles and hunting the roan antelope. Gorst
had a "touch of fever" on December 15 but it did not
slow him down. At the town of Fashoda in the
Sudan he was treated to a "great Shilluk dance." [93]

Despite his wife's troubles and his own illnesses,
the surviving evidence indicates that neither his energies nor his spirits had been significantly affected.
Throughout 1909 Gorst skillfully and energetically
managed Egyptian affairs; but there were few, whether
nationalists or British officials or European businessmen, who liked him or understood what he was doing.
The Foreign Office alone was grateful. Hardinge wrote

in the spring of 1909 : "We have as you say, had a terrible time during this past winter; but happily we are
in smooth waters at last. I should add that we are
extremely grateful to you for having spared us from
any bother or trouble during our recent time of stress."
Grey also assured Gorst that Kitchener's provisional
appointment to the Mediterranean command in August
1909 would give the imperious field marshall no authority to meddle in Egyptian affairs.[94]

All in all, Gorst seemed to be in solid control
of Egyptian affairs as 1909 closed. There were, of
course, rumblings of discontent from many officials
and the nationalist press fulminated when it could,
but its voice seemed relatively unthreatening.[95] The
nationalist leadership was generally inept, and it
seemed unlikely that there would be any issue that
might be beyond Gorst's control. The French were
busy in Morocco, the Germans were ineffective and
involved in Turkey, and the Young Turks were not prepared to interfere in Egypt.[96] As the year closed,
only the proposed revision of the Suez Canal Company
concession remained unsettled. Judging from his record it seemed likely Gorst would manage this delicate
and complicated proposal with success.

Chapter Twelve

CRISES IN EGYPT: 1910

*The British in Cairo could thus enjoy themselves. The
rich Europeans and Egyptians entertained lavishly, the
middle classes lived like well-kept domestic gods, and
the soldiers got drunk in the cafes and enjoyed the
brothels. It was soft, pleasant, succulent, boring;
yet always rather edgy because of the Egyptians, who
could not be quite forgotten.*

James Aldridge, 1969[1]

In 1909 Gorst set out to negotiate the revision of the
Suez Canal Company's concession with one major objective in mind—money for the Sudan. He needed a large
amount, between four and six million pounds, to finance development projects. Some financial mismanage-
ment during Cromer's last years had been quietly rec-
tified. The worldwide financial crisis in 1907 coin-
cidentally occurred just as Gorst returned to Egypt,
and the Egyptian economy did not fully recover from
the effects of the crisis until 1914; 1908 was a year
of retrenchment for the Egyptian administration.[2]
Kept under careful supervision by Gorst and the new
financial advisor, H. P. Harvey, the budgets in 1907,
1908, and 1909 were brought into balance, but the income growth was reduced from the previous boom decade.[3]
As a result, surpluses for large-scale development
projects were not available. The necessity to allo-
cate larger amounts to departments such as education,
which did not generate significant income, reduced the
extra funds accessible to Gorst and Harvey. Moreover,
the financial crises had caused a recession, and the
value of the securities in the Egyptian reserve fund
had by mid-1908 depreciated by 319,911 Egyptian pounds;
this generated some disquiet at the Foreign Office.[4]

Later that summer, while in Britain on holiday,
Gorst attempted unsuccessfully to persuade the British
government to guarantee a Sudan loan or to assist him
in procuring funds that were "indispensable for the

development of the country."[5] What the Sudan needed
most was capital to invest in its infrastructure, particularly its communications system. Gorst, supported
by Wingate, submitted a memorandum to the Cabinet
stressing that the security of the vast Sudan would
require an increase either in the garrison's numbers
or in its mobility. That meant that railroads had to
be constructed. Not only were Egyptian government reserves down, but the Egyptians were resentful at British domination of the Sudan and would resist paying
any further development costs there, especially if
expenses appeared to increase the British monopoly of
control in an area that the Egyptians regarded as be-
longing to Egypt.[6]

Failing to get the guarantee for necessary funds
from the British government, Gorst cast about for
other sources. Through the Foreign Office, he began
negotiations with the Young Turks to remove Ottoman
restrictions on Egyptian borrowing power. Various
firmans during the financial heyday of Khedive Ismail
had set debt limits on the Egyptian government.[7] Since
the Ottoman sultan remained the *de jure* sovereign over
Egypt, it was necessary for the Egyptian government
to negotiate with the Porte for release from these
limits. Naturally the negotiations were lengthy and
complicated : the British government, the khedive, the
Egyptian government, and other interested foreign powers had to be consulted. The uncertain situation of
the newly established Young Turk regime further complicated the matter. Gorst kept the Egyptian government in the negotiations during 1909 and on into 1910,
but in the meantime he found another possible source
of funds in the Suez Canal Company.[8]

The Canal Company sought in 1908 to extend its
extraordinarily lucrative concession for another forty
years. In return the directors of the company were
willing to provide the Egyptian government with a considerable amount of money immediately, and eventually
to concede to Egypt a small share of the profits of
the canal, which had been built with large amounts of
Egyptian effort and money. Gorst thought that he and
Harvey could drive a good bargain for Egypt, and they
plunged into complicated negotiations with the British
official directors of the canal, the Foreign Office,
the board of trade, and the treasury. Gorst had demonstrated his negotiating skill, particularly in the
diplomatic preliminaries to the Anglo-French Entente

in 1904. He and Harvey, working mainly through the
three official directors—Sir H. Austin Lee, Sir H. T.
Anstruther, and Sir William Garstin—arrived by the
fall at what he judged "an excellent bargain for
Egypt."[9]

In the process serious opposition to the proposals
arose in Britain. The British government's interests
in the Suez Canal Company were not unitary. The extraordinary profits that the Canal Company had derived
since 1881 caused the British treasury and the British
directors to pay more attention to maximizing profits
than to representing the interests of the British
Empire or, at another level of concern, the interests
of the smaller British shipowners. At the same time
the Foreign Office was under some pressure from the
owners of tramp ships to press for lower tolls, which
would reduce the costs for the individual shipowners
and some merchants and still provide a kind of invis-
ible subsidy for British shipping.[10] British tonnage
since the opening of the canal in 1869 had never fallen below fifty-seven percent of the total (in 1899)
and averaged about seventy-five percent through 1908.
The increase in *total* tonnage carried was very substantial—from roughly one million tons in 1872 to
almost nine million by 1909. The British increase
between the years 1875 and 1905 was thirty-seven
percent greater than those of all the other flags
put together.[11]

Clearly the stakes for the various parties were
great. The treasury especially, since it was under
pressure to find funds for new social programs in
Britain, did not regard the proposals of the Egyptian
government with much favor. By March the directors
of the company and Gorst had arrived at an acceptable
proposal. It was necessary, however, to refer the
scheme to the Cabinet for final settlement. The treasury objected and opted for the status quo, since the
risks were judged too great in an unsettled time.[12]
Cromer, consulted by the Foreign Office on the proposal,
was opposed to prolongation as he had been in 1899,
and for the same reason: it was "altogether premature
to raise the question" and "it ought to be postponed
for the future generation." Cromer went on:

I can quite understand that under present
conditions Gorst should be inclined to look
favourably upon the proposal and if it's

rejected I hold very strongly that it is
more important than ever to take up seriously the question of providing capital
expenditure in Egypt and the Sudan.[13]

In 1899, when he had refused to consider a prolongation of
the Canal Company concession, he had remarked: "The
Egyptians will never willingly consent to prolong,
unless favourable terms are made for them, and I think
it would be very undesirable to cram a settlement,
which they would think unjust, down their throats."
The retired proconsul did think it would be possible
to obtain Egyptian agreement to discounting that country's
future, but not for a trifling sum. He recommended
that the canal tariff be reduced substantially, that
an immediate profit of at least three million pounds
Egyptian be offered for the Egyptian treasury, and
that more be added for the years of the proposed extension. He also backed Gorst's efforts to free Egypt
from the Ottoman restrictions on borrowing money.[14]
At this point the negotiations with the company broke
down.

Meanwhile, rumors of the negotiations had reached
J. M. Robertson, who asked Grey in the House of Commons
on May 20 if there were talks in progress on an extension. Robertson's questions were not pointedly phrased
and Grey, somewhat equivocally, said no. Gorst and
Harvey in fact resumed their talks with the British
directors of the Canal Company, and they worked out an
agreement which all the directors and the Foreign
Office found acceptable.[15] It was never put before
the shareholders.

The main outline of the agreement was as follows:
In return for the prolongation of the concession for
forty years from 1968 to 2008, the Egyptian government
was to receive four million pounds Egyptian in cash
over the next four years, and a share of the profits
beginning in 1921 at four percent and rising eventually to fifty percent in 1969. After 1968 the Egyptian government would also be entitled to three seats
on the board of directors. The Canal Company agreed
to assume certain costs for improvements and received
rights to the Egyptian government's allotted share of
fifteen percent of the profits after 1968. It should
be noted that the Egyptian government had not received
its share of the profits since 1880, when its fifteen
percent had been sold off to a French bank, which

promptly sold it to the Canal Company.[16]

The treasury opposed the agreement on financial grounds; as Sir George Murray told the Cabinet: "I do not know what concerns of policy (either towards the Egyptian Government or the Canal Company) may demand: but as a purely financial transaction the proposal seems to have nothing to commend it; and I think the British directors should be instructed to oppose it."[17] Hardly renowned for its imaginative policies at this period of its history, the treasury simply preferred not to speculate. Winston Churchill at the board of trade couched his ministry's objections in a larger context. He argued that, in the interests of the British Empire and British trade, the real necessity was for dues reduction and for cheap, easy communications and commerce with India and the Far East, especially Australia and New Zealand. He pointed out: "On general grounds it would be better for the Canal to revert as speedily as possible into the hands of a weak military state, which would be allowed by international pressure to exact only a moderate toll for the upkeep of the water way."[18] Britain, as the controlling power and the greatest shipper, was, of course, in an excellent position to exert pressure for her interests.

Despite the strong objections from the treasury and the board of trade, the Cabinet decided to allow Gorst and the Egyptians to go ahead with the renewal of the concession. Grey wrote to Gorst early in November: "We have somewhat reluctantly decided to instruct the British official directors to vote with the rest of the Board [of Directors] for extension of the Suez Canal concession if we obtain satisfactory assurances as to reduction of the rates on shipping."[19] Backing the renewal would help the British government to regain its influence in filling vacancies amongst the unofficial British members of the board of directors.

At this critical moment, the negotiations broke down. The Egyptian Cabinet refused to ratify the agreement because they disagreed with the compensation offered. Gorst recorded in his diary: "Suez Canal arrangement [is] causing great difficulties as some of the [Egyptian] Ministers are hostile."[20] It looked as if a deadlock had been reached. In Paris news of the impending prolongation of the concession had leaked,

and the price of Canal Company shares rose substantially.[21]   This development must have further increased
the enthusiasm of directors and shareholders for the
renewal agreement.

    In Cairo, however, word of the agreement aroused
a storm of protest from the Egyptians. The nationalist press was violently opposed. Ronald Storrs, the
new Oriental secretary under Gorst, wrote home: "Heavy
weather is going on here owing to the projected extension of the Suez Canal concession to 2008. . . . Egypt
gains in many ways, but the people don't see it, and
are crying aloud and spending large sums on telegrams
to those in high places."[22] Gorst reported to the Foreign Office that the Egyptian Cabinet was reluctant
to spend Egyptian money in the Sudan. Yet what were
they to do, since that was where it had to be spent?
It would be necessary, he thought, to delay, because
"the Oriental mind needed time to make itself up."[23]
Meanwhile Gorst applied pressure to bring the Egyptian
Cabinet around.

    Grey in London refused to raise the question in
the House, since he said it was not a matter that was
under the control of the British government.[24] In his
response, the convenient fiction of the independence
of the British directors was maintained, as was the
fiction of the independence of the Egyptian government.
Churchill, in private, had been much more frank: "Egypt
is Gorst and Gorst is you [i.e., the Foreign Office]
and you are us so we are responsible in a certain sense
for doing the right thing by her. I do not think we
can treat 'Egypt' as a separate responsible power whose
view about her own interests may for good or ill be
accepted as final." Churchill noted that the influential financier Sir Ernest Cassel was against granting
reversionary rights or interests in the Suez Canal to
the Egyptians. He warned Grey that the British should
delay and relax their pressure on the Egyptian ministers. "Above all do not let us get into the position
where we may be accused of having cajoled or coerced
the Egyptians into selling their birthright for a railway in the Sudan."[25]

    Meanwhile Gorst had decided to submit the draft
renewal to the Egyptian General Assembly. In his
diary he noted: "Saw Boutros [sic] & Harvey as to sub-
mitting Suez Canal arrangement to General Assembly &
decided reluctantly that we must do it."[26] This was an

unprecedented and fateful decision. This body had
been largely moribund during the Cromer period. Neither Gorst nor the Egyptian Cabinet had any legal obligation to consult the General Assembly. Its members
had not been party to the long and tortuous negotiations. The Organic Law did not say the Assembly must
be consulted on every public loan, and Gorst construed
the draft renewal of the Canal Company's concession as
a loan. He chose to allow the General Assembly to advise the Egyptian government as a tactic to extricate
himself and save the agreement with the Canal Company.
It was a disastrous choice.

The khedive and Butrus "cordially affirmed" the
scheme, but the other Egyptian ministers disliked it.
Despite Cromer's warning, Gorst also had not anticipated the impact of the vociferous opposition of the
Egyptian Cabinet. During 1909 there had been opposition in the Egyptian press and the Legislative Council
to grants to the Sudan, and considerable agitation in
the Council and in the press for a constitution for
Egypt. Gorst had firmly but quietly informed the
Egyptian ministers and Prince Husain, president of the
Legislative Council, that the British government would
not contemplate any organic changes in the present
Egyptian constitution until the changes already wrought
were studied.[27]

Gorst was fully aware of the resentment and fear
that many Egyptians felt about their exclusion from
the Sudan, and their disgust at being almost totally
barred from the operations or the profits of the Suez
Canal. With this knowledge, it would have seemed
sensible to let the negotiations lapse when he encountered opposition within the Egyptian Cabinet. Instead
he sought to persuade the recalcitrant Cabinet members
to accept the draft renewal. Apparently Gorst thought
that if he involved both the Egyptian Cabinet and the
General Assembly, public opposition to the proposed
renewal of the concession would be overcome. "Independent native opinion" was not adverse, he wrote to
Grey in November; rather, "a strong and universal feeling prevailed that the General Assembly should be
specially convoked, as provided by the Organic Law, to
give its opinion before the arrangement is definitely
concluded." Furthermore, if the agreement were rati-
fied by the General Assembly, it would have been easier to
defend in the British Parliament. Gorst calculated
that his influence with the khedive and the prime

minister, and their backing of the measure, could
bring members of the General Assembly into line with
what he had referred to as independent native opinion.
After a tactical delay followed by public announcement
of the details of the draft agreement, he assumed the
usually docile General Assembly's good sense would
prevail over its emotions.[28]

The negotiations with the reluctant ministers
took the rest of the year. Meanwhile public discussion of the issue did not abate. The Legislative
Council met in November. Gorst had certain limitations "prescribed" on its members to "ensure regular
and orderly debate." The president of the Legislative
Council was given the right to disallow or modify any
questions that might be of a personal nature, or disturb the internal tranquility of Egypt, or that dealt
with relations between Egypt and the Powers. Five days'
notice had to be given on all questions, and no discussion was permitted on the answers, if any were
given. Members resented these restrictions. As one
English observer put it: "Everything that emanated
from the Egyptian Government and was not framed as a
law and promulgated by Khedival decree was to be received with distrust and suspicion."[29]

Gorst's policy of conciliation had not succeeded.
In fact his excellent working relationship with the
khedive and Butrus Ghali, the prime minister, may have
contributed to the miscalculation of his ability to
maneuver the Legislative Council. Moreover, Gorst apparently decided to put the policy of conciliation on
trial. To let the Egyptians, through the long moribund General Assembly, express their feelings on this
vital issue would demonstrate both in Egypt and in
Britain that the British were willing at least to listen to informed and responsible Egyptian opinion.
Even if the General Assembly failed to act favorably,
British magnanimity would have been demonstrated.

Gorst was able to overcome the objections of the
various Egyptian ministers by late January, and told
Hardinge he was optimistic on the outcome when the
matter was submitted to the General Assembly. The
next day he met Butrus and Rocca Serra, chief legal
advisor, to arrange the khedive's speech on the proposed Canal Company renewal. In a letter to the skeptical Cromer a few days later, his tone was cautious
but not pessimistic:

>The Suez Canal Negotiations are coming to
>the fore again next week. . . . After a
>great deal of trouble, I have got all the
>Ministers into line, and as long as the
>G.A. does not give an absolute veto, I
>think the matter will go through. If how-
>ever their opinion is distinctly adverse, I
>do not think the British Government will al-
>low us to *passer outre* and from their point
>of view I can hardly blame them. The advan-
>tages of the project are entirely Egyptian
>and if these people here are such fools that
>they won't accept it it can hardly be ex-
>pected that the British Government should
>cram it down their throats.[30]

The poet and anti-imperialist Wilfrid Blunt, who
kept in touch with the nationalist movement in Egypt,
had a different forecast. He accurately sensed the
Egyptians' deep indignation and predicted the General
Assembly would condemn it unanimously since it could
seriously prejudice Egypt's future political position.
A British journalist then in Egypt, H. Hamilton Fyfe,
also reported the rising tide of opposition. He called
in February 1910 for a "sane frame of mind" among the
Egyptians in the next few weeks. The General Assembly
was itself on trial, since it had never during the
British occupation been allowed to fulfill a real legislative function. "If it allows itself to be swayed
by passion and fanaticism it will make itself impotent
for years to come and strengthen mightily the arguments of those who declare the nationalists are not
fit to take part in the government of their country."[31]

The General Assembly was convened by the khedive
on February 9. After speeches in support of the proposal by the khedive and prime minister, a committee
was selected to consider the documents presented by
the Egyptian government on the matter. Four of the
nineteen members promptly resigned— not an auspicious
sign. The khedive told the notables in the assembly
that the exceptional nature of the Canal Company proposal had occasioned the submission of the matter to
the General Assembly for its advice. Gorst meanwhile
informed the Foreign Office that the advice of the
General Assembly did not commit the Egyptian government in any specific way to the renewal proposal. The
Egyptian government—which of course meant Gorst and
his British advisors— in consultation with the khedive

and the Egyptian ministers would subsequently decide
what action to take. Should the General Assembly be
opposed and the Egyptian government decide to ignore
its advice, then Gorst would ask the British government for its approval. By then Gorst noted pessimis-
tically in his diary, "It is supposed that G.A. will
throw out the Suez Canal arrangement."[32]

Despite the intensity of the nationalist reaction
against the proposed agreement, and its ability to
mount an intensive anti-British public campaign in the
Egyptian press, Gorst had judged that the Egyptian
government could quickly maneuver the General Assembly
into a vote of support. There was powerful opposition
to the project in Britain. Convinced of the scheme's
merits, Gorst sought to obtain the support of Egyptian
public opinion. In his autobiographical notes he wrote:

> The scheme, wh. was cordially affirmed by
> Boutros and the Khedive but disliked by the
> other Ministers, was such an excellent bar-
> gain for Egypt, and it was so clear that un-
> less it passed speedily an interested
> agitation would arise against it from Brit-
> ish and foreign shipowners, that I endeav-
> oured to push it through without perhaps
> realizing that it would give an opportunity
> to the nationalists to arouse a really
> strong and universal feeling against us.
> No doubt I committed some blunders in my
> management of what was a very difficult
> (perhaps impossible) business, and perhaps
> the decision to submit the scheme to the
> General Assembly was one of the chief mis-
> takes, but it is easy to be wise after the
> event, and who can say what would have hap-
> pened if I had fought the matter through to
> the bitter end?[33]

The depth of Egyptian opposition manifested itself only ten days after the General Assembly was convened. On Sunday, February 20, Gorst had arranged a
visit via boat to Saqqarah for Ronald Storrs's uncle,
Harry Cust, and his wife. Gorst had known Cust at
Eton. Storrs, who was along, recalled: "We were returning from Saqqara when the local stationmaster,
very white, suddenly appeared speeding over the plain,
a telegram in his hand. Sir Eldon, who was luckily
riding an Arab pony (the rest on donkeys) galloped to

the station, where a special train whirled him to
Cairo."[34] The Custs and Storrs were left behind, not
knowing what had happened. A young Muslim, Ibrahim
al-Wardani, had just shot the prime minister, Butrus
Ghali, on the steps of his ministry. He died the next
day. Al-Wardani justified the killing as necessary to
prevent the ratification of the Canal Company renewal.
His six bullets snuffed out the pliant Copt's life,
and with it the renewal scheme and the policy of conciliation. Storrs put it succinctly: "His revolver
was mortal not only to Butrus but also to the hopes of
Gorst." The young assassin was a member of the Nationalist Party, and belonged to a secret society formed
to oust the British from Egypt, if necessary by
violence.[35]

        Butrus's assassination, the first political mur-
der of a major figure in thirty-eight years, coalesced
opposition against the course Gorst had been steering.
In Egypt the nationalists made the young druggist a
hero in the battle against the hated British occupation and the Canal Company proposal.[36] The Coptic community, split during much of the Gorst period by inter-
necine feuds, took fright and rallied behind the British for protection from the Muslim majority's threat
to its strong position in Egypt. The Copts unleashed
a sizable protest movement against Gorst's policies
to the Foreign Office, the British public, and such
groups as the missionaries and their supporters. The
Copts were joined in their protests by the anglophile
Arabic press such as *al-Muqattam*, the local British
press, and many officials who had long distrusted
Gorst's policies of limited self-government for Egypt.
All used the pretext of Ghali's assassination to
attack Gorst. A recent historian of the Copts in
Egypt remarked:

        In life Ghali had proved his usefulness by
        struggling against the Nationalists. In
        death Ghali would be used to finally dis-
        credit any attempt at extending self-
        government in Egypt. By dying he had kept
        alive in the hearts of many the hope that
        soon the liberal aberrations of Gorst would
        be scrapped. Regrettable that Ghali died
        they forever said; highly appropriate that
        he did they forever implied.[37]

Shocked by the murder of Ghali and flooded with protests, the Foreign Office began to reconsider the policy of liberalization and conciliation. Suddenly Egypt appeared to be drifting rapidly toward a state of chaos. Gorst, too, was deeply shaken. After Butrus's funeral Gorst wrote in his diary: "This sad occurrence has upset me very much. I feel that Butrus was a victim of his loyalty to British policy." He had depended heavily on Butrus, who had been an able agent of the British policy. Gorst expressed his despair to Cromer a few days later:

> Butros' assassination was a terrible business and, so far as I am concerned, an irreparable loss, for he was the only Egyptian left in whom one could have entire confidence, and who was able to understand how public affairs have to be managed. I feel very deeply that he was a victim of our policy, and as regards the four reasons which the murderer gave for his act, he ought to have shot you for the first two and me for the second two. [38]

Gorst's shock and despair did not deter him from acting quickly to find a new prime minister, a man who might help to allay the communal and political tensions that had just burst into violence. In consultation with the khedive, he settled on Muhammad Said, the interior minister in the present cabinet:

> Neither His Highness nor I can think of any other possible candidate and though he [Mohamed Said] has the reputation of not being very friendly to the occupation, there are fewer objections to his appointment than to that of anyone else. . . . He will be given clearly to understand, both by His Highness and myself, that cordial cooperation in our work will be an essential condition to his remaining in office. [39]

Sections of the British community in Egypt objected to the Foreign Office over Said's appointment, alleging that his nationalist sympathies would endanger British interests in Egypt. Gorst did not deny that Said might be glad to see the British leave, but

he defended the selection on the grounds that a Muslim
with known nationalist sympathies as prime minister
might reduce the tension and particularly the anglophobia then disturbing Egypt—provided he worked harmoniously with the British, as he had done in the past.
Gorst also took the opportunity to reshuffle the Cabinet to make it more useful to the British. The only
new appointment was Yusuf Saba, a Christian, to the
finance ministry. Gorst told Cromer that he chose
Saba to show the Muslims they had not gained a victory.[40]

     Neither the old ministers nor the presence of a
Muslim prime minister with nationalist sympathies
abated the clamor that had been aroused against the
proposed renewal of the Canal Company's concession.
The committee selected from the General Assembly in
February to study the draft proposal met for about a
month. By the end of the first week in March it was
apparent to such informed observers of Egyptian affairs
as Captain G. F. Clayton—the Sudan agent and director
of military intelligence in Cairo—and Wilfrid Blunt
in England that the Egyptians were going to reject the
renewal scheme. Clayton—an acute, calm, and experienced scrutinizer of the Egyptian scene—informed his
superior, Wingate, in Khartum, that the nationalists
and the Legislative Council were not willing to spend
any money on the Sudan. Britain was not willing to
provide money. "As Egypt has not money to spare for
the Sudan," he concluded, "and still less now that
there is every probability that the new Suez Canal
Convention will be thrown out, we shall be very soon
on our own beam ends."[41] Blunt noted the resignation of
Prince Husain as president of the Legislative Council,
apparently out of frustration at the unruly opposition
he encountered to the British and the Egyptian government; it was an indication, thought Blunt, that the
Egyptian General Assembly would reject the renewal of
the Canal Company's concession. Gorst was very annoyed
at Husain's resignation: "I am struggling along with
my [Annual] Report in the midst of all the confusion
& worry caused by all these changes." The prince's
resignation meant that "I have wasted time in trying
uselessly to get him to reconsider his decision."[42]

     By the time the General Assembly reconvened on
April 4, the unanimous negative recommendation of the
committee was known. With crowds in the streets and
the gallery, the committee members placed their objections before the assembled notables and the Egyptian

Cabinet. They found both financial and political
grounds for their opposition and saw no urgent financial necessity to mortgage the future to the detriment
of Egypt's posterity.[43] Muhammad Said, Zaghlul (now
minister of justice), and Ismail Sirri, minister of
public works and war, spoke in support of the scheme.
Said affirmed that the Egyptian government would abide
by the decision of the General Assembly in the matter.
After two speeches by members who opposed the scheme,
the General Assembly was adjourned until April 7. The
three-day delay served only to harden further the
opposition of the notables.[44] Influenced by the pas-
sionate objections of the Egyptian press and many of
their knowledgeable countrymen, the General Assembly
shouted down Zaghlul and rejected the proposal overwhelmingly. Only the Cabinet ministers and one lonely
Coptic member, Murqus Simaika Bey, supported it. The
British had suffered a considerable rebuff.

Although not surprised, Gorst was very unhappy:
he had returned from an ibex shooting expedition to
learn of the General Assembly's outright rejection.
The next day, after a talk with the financial advisor
Harvey, he wrote: "Felt much depressed at general
situation & at failure of our efforts to encourage
Egyptians to take part in their affairs. The Ministers show great weakness & their only idea is to take
the line of least resistance." In a deeply troubled
letter to Grey, he ignored the substantial objections
that the committee from the General Assembly had put
forward. Instead he condemned the current generation
of Egyptian ministers as "incapable" and the Legislative Council and General Assembly as dominated by an
anglophobe press. Although he acknowledged that he
had made some mistakes, Gorst never questioned the
basic idea of renewing the concession. The Egyptians
involved, he thought, were simply irresponsible fools
who let their passions blind them to an excellent
bargain.[45]

Arnold Wilson, a proconsul in his own right, succinctly summarized the reaction of the British in Egypt
and at home— looking back on the episode about twenty
years later:

The opinion was widely expressed at the time
that the scheme, thus unequivocally condemned,
had been inadequately studied and had never
received impartial consideration at the hands

of experts. It is difficult to resist the
conclusion that the General Assembly decided rightly in rejecting the Convention,
although, in fact, the vote was intended
to be an indication of hostility to Britain,
and of the intention of the Notables to condemn every scheme, irrespective of its merits, proposed by the Government.[46]

Even if the Egyptian notables had offered a counterpro-
posal, it is doubtful that Gorst and the British would
have relinquished their conception of the Egyptians'
role in their own government.   Gorst had sought their
acquiescence, not their substantial advice or criticism.

The nearly unanimous rejection of the draft proposal, riding on the wave of anti-British propaganda,
nationalist demands for a constitution, and the murder
of Butrus, further convinced Gorst that the experiment
in conciliation and liberalization of the Egyptian
government had failed.   Early in April, he sadly wrote
to Grey:

The rejection of our proposals by the General
Assembly was a foregone conclusion, but I did
not anticipate such an open and indecent refusal even to discuss the question. . . . From
first to last, the attitude of the members
has been nothing more than an acute manifes-
tation of Anglophobia, and the real hostility
to the project is due to the fact that it was
negotiated and prepared by the English advisors to the Egyptian Government.   It will be
impossible to adduce a clearer proof of the
present incapacity of the Egyptians for any
sort of autonomy, and of the futility of ex-
pecting from them reasonable discussion or
argument on important matters of public
interest.

I do not see we could well have avoided trying the experiment of allowing these people
to have rather more say in the conduct of
their own affairs, but I am gradually coming
to the conclusion that it has been a failure,
that in our future policy we shall have to
reconcile ourselves to this fact. . . . The
only remedy that I can see is that we, the
English, should come out more into the open.[47]

At the Foreign Office Grey and Hardinge agreed with Gorst. Hardinge revealed he had been pressing Grey for about a year and a half to change the policy in Egypt, "but I have always had to give way owing to the feeling which there is in this Radical Government in favour of self-government for all communities, whether they are capable of governing themselves or not." British and foreign interests in Egypt were too great, he felt, "to allow the Egyptians to be the plaything of the Utopian fancies of a few faddist members of Parliament."[48]

Change in the direction and emphasis of British policy in Egypt was in the works, but first it was necessary to deal with the aftermath of the Egyptian prime minister's murder. A troubled Gorst did his best to keep the Foreign Office informed of the realities of the situation in Egypt that spring. He did not play down the complications that had arisen out of the Butrus murder and the rejection of the Canal Company proposal, but he assured the authorities that al-Wardani could be prosecuted without undue disturbance, and that the communal tensions were not so exacerbated as to warrant an increase in the British garrison. More British soldiers would excite rather than calm the tensions within Egypt. Grey and Hardinge both wanted to send troops, but Gorst assured them that was not necessary. "This was one of Lord Cromer's favorite panaceas in times of difficulty, but I never myself thought that the effect produced was commensurate with the perturbation which it occasioned." He was far more concerned about the hostile press and its deleterious effect on public and official opinion in London. He firmly asserted: "From a practical point of view, the idea which is gaining ground in the British press, that British authority is at a low ebb here is absurd."[49]

Certainly the British officials reacted firmly to quiet the furor and to tighten their control. Under the Press Law they took action against some of the offensive nationalist newspapers, warning their management or suspending their publication if they were not protected by the Capitulations. As before, the effectiveness of the Press Law was limited by the reluctance of a few of the Powers, particularly France, to cooperate and withdraw protection from their nationals who owned newspapers or periodicals. Eventually, in 1911, the Egyptian government sought to prevent

disapproved periodicals from reaching the public by
forbidding them access to the mails or railroads.[50]
Measures were taken, over resistance from the Legislative Council, to modify the Egyptian penal code so as
to prosecute secret societies such as the one to which
al-Wardani had belonged and to deport undesirable
troublemakers, such as Shaikh Shawish. Laws were
strengthened to tighten discipline in the schools, and
to prosecute anyone who threatened public officials.[51]
Al-Wardani's trial began on April 21, and early in May
Gorst noted in his diary, "If Wardani trial does not
end satisfactorily, I've proposed to deport the Nationalist leaders."[52] The sensitive case of al-Wardani,
who had become a hero to the nationalists, was managed
without resorting to a major show of force or to special courts outside the Egyptian judicial system.
Despite considerable disquiet and threats against the
lives of the Egyptian Cabinet and the judges assigned
to al-Wardani's trial, and despite pressure from officials in Egypt and in Britain for strong measures from
the Agency, Gorst resisted what he called the "panic
mongers." He saw to it that the assassin was sen-
tenced to death in the Egyptian courts. Public demonstrations were avoided, the assassin executed in private, and his body buried quietly.[53]

     Gorst, now committed to overt action in support
of the British occupation, was able to deal with the
trial of al-Wardani and agitation by the nationalists.
But he could not censor, suppress, or directly influence the chorus of complaints against his policies
that appeared in the British press or in Parliament.
The shocked Coptic community, the Egyptians who had
previously favored the British occupation, and elements
of the British press used the murder to discredit
Gorst's policies.[54] He already had his detractors in
Egypt among the English press, the business community,
and the Anglo-Egyptian civil service, and in London in
the City and in Whitehall. Critical articles had appeared the year prior to the Butrus murder in London.
The Saturday Review in July 1909 had cited, for example,
the increase in crime in Egypt and inefficiency in the
Egyptian administration as reasons why Gorst should be
replaced. It called for a despot to save Egypt.[55] Gorst
lacked his predecessor's aura of omnipotence; in fact
he deliberately avoided the limelight. He also lacked
Cromer's influential supporters. As a public servant,
he could not respond openly to attacks like that of
The Saturday Review. Thus, when the attacks intensified

Gorst, the high wire artist.

in the spring of 1910, Gorst had to depend on the Foreign Office to support him, but its support was neither as swift nor as firm as he needed. As a result, Gorst and his supporters in Egypt became disillusioned and discouraged. [56]

A number of captious articles suddenly appeared. Few were as close to libel as that in *The Saturday Review* of April 16 where Gorst's policy was described as evil and a disaster. It accused Gorst of undermining British prestige in Egypt, of undignified personal behavior, and of anti-imperial opinions in his dangerous relationship with the khedive. The magazine demanded, again, his recall.[57] This article, entitled "The Case of Sir Eldon Gorst," came to his attention on April 24. He wrote angrily: "Read an infamous libel on me published in *The Saturday Review*, and wired to the F.O. for permission to bring an action against the newspaper." The next day he learned to his fury, "There is no doubt that the libellous article was written by Lady Sykes & founded on exaggerations & good stories emanating from Mark's [Sykes] fertile mind." Mark Sykes and his wife, Gorst's sister Edith, had visited Egypt that winter and were there when the nationalist agitation and Butrus's murder occurred. Early in May Gorst noted that "Mark Sykes has tried to make the 'amende honorable' by replying to *The Saturday Review* effusion."[58] Though Gorst thought that the exaggerations and "violence" to him and his policy had done some local good by causing a favorable reaction, the irony of this episode is evident.

Twenty years before, Lady Sykes had supported, encouraged, and— one would guess— loved the young Gorst. He had gratefully acknowledged her crucial role in his maturation. Congreve put it neatly: "Heaven has no rage like love to hatred turned, Nor hell a fury like a woman scorned." Gorst had ended their intimacy long ago though he continued to see her socially, and his sister Edith had married Mark. Jessica's hatred must have been deep and abiding. An Italian folk saying goes, "Revenge is a dish that tastes best when it's eaten cold." She had her cold plate. Her "effusion" alone would not have been so damaging. However, *The Times, The Daily Express, The Pall Mall Gazette, The Spectator, The Daily Mail,* and *The Daily Telegraph* also carried articles and letters that were hostile to Gorst and his policies in Egypt.[59]

Gorst was most often accused of weakness that had fostered violence. In reality the only violence Gorst could not manage came from these hostile writings and speeches. His correspondence with the Foreign Office that spring reflected his deep concern with the effect that this hostile opinion was having on the British position in Egypt. It also reflected his increasing frustration, since he had no recourse as a public servant but to remain quiet, even when clearly libeled. He twicé asked the Foreign Office for permission to sue *The Saturday Review*. It was refused on the grounds that the article referred to sensitive political questions that could not be adjudicated. Gorst acquiesced "with extreme reluctance."[60]

The government was sensitive to criticism on Egypt, but troubled by other matters. Gorst had to spend much of his time that spring convincing the Foreign Office not to send troops in response to the unrest. Often the reports received at the Foreign Office were exaggerations of real incidents, sometimes stirred up by the Coptic and Syrian reporters for the minor English newspapers in Egypt. These men, Gorst told the Foreign Office, were "all anxious to stir up trouble and make out they are in constant danger of massacre."[61]

Elements in the Coptic community had reacted to the murder of Ghali by starting a noisy and, from the evidence now available, ill-founded campaign against Gorst. They imagined that Ghali's assassination signaled the start of a Muslim effort to persecute their community, and they blamed Gorst's "low profile" and his conciliatory policies for the resurgence of religious fanaticism. A recent study has found that although the Coptic community did not present a united political front during the British occupation, most of its politically active and articulate members since 1903 had opposed the nationalist movement. There were good reasons for this stance. The Copts feared fanaticism, were repelled by the nationalist appeal to Ottoman power, feared the loss of their special position and privileges if the occupation were terminated, and foresaw the end of their considerable economic progress. Their fears had been further aroused by the virulent diatribes against them in the nationalist press in 1908.[62] A short-lived "Independent Egyptian Party" led by a wealthy Copt, Akhnukh Fanus, was formed

to promote independence and a real friendship with
Britain.[63]   At that point in 1908, when the Copts and
the nationalists were severely estranged, Butrus Ghali
was appointed prime minister by Gorst.

The nationalists despised Ghali for having been a
faithful servant of the khedive, the British, and his
community. He had never been forgiven for his signature on the Sudan Condominium Agreement in 1899 and
his participation in the Dinshawai special tribunal in
1906. Although it appeared that Ghali was more interested in remaining in office than in exploiting his
powers for his community, the Muslim majority resented
his appointment, and were not prepared to trust any
power the British allowed to a Christian Egyptian
prime minister.   Ghali's career has been neatly summarized in a recent study of the Copts under British
rule:

> To the Egyptians he appeared to dissemble,
> claiming to represent their aspirations,
> but in reality serving as an instrument
> for a power determined to thwart the ful-
> fillment of any Egyptian aspirations. In
> fact he did dissemble, becoming a politi-
> cian of no stand, but many performances.[64]

His final performance, when he was on the steps to his
office, served mainly to frighten his community, and
provided grounds for agitation that helped to destroy
the policy of his protector, Sir Eldon Gorst.

The Copts as an active Christian minority in
Egypt could elicit a good deal of sympathy and support
in Britain. One of the minor justifications given for
the British presence in Egypt was to protect them.
Cromer, as we have seen, had in his last years made
efforts to gain the support of the various minorities
in Egypt, including the Copts, since he did not feel
the Muslim Egyptians were capable of any significant
responsibility for their country. Gorst's major concern in appointing a prime minister appears to have
been the policy of the liberalization of the Egyptian
government. Ghali was a pliant instrument for that
policy. Gorst, however, did not regard the Copts as
an important prop for the British rule, nor did he
fear the reputed fanatical tendencies of the nationalists.[65] He underestimated latent religious and communal
tensions and the capacity of some influential Coptic
leaders to exploit this hostility.

Their outcries against Gorst after Butrus's mur-
der quickly reached the ears of the Foreign Office.
Gorst advised Hardinge in late March to ignore the
Coptic pleas for help:

> Ever since the assassination of Butros
> Pasha, the Copts have been getting up a
> very foolish and violent agitation, and
> doing their best to promote ill-feeling
> between themselves and the Mohammedans.
> In case you receive telegrams on the sub-
> ject, I repeat emphatically that there
> are no indications of fanaticism on the
> part of the Mohammedans, and that reli-
> gious feeling had nothing to do with the
> murder. All that can be said is that
> the mass of the population do not con-
> sider the crime of the same gravity as
> if the Prime Minister had been a Moslem.[66]

Gorst rejected the outcry of the Copts on the basis
of the evidence he had; he felt their grievances had
little substance. The fear of unrest was in the minds
of the insecure minority communities in Egypt, who
were simply undergoing one of their periodic fits of
alarm. Unless the mass of Muslims was disturbed,
Gorst informed the Foreign Office, he and General
Maxwell, commander of the army of occupation, were
confident that the army could handle the situation.
Once al-Wardani was hanged, "the present state of unrest would disappear."[67]

Although the unrest did subside as Gorst had predicted,
the campaign against him and the policy he had been
implementing did not. The Copts were not assuaged
and they elicited widespread sympathy for their campaign in Britain. Others jumped onto the anti-Gorst
bandwagon for a variety of reasons. Criticism was
especially stimulated by two speeches by Theodore
Roosevelt. The vigorous ex-president of the United
States happened to emerge from a months-long safari
in East Africa that spring and returned home through
Khartum, Cairo, and London. Two of his speeches, one
in Cairo at the Egyptian University and the other at
the Guildhall in the City of London, were highly critical of the nationalist activity and the weak British
rule in Egypt. They raised a considerable stir among
two groups: the nationalists and their sympathizers
in Egypt, and the hard-line critics of Gorst in England.
Only the Copts were elated by Roosevelt's admonitions

to the Egyptian students. The students themselves,
once they had grasped the substance of Roosevelt's
message, burst out in a storm of protest.[68]

It was unusual—and some of the British considered it impolitic—for the ex-president, an outsider,
to criticize either the nationalists or the nature of
British rule. But Roosevelt had discussed the speech
in Egypt with Gorst before he gave it, and had his encouragement. Gorst, now discouraged by the Egyptians'
response to his policies, informed Hardinge that
through Roosevelt he sought to administer a warning to
the nationalists:

>   You will have seen in the papers that
>   Roosevelt delivered an address at the
>   Egyptian University, which has caused
>   great dismay in the nationalist ranks.
>   He pointed out, with great emphasis, that
>   you could no more confer the capacity for
>   self-government on people by a decree, than
>   you could make a man educated by the same
>   process. He also rubbed in pretty severely
>   the disgrace of political assassination or
>   of any half-hearted endeavor to condone
>   crimes of this nature. He showed me before
>   hand what he was going to say, and I encour-
>   aged him to administer this unpalatable med-
>   icine. When the first feelings of irrita-
>   tion have worn away, this plain speaking
>   may do some good to those who are not en-
>   tirely beyond redemption.[69]

Gorst called the speech itself "a splendid performance." Wingate, the governor-general of the Sudan,
was pleased with Roosevelt's speech; he predicted to
Gilbert Clayton, his intelligence officer, that it
would help to awaken the policymakers in Britain to
the dangerous conditions in Egypt: "[Roosevelt's]
words will travel all over the world and will do more
than anything else to make our sleepy people realize
that the situation in Egypt is not as it should be and
that a strong hand is absolutely necessary."[70]

Roosevelt elaborated on this theme in London. At
the Guildhall late in May he made a rousing speech,
punctuated by cheers, in which he exhorted the British
as guardians of civilization to rule Egypt with vigor
and firmness. He reminded his audience also of their

own interests. Weakness and sentimentality by the
imperial power might cause more harm in a country
filled with uncivilized and fanatical peoples than
violence and injustice. The recent behavior of the
Egyptians, in particular the nationalists, had shown
that they were unworthy and incapable of self-government.
The British had originally occupied Egypt to provide
order. He told his audience they had better make up
their minds:

> Now either you have the right to be in Egypt
> or you have not; either it is or it is not
> your duty to establish and keep order. If
> you feel that you have not the right to be
> in Egypt, if you do not wish to establish and
> to keep order there, why then by all means
> get out of Egypt. . . . You are in Egypt for
> several purposes, and among them one of the
> greatest is the benefit of the Egyptian peo-
> ple. You saved them from ruin by coming in,
> and at the present moment, if they are not
> governed from outside, they will sink into a
> welter of chaos. Some nation must govern
> Egypt. I hope and believe that you will de-
> cide that it is your duty to be that nation.
> [loud cheers] [71]

This bombast was delivered after discussion with the
Foreign Office. Hardinge met with Roosevelt before
he spoke in London and cautioned him only that any
reflection on Gorst would be unfair. [72]

The speech aroused considerable attention in
Britain and Egypt. Many agreed but some resented it,
including Gorst, who felt it helped to confirm the
critics of his efforts in Egypt. Worriedly he wrote:
"Roosevelt appears to have made some mischievous remarks about Egypt in his Guildhall speech, subsequently
backed up by H. Chaplin [a right-wing Tory M.P.] in a
letter to *The Times*." [73] Lord Elgin, the ex-colonial
secretary involved at the time in the reassessment of
the government's policy in Egypt, thought the Roosevelt
speech "a pity" since it would provoke resentment on
the part of many who might have agreed with its substance but not with its oversimplification of the
issues.

> I don't agree with his diagnosis that it is
> "sentiment" that does the mischief [in Egypt].

> . . . I regard that as superficial view,
> because I believe that Bayless and
> MacKarness [Radical MPs sympathetic to
> Egyptian self-rule] are almost as scarce
> as the white rhinoceros (of which Mr.
> Roosevelt killed too many, I fear) and that
> the harm comes not from a moral source, but
> from intellectual indolence, which misap-
> plies political maxims in countries like
> Egypt by treating them as if they were fun-
> damental truths.[74]

Grey, however, thought the speech would have a salutary effect at home and abroad. He told Lord Crewe,
the colonial secretary:

> Roosevelt's speech was really a great trib-
> ute to our work in Africa generally, and
> the effect outside ought to be very good.
> Inside this country some people will be an-
> noyed by what he said about Egypt; but I
> think it is healthy that that particular
> sort of person should be shocked by someone
> else, as well as by his own government oc-
> casionally, and Roosevelt's analysis of the
> situation is much the same as I had come to.[75]

In the same letter Grey mentioned that Cromer was "very
pessimistic about Egypt" at that moment, and "fears
all his work will be undone, which must not be."

Grey at that moment was working with Elgin, Crewe,
and others on tactics and timing for a defense of the
government's policy, and on efforts to see that Cromer's
work was not "undone." By early June Gorst and Grey,
in consultation with various officials, had decided
the events in Egypt that winter and spring indicated
the need for a change in policy. It was necessary,
however, to reaffirm British intentions to remain
firmly in control of Egyptian affairs, in order to
quiet the criticism that had erupted in the public
press, Conservative circles, and Parliament. A series
of letters from Cromer to Grey and to Gorst during
that spring illuminated the serious concern that had
arisen in Britain and the various measures, official
and unofficial, that had been taken to allay the disquiet on the home front. Cromer himself intervened
with Balfour and others to prevent concern about Egypt
from becoming a party issue. He also prevailed upon

Lord Rosebery not to bring forward any resolutions on the issue in the House of Lords. Cromer's letters to Gorst are friendly but full of frank criticism, genteelly expressed.[76]

Gorst in Egypt was no less troubled at the events of the winter and spring. He had miscalculated badly in thinking he could convince the Egyptian Assembly to extend the Canal Company concession. With the murder of Butrus and the rejection of the Canal Company proposal, Gorst lost "the only Egyptian left in whom one could have entire confidence, who was able to understand how public affairs have to be managed," and he lost all confidence in the Egyptians' capacities to cope with even limited self-government.[77] His letters to the Foreign Office in April, May, and June reveal the trend of his thinking. With backing from London, he decided to call a halt to the policy of liberalization.

Grey summed up the British attitude when he wrote Gorst early in May:

> As for recent attempts to develop the government of Egypt by means of Egyptians (for recent steps in this direction I take the entire responsibility, though the policy itself is the policy of Lord Cromer). So far as I can see the Egyptians have taken advantage of our attempts, not to further good government in Egypt but to agitate against the British occupation.[78]

Grey then directed Gorst to put his thoughts on the matter into a memorandum. Gorst immediately did so. This document, entitled "Memorandum Respecting Self-Government in Egypt" elicited Grey's swift approval, and he had it sent to the prime minister, Lord Cromer, and the Cabinet. He informed Gorst: "If we have a debate in Parliament, I shall for my own part adopt the views of the memorandum."[79]

Gorst's memorandum deserves discussion, for it provides insight into Gorst's attitude toward the turmoil that he had helped to stimulate, and the basis for the change in policy that resulted. He outlined the two methods he had worked out to provide a measure of self-government for the Egyptians. It was too early to judge the effect of what he called "reforming the constitution" and enlarging the scope of the provincial

councils. But the attempt to allow the General
Assembly and Legislative Council limited participation
in the governing of Egypt had been "extremely disap-
pointing." These two bodies managed to act respon-
sibly on nonpolitical matters, but they displayed an
increasing tendency "to become mere instruments of the
Nationalist agitation against the occupation." They
made periodic demands for a constitution, attacked the
Egyptian government during debates on the budget and
the Sudan, and were unreasonably hostile and suspi-
cious during their discussion of the Suez Canal scheme.
It was, according to Gorst's analysis, all part of the
anglophobia stirred up by the nationalists and designed
to bring the occupation to an end by making the British task in Egypt an impossible one.

The khedive's support was of little value to the
British, as his political influence had come to an end
when it was no longer directed against the occupation.
The Egyptian ministers had had no success in building
a group sympathetic to Britain within the Legislative
Council, whose consistent hostility adversely affected
relations between the Egyptian ministers and the British officials. These ministers, although no longer
the "complete dummies" of the Cromer era, were ham-
pered by violent attacks in the Legislative Council
and the Egyptian press from showing the initiative
Gorst encouraged. The nationalists regarded any deference to the British view as offense. Since the ministers were unable to resist nationalist pressures,
the administrative machinery could not work well. And
since the country was overwhelmingly illiterate, real
representative institutions were "obviously impossible." Somewhat bitterly, Gorst outlined the misunderstanding and opposition of the officials and foreign
communities in Egypt:

> With the possible exception of the Khedive
> and his Ministers, not only the British com-
> munity and all of the European colonies, but
> even the Egyptians themselves, are firmly con-
> vinced that this policy is a concession to
> clamour, and represents a diminution of Brit-
> ish authority. Until therefore the lesson
> had been learnt that the rate of progress to-
> wards autonomy must depend on the decisions
> of the British, and not the Egyptian people,
> the inevitable result of further concessions
> could only be to provoke further agitation. [80]

The time had come, he felt, to cry for a halt; no further concessions would be made. It would be "a suici-
dal policy" to grant any more real power to the as
then constituted Legislative Council. If his conclusions met with the British government's approval, an
official pronouncement on the matter would be called
for. He ended with these words:

> To sum up in a few words the views submitted
> in this memorandum, I consider it would
> greatly ease the situation, facilitate our
> relations with the native ministers, and re-
> move the obstructions now placed in the way
> of continuing the policy of administrative
> reform if it could be laid down categorically
> that, inasmuch as the Egyptians are very far
> from the stage when they could govern them-
> selves without foreign assistance, the occu-
> pation must continue, and that the experience
> of the last two years has shown that even the
> gradual development of existing institutions
> is out of the question so long as these insti-
> tutions are liable to be used as an instru-
> ment of agitation against the occupation.[81]

Gorst was not the type of man who sought to avoid
blame for his own errors. Before the debate in the
House of Commons on Egyptian affairs took place in
June he admitted to Grey that he had made a mistake
with the handling of the Suez Canal Company scheme.
"I fear that my *apologia* for the Suez Canal Company
business is rather weak, and by the light of subsequent events it is easy to see we made one or two
really bad mistakes. I do not know whether I ought to
have been able to force them at this time." Furthermore, he told Grey not to act as a buffer for him during the impending debate:

> I hope you will state very emphatically that
> I have always concurred in all that has been
> done here and in most cases been responsible
> for proposing it to you. I see no reason why
> we need any of us be ashamed of an honest at-
> tempt to carry out our past promises, even if
> it has failed owing to the stupidity of the
> Egyptians themselves.[82]

Grey, armed with the Gorst memorandum and a consensus
among his advisors, had decided it was time for firmness,

what he called "a new departure in the direction of strong and arbitrary measures" in Egypt.[83] Although the government would have preferred to avoid all discussion of Egyptian affairs, and had done so that spring, it was necessary to make a statement to reassure their Conservative and imperialist critics in England, and to quiet the nationalist clamor in Egypt.

The debate over Egypt that June was muted partly through the influence of Cromer. Deeply concerned lest his years of effort in Egypt be overturned, Cromer outlined the influence he would exert in a letter to Gorst on May 30:

> As regards the Egyptian debate, I do not think it is likely to be brought forward in the House of Lords unless I do so myself, and the objections to this are two-fold. In the first place, it would be extremely disagreeable to me, and I would very much rather hold my tongue: this point, however, I should be, if necessary, prepared to yield. The other objection is more serious. It is that the Foreign Office is practically not represented in the House of Lords, and that it is very desirable that Grey himself should make a statement on the subject, which he is anxious to do, and which he can, of course only do in the House of Commons. I should think, therefore, the debate would probably come off upon the Estimates some time in the course of June or early in July. I can do a good deal behind the scenes in the way of preventing it degenerating into a party discussion, and as it seems probable that a General Election will now not take place yet awhile, I should think I ought to be successful.[84]

The recent events in Egypt and the government's policy there were raised during the estimates in June by both Conservatives and Liberal imperialists who were disturbed by the turmoil and the apparent loss of British authority and prestige. They called for an end to the experiment in limited self-government and the reinstitution of respect for British authority by drastic measures where necessary. They felt the Liberal government had been weak, allowing Egypt to drift into a state of chaos. Now it was time to reverse

this trend and resume the responsibilities of Empire
which Britain had let slide in the last few years. Former
President Roosevelt's admonition to rule Egypt or
leave it was cited by the critics of the government
as evidence of the seriousness of the situation.[85]

Only the Radical J. M. Robertson arose in the
House to defend the experiment in self-government.
The critics of the government's policies did not take
kindly to his suggestion that Britain had, in fact,
not given enough self-government to Egypt, or that it
had been guilty of neglecting its responsibilities to
that country. The critics were guilty, he declared,
of a double standard in politics: one set of rules
for the British and another for the subject races. He
also chided them for lauding Roosevelt simply because
he happened to say things about Egypt they agreed with,
and for their offensive language against the British
government, which only served to teach the Egyptians
"a lesson in the art of vituperation."[86]   There was
irony in Robertson's words. Since 1906 he had been a
major critic of the policies of Sir Eldon Gorst and
the Liberal government; now he found himself speaking
in their defense.

The next speakers dismissed Robertson as ignorant
of Egyptians, and as a faddist and sentimentalist.
Finally Balfour, the leader of the opposition, intervened to speak before Grey, giving his view of why the
British were in Egypt. Countering Robertson, he asserted that problems there were different from those
of the shires in Britain. It was not a question of
racial inferiority or superiority, but of two peoples
in different places on the scale of political development. The Egyptians had never had self-government,
and it would take longer than thirty years to teach it
to them. Consequently the British had a vital mission:

> We are in Egypt not merely for the sake of
> the Egyptians, though we are there for their
> sake; we are there also for the sake of Eu-
> rope at large. If this be the task which,
> as it has been thrown upon us we ought to
> take up, as it is a task which is of infinite
> benefit to the races with whom we deal.[87]

Since the British had made sacrifices in sending their
very best men to govern under trying and difficult
circumstances, it was the duty of the nation to support

these men. "These officials can do that work, I believe, better than anybody, if they merely have the
sense that they are being supported. If they lost
that sense, rightly or wrongly—sometimes it is
wrongly—their whole position is undermined." Balfour
told the House that he had consulted people who had
long and intimate experience of Egypt: "All these people have agreed with one voice that the position in
Egypt is now eminently unsatisfactory . . . because
the authority of what they frankly say is the dominant
race—and as I think ought to remain the dominant
race—has been undermined." The sense of order was a
prerequisite for civilizing the natives, and the sense
of authority was a prerequisite for conferring the
benefits of the dominant race.   These depended, said
Balfour, on the confidence and ungrudging support of
the country that sent its agents to Egypt.   The British officials' loss of confidence in that support was
undermining their work. Balfour called upon the government to secure "the greatest task that can fall to
their lot," that is, of seeing that the civilizing
work in Egypt, "carried on as it is by a mere handful
of our countrymen, shall not suffer even the smallest
degree by a feeling, well or ill-deserved, that they
do not have from home that support without which they
are helpless indeed." [88]

     Grey spoke immediately after Balfour. He thanked
the opposition leader for the tone and substance of
his speech, which was a "valuable contribution" to every
thoughtful mind in regard to "the problems with which
we have to deal." The problems in Egypt were not
Gorst's fault and attacks on him in some of the press
were "most unfounded, most unjust, and most untrue."
The government, whose instructions Gorst was following,
should be held responsible. "No one could have carried
out this policy or any policy in Egypt with more knowledge and ability and skill than Sir Eldon Gorst." [89]

     Grey admitted also that Roosevelt had met with
him before his Guildhall speech and disclosed his views
on Africa. "I seldom listened to anything with greater
pleasure," Grey remarked. He reminded the House that
most of what Roosevelt said had been complimentary. The
government, too, had been concerned with recent events
in Egypt, but the situation was not nearly so grave as
the rumors held. In consultation with Gorst, he had
determined that crimes such as Butrus's murder would
be rapidly and justly handled, or else the army of

occupation would have to intervene. Special methods to deal with crime had recently been instituted, and the results were encouraging. The Sudan, he pointed out, had been doing well under Wingate's tutelage.

Grey then explained the general policy of government in Egypt and denied it had undermined the authority of the British there. More involvement of Egyptians in their own administration was a natural process; even Cromer had taken one step in that direction with the appointment of Zaghlul. He thought the government might have been going too fast in that direction recently. Still, sincere and thoughtful changes had been made, and the increase in Egyptian responsibilities at the provincial level looked promising.

The trouble at the moment, according to Grey, lay not with the British policy but with the Egyptians, particularly the small nationalist minority who were abusing the privileges granted to the Egyptian ministers by using the opportunity for constructive criticism to agitate against the British occupation. Since Egyptian progress was, in Grey's mind, directly associated with British needs in Egypt, any such criticism was simply not tolerable, and there could be no progress in the development of self-rule as long as agitation against the British occupation continued. He echoed Balfour's assertion that the British were trustees in Egypt for Egyptians, for good order and public security, and for the interests of Europe.

> The British Occupation must continue in
> Egypt more so now than ever. It is not
> a question of British interests in Egypt.
> It is simply this, that we have gone on
> in Egypt doing more and more good work,
> year after year, that that good work de-
> pends on our staying there, and that we
> cannot abandon Egypt without disgrace to
> ourselves.[90]

Thus the British were not going to leave or yield to any agitation, since in the end they would determine what the Egyptian needs really were. When the Egyptians "who would desire to see their country progress under British advice and British care have their views accepted and not denounced by the great majority of their fellow-countrymen," then there would be further progress towards self-rule.

Grey assured the House that the disquiet in Egypt
had been less in recent weeks, and it was not necessary at the moment to take any drastic steps to assert
British authority. But he warned the House:

> I do think it necessary and desirable to
> give this warning that the symptoms which
> we have seen and the agitation against the
> British occupation, if it is rekindled and
> continued, will make it necessary for any
> British Government to make it clear that
> their first object is to assert their au-
> thority and to protect Egyptian Ministers who
> follow their advice, and that there will be
> no further progress in Egypt until they put
> an end to the agitation against British
> occupation.[91]

This warning by Grey heralded the end of the
Liberal government's "experiment" in liberalization
that had begun when Gorst replaced Cromer in 1907.
The policy had failed, and Gorst, despite Grey's attempt to defend him, was blamed for the failure.

History has judged Gorst's administration in this
light. His record as proconsul has long suffered from
the rash of criticism, much of it partisan, self-
serving, and misconceived, that erupted when Butrus
Ghali was murdered and the Egyptian General Assembly
rejected the extension of the Suez Canal Company concession. Cancer cut short his career, and Gorst was
dead barely a year later.

Chapter Thirteen

CONCLUSION: THE FAILURE OF VISION

These rotten states, backward and venal as they are,
must be seriously thought about; they cannot be held
together just by encouraging what is weakest and
most corrupt in them, as we appear to be doing.

Pursewarden to Mountolive[1]

After the sound and fury of the events of the winter
and spring of 1910, Gorst's last year in Egypt had an
element of anticlimax. Despite the alarmists at home
and in Egypt who feared, expected, and predicted further trouble for the British occupation, little or
nothing occurred. Although his health deteriorated
rapidly, Gorst's control over the situation did not.
Once the experiment in self-rule had been shelved, it
was enough on the political front for the Agency to
warn certain nationalist agitators, censor where possible certain offensive periodicals, and indulge in a
limited amount of counterpropaganda to maintain and
affirm British control.[2]

Gorst sought to cultivate a more sympathetic
English press at home and in Egypt. He courted
Valentine Chirol, director of the foreign department
of *The Times*, when Chirol visited Egypt for a fortnight late in May 1910. And in London that summer
he attempted without success to persuade George Allen,
editor of the weekly *The Near East*, to publish a
"respectable English paper in Egypt." However, when
Gorst died the next year that journal did publish
leaders and several articles that were sympathetic
to him and to his policies.[3] The movements and activities of nationalist leaders and their sympathizers
inside and outside Egypt were also more carefully
monitored. Gorst was able to report to Grey in November 1910 that Egypt had been quiet for some little
time, but he warned that there might be a revival of
agitation against the British in the press:

We must be prepared to drop on them at once
with vigour at an early stage if we wish to
prevent a repetition of the agitation of
last year. The Ministers have been working
quite harmoniously together, and also with
us, and they are prepared, I think, to do
what they can to keep things quiet, and to
stimulate a certain amount of native support on our side amongst the respectable
members of the community.[4]

The principal annoyance to Gorst and the British
in Egypt after June 1910 came not from the nationalist
agitation, but from an activist element within the
Coptic community. Support for the Coptic demands in
Egypt came from such anti-Gorst circles as the management of *The Egyptian Gazette,* the various Christian
missionary groups, and, it was alleged, the khedive.
This opposition further discredited the policy Gorst
had been implementing. Coptic accusations continued
to appear in British periodicals; telegrams, letters,
and delegations of Copts were sent to London to lobby
the British government for special treatment and protection for their community.[5] During his final year
in Egypt Gorst had to spend much of his precious time
countering the Coptic assertions and discounting their
grievances, which had, he thought, little substance.

In January 1911 Gorst toured the Egyptian provinces and assured the Foreign Office once again that
the Coptic complaints had little foundation or public
support. It must have annoyed him considerably to
have to deal with their constant criticism. Coptic
employment in the Egyptian government far exceeded
the percentage their numbers would warrant, and the
British were careful to see that the state-supported
lower schools in Egypt provided religious instruction
for Coptic as well as Muslim children.[6]

The Copts' campaign to be treated as a privileged minority, however, might easily have inflamed the Muslim
majority and accelerated into actual violence between
the two communities had Gorst not been careful.
They sought to intensify their protest movement by
staging a congress in Asyut in March 1911.[7] The Muslims responded by organizing an "Egyptian" congress
in Heliopolis in early May. Had the nationalists at
this later assembly been able to air their grievances
against the British occupation and the Copts, they

might have precipitated serious disturbances among the masses of *fellahin*. Gorst and his officials cooperated with the prime minister and the interior minister to manipulate the "Egyptian" congress so that all its meetings were devoid of threatening religious and political content. The chairman of the congress, Mustafa Riaz Pasha, ex-prime minister, was chosen by the British Agency. He still retained considerable prestige as "a grand old man of Egyptian politics." Riaz and the moderate Ummah Party, with the encouragement and support of the Agency and the Egyptian ministers, obtained control of the congress and kept the program from focusing on issues that might exacerbate either communal tensions or opposition to the British occupation.[8] It is noteworthy that it took the Coptic protests and demands to bring the quarreling groups of nationalists together. At that time the only issue the majority could agree on was the Islamic foundation of the state:

> The speeches delivered are conclusive evidence that the delegates did not extoll Islam and indulge in an indignant denunciation of the Copts, yet it is clear that all the speakers with hardly any exception were zealous in defending the Muslim character of the state. If the common theme of the Coptic Congress was a plea for justice, that of the Egyptian Congress was an insistence upon the inviolable Islamic nature of the state.[9]

In maintaining British control in Egypt, Gorst did not consciously foster religious discontent or tension among the sects. But the policy of liberalization meant that more attention and influence had been granted to the Muslim majority. The Coptic campaign against Gorst contributed to the end of this policy and generally obscured the achievements of his last year in Egypt. Emanations from this campaign reached the ears of the novelist Lawrence Durrell, who served in Egypt more than twenty years later, an era of manifest decline in British power and influence. In the novel *Mountolive*—part of *The Alexandria Quartet*—the young English diplomat David Mountolive has been befriended by a prominent Coptic family. Invited to stay at the family estate in the Nile Delta in order to perfect his Arabic, he made a thoughtless remark at the dinner table that lumped Copts with

Muslims. This act provoked a diatribe from the Hosnani
family patriarch, a crippled and bitter old man. Shak-
ing his finger at the embarrassed young guest, he said:

> I see nothing to smile at. Nothing at all.
> The slip exactly expresses the British point
> of view— the view with which we Copts have
> always had to contend. There were never any
> differences between us and the Moslems in
> Egypt before they came. The British have
> taught the Moslems to hate Copts and to dis-
> criminate against them. Yes, Mountolive, the
> British. Pay heed to my words.[10]

He went on with rising anger to give the diplomat a
lecture on the Coptic contributions to modern Egyptian
history, which included: "The British changed it [the
Coptic role] with their hatred of the Copts. Gorst
initiated a diplomatic friendship with Khedive Abbas,
and as a result of his schemes not a single Copt was
to be found in the entourage of the Court or even in
the services of its departments."[11] One wonders if
Gorst ever dreamed that his machinations, however misunderstood, might contribute to the plot of a famous
twentieth-century novel.

Disappointment and frustration with the events
of the spring of 1910 and the consequent Coptic activities did not prevent Gorst from acting positively in
other areas. The disastrous cotton harvest in 1909
made the Egyptian government realize that private
enterprise could not be entrusted, as it had been
under Cromer, with the complete responsibility for
this crucial staple. In 1910 a department of agricul-
ture was created with G. C. Dudgeon, an official with
experience in East Africa, as its director general.[12]
Under Kitchener, Gorst's successor, the department
became a full-fledged ministry.

Another reform that Gorst pursued up to the end
of his term was modification of the Capitulations.
Gorst had abandoned Cromer's scheme of a cosmopolitan
legislative body that would assume responsibility for
the interests of foreigners in Egypt. In June 1910
Gorst informed Grey that there had been almost universal opposition to such a proposal, and its advantages
were "very problematical." In December of that year
he emphasized the necessity for action on the matter
in a letter to Arthur Nicolson at the Foreign Office:

> Unless we maintain the hold which we have
> now obtained over the native press, it is
> not fair to hold me responsible for the
> condition of public security in this coun-
> try. If we allow the Arabic newspapers to
> stir up all the violent passions of the
> mob, we shall be heading straight for dis-
> aster and bloodshed, and if the Capitula-
> tions really stand in the way of our taking
> efficacious measures in this respect, then
> I say that for any English Government much
> the lesser evil is to sweep them away.[13]

Early in January 1911 he informally outlined to the
Foreign Office his plan for the modification of the
Capitulations along with the suggestion that the
British offer a quid pro quo to the French in order
to obtain their acquiescence. Give them British
Gambia, as Cromer had originally suggested in 1904,
and the French, Gorst thought, would come around:

> Roughly speaking, it [his plan] may be de-
> scribed as abolishing the Capitulations; main-
> taining the Mixed Tribunals, with civil and
> criminal jurisdiction over foreigners; re·
> placing the legislative control of the Powers
> by that of H.M.G. acting on their behalf; and
> guaranteeing to all foreigners most-favoured-
> nation treatment in all respects with Brit-
> ish subjects; the whole system to be in force
> only as long as the British occupation lasts.
> I have so far not submitted the scheme to the
> F.O. as the psychological moment has not yet
> arrived, but whenever that moment does come,
> I am ready to put it forward officially.[14]

While awaiting that moment (which never came),
the Egyptian government secured an agreement from the
Powers to modify the mixed civil code. A new legislative assembly was established, composed of judges
from each treaty Power not already in this court.
This body was empowered to enact legislation, after a
rather complicated lease process, that would apply to
the civil disputes of foreigners in Egypt. Lord Lloyd,
a successor of Gorst's in the 1920s, asserted that this
measure was a significant benefit to the Egyptian government.[15] Also passed during Gorst's last year was a
law—the organic statute of al-Azhar—which lasted
until 1930. Zaghlul, with Gorst's support, had

struggled against heavy opposition from entrenched and
reactionary Azhar leaders to reform the administration and
curriculum of al-Azhar and its school for Qadis, the
religious judges.[16]

     Egypt's financial prospects improved during
Gorst's last year despite the turmoil over the refusal
of the Egyptian General Assembly to approve the proposed renewal of the Canal Company concession. The
financial advisor, Harvey, reported that 1910 closed
with more favorable prospects than had been expected.
Cotton production improved after the disastrous crop
of 1909, and there was a year-end surplus of one and
a quarter million pounds Egyptian. The Egyptian government, even before the budgeted increase for 1911,
was living within its income.[17] Under Gorst, Egyptian
finances were soundly managed—if the records available are to be believed. This accomplishment, however,
is often forgotten when his career is assessed.

     Gorst's ill health, especially during the last
year of his tenure as Consul-General, also needs to
be emphasized in an assessment of his effectiveness.
According to his own testimony, when he replaced
Cromer in 1907 he was in excellent health and spirits.
His physical vigor seems to have continued throughout
1908, and the sanguine tone of his correspondence and
his autobiographical notes lasted at least through
July 1909. Even the nervous breakdown of his wife in
the fall of 1908 did not appear to dent his confidence
or his powers.[18] In January 1909 he suffered from what
his doctor called a mild attack of typhoid fever, and
in March of that year he took a month's holiday to the
Lebanese mountains for a rest and a change of air.
Harry Boyle noted that Gorst returned from the Lebanon
restored to his "usual robust health." Little more
than two years later Gorst was dead of cancer.[19]

     Before the onset of the malignancy in 1911, he
suffered a serious stroke due to the stress and
strain of the troubled winter and spring of 1910.
Gorst was intolerant of weakness in other men, and
could easily have let the very real strain of the
negotiations obscure the deterioration in his physical
condition. The onset of illness may have contributed
to his admitted blunders. In June 1910 Gorst informed
Grey he had had "a touch of the sun" for a fortnight
and had to postpone serious discussion of Egyptian
affairs. Several days earlier Cheetham had informed

the Foreign Office that Gorst was too ill to write.[20]

What actually happened was more serious: he had been working nonstop for several months under quite terrible pressures. To add to this, his mother came down with pneumonia during the Ghali assassination. On June 9, while in the final stages of drafting the memo on self-government for Grey, Gorst felt "seedy" after an afternoon of fishing near Alexandria. "I really got sun stroke, but this did not develop 'til later." He worked on, and then admitted that he was not well: "There is no doubt that these three days of hard work on top of the sunstroke finished me off." That same day he finished his memorandum to Grey. Two days later he was dressing to go swimming and "suddenly fell down—my left arm and leg paralyzed. When Dr. Morrison arrived I was better and the attack seemed to have passed away." He did some business with the financial advisor, Harvey, but later that day his leg and arm became "quite useless." The diagnosis was "a broken small blood vessel in the brain, or the brain is congested for some reason." In short, he had had a stroke. "Perfect quiet" and ice packs on his head were prescribed by the attending physician.[21]

He made "slow progress" through the rest of June. By the end of the month he conducted some business, played poker with the Agency staff, and made plans to go to England for the summer holidays. He left early in July and arrived in London sounding rather exhausted and dispirited, and was uncharacteristically relieved to hear that he would not have to see either Grey or the king immediately. His physician prescribed "perfect rest—mental and physical—for the present." Gorst and his family went to Castle Combe, but his progress by the end of the month was "very slow indeed." Visits to the Foreign Office to see Hardinge and Grey, and to Cromer at the end of the month, seem to have depressed him. At the Foreign Office he noted: "Got through the ordeal fairly well. They all seemed quite satisfied with my proceedings." The visit to his former mentor was less pleasant. "To see Lord Cromer who was rather severe on me & our proceedings. I did not feel up to arguing with him."[22]

After another medical consultation early in August, Gorst was informed that he might have another stroke were he to risk a further siege of strain and anxiety. A very depressed Gorst for the first time

contemplated giving up his proconsulship. "Under
these circumstances I shall have to consider whether
to ask the F.O. for a less strenuous post than Cairo."
The purchase of a new car—a 15-horsepower Daimler—
did something to brighten his spirits. Still, he took
the precaution of making a new will and resettled the
estate of Castle Combe in the middle of August. Some
gradual improvement in his health was indicated by his
increased activity. In August he toured North Wales
for several days in his new car, then spent most of
September in Scotland at his father-in-law's estate.
On September 13 he recorded that his sister Dolly
would accompany his family to Cairo in the fall. Early
in October he was driven to Lincolnshire for a weekend
with the Monsons, their guests, and his godchild
Margaret Turnure. Kitty even joined the house party.
Margaret was "very fit." There was no mention of
Romaine.[23]

        Back in London, he changed doctors. The new
physician, Addinsell, was much more encouraging about
Gorst's future. Gorst had informed Hardinge at the
Foreign Office that he did not think he could do more
than another winter in Egypt. In a conversation with
Romaine's husband, Lord Monson, he had indicated his
interest in shifting to the embassy at Constantinople.
After the interview with Hardinge he had two more
talks with Grey. Signs of his failing health and
spirits were evident. He informed Grey he wanted to
leave Egypt because of his health. The foreign secretary promised to do what he could, but reminded the
dispirited Gorst that he would have to wait for a
"suitable vacancy." In the second interview Gorst
sounded untypically self-pitying: "ventilated the
hardships of my lot. He was sympathetic and encouraging."[24] One gets the feeling that Gorst was a little
self-deluded at this time.

        The long vacation was not enough and Gorst was
still ill when he returned to Egypt that fall. "I
arrived here Tuesday 1st," he informed Grey, "and took
over the Agency from Cheetham. I find it somewhat
irksome getting into the saddle again, and am obliged
for the present to work half-time; so I trust any
failings on my part may be viewed with a lenient eye."[25]

        Even on half-time he was able to keep on top of
his job. He found a suitable Swedish masseur in Cairo.
His recreation was confined largely to motoring and

croquet. Throughout the remainder of the year and
into January 1911 the diary showed no specific complaints. His friend the khedive made a special trip
to Cairo from Alexandria to accept Gorst's new letters of credence. By the end of the year he was re-
suming most of the normal official routines and had
begun to entertain again. There was one minor negative note: at the annual meeting of the Khedivial
Sporting Club, Gorst (the chairman) found it boring;
the meeting, he wrote, involved "several wearisome
discussions." In December he made plans to buy "some
fine Aubusson curtains" in Cairo. Kitchener, more or
less out of work, made a short visit and Gorst entertained his old adversary. Since this cagey soldier
was angling for a new position, he may well have come
to ascertain the state of Gorst's health and spirits;
it was not entirely coincidental that he was selected
as Gorst's successor barely seven months later.[26]

Early in January Gorst made an official inspection trip by boat up the Nile as far as Aswan. All
went well, and he appeared to be on the road to recovery. On February 19 the first symptoms of his
fatal illness are recorded in his diary. He felt
"seedy" but went ahead with his busy schedule, entertaining eleven for dinner on the 20th. He labeled his
pains neuralgia and, feeling worse, consulted a doctor.
He decided to spend a few days at the spa at Helwan.
A doctor there, who might better be called a quack,
told Gorst that his "neuralgia" was due to faulty di-
gestion and prescribed some sort of "electric treatment."[27] His condition worsened, so that after about
a week in Helwan he returned to Cairo. Another shift
of scene to a camp on the desert did little good.
Despite increasing pain and lack of sleep he doggedly
kept working on the annual report for 1910. In March
he sent Grey a draft and told the foreign secretary
that his "neuralgia" continued and he found it hard
to get through a day's work. "My doctor attributes
my being generally run down to my having resumed work
too soon after my last summer's illness."

The illness had distinctly affected his attitude
toward his job. In the same letter to Grey he asked
to be relieved as soon as possible.

> In May 1912, I shall have served in this
> country for 23 years and shall have com-
> pleted 5 years in my present post which

is probably the most arduous and certainly
the most ungrateful place in the British
Empire, and if I remain here longer I shall
(probably) break down [word not clear] and
be of no use to anyone. I trust therefore
you will see your way then to transfer me
to an easier billet. What I should like
would be one of the embassies where there
is useful work to be done—not one of the
ornamental ones. The two for which I consider my past experience best fits me are
Paris and Constantinople. I should like to
be considered for either if you have nobody
better in view whenever a vacancy occurs.[28]

Gorst's energy had dissipated along with his ambition and he asked Grey's permission for a long leave
of five or six months. His pain worsened so drasti-
cally towards the end of March that he pushed ahead
his plans to leave as soon as possible. Meanwhile, in
a private telegram, Grey had assured him that a new
post would be found after his recovery. He left Egypt
on April 8, 1911, for the last time, seen off by a
large crowd. The handwriting in his diary had already
begun to falter.[29]

In terrible pain, he went directly to the mud
baths at Acqui near Genoa, Italy, and was met there
by his London doctor, Addinsell. Addinsell and the
Acqui staff doctor decided that his inflamed stomach
made it too dangerous for him to take the baths immediately. Heavily drugged with aspirin, he entrained
with the physician for London and a nursing home where
the regime seemed to have some good effect. He was
able to reduce his daily consumption of aspirin to ten
grams, and he had "less pain." His diary entries,
formerly written every day, now began to dwindle. On
April 21 he started to record his weight: he lost
about nine pounds in a month—from 9 stone 9-3/4 pounds
(135 pounds) to 9 stone (126 pounds) on May 20. Though
apparently he had been able to leave the first nursing
home and do some touring by car for pleasure, his condition continued to worsen and late in May he went to
another nursing home at Hindhead. There was no improvement, and the specialist, Victor Horsley, was
called into consultation. Gorst recorded his verdict:
"He considers that neuritis etc. is all due to gastric
trouble near duodenum & advises operation to wh. of
course I agreed." His handwriting by now had become

extremely weak, and his weight had fallen to 8 stone
9 pounds (121 pounds). Less than a week later he
could hardly write: "Consultation of leading medicos
decided on exploratory cooperation [*sic*]." Addinsell
and Lane operated on June 9. Gorst scrawled: "Result
is cancer of the pancreas & liver. I have about 2
months to live." The next day he scrawled: "Decided
to go down to C.C. to die as soon as I have sufficiently recovered from operation. Resigned my place."[30]
That was his last entry.

He endured his last pain-filled days bravely. In
a letter to the counselor at the Cairo Agency, Sir
Milne Cheetham, Cromer remarked admiringly: "I never
knew anyone so plucky as he is. It is however a great
pity that, as he nearly collapsed under the chloroform,
the Doctors were not merciful enough to let him do so
altogether." Gorst added one codicil to his latest
will, made out the previous September, which made his
sister Dolly joint guardian of his daughter Kitty.
His marriage to Evelyn "Doll" Rudd had been troubled.
This terrible last year so disturbed her that she
rarely spoke again of her husband to Kitty. And she
left her upbringing to Dolly.[31]

Gorst was visited in his last days by several of
his old friends, among them the famous hydraulic engineer Sir William Garstin, who was so moved by the
visit that he retreated into stunned silence. In a
letter which Gorst probably never saw, he wrote:

My dear Gorst
    I must write you one line of farewell.
I was so tongue-tied today when I saw you
& could find no words. It was such a shock
to me to see you lying there & to know that
we should not meet again. I never realized
it before. You and I have been friends for
more than 24 years & good friends always.
I have always felt that I could count upon
your friendship to help & you have shown it
to me in many ways in the past. Now I feel
as if something had been torn up in my life.
    May I tell you what good it did me to
see you so calm and brave—Meeting the end
in the way that man should do. . . . You
know my dear friend that if ever I can do
anything for Lady Gorst or any of your sisters they can absolutely count upon me.

> . . . I just want you to know that I shall
> <u>never</u> forget you and that I shall miss you
> <u>always</u>. You are going now to learn the
> great secret. I am one of them who believe
> that we shall meet again. I am not reli-
> gious but I do hold to this conviction.
>
> > Goodbye my very very dear friend,
> >
> > W. Garstin [32]

Another friend, Khedive Abbas Hilmi, rushed across the
channel to succor Gorst. In a letter to the bereaved
father, he said:

> It is a consolation to me to have been able
> to visit Sir Eldon in his house, and to have
> been recognized by him; and I shall endeavor
> to retain the friendship of yourself and fam-
> ily by always showing to your daughters,
> whose husbands are established in Egypt, in
> me they have a friend who will endeavor to
> replace their brother. [33]

There is a family legend that when the khedive entered
the manor library, the dying Gorst sat up and they
greeted each other in Arabic. In a previous letter to
the elder Gorst, Abbas had said: "His services in my country will be long remembered, and personally I shall
always look upon him as one of my best friends." Not
an epitaph to be scorned. On July 12, 1911, at the
age of fifty-one, Gorst was dead. The khedive went
to Castle Combe every year to lay a wreath on his
grave. [34]

Gorst's death killed what faint hope might have
existed for further experiments in the liberalization
of British rule in Egypt. Lord Kitchener, who succeeded him as Consul-General, was cut from an imperious and autocratic mold, and the priorities of the
British government had changed since 1907. Plagued
now by a plethora of domestic and foreign problems,
London learned from Gorst's experience that the
Egyptians were still unworthy and unable to cope
even with carefully limited responsibility for their
own affairs. Gorst himself had been bitterly disillusioned with the Egyptians, whom he thought irresponsible, and with the British officials and the
European communities whose selfishness and lack of
imagination led to clamor and backbiting which he felt

contributed to the demise of the new policy.

Most critics have blamed Gorst for the failure of the new policy in 1907-1911, although few understood what his policy was. Even fewer understood his tactics. His admitted blunders over the management of the Canal concession scheme have obscured the overall picture. What we now know, from examining his papers and correspondence along with other relevant sources, is that he proposed genuine changes in the pattern of rule established by Cromer. These changes would have meant that selected Egyptians would be encouraged to act on their own responsibility in internal affairs. Certain semirepresentative institutions, long moribund under the tutelage of the autocratic Cromer and his officials, would also be given some limited powers. In the process the British presence and direct influence would have been reduced, as would the influence of the other foreign communities.

Like Cromer, Gorst had little use for the nationalists, but he did see justification for certain of their grievances. Unlike Cromer, he did not need to be a bully or depend on a show of power to obtain what he wanted, and he thought it worthwhile to experiment with a guided and watchful cooperation with the khedive. If nothing else, this would prevent the khedive from stirring up with the nationalists or anyone else intrigues that might threaten British interests in Egypt. He also sought to reduce Anglo-Egyptian tensions that had been aggravated by arrogant British behavior during Cromer's last years in Egypt.

An earlier Liberal Cabinet had blundered the British into the occupation of Egypt in 1882 because its members did not— as Robinson and Gallagher point out in *Africa and the Victorians*[35] —comprehend the Egyptian nationalist movement. Gorst, in effect the agent of another Liberal Cabinet twenty-five years later, showed some increased awareness of the nature of Egyptian grievances and attempted in a limited fashion to deal with them. During his tenure of office the insidious game of political chess involving the British Agency (later the residency and the embassy), the nationalists, and the palace began to take shape. Gorst manipulated the system quietly and deviously, but made two serious tactical errors. Kitchener, his successor, sought to divert the Egyptians' attention from self-rule and nationalism; but

his interventions in the economy and administration—
and his restructuring of the feeble political system
only to further weaken it—confirmed the British illu-
sion that their presence in Egypt was necessary.

The British inclination to interfere in Egyptian
politics, while not surprising, had the effect of
weakening Britain's clients, the system itself, and
any viable "legal" opposition.   Intervention thus came
to provide its own justification.   Gorst's policy of
self-effacement, along with his deviousness and cynicism, alienated or confused many British officials and
members of the other foreign communities.   They simply
did not know whether he believed in what he said, and
misunderstood his tactics. Too many of these men,
their imagination and political sensitivity deadened
by force of habit, were unable to comprehend what
Gorst was attempting to do.   Elizabeth Monroe accurately characterized the situation in Egypt during the
British occupation: "No other country affords such
clear proof that force of habit kills political sensitivity and imagination."[36]

Gorst made two major mistakes.   First, he chose
Butrus Ghali as prime minister.   Butrus was an able
man, but he was hated by the nationalists for his record and
distrusted by many Muslims for his Christian faith.
Second, Gorst sought to extend the Canal Company's
concession and ended by losing Ghali, the scheme itself, and the experiment in limited self-rule.   To
Gorst, the renewal of the Canal Company's concession
was fair and necessary for Egypt.   He assumed he could
persuade the Egyptians to support this proposal since
it was for their own good.   All his efforts would not
suffice.

Cleverness, as Samuel Hynes noted in his study
of the Edwardians, "seemed to frighten and offend the
English ruling class" in that era.[37]   Moreover, the
late Victorian and Edwardian eras were periods when
hypocrisy was something of a moral imperative for a
successful politician or imperial administrator.
Gorst failed in part because he could not plausibly
equivocate.   He believed in the British Empire, but
he did not accept the necessity for the autocratic
style that Cromer had developed.   He also never had
the leisured retirement, as did Cromer, to describe
his own theories and practice of imperialism.

When he instituted two repressive measures, the
Press Law and the Criminal Deportation Act, he worked
with the Egyptian Cabinet rather than simply enforcing
his power as the British Agent. By his standards
these measures were essential to Egyptian security.
He had his own conception of Egypt's needs, and he had
a clearer knowledge of Egyptians than his predecessor.
He may have miscalculated the strength of nationalist
sentiment, but he did not discount it. The measures
of repression express his appreciation of the nationalists' capacity to make trouble for the British occupation and to disturb the tranquillity of Egypt.

He refused, at the price of a bad press and the
enmity of some powerful financial interests in Egypt
and in England, to subordinate the domestic needs of
Egypt to the demands of some beleaguered speculators.
Ronald Storrs, one of his protégés in Egypt, has written: "The appeal to Empire sentiment is a mockery
worse than useless unless accompanied by the offer of
Imperial opportunities."[38] Gorst had the sense to realize that the Egyptians could not be expected to remain
content unless they were given real responsibility for
their country's affairs.

The imperialists at home were blind in their own
fashion to Egyptian realities. They never grasped
that in Egypt there were few knowledgeable men, especially after 1895, who accepted the imperial idea that
the British came as saviors and agents of European
civilization. In rejecting the Canal Company's draft
concession renewal, the General Assembly conveyed a
message to its British masters. It was not heeded.
Instead the imperialists, including Gorst, blindly
asserted that the new policy in Egypt had been too
much for the Egyptians and initiated too soon. In
fact, Gorst failed because he gave too little and it
was already too late.

Appendix 1

GENERAL INSTRUCTIONS AND REQUIREMENTS FOR
CANDIDATES FOR THE ANGLO-EGYPTIAN AND
SUDANESE CIVIL SERVICE IN 1906[1]

Civil Service

Egyptian and Sudanese Governments

The following precis of information on the Conditions
of Service and prospects of Government Civil Servants
in Egypt and the Sudan has been prepared in answer to
the numerous enquiries received by the Egyptian and
Sudanese Authorities:--

The Candidates desired are Gentlemen who have
just finished their University course, and are about
23 years of age.

Candidates will be examined by a Medical Board
both before selection and in the following year prior
to appointment. No Candidate will be selected or appointed who is not reported by the Medical Authority
to be physically fitted in all respects for work in a
tropical climate. The selection will take place in
the month of July. Applications should reach Egypt
by April 15. The application must in all cases be
made on one of the forms issued by the Egyptian and
Sudanese Governments. A Candidate who is in for his
Final Schools in June and July is not excluded by the
requirements (p. 10 of authorized form of application)
of the statement of his Degree. The circumstance
should be explained and the name sent in provisionally, and a supplementary statement forwarded immediately after the Class List appears. No married man

---

[1]F.O. 371, Vol. 67, file 27092 (August 8, 1906),
pp. 459-67.

should apply for these appointments, and an Official
who wishes to marry within the next ten years or so
will probably find it difficult to fit in his duties
with family life. The probationary year in England
and the examination at the end of it are sufficiently
described in the official document (enclosed). They
are the same for the Egyptian and Sudanese Service.
Every candidate who passes the examination and complies
with the conditions will be offered an appointment,
though it cannot be decided beforehand whether it will
be in Egypt or the Sudan. A Candidate may put down
his name for either or both Services, or may state his
preference for one or the other. The number of posts
to be allotted every year is necessarily small. All
information as to the date and place of meeting of the
Selection Board and any information which may be required in addition to that given below may be obtained
from the Secretary to the Selection Board, Finance
Ministry, Cairo; or the Secretary, University Appointments Committee, at either Oxford[,] Cambridge or
Dublin (Trinity Coll)[.]

     1. Egyptian Service.--Setting aside the more
technical Departments (Public Works, Medicine, Justice)
and the Educational Department, which is on a different footing, the careers for selected Candidates will
be mainly in the Departments of the Interior and of
Finance.

     On arriving in Egypt the approved Candidate will
probably receive an appointment as Assistant Inspector.
His salary will begin with at least ₤E.240; he will
likewise have traveling allowances, which are calculated on so liberal a scale as to make a substantial
addition to the salary. His residence will be in
Cairo, which will be his headquarters, but he will
probably spend at least 20 days in each month travelling in the Provinces. Resthouses are provided in
many places, and living will be less expensive than
in Cairo. A man will be able to live, quietly but in
fair comfort, on his first salary with the travelling
allowance.

     The main duties of the Inspector are to overlook
the work of the Native Officials, to examine registers,
to collect information and to report to the Central
Department. He will likewise have to give advice to
the Native Mamurs (District Governors) and to consult
with the Native Mudirs, or Governors of Provinces, who

are always his superiors in rank. In all these matters he will be guided by instructions issued from his
Department. In some cases the Inspector is specially
commissioned to enquire into a case which [h]as been
brought before the Department by way of petition. In
the Finance Department there is some executive work
(Land claims, Assessments of Taxation, etc.) not unlike that of the Settlement Officer in India. The
rise in salary depends on the efficiency of the Official, but there is a probability that in from five to
ten years' time an Inspector will be drawing ŁE.600 to
ŁE.700. There are certain higher posts (Police, Customs, &c.) with salaries of from ŁE.800 to ŁE.1,500,
which have hitherto generally been filled by promotion.

For the first year an Official is considered to
be a probationer, and may be discharged if not likely
to be a success. After that he can only be deprived
of his appointment for ill-health, misconduct or suppression of post.

Subject to the exigencies of the Service, furlough
(which may not be taken in the first year) is given
for two months every year on full pay, and a third
month may be allowed on half pay. Leave may be accu-
mulated, but not more than three and a half months may
be taken in any one year.

All salaries are subject to a 5% reduction for
pension. To earn a pension a man must have been under
35 at date of appointment; he must have served 25 years
and be 55 years of age, unless he has been retired
from Service after not less than 15 years for ill-
health or suppression of post. The pension is calculated on the average of last three years' salary, at
the rate of 1/60th of such average for each year of
Service, provided that no pension can exceed ŁE.600
a year.

In case of retirement on the grounds of ill-
health or suppression of post, before the completion
of 15 years' Service, there is no pension, but a lump
sum down of one month's salary for each year of Service up to ten and of three months' salary for each
year between ten and fifteen.

2. Sudanese Service.--There is a year's probation as in the Egyptian Service. The newly arrived
Official will proceed at once to Khartoum where he

will go through a three months' course to learn his
future duties.

As soon as his superiors consider him fit, he
will be transferred to one of the Provinces as Deputy
Inspector. At the completion of two years' service in
the country he will be required to pass a further examination in Arabic (chiefly colloquial and technical)
and in Law (the Sudanese codes). If he is successful
and is well reported on he may at the end of four
years' service in the Sudan be promoted to the rank of
Inspector.

When doing duty in a Province his duties will be
of an administrative nature and he will also sit as a
Magistrate to deal with civil and criminal cases. His
duties will necessitate an active life and a good deal
of his time will be spent in travelling on horse or
camel back from place to place, as his duties lead him.

At present the appointments as Governors of Provinces are held exclusively by selected British Military Officers who are generally of the rank of Major
or Lieutenant-Colonel in the British Army. British
Officers, usually drawn from those attached to the
Egyptian Army in which they hold Field Rank, also fill
certain of the appointments as Senior Inspectors and
Inspectors.

A scheme for regulating the relative seniority of
Civilian Officials and Military Officers in the ranks
of Senior Inspector and Inspector is in the course of
preparation.

In the course of time it is hoped that Civilian
Officials will become qualified for the posts of
Senior Inspectors and be eligible for eventual selec-
tion from this rank for the appointments as Governors
of Provinces at a salary of (as at present fixed)
£E.1,000 to £E.1,200 per annum.

On joining the service the lowest pay is £E.360
per annum with certain allowances for travelling, etc.,
which enables the Official to live on his pay, and
though as in the Egyptian Service the increase of pay
within the limits of a particular rank is not fixed,
a scheme is under consideration for the establishment
of three grades in each rank, through which an official
will rise in due course, obtaining a corresponding
increase in his salary. A Law regulating the Pensions

and Retirement of Officials is now in the course of settlement. It is understood that though on the same lines as the Egyptian Pension Law, it will be more liberal in its provisions.

If the exigencies of the Service permit, leave of absence is granted (after the first year) at the rate of 90 days per annum, counting from the departure of the Official proceeding on leave from Cairo, until his return to that place. During the remaining 9 months of the year the work is often hard and continuous.

The climate varies considerably in different parts of the Sudan and is trying for Europeans every-where South of Khartoum, more especially in the Bahr El Ghazal Province. To the North of Khartoum the climate is dry and bracing, although very hot in Summer, and is comparatively healthy.

3. General remarks.--In estimating the desirability of these careers, it must be remembered that one has not to deal with an old-established system like that of India, in which (apart from the great prizes) the position which each man may expect to attain, if he behaves himself, at the end of a given number of years, can be pretty accurately laid beforehand. On the other hand one has in Egypt an excellent climate and pleasant society; in the Sudan very interesting and responsible work, and in both the chance of promotion to important posts if a man shews himself really capable. Probably for the average man who is just able to do his duty neither better nor worse than his fellows, these careers offer fewer advantages than the Civil Service in India, Ceylon, etc. He will probably stick at a much lower point than if he had gone to India, or even to Ceylon. On the other hand, the very indefiniteness of the situation in Egypt (as in some of the frontier Provinces in India) gives great chances to a man of real energy and administrative ability. There is no red tape to interfere with selection. It is a matter of vital importance to those responsible for the welfare of the country that the great posts should be filled by men of practical ability and efficiency. An Official in the lower grades may be sure that his work and conduct will be carefully scrutinised by his superiors, and that merit will not be disregarded. Any day may bring out a chance for him.

Cairo, 1st May 1904.

General Instructions to Candidates selected for
Service under the Governments of Egypt and
the Soudan, subject to their passing
a Test in Arabic at the end of
their Year of Probation

I.--Probation

SELECTED candidates will, as a rule, be informed
of their provisional selection a few days after they
have been interviewed by the selecting officials, but
the definite appointment of selected candidates will
take place about a year after their selection, and
will be conditional--

(a.) On their passing a medical test;
(b.) On a continued record of diligence and
good conduct;
(c.) On their passing a test in Arabic.

II.--The Arabic Test

Having regard to the unity of the literary language throughout all Arabic-speaking (and indeed all
Mahommedan) countries, and its general employment in
the former in the press, the law courts, the schools,
and for correspondence, a knowledge of this, and not
of any colloquial dialect, will be required of the
selected candidates. Due credit will, however, be
given for any knowledge of the Egyptian vernacular
which a candidate may possess in addition to a sound
knowledge of the literary language.

In the final examination the knowledge of the
candidates will be tested in:--

1. Reading and translation of--

(a.) Specified printed texts, pointed and
unpointed;
(b.) Easy unspecified printed texts, pointed
and unpointed;
(c.) Easy manuscript in the hand ordinarily
employed in correspondence in Egypt.

2. Ability to write a legible hand--

(d.)　In copying a printed or manuscript document;

(e.)　In writing from dictation.

3.　Translation (f) oral, or (g) written, of simple English sentences, or short and easy prose passages into literary Arabic.

Additional credit and marks of distinction will also be given for--

(h.)　Correct pronunciation;
(i.)　Good handwriting;
(j.)　Ability to converse in Arabic;
(k.)　And, as remarked above, any knowledge which a candidate may have been able to acquire of the Egyptian vernacular.

Every candidate will be expected to show a respectable knowledge of the principles of Arabic grammar.

The examination will take place at Cambridge (or such other locality as may be from time to time notified), probably during the first fortnight of June, and will be to a large extent conducted orally by the Professor of Arabic and the Sheikh who assists him, and any other examiner whom it may from time to time appear desirable to add to these. Owing to the difficulty which is anticipated in finding any single time, especially at this season of the year, which will suit all the candidates, resident and nonresident, as well as the examiners, each candidate will be separately examined by the examiners, acting conjointly or successively, at such time within a given period of a week or ten days as may be agreed upon between him and them, such examination being continued in each case until each examiner has satisfied himself as to the proficiency of the candidate in each of the branches of knowledge enumerated above. A record of the examination of each candidate shall be kept by the examiners, who will report the result of the examination to the Egyptian and Soudanese Governments as soon as practicable after the conclusion of the examination. Selected candidates who fail to satisfy the examiners that they have acquired such knowledge of Arabic as may reasonably be expected in a year's diligent study are liable to rejection, which may be final and

absolute, or temporary and conditional on their passing the required test at a subsequent date as the two
Governments may from time to time determine. Excel-
lence in the examination, on the other hand, will,
caeteris paribus, increase a selected candidate's
chance of earlier and more desirable employment. The
final decision rests in all cases with the Egyptian
and Soudanese Governments, after taking cognizance of
the examiners' report.

III.--Books Prescribed or Recommended
to the selected Candidates for
the study of Arabic.

[N.B.--Books to the titles of which an asterisk is
    prefixed are supplied gratuitously to each selected
    candidate by Professor Browne, Pembroke College,
    Cambridge (to whom all further applications for
    them or for further information as to the study of
    Arabic should be addressed), on behalf of the Egyp-
    tian Government. Books not thus distinguished must
    be obtained by the candidate at their own charges
    from Messrs. Luzac, 46, Great Russell Street,
    London, W.C., or some other Oriental bookseller.]

1.--Grammars

Of the larger and more systematic grammars of
literary Arabic, the most complete and accurate is
that of the late Dr. Wright (third edition revised by
the late Professor M. J. de Goeje; Cambridge University Press, 1896). This, however, is more detailed
and minute than most learners will require or desire
in the earlier stages of their study. A convenient
abridgment of it, privately printed by the late
Frederic Du Pre Thornton, under the title of "Elemen-
tary Arabic: a Grammar," is shortly to be reprinted
by the Cambridge University Press, where a few copies
of the former edition are still kept in stock. These,
however, are not at present on sale, and, pending the
publication of this book, Socin's "Arabic Grammar"
(English edition, published in the "Porta Linguarum
Orientalium" Series) is, on the whole, recommended.
The late Professor E. H. Palmer's "Arabic Grammar" and
"Arabic Manual" may also be studied with advantage.
Green's "Practical Grammar of Egyptian Arabic" (Oxford
University Press) contains valuable material, but must

be used with great caution, since in it forms peculiar
to the literary and colloquial dialects respectively
are constantly combined in a single sentence, as no
Arabic-speaking or Arabic-writing people has ever
combined them.

Candidates are advised, if they wish to use one
grammar only, to use De Pre Thornton's, if they can
obtain it, and, failing that, Socin's.

2.--Dictionaries

For those who read French, the best dictionaries
(short of the large and expensive lexicons of Lane,
de Biberstein Kazimirski, Badger, and the like) are
the "Vocabulaire Français-Arabe" and the "Vocabulaire
Arabe-Français" (or the larger "Dictionnaire Français-
Arabe")of le Père J. Belot, published at very moderate
prices (about 8 fr. for the first, 3 fr. 50 c. for the
second, and 18 fr. for the third) by the "Imprimerie
Catholique" of the Jesuit Missionaries at Beyrout, who
have also published an Arabic-English Dictionary compiled on the same plan by le Père J. Hava (price 21 fr.).
Less complete and trustworthy, and slightly more expensive, are the two Dictionaries of Wortabet and
Porter, the smaller containing in one volume an Arabic-
English and an English-Arabic Vocabulary, the larger
consisting of an Arabic-English Vocabulary fuller than
that contained in the other volume.

3.--Reading Books

The books provisionally chosen as set subjects
for candidates selected in July 1903 are:--

*(a.)   The first volume of the "Majani'l-Adab" (a
fully vocalized chrestomathy of Arabic prose selec-
tions, compiled by le Père Cheikho).
*(b.)   The first volume of the "Alf Layla wa
Layla," or "Thousand and One Nights" (Beyrout edition).
*(c.)   "The History of Al Fakhri" (Cairo edition,
printed at the Mu'ayyad Press; or, if preferred, the
edition of Aldwardt or Derembourg).

Portions of these books will be prescribed.
Those at present prescribed in vol. 1 of the "Majani'l-
Adab" (which, being fully vocalized, is easier than

the others, and will therefore be taken first) are as
follows:--

    Pp. 24-30 (ch. iii, Proverbs, 73-4), pp. 47-54
(ch. v, Virtues and Vices, 122-137), pp. 72-87 (ch. vi,
Anecdotes, 191-219), and pp. 137-168 (ch. ix, Travels,
313-322).

    Candidates will be informed at a subsequent date
as to what portions of the two other books have been
specified.

    Other publications of the "Imprimerie Catholique"
at Beyrout recommended as specially useful to those
who study the Arabic language for practical purposes
are:--

    (d.) "Spécimens d'Écritures Arabes pour la
Lecture des Manuscrits anciens et modernes," publié
par P. L. Cheikho, S.J.; the specimens alone, 1 fr.
50 c., the same with key, 2 fr. 50 c.
    (e.) "Nouvelle Méthode de Calligraphie Arabe,"
in twelve copy-books ("cahiers"), costing 3 fr. 50 c.
(with postage, 5 fr. 10 c.), the packet of fifty.
    (f.) "L'Arabe moderne étudié dans les Journaux
et les Pièces officielles," compiled by Mr. Washington
Serruys (7 fr.).

    Many other publications of the Press are of the
greatest use to the practical students of Arabic. The
"Catalogue Spécial" of the Press (dated 1904, and com-
prising about seventy pages) can by obtained by apply-
ing "Au Directeur de l'Imprimerie Catholique, Beyrouth
(Syrie)."

    The English Agent of the "Imprimerie Catholique"
is James Parker, 27, Broad Street, Oxford; the French
Agent, Ernest Leroux, 28, Rue Bonaparte, Paris; the
German Agent, Otto Harrassowitz, 14, Querstrasse,
Leipzig.

            4.--Books on the Egyptian Vernacular

    For reasons already stated, selected candidates
are not recommended to devote much attention to the
vernacular until they have arrived in Egypt and know
in what district their work will lie. For those, however, who may desire to obtain some insight into the

peculiarities of colloquial Egyptian Arabic, the
Grammars of Willmore or Vollers (English translation
by F. C. Burkitt; Cambridge University Press) and
Spitta Bey's "Contes Arabes" are the most useful
books.

November 1903.

Notes

INTRODUCTION

1. Jemal Mohammed Ahmed, *The Intellectual Origins of Egyptian Nationalism* (London: Oxford University Press, 1960), p. 75.

2. Baron R. G. Vansittart, *The Mist Procession* (London: Hutchinson & Co., Ltd., 1958), p. 95.

3. The diaries begin in 1890; two years, 1893 and 1896, are missing, and a few pages have been excised in two others. They and a few other papers are in the possession of Gorst's daughter, Mrs. K. R. Thomas, of Castle Combe, Wiltshire. They will be cited hereafter as "Gorst Diary," with the date of entry.

4. Elizabeth Monroe, "Review of *Modernization and British Colonial Rule in Egypt*, by Robert L. Tignor," *Middle East Journal* 22 (1968):96.

5. Milner to Curzon, August 19, 1920, Milner Papers.

6. Sir Evelyn Baring was created Baron in 1891, Viscount in 1899, and Earl of Cromer in 1901.

7. Marquess of Zetland, *Lord Cromer* (London: Hodder and Stoughton, Ltd., 1932), p. 16.

8. Earl of Cromer, *Modern Egypt*, 2 vols. (London: Macmillan and Co., Ltd., 1908), 2:123, 130. The imperialist viewpoint is summarized ably in A. P. Thornton, *The Imperial Idea and Its Enemies* (London: Macmillan & Co., Ltd., 1959), pp. 241-42 *passim*.

9. Cromer, *Modern Egypt*, 2:569.

10. See Afaf Lutfi al-Sayyid, *Egypt and Cromer* (New York: Frederick A. Praeger, 1969), p. 144.

11. Peter Rowland, *The Last Liberal Governments* (New York: The Macmillan Company, 1968), p. 90.

12. See Bernard Porter, *Critics of Empire* (London: Macmillan & Co., Ltd., 1968), *passim*, for a discussion of the changes in British radical attitudes from 1895 to 1914.

13. J. P. Priestley, *The English* (Harmondsworth: Penguin Books Ltd, 1975), p. 210.

14. Peter Malcolm Holt, *Egypt and the Fertile Crescent, 1516-1922* (London: Longmans, Green & Co., Ltd., 1966), p. 226.

CHAPTER ONE

1. Sir Eldon Gorst, Autobiographical Notes, 2 vols., 1:1.
Hereafter referred to as "Gorst Notes." A family tree held by
Mrs. K. R. Thomas of Castle Combe, Wiltshire, traces the Gorst
lineage back as far as the late seventeenth century.

2. John Gorst, who had expected to be first, was consoled
by his coach: "I never knew a man take so high a mathematics
degree who knew so little mathematics as you." Harold E. Gorst,
The Fourth Party (London: Smith, Elder & Co., 1906), p. 24;
J[ohn] E[ldon] Gorst, *The Maori King* (London: Macmillan & Co.,
1864), p. 1.

3. Keith Sinclair, *A History of New Zealand* (Harmondsworth: Penguin Books Ltd, 1959), p. 110.

4. Harold Gorst, *The Fourth Party*, pp. 30, 355.

5. E. J. Feuchtwanger, "J. E. Gorst and the Central
Organization of the Conservative Party, 1870-1882," *Bulletin of
the Institute of Historical Studies* 32 (1959): 192-208.

6. Harold Gorst, *The Fourth Party*, p. 23; Clinton Dawkins
to Milner, Lima, Peru, January 4, 1892, Milner Papers, box 187.

7. Robert Rhodes James, *Lord Randolph Churchill* (London:
Weidenfeld & Nicolson, 1959), pp. 81, 371; Harold Gorst, *The
Fourth Party*; Bentley Brinkerhoff Gilbert, "Sir John Eldon Gorst:
Conservative Rebel," *The Historian* 18, no. 2 (1956): 151-69;
Myra Curtis, "John Gorst," *Dictionary of National Biography*
(Oxford: Oxford University Press, 1927), pp. 1912-21. See also
the forthcoming study by Neil Daglish on John Gorst.

8. Gorst Notes, 1:1-2.

9. Ibid., 1:3-5.

10. Ibid., 1:5-7.

11. Cyril Connolly, *Enemies of Promise* (Garden City:
Doubleday & Company, Inc., 1960), p. 221.

12. Samuel Hynes, *The Edwardian Turn of Mind* (Princeton:
Princeton University Press, 1968), p. 234. "But in fact cleverness seemed to offend the English ruling class. . . ."

13. Gorst Notes, 1:6-7.

14. Ibid., 1:9-12.

15. Ibid., 1:12.

16. T. R. Harrison, et al., eds., *Principles of Internal
Medicine* (New York: McGraw-Hill Book Company, 1966), pp. 1512-13.

17. Gorst Notes, 1:11.

18. Ibid., 1:13.

19. Ibid., 1:15-16.

20. Ronald Storrs, *Orientations* (London: Nicholson &
Watson, 1945), p. 66.

21. Vansittart, *The Mist Procession*, p. 86.

22. Gorst Notes, 1:16-19.

23. Ibid., 1:19-20.

24. Ibid., 1:18.

25. David Piper, *The Companion Guide to London* (London: Fontana Books, 1970), p. 164.
26. Sydney H. Zebel, *Balfour: A Political Biography* (Cambridge: Cambridge University Press, 1973), pp. 40-43.
27. Gorst Notes, 1:25.
28. See Zebel, *Balfour*, pp. 42-43; James, *Lord Randolph Churchill*, p. 7.
29. Gorst Notes, 1:24-26.
30. Zara S. Steiner, *The Foreign Office and Foreign Policy, 1898-1914* (Cambridge: Cambridge University Press, 1969), pp. 16-19.
31. Gorst Notes, 1:26-27.
32. Ibid., 1:27-30.
33. Ibid., 1:30-31.
34. Steiner, *The Foreign Office*, p. 11.
35. Gorst Notes, 1:31-32.
36. Ibid., 2:1-2.
37. Ibid., 1:33-34.
38. Ibid., 1:32-33.
39. Ibid., 2:2-3.

CHAPTER TWO

1. Lord Lloyd, *Egypt since Cromer*, 2 vols. (London: Macmillan & Co., Ltd., 1933), 1:2.
2. Viscount Grey of Fallodon, *Twenty-Five Years*, 2 vols. (London: Hodder & Stoughton, Ltd., 1925), 1:11. Grey described how the Germans had blackmailed the British for railway concessions in the Ottoman Empire by threatening to open the Egyptian Question in 1892.
3. Cromer to Coles, March 8, 1911, Cromer Papers, F.O. 633, vol. 20, pp. 225-26. Hereafter referred to as "Cromer Papers."
4. Ibid.; Cromer, *Modern Egypt*, 2:123-65. Other historians have disputed this judgment. See Lutfi al-Sayyid, *Egypt and Cromer*, pp. 60-64.
5. The Capitulary Powers were Great Britain, France, Italy, Germany, Austria-Hungary, Russia, Holland, Spain, Sweden, Denmark, Belgium, Portugal, Greece, the United States of America, and Brazil.
6. Lloyd, *Egypt since Cromer*, 1:21-27; Alfred Milner, *England in Egypt*, 4th ed. rev. (London: Edward Arnold, 1907), pp. 37-51; Jasper Yates Brinton, *The Mixed Courts of Egypt* (New Haven: Yale University Press, 1930), pp. 1-19.
7. The descendants of Mamluk—slave warriors—and Turkish-Balkan soldiers who had effectively ruled Egypt since the Middle Ages. Tom Little, *Modern Egypt* (New York: Frederick A. Praeger, 1969), pp. 57-58, 60-61; Milner, *England in Egypt*, pp. 319-22.

8. Milner, *England in Egypt,* pp. 184-220; Cromer, *Modern Egypt,* 2:443-45; Robert L. Tignor, *Modernization and British Colonial Rule in Egypt, 1882-1914* (Princeton: Princeton University Press, 1966), pp. 80-82.

9. Gorst Notes, 2:7.

10. Ibid., 2:9-12 *passim.*

11. Cromer to Rosebery, Cairo, March 4, 1893, Cromer Papers, vol. 7, p. 398; Gorst Notes, 2:9-10, 13-14.

12. Milner to Percy Matheson, Cairo, October 25, 1890, Milner Papers, box 183.

13. Janet L. Abu-Lughod, *Cairo: 1001 Years of the City Victorious* (Princeton: Princeton University Press, 1971), p. 115, col. 2.

14. Karl Baedeker, ed., *Lower Egypt* (London: Dulac & Co., 1885), p. 233.

15. Baring to Salisbury, Cairo, March 19, 1887 (Private), Cromer Papers, vol. 6, p. 107.

16. Gorst Notes, 2:3-6.

17. Ibid., 2:4.

18. Sir John Gorst to Baring, India Office, London, May 4, 1888, Cromer Autographs, 1:163.

19. Milner to Edith Gell, Maison Rollo, Cairo, December 27, 1889, Gell Papers, MIL-1/262/ii.

20. Ibid.

21. Princess Nazli to Milner, Cairo, August 20, 1891, Milner Papers, box 186; Storrs, *Orientations,* p. 87; Gorst Notes, 2:11.

22. Gorst Notes, 2:11.

23. Ibid., 2:18-19, 20.

24. Roger Adelson, *Mark Sykes: Portrait of an Amateur* (London: Jonathan Cape, 1975), pp. 19, 25. This excellent biography has a full and frank portrait of this remarkable woman facing p. 32.

25. Ibid., p. 19.

26. Baring to Vincent, Cairo, January 21, 1890 (Private), D'Abernon Papers, B.M. 48938, pp. 3-5.

27. Gorst Diary, December 31, 1890 and 1891. See also Adelson, *Mark Sykes,* pp. 35-36.

28. Philip Magnus, *King Edward the Seventh* (New York: E. P. Dutton & Co., Inc., 1954), p. 220.

29. Milner to Edith Gell, Maison Rollo, Cairo, April 4, 1890, Gell Papers, MIL-1/273/i.

30. Gorst Diary, April 16, 1890.

31. Ibid., August 19, 1890.

32. Ibid., September 8, 1890.

33. Ibid., December 9, 1890, February 11, July 23, 1891.

34. Ibid., Accounts, end of 1897.

35. Adelson, *Mark Sykes,* p. 69.

36. Ibid., pp. 67, 35, 54-59 (the legal problems are

effectively described by Adelson); also interview with Archibald Hunter, July 1971.

37. Gorst Notes, 2:20-21.

CHAPTER THREE

1. Gorst Notes, 2:22; see also *Egypt No. 1* (1890).
2. Joseph Chamberlain to Baring, Cairo, January 25, 1890, Cromer Papers, vol. 11.
3. Zetland, *Lord Cromer*, p. 142.
4. H. S. Deighton, "The Impact of Egypt on Britain: A Study of Public Opinion," in P. M. Holt, ed., *Political and Social Change in Modern Egypt* (London: Oxford University Press, 1968), pp. 247-48.
5. For the public relations campaign of Sir Reginald Wingate on behalf of British policy in the Sudan, see Richard Hill, *Slatin Pasha* (London: Oxford University Press, 1965), pp. 30-42, 110; Normal Daniel, *Islam, Europe and Empire* (Edinburgh: The University Press, 1966), pp. 424-59. Daniel discusses, with relevant examples, the distorted image of Islam created in the minds of the British public by British accounts of the Mahdist movement. See also P. M. Holt, "The Source-Materials of the Sudanese Mahdia," *St. Antony's Papers*, no. 4, *Middle Eastern Affairs*, no. 1, edited by Albert Hourani (London: Chatto and Windus, 1958), pp. 112-15.
6. Deighton, "The Impact of Egypt on Britain," p. 247.
7. Milner to Philip Gell, London, August 30, 1884, Gell Papers, MIL-1/126.
8. Milner to Goschen, Cairo, November 2, 1890, Milner Papers, box 182.
9. Cromer to Bell, Cairo, April 3, 1890, Moberley Bell Papers.
10. Ibid.
11. Baring to Bell, May 11, 1890 (Very Private), Moberley Bell Papers.
12. Ibid.
13. Ibid.
14. Baring to Bell, May 30, 1891, Moberley Bell Papers.
15. Archives of *The Times*.
16. Gorst Notes, 2:23-24; *The History of the Times, 1884-1912*, vol. 3: *The Twentieth Century Test* (London: Printing House Square, 1947), p. 773.
17. C. E. Coles, *Recollections and Reflections* (London: St. Catherine Press, 1918), pp. 170-71.
18. The Arabic press was allowed considerable freedom, and became a training ground for the Arab world press. It also educated many Egyptians. The British liberal tradition of freedom of the press was compatible with this policy, and for a long

while the British did not appreciate the effects this latitude would have on their control of Egypt.

19. Sydney A. Moseley, an English journalist in Egypt, recommended Cromer's press policy. He suggested that Gorst "breathed pessimism into his [annual report] and the spirit caught the people in forming their judgement of him." From reading Cromer's reports one is fully aware of his self-confidence and self-justifications. *With Kitchener in Cairo* (London: Cassell and Company, Ltd., 1917), p. 38. See also Lutfi al-Sayyid, *Egypt and Cromer*, p. 64.

20. Lutfi al-Sayyid, *Egypt and Cromer*, pp. 186-87.

21. Sir James Rennell Rodd (*Social and Diplomatic Memories, 1894-1901*, 2 vols. [London: Edward Arnold & Co., 1923], 2:100) reported that while Cromer was in Britain on one of his usual long summer vacations some "violent and gross attacks on the Queen" were made in two journals in Egypt. He obtained permission to suspend the two journals and arrested their editors. "The police courts did their duty and they were condemned to the maximum penalty, a fine and eighteen months imprisonment. . . . These prosecutions had a salutary effect, and they were in my opinion absolutely necessary." Rodd, like Cromer, blamed the khedive as "largely responsible" for this incident.

22. Sir William Willcocks, *Sixty Years in the East* (Edinburgh: William Blackwood & Sons, Ltd., 1935), pp. 116-17.

23. Ibid.

24. Gorst to Grey, Cairo, February 16, 1911 (Private), F.O. 371, vol. 1112, file 7732. David Rees, the Reuters correspondent in Cairo, was alleged to be Harry Boyle's best friend there. Boyle pulled him out of some financial difficulties, and Cromer is alleged by Mrs. Boyle to have lent Rees two thousand pounds. Rees was allowed free entry into the Agency, the only correspondent accorded that privilege. Clara Boyle wrote that "Harry and his colleagues never had the slightest occasion to regret the liberty this accorded to him [Rees]." Clara Boyle, *Boyle of Cairo* (Kendal: Titus Wilson & Son, Ltd., 1965), pp. 114-18.

25. Hill, *Slatin Pasha*, p. 110.

26. Boyle to Cromer, Berlin, May 31, 1912, Cromer Papers, vol. 21. "As regards Faris [Nimr] of course he was cut off at the same time, but that did not matter, first because the *Mokattam* was rich; and secondly, because Faris was going to give up the subvention anyway, as his paper could no longer support the policy which was being adopted by the Agency" (p. 123).

27. Lutfi al-Sayyid, *Egypt and Cromer*, pp. 96, 111, 113, 171; Willcocks, *Sixty Years*, p. 116. "At the time I had no idea that the 'Mokattom' was the mouthpiece of the British Agency."

28. J[ohn] E[dwin] Marshall, *The Egyptian Enigma, 1890-1928* (London: John Murray, 1928), p. 23. See also p. 28, where

he states that the proprietors of *al-Muqattam* "were for many years staunch supporters of the British occupation."

29. Boyle to his mother, Cairo, December 9, 1906, Boyle Papers.

30. See Joachim O. Ronall, "Julius Blum Pasha: An Austro-Hungarian Banker in Egypt, 1843-1919," *Tradition: Zeitschrift für Firmengeschichte und Unternehmerbiographie* 2 (1968), *passim*.

31. Baring to Barrington, Cairo, June 14, 1890, Cromer Papers, no. 438.

32. Gorst Diary, July 5, November 8, 1890.

33. Ibid., November 10, 1890.

34. Gorst Notes, 2:26-27.

35. Ibid., 2:25-26.

36. Gorst Diary, December 13, 1891.

37. Gorst Notes, 2:29.

38. Baring to Bell, Cairo, March 23, 1891, Cromer Letters.

39. John Marlowe, *Cromer in Egypt* (London: Elek Books, 1970), pp. 149-51.

40. Baring to Bell, Cairo, March 23, 1891, Cromer Letters.

41. Milner to Goschen, Maison Rollo, Cairo, June 4, 1890, Milner Papers, box 182, p. 3.

CHAPTER FOUR

1. Baring to Salisbury, Cairo, January 11, 1892, Cromer Papers, vol. 7, p. 388.

2. Baring to Bell, Cairo, January 9, 18, 1892, Cromer Letters. See also Milner to Beatrice Goschen, Beni Souf, February 26, 1892, Milner Papers, box 183.

3. See Lutfi al-Sayyid, *Egypt and Cromer*, chapters 6, 7 *passim*.

4. Cromer, *Modern Egypt*, 2:chapters 24, 25 *passim*.

5. Hardinge to Grey, Memo, Corfu, April 13, 1906 (Very Confidential), Hardinge Papers, vol. 8, pp. 213-14; also in Grey Papers, vol. 92.

6. Earl of Cromer, *Abbas II* (London: Macmillan & Co., 1915), p. 68.

7. Cromer to Lansdowne, Cairo, November 9, 1900, Cromer Papers, no. 328, vol. 6.

8. Lutfi al-Sayyid, *Egypt and Cromer*, p. 146.

9. Abbas in 1904 accepted a British officer as one of his ADCs, and on King Edward's birthday in November appeared—he claimed by accident—at the Abdin Palace and on Cromer's invitation reviewed the troops of occupation. This "accident" happened the next year. See Lutfi al-Sayyid, *Egypt and Cromer*, pp. 163-64; Mohamad El-Mesaddy, "The Relations between Abbas Hilmi and Lord Cromer" (Ph.D. dissertation, University of London, 1966), pp.300-9.

10. Lutfi al-Sayyid, *Egypt and Cromer*, p. 164.

11. Cromer to Grey, "Memorandum on the Present Situation in Egypt," September 1906, Consular Files, F.O. 407, vol. 169, September 1906, pp. 5-6.

12. Gorst Notes, 2:32-33.

13. Ibid., 2:36.

14. Gorst to Milner, Cairo, February 3, 1893 (Confidential), Milner Papers, box 187.

15. Gorst to Milner, Cairo, November 23, 1893, Milner Papers, box 187.

16. Ibid.

17. Cromer to Rosebery, Cairo, April 15, 1893 (Private), Cromer Papers, no. 191, vol. 6.

18. Gorst Notes, 2:38.

19. Dawkins to Milner, Cairo, August 16, 1896, Milner Papers, box 190.

20. Gorst Notes, 2:37-38.

21. Ibid., 2:39.

22. Baring to Bell, Cairo, February 11, 1892 (Private), Cromer Letters.

23. Gorst Notes, 2:40-41.

24. Cromer to Kimberley, Cairo, December 9, 1894, Cromer Papers, no. 229, vol. 7.

25. Garstin to Milner, Cairo, April 19, 1895, Milner Papers, box 189.

26. Peter Mansfield, *The British in Egypt* (New York: Holt, Rinehart and Winston, 1971), p. 123.

27. Gorst Notes, 2:39.

28. See Sir Thomas Russell Pasha, *Egyptian Service, 1902-1946* (London: John Murray, 1949) *passim;* Tignor, *Modernization,* pp. 184-85.

29. Tignor, *Modernization,* p. 183.

30. Baring to Bell, Cairo, February 11, 1892, Cromer Letters.

31. See Lord Edward Cecil, *The Leisure of an Egyptian Official* (London: Hodder and Stoughton, Limited, 1921). In this frankly racist yet humorous account, Cecil, who served under Gorst, Kitchener, and Wingate when they were proconsuls in Egypt, described the French used by Anglo-Egyptian officials: "Our 'French' is the most remarkable language, except perhaps pidgin English, in the world. It should be spoken with a strong accent to show your own independence, and is a literal, or as near a literal translation into French of the words of your own language in the order they usually occur. If you don't know the French for any word, you can either say it in our own tongue rather loud (to help the benighted foreigner to understand) or you can use any French word of somewhat similar sound, if not meaning; or again you can simply gallicize the word itself by giving it what is here believed to be a French pronunciation, thus enriching that restricted language with a new word" (pp. 102-3).

32. Interview with Archibald Hunter, Castle Combe, July 1971.

33. Clinton Dawkins, "England in 1898," in Milner, *England in Egypt*, pp. 389-90.

34. Gorst Press Cuttings, 1893-1902, vol. 1: *The Times* (London), April 29, 1890; *Le Figaro* (Paris), August 31, 1892; *New York Herald*, April 11, 1893; *Le Temps* (Paris), November 1, 1894; *The Times* (London), November 1, 1894; *The Home News*, November 2, 1894; *The Pall Mall Gazette* (London), November 27, 1894; *The African Review*, November 12, 1895; *The Globe* (London), November 12, 1895.

35. Gorst Notes, 1:46.

36. Hill, *Slatin Pasha*, p. 73.

37. Gorst Notes, 2:57. In 1896 he had a conflict over Sudanese finances with the imperious Sirdar, Kitchener. "A month later all the other parties concerned had forgotten the affair, but the sense of injustice with which I was treated has rankled in my mind ever since, and I can never again treat as a friend the Sirdar to whose duplicity and falseness I owe this unwarranted censure" (ibid., 2:49-50). See also Cecil, *Leisure of an Egyptian Official*, p. 177.

38. Storrs, *Orientations*, p. 66.

39. J. Rennell Rodd, "Milner Mission to Egypt," chapter 10, pp. 2-6, Rodd Papers. This material was never published due to a Foreign Office request.

40. Ibid.; E. S. Herbert, Gorst's brother-in-law, wrote that Gorst's weak point was "his intense cynicism." E. S. Herbert to General Maxwell, Wingate Papers, 290/2/2.

41. Vansittart, *The Mist Procession*, p. 85.

42. Dawkins to Milner, Cairo, January 9, 1896, Milner Papers, box 190.

43. Dawkins to Milner, Cairo, August 16, 1896, Milner Papers, box 190.

44. Gorst Notes, 2:43-44. In his diary for July 3, 1895, Gorst wrote: "Heard in Reuters telegram that my father had been appointed Vice President of Council (Education Minister) without seat in Cabinet. Very pleased, especially as I feared that the New Zealand Loan Company affair might be used as a pretext to leave him out in the cold."

45. Gorst Notes, 2:46.

46. Gorst Diary, June 22, 1895.

47. Ibid., September 21, December 21, 1895.

48. Dawkins to Milner, Cairo, August 16, 1896, Milner Papers, box 190.

49. Gorst Notes, 2:49.

50. Ibid., 2:46-47.

51. Ibid., 2:52-53.

52. Ibid., 2:54; Gorst Diary, January 11, 1897. K.C.M.G. is a knighthood in the Order of St. Michael and St. George, one of several orders of honors evolved by the British government,

especially in the nineteenth century.

CHAPTER FIVE

1. Gorst Notes, 2:51.
2. Ibid.
3. Interview with Archibald Hunter, Castle Combe, July 1971. Mattie Rees's photo appears in one of Gorst's scrapbooks for that era.
4. Gorst Notes, 2:29-30.
5. Gorst Diary, April 23-25, 1893.
6. Ibid., January 1, 15, 22, 24, 1894. Margaret Turnure Bevan's daughter, Mrs. Prudence de Lobinière, has photos of her grandmother; Baron and Lady Monson also have photos, plus a portrait of Romaine.
7. Ibid., March 28, April 5, 1894.
8. Ibid., May 1, 1894: "found her as charming as ever."
9. Ibid., May 4, 1894.
10. Ibid., May 12, 15, 1894.
11. Ibid., May 21, 1894.
12. Ibid., May 28, June 1, 1894.
13. Ibid., June 9, July 1, 9, 1894.
14. Ibid., July 17, 1894.
15. Ibid., March 22, 26, 29, 1895.
16. Ibid., April 2, July 26, 1895.
17. Ibid., July 16, August 19, September 2, 4, 1895.
18. Ibid., September 16, 21, 26, 1895.
19. Gorst Notes, 2:51.
20. Gorst Diary, February 4, 13, 20, June 6, 1897.
21. Gorst Notes, 2:53-54; Gorst Diary, July 20, 1897.
22. Gorst Diary, July 22, August 6, 7, 1897.
23. Ibid., September 9, 24, 1897.
24. Gorst Notes, 2:51.
25. Gorst Diary, December 18-30, 1897, January 23, 1898.
26. Gorst Notes, 2:56-57, 59-60.
27. Ibid., 2:57.
28. Ibid., 2:58: Gorst Diary, May 31, 1898.
29. Gorst Diary, June 11, 1898; Gorst Notes, 2:58.
30. Gorst Diary, July 6, 10, 1898.
31. Gorst Notes, 2:62-63.
32. Ibid., 2:63-64.
33. Gorst Diary, July 6, 9, 1899.
34. Gorst Notes, 2:70
35. Ibid., 2:70-71.

CHAPTER SIX

1. Gorst Diary, September 3, 1898.
2. Gorst Notes, 2:60-61; see also *Egypt No. 3* (1899), pp. 27-28.
3. Ibid.
4. His ex-partners were "Tommy" Allen, who left Egypt in the spring of 1899, and Valensin, who remained as Gorst's trainer. Gorst Notes, 2:72.
5. Ibid., 2:62.
6. Ibid., 2:60.
7. Storrs, *Orientations*, p. 66.
8. Gorst Notes, 2:76. Present-day lore in the Treasury echoes Gorst's assessment of the relative merits of the two orders. A Treasury official told the author in 1974 that one of his seniors advised him to "Get in the Bath and stay in the Bath." Interview with C. J. Carey, June 1974.
9. Gorst Notes, 2:77.
10. Gorst Diary, September 13, October 7, November 1, 1900; Gorst Notes, 2:76-77.
11. Gorst Notes, 2:79. Cromer was not a favorite of Edward VII, and Gorst may have suffered from his connection with Cromer.
12. Ibid., 2:85; Gorst Diary, December 16, 17, 1901.
13. Ibid., 2:78, 90-91.
14. Gorst Diary, August 24, 29, 30, September 9, 1901.
15. *The Candid Friend*, August 31, 1901, Gorst Press Cuttings, vol. 1.
16. Harold Gorst, *Much of Life is Laughter* (London: George Allen & Unwin, Ltd., 1936), pp. 204-5.
17. Gorst Diary, July 25, 1902.
18. Ibid., January 28, 29, February 15, 1903.
19. Interviews with Mrs. Prudence de Lobinière, granddaughter of Margaret Turnure, and Lady Emma Monson, wife of the present Baron Monson, July 1976.
20. Gorst Diary, March 7, 10, 15, 1903.
21. Ibid., June 24, 1903.
22. Gorst Press Cuttings, vol. 2: *The Morning Leader* (London), June 26, 1903; *The Queen* (London), July 4, 1903; *The Daily Mail* (London), June 26, 1903. Gorst's best friend from Eton, Guy Oswald Smith, would appear to have been the logical choice to be best man; from the papers Gorst left, Machell never was a close friend.
23. Gorst Diary, June 25, July 29, August 3, October 1, 1903. The car cost seven hundred eleven pounds.

24. Gorst Notes, 2:82.
25. Lansdowne to Cromer, December 7, 1903, Cromer Papers, no. 11, vol. 6, p. 359.
26. Gorst to Cromer, December 17, 1903 (Private), Cromer Papers, no. 14, vol. 6, p. 363.
27. Lansdowne to Cromer, January 5, 1904 (Private), Cromer Papers, no. 17, vol. 6: "Gorst's visit to Paris was most useful and he seems to have proceeded with great judgement and tact" p. 366; Cromer to Lansdowne, Cairo, January 15, 1904 (Private), Cromer Papers, vol. 6, p. 370: "He [Gorst] seems to have done his work extremely well."
28. Cromer to Lansdowne, February 26, 1904 (Private), Cromer Papers, no. 23, vol. 6, p. 372.
29. Cromer speech, Cairo, April 22, 1904, Cromer Papers, vol. 25, p. 81 (as printed in the collection of his speeches).
30. *The Times* (London), August 2, 1904, Wingate Papers, 234/2, 1904, marked by hand "very important."

CHAPTER SEVEN

1. Piper, *The Companion Guide to London,* p. 149; Gorst Diary, January 19, March 1, 1904.
2. Gorst Diary, Accounts 1904.
3. Gorst Notes, 2:96, 97; Gorst Diary, June 24, July 9, November 21, December 25, 1904; May 22, 1906.
4. Gorst Diary, February 11, March 26, June 3, 1905; December 8, 1906; March 16, 1907.
5. Ibid., December 22, 1905; September 29, October 23, 1906.
6. Ibid., January 5, 1907.
7. Gorst Notes, 2:98.
8. Ibid., 2:95. The countries were Belgium, Denmark, the Netherlands, Sweden, Norway, and Switzerland. See Godfrey P. Hertslet, ed., *The Foreign Office List* (London: Harrison & Sons, 1905), pp. 6-7.
9. Gorst Notes, 2:95.
10. Storrs, *Orientations,* p. 66.
11. Gorst Notes, 2:97.
12. Steiner, *The Foreign Office,* p. 107.
13. Gorst Notes, 2:95.
14. [Louis] Mallet to [Sir Francis] Bertie, January 27, 1905, Bertie Papers, vol. 174, ME/05/2, p. 25.
15. G. W. Monger, *The End of Isolation* (London: Thomas Nelson and Sons, Ltd., 1963), p. 264; Steiner, *The Foreign Office,* p. 74; Gorst Diary, November 1, 1904: "Talked to Drummond Wolfe who had been told I was to succeed Sanderson at the F.O."
16. Cromer to Grey, May 16, 1906 (Private), Grey Papers,

vol. 46, p. 106. See Robert O. Collins, *King Leopold, England and the Upper Nile, 1899-1909* (New Haven: Yale University Press, 1968), pp. 262-71, for a summary of the negotiations.

17. Gorst Notes, 2:96, 99, 104; Gorst Diary, November 15, 1904; July 22, 1905. Sir Reginald Wingate was Sirdar and governor-general of the Sudan, and Sir William Brunyate was the judicial advisor to the Egyptian government.

18. Gorst Diary, August 29, 1906; Gorst Notes, 2:101, 104.

19. Daniel, *Islam, Europe and Empire*, pp. 425-26; Hill, *Slatin Pasha*, p. 39; Deighton, "The Impact of Egypt," pp. 246-47.

20. Gorst, "The Oriental Character," *Anglo-Saxon Review* 2 (1899):47-55. A copy is in Gorst Papers.

21. Ibid.

22. Gorst, "Lord Cromer in Egypt," *The Empire and the Century* (London: John Murray, 1905), p. 766.

23. Ibid.; Cromer, *Modern Egypt*, 1:6-7, 567.

24. Gorst, "The Oriental Character," p. 9.

25. Gorst, "Lord Cromer in Egypt," p. 766.

26. Gorst, "The Oriental Character," p. 90.

27. Gorst, "Lord Cromer in Egypt," pp. 769-71.

28. Gorst, "Egypt in 1904," in Milner, *England in Egypt*, Appendix 3, pp. 413-14, 421.

29. Gorst, "Egypt: The Old Problem and the New," *Edinburgh Review* 205 (January 1907):75-76.

30. Gorst, "Lord Cromer in Egypt," p. 772.

31. Gorst Notes, 2:109.

32. Wilfrid Scawen Blunt, *My Diaries*, 2 vols. (London: Martin Secker, 1921), 2:166. Blunt also noted that Mustafa Kamil, the Egyptian nationalist leader, had told him in December that Gorst was preferable to an outsider to succeed Cromer.

33. Boyle to his mother, March 27, 1907, Boyle Papers.

34. Cromer to Grey, March 28, 1907 (Private), Cromer Papers, vol. 13.

35. Grey to Cromer, April 6, 1907, Campbell-Bannerman Papers; Campbell-Bannerman to Grey, Cannes, April 7, 1907, Grey Papers, vol. 100.

36. Gorst Diary, April 9, 1907; Gorst Notes, 2:108-9.

37. *The Egyptian Gazette* (Alexandria), April 10, 12, 1907, B.M. misc. 1291.

38. Gorst Press Cuttings, vol. 2: *The Saturday Review* (London), April 13, 1907; *The Sketch* (London), April 17, 1907; *The Methodist Times* (London), April 18, 1907; *The Bystander* (London), April 24, 1907; *The Morning Post* (London), April 26, 1907.

39. Reverend Rennie MacInnes (Cairo) to Mr. Baylis (London), April 12, 1907 (Private), nos. 13, 14, Church Missionary Society Papers, G. 3 E./05, pp. 1-2.

40. As quoted in MacInnes to Baylis, no. 17, Church Missionary Society Papers, G. 3 E./05, 1907, p. 2.

41. Storrs to his mother, Cairo, April 11, 1907, Storrs Papers.
42. Sir John Gorst to Cromer, April 18, 1907, Cromer Autographs, vol. 1, p. 58.
43. Gorst Notes, 2:109-10.
44. Gorst to Cromer, April 12, 1907, Cromer Papers, vol. 12, pp. 311-12.

CHAPTER EIGHT

1. Storrs, *Orientations*, p. 19.
2. Frederick C. Penfield, *Present-Day Egypt* (New York: The Century Co., 1903), pp. 52-53.
3. Cromer, *Modern Egypt*, 2:280-84; Milner, *England in Egypt*, p. 27.
4. Cromer, *Modern Egypt*, 2:327-33. Cromer described Taufiq as a man who "developed a considerable talent for trimming" (p. 331).
5. Arthur Goldschmidt, Jr., "The Egyptian Nationalist Party: 1892-1919," in P. M. Holt, ed., *Political and Social Change in Modern Egypt* (London: Oxford University Press, 1968), pp. 309-12; see also Lutfi al-Sayyid, *Egypt and Cromer*, chapters 6-8 *passim*.
6. Cromer to Errington Baring, Cairo, March 15, 1907, Cromer Additional Papers, 4MC A/3.
7. Charles Issawi, *Egypt: An Economic and Social Analysis* (London: Oxford University Press, 1947), p. 26; Little, *Modern Egypt*, p. 258; Tignor, *Modernization*, pp. 219-23.
8. For a description of the reorganization of the Egyptian army, see Arthur Silva White, *The Expansion of Egypt under Anglo-Egyptian Condominium* (London: Methuen and Company, 1899), pp. 287-95.
9. Vansittart, *The Mist Procession*, p. 49. Vansittart was a third secretary in the Cairo Agency in 1904; he later became permanent under secretary in the Foreign Office.
10. "Declaration respecting Egypt and Morocco," F.O. 371, vol. 68, file 39795, pp. 545-47.
11. Cromer, *Modern Egypt*, 2:262.
12. Boyle to "My Dearest Tommy," Cairo, October 30, 1899, Boyle Papers.
13. Boyle to his mother, Cairo, January 14, 1904, Boyle Papers.
14. Rodd, *Memories*, 2:19.
15. Cromer spent two periods in India: the first (1872-1876) as secretary to his cousin Lord Northbrook, the viceroy; the second (1880-1883) as financial member under Lord Ripon. For a discussion of the effects of these experiences on Cromer, see Roger Owen, "The Influence of Lord Cromer's Indian Experience

on British Policy in Egypt, 1883-1907," *St. Antony's Papers*, no. 17, *Middle Eastern Affairs*, no. 4, ed. Albert Hourani (London: Oxford University Press, 1965), pp. 109-39.

16. Zetland, *Lord Cromer*, pp. 53, 180-81.

17. Rodd, *Memories*, 2:5.

18. Willcocks, *Sixty Years*, pp. 116-17, 119.

19. P. G. Elgood, *The Transit of Egypt* (London: Edward Arnold & Co., 1928), p. 148.

20. Viscount D'Abernon, *Portraits and Appreciations* (London: Hodder and Stoughton, Ltd., 1931), p. 17.

21. Gorst Notes, 2:128; Owen, "British Policy in Egypt," pp. 128-29; Rodd, *Memories*, 2:19; Willcocks, *Sixty Years*, p. 118.

22. "Report of the Special Mission to Egypt" [the Milner Mission], *Egypt No. 1* (1921), p. 30; Owen, "British Policy in Egypt," p. 131; Cromer, *Modern Egypt*, 2:134-40.

23. P. J. Vatikiotis, *The Modern History of Egypt* (New York: Frederick A. Praeger, 1969), p. 239; Cromer, *Modern Egypt*, 2:260-64. See also Harold Nicolson, *Portrait of a Diplomatist* (New York: Harcourt, Brace & Co., 1930); Steiner, *Foreign Office and Foreign Policy:* Lord Hardinge initiated some long overdue administrative reforms in the Foreign Office machinery when he was permanent under secretary from 1906 to 1910. The diplomatic and consular corps, "also in crying need of reform," according to Nicolson, then a very junior member of the Foreign Office, conducted its business well into the 1920s on a system devised for conditions of diplomacy in the 1840s (p. 238).

24. Storrs, *Orientations*, pp. 18-19, 22-23, 143.

25. Coles, *Recollections*, pp. 170-71.

26. Rodd, *Memories*, 2:29.

27. For an example, see Lutfi al-Sayyid, *Egypt and Cromer*, pp. 143-44.

28. D. G. Hogarth, "Lord Cromer Today," *Fortnightly Review* 110 (September 1921):470.

29. Cromer to St. Loe Strachey, Cairo, April 3, 1906, Cromer Papers, vol. 8 (Cromer refused partly because his health was declining, but also because, as he wrote to Strachey, editor of *The Spectator:* "I greatly feared I should become responsible for socialist legislation which would run counter to all my most cherished convictions." He thought that the Liberal government would misgovern South Africa, and that India was in bad shape through no fault of Curzon's; he did not want to be involved.).

30. Lutfi al-Sayyid, *Egypt and Cromer*, pp. 65-67; Cromer, *Modern Egypt*, 2:325-26, 567: the result of British withdrawal, he wrote in his apologia, would be "a personal rule of the Oriental type"; the irony is that Cromer had created much the same system as he claimed to be avoiding; Hogarth, "Lord Cromer Today," p. 470.

31. In 1905 Cromer was granted extra leave by the Foreign

Office when his doctors advised him to get more rest, since he had been "living on his capital"; Cromer to Lansdowne, Cairo, April 30, 1905, Cromer Papers, vol. 6. The death of his first wife had profoundly affected his morale and, despite a second marriage, he attributed his flagging energies to that loss: Cromer to Grey, Cairo, March 28, 1907, Campbell-Bannerman Papers, B.M. add. 41218. See also Zetland, *Lord Cromer*, 2:286-89; Clara Boyle, *A Servant of the Empire* (London: Methuen & Co., Ltd., 1938), p. 62.

32. See Robert Rhodes James, *Rosebery* (London: Weidenfeld & Nicolson, 1963), pp. 277-80, for a description of Cromer's overreaction in an earlier crisis in the 1890s.

33. General Sir James Marshall-Cornwall, "An Enigmatic Frontier," *The Geographical Journal* 125 (September-December 1959):459.

34. Ibid.; see also Cromer, *Modern Egypt*, 2: "It was undesirable to bring Turkish soldiers down to the banks of the Suez Canal" (pp. 268-69).

35. Cromer, *Modern Egypt*, 2:269.

36. Cromer to Grey, Cairo, March 17, 1906, Grey Papers, vol. 46, p. 30; Lutfi al-Sayyid, *Egypt and Cromer*, p. 166. The Jennings-Bramly Papers, Royal Geographical Society, London, "Correspondence respecting the Turco-Egyptian Frontier," contains the official letters and private papers of W. E. Jennings-Bramly, who led the Anglo-Egyptian detachment to Aqabah in January 1906.

37. Cromer to Grey, Cairo, March 17, 1906, Grey Papers, vol. 46, p. 33; Findlay to Hardinge, Cairo, March 24, 1906, Grey Papers, vol. 46, p. 39; Vatikiotis, *Modern History of Egypt*, p. 212; Farhat J. Ziadeh, *Lawyers and the Rule of Law and Liberalism in Modern Egypt* (Stanford: Hoover Institution Publications, 1968), p. 65; Lutfi al-Sayyid, *Egypt and Cromer*, p. 169.

38. In the finest traditions of gunboat diplomacy, the massing of elements of the British fleet in the eastern Mediterranean and the presentation of an ultimatum to the Sublime Porte to evacuate the troops from the area in dispute and to submit the issue to a British-controlled arbitration commission led to the sultan's capitulation on May 10. The Jennings-Bramly Papers contain a significant disagreement with the official accounts of the "Aqabah" [Tabah] dispute:

W. E. Jennings-Bramly, described in his obituary (*The Times* [London], March 12, 1960) as "among the last of the romantic eccentrics of the Arab world, where now nationalism allows no time for such men to work their good," was sent by Cromer to Sinai with some Egyptian troops to reconnoiter in January 1906. Cromer's verdict is that "he did not do well, but that was because he did not understand dealing with the Turks" (Cromer to Lord Crewe, Cromer Papers, vol. 23, pp. 201-02). Jennings-Bramly may not have "done well" in Cromer's judgment because he

felt that the British claims for the Egyptians in the area were
false, as was indicated in his papers in the Royal Geographical
Society. In a gloss on the Cromer report on the crisis he wrote:
"The contention from beginning to end of this report is not to
consider Turkey's claim as correct but to consider if Turkey's
claim would be prejudicial to our British interests in the canal
zone" (p. 10 attached to *Egypt No. 2* [1906], "Correspondence on
the Turco-Egyptian Frontier," in the Jennings-Bramly Papers).
Jennings-Bramly alleges that the Germans advised the Porte, on
the basis of an 1841 map that showed the territory allotted to
Muhammad Ali, to claim all the territory south of the Suez-
Rafah line. "The line Tabah-Akabah was the invention of a
moment, probably Harry Boyle, it had never been heard of before"
("A Short Account of the Boundary Dispute and the Probable
Effect on the Tribes," Jennings-Bramly Papers, p. 219). In 1927
he wrote, "I have never understood why Turkey did not produce the
[1841] map." The map was lost or had "disappeared" in Egypt,
but "when [Ahmad] Ziwar [Pasha, the Egyptian prime minister]
applied to Turkey for it in 1925, it was produced in a very
short time . . . and it was printed by the Egyptian Government
and attached to the agreement between Egypt and Italy concluded
for that year [1927]" (p. 10 attached to *Egypt No. 2* [1906],
Jennings-Bramly Papers).

Cromer admitted to the Foreign Office on May 16, 1906 that
the Egyptian claim to the area may have been weak. "If he
[Mukhtar, the Ottoman high commissioner in Egypt] had kept
tinkering on over Taba alone, he would have put us in considerable difficulty, for it would have been difficult to justify
strong action on this small incident" (Cromer to Grey, Grey
Papers, vol. 46, p.104).

39. Cromer to Grey, Cairo, May 5, 1906, Grey Papers,
vol. 46, pp. 85-86. Lord Hugh Cecil, a son of the Marquess of
Salisbury,was one of the most fanatical defenders of the prerogatives of the titled class in England in the Edwardian era, but
on the basis of intense intellectual and religious beliefs.

40. Humphrey Bowman, Egypt, May 1, 1906, in Journal: September 1905-March 1910, Bowman Papers.

41. Findlay to Hardinge, Cairo, March 24, 1906, Grey
Papers, vol. 46, p. 39.

42. Minto to Morley, May 7, 1907, Grey Papers, vol. 98.
Lord Minto, viceroy of India, observed that under the present
circumstances there need be no anxiety about the employment of
Indian Muslim troops against the Turks, but should a holy war be
declared there would be cause for serious anxiety in India. A
copy of a memorandum of the Government of India on the fanatical
feelings of Muslims in India in response to recent pressures on
Turkey and the sultan includes reports of chief executives of
provinces in the Indian Civil Service (F.O. 371, July 26, 1906,
no. 25468 and Simia, Foreign Dept. no. 85, June 28, 1906,

vol. 67, pp. 411-26). See also Lloyd, *Egypt since Cromer*, 1:45.
There had been anti-partition riots in Bengal in 1905-1906 and
the wave of violence turned into a terrorist movement in 1907.
See B. N. Panday, *The Break-up of British India* (New York:
St. Martin's Press, 1969), p. 69.

43. O'Conor to Grey, Constantinople, May 15, 1906 (Private),
Grey Papers, vol. 79: O'Conor, the British ambassador to the
Sublime Porte, wrote: "I regard the political result as very
important as it clearly establishes the principle of our right
to interfere in all matters concerning Egypt." Cromer to Grey,
Cairo, May 16, 1907, Grey Papers, vol. 46, pp. 102-03.

44. General Staff Memorandum, CID, Cab. 3812, June 26,
1906. This document indicated that the British garrison numbered 4,010 in April 1906, and about 5,400 after reinforcement.
About 3,500 troops were stationed in Cairo; the remainder, ap-
proximately 1,900, in Alexandria.

45. General John Maxwell to Gorst, Cairo, November 29,
1910, F.O. 371, vol. 895.

46. Cromer to Wingate, Halkirk, Scotland, July 24, 1905,
Wingate Papers, 473/4, pp. 2-3. The Egyptian army was kept
under British supervision until 1936. The late President
Nasser was among the first class of cadets admitted to the
Egyptian military academy after British control over officer
candidates was relaxed.

47. Maxwell to Gorst, Cairo, November 29, 1910, F.O. 371,
vol. 895.

48. Cromer to Grey, Cairo, May 30, 1906, F.O. 141, vol.
397, pp. 267-69. In his dispatch Cromer also complained that
an excessive number of dependents arrived with the reinforcements.

49. Cromer to Grey, Cairo, June 14, 1906, F.O. 371, no. 190,
vol. 66, p. 1; Cromer to Grey, Cairo, June 17, 1906, F.O. 371,
vol. 66, pp. 46-47.

50. Rodd, *Memories*, 2:301-3; Zetland, *Lord Cromer*, p. 29.
Both describe the handling of such incidents. Rodd asserted
that British dignity had to be upheld, even at the cost of
stretching the law.

51. *Egypt No. 3* (1906), "Correspondence respecting the
attack on British officers at Denshawai," vol. 137, Cd. 3086,
July 1906, pp. 3-4.

52. Arthur E. P. Brome Weigall, *A History of Events in
Egypt from 1798 to 1914* (London and Edinburgh: William Blackwood
& Sons, 1915), p. 203.

53. Boyle to his mother, Cairo, June 18, 1906, Boyle
Papers.

54. Cromer to Grey, Cairo, June 19, 1906, F.O. 371,
no. 194, vol. 66.

55. *The Egyptian Gazette* (Alexandria), June 19, 1906, B.M.
1291. Ghali's career is described in S. M. Seikaly, "The Copts
under British Rule, 1882-1914" (Ph.D. dissertation, University

of London, 1967), pp. 161-225.

56. Lutfi al-Sayyid, *Egypt and Cromer*, p. 171.

57. A Lieutenant Smithwick acted as commander of the rear guard to the column that escorted the prisoners to Dinshawai; apparently this is the same Lieutenant S. J. Smithwick who was one of the five officers of the Royal Dublin Fusiliers assaulted at the village on June 13, 1906. The gallows were brought from Cairo the day of the sentencing, June 27. See *Egypt No. 3* (1906), p. 18, and *Egypt No. 4* (1906), pp. 60-61; *The Egyptian Gazette* (Alexandria), June 29, 1906; another description of the collective punishment of the Dinshawai villagers can be found in Mansur Mustafa Rifat, "Lest We Forget" (Hoover Institution, Middle East Collection, Stanford), a pamphlet that contains photographs showing the prisoners being flogged and hanged.

58. Lloyd, *Egypt since Cromer*, 1:47.

59. This discussion of the Dinshawai incident has drawn heavily on the impressions conveyed in the reports from Egypt by British officials in the Foreign Office Archives and from A. H. Hourani, *Arabic Thought in the Liberal Age* (London: Oxford University Press, 1962), p. 201; Lutfi al-Sayyid, *Egypt and Cromer*, pp. 169-75; Ahmed, *The Intellectual Origins of Egyptian Nationalism;* Vatikiotis, *The Modern History of Egypt*, pp. 194-95.

60. There were exceptions: Sir Charles Dilke was a lonely example of a Liberal M.P. concerned with native problems. See Porter, *Critics of Empire*, chapter 3 *passim*.

61. Thornton, *The Imperial Idea*, p. 125 *passim*; Porter, *Critics of Empire*, pp. 293-94.

62. Memorandum by the Earl of Cromer, July 12, 1906, *Egypt No. 3* (1906) p. 20.

63. George Bernard Shaw, *John Bull's Other Island and Major Barbara* (New York: Brentano's, 1907), pp. xlvi-lxii. Shaw's description, or reconstruction, of the hangings and floggings is particularly sarcastic and funny.

64. The press reaction to the Dinshawai incident is outlined in El-Masaddy, "The Relations between Abbas Hilmi and Lord Cromer," pp. 366-70.

65. Great Britain, *Parliamentary Debates* (Commons), 4th ser., 160(1906): 314-17.

66. As early as July 14, 1906, doubts about the evidence on which the sentences were based had begun to appear in Foreign Office correspondence. On that day Gorst minuted on a dispatch by Findlay from Cairo: "We shall have to decide whether to omit the opinion of W. Hayter and Judge Bond when Findlay's No. 196 is published. I am afraid the case for 'premeditation' is not as strong as could be wished." Findlay to Grey, Cairo, June 27, 1906, no. 196, F.O. 371, vol. 66. In his memoirs Grey admitted: "When the full facts were before me I felt that what had been done was open to question." Grey, *Twenty-Five Years*, 1:133.

67. Memorandum of the Earl of Cromer, London, July 12, 1906, no. 15, *Egypt No. 3* (1906), p. 20.

68. Cromer to Gorst, Cairo, October 19, 1906, Grey Papers, vol. 46, pp. 171-72; Cromer to Grey, Cairo, October 24, 1906, no. 186, F.O. 371, vol. 68, p. 362a.

69. Cromer to Grey, Cairo, October 24, 1906, Cromer Papers, vol. 13.

70. Cromer to Grey, Cairo, December 13, 1906, Cromer Papers, vol. 13, pp. 16-17. See also Cromer to Grey, Cairo, November 15, 1906, Cromer Papers, vol. 13, p. 8; Grey to Cromer, London, January 18, 1907 (Private), Cromer Papers, vol. 13, p. 14.

71. Grey to Cromer, London, March 1, 1907, Cromer Papers, vol. 13, p. 14.

72. Cromer to Grey, Cairo, March 7, 1907, Cromer Papers, vol. 13; this letter is also found in the Grey Papers, vol. 46.

73. Grey to Cromer, London, March 15, 1907, Grey Papers, vol. 36; Cromer to Grey, Cairo, March 22, 1907, Grey Papers, vol. 36, p. 341.

74. Grey, *Twenty-Five Years,* 1:133-34. Both Grey and Cromer felt it more important to uphold authority on the spot, for they judged that not supporting the officials would undermine their confidence and encourage further unrest on the part of the Egyptians.

There are indications that one of the judges, Walter MacGeough Bond, vice-president of the native court of appeal, may have been partially responsible for the extreme harshness of the sentences. J. E. Marshall, a judge who served under Bond on the native court of appeal, described in *The Egyptian Enigma* the latter's conduct as a member of the Dinshawai special tribunal: "Bond virtually conducted the proceedings. . . . The case was conducted with such a want of method that when minutes of the proceedings were called for by Parliament in London, they had to be compiled from reports made by native journalists for their papers" (p. 83).   There is some correspondence about Bond in the Foreign Office files. Findlay wrote to Grey in early July 1906 that Bond and William Hayter, another judge, had objected to being quoted by Grey in the House of Commons as having no doubts that an English court would have convicted the first six men. Grey had quoted in the House what Findlay had reported to him earlier. A letter from Bond to Findlay appears to be more self-justification than denial. Findlay wrote that it was advisable to placate Bond, "as his influence with Egyptian judges would be impaired" if it was not done. "He has been most useful." W. MacGeough Bond to Findlay, Cairo, July 6, 1906, F.O. 141, vol. 404; Findlay to Grey, Alexandria, July 13, 14, 1906, nos. 217, 219, F.O. 371, vol. 66, p. 203.

In a 1909 letter to Grey concerned with Egyptian judicial reforms, Cromer described the foreign judges as underpaid and incompetent, and went on to illustrate his point: "When I tell

you that Bond, who was really more than any other individual
responsible for getting us into the Denshawai trouble, was the
best among the Judges, you will be able to form a very correct
idea of the capacity of the remainder." Cromer to Grey,
October 29, 1909, Cromer Papers, vol. 14, p. 106.

75. Cromer to Grey, August 2, 1907 (Private), Grey Papers,
vol. 106: "I admit the difficulty of defending the great severity of the sentences, but I hope you will not go too far in the
way of concessions."

In 1911 he wrote to "My Lady Khan" of her book (Gertrude
Bell, *Amurath to Amurath* [London: Macmillan & Co., 1924]): "It
was a bitter pill for me when, as you very truly say (p. 196)
the folly of a few young officers and the lies of those Englishmen who are friends of every country but their own, went far to
wreck the good, outside Egypt, which might have been done by
Egyptian example." Miss Bell had discussed on p. 196 the reaction of a dervish leader in Bagdad to the Dinshawai incident.
Cromer to "My Lady Khan," January 14, 1911, Cromer Papers,
vol. 20, pp. 157-58.

76. Findlay to Foreign Office, Alexandria, September 10,
1906, no. 158, F.O. 371, vol. 67, p. 115; Findlay to Grey, Cairo,
February 16, 1907, Grey Papers, vol. 46, pp. 271-72; Ronald
Storrs wrote: "Ronald Graham succeeded Charles de Mansfeld
Findlay, remembered in Egypt chiefly for his misfortune in having
having acted for Lord Cromer throughout the Denshawai incident of
of 1906." *Orientations,* p. 64.

CHAPTER NINE

1. Findlay to Hardinge, Cairo, March 24, 1906, Grey
Papers, vol. 46, p. 39: "One must live in Egypt to understand
the phenomenal weight of Lord Cromer's prestige," Admiralty to
Foreign Office, July 16, 1906 (Admiralty M-0992), F.O. 371,
vol. 67, p. 302; Findlay to Foreign Office, Alexandria, July 24,
August 20, 1906, F.O. 371, vol. 67, nos. 228, 238, pp. 238, 311.

2. Findlay to Foreign Office, Alexandria, July 13, 20,
1906, nos. 125, 215, F.O. 371, vol. 67, file 26092, pp. 436-39.

3. Admiralty to Foreign Office, October 18, 1906
(Admiralty M-01272), F.O. 371, vol. 67, p. 320.

4. *Al-Muqattam* was receiving a subvention from the Agency
during this period.

5. Boyle to Cromer, Cairo, September 10, 1906, Hardinge
Papers, vol. 8, pp. 40-42.

6. Findlay to Foreign Office, Alexandria, September 15,
1906, no. 254, F.O. 371, vol. 68.

7. Bowman Journal, September 27, 1906, Bowman Papers.
Bowman became an inspector of schools in the department of education in April 1906.

8. Cromer, "Memorandum on the present situation in Egypt," F.O. 407, vol. 167, pp. 12-13. John Morley, secretary of state for India, had some significant and critical observations on the memo: "I have read and re-read Cromer's Memo. The parallel with Indian difficulties is almost startling. But I note what I take to be essential differences, eg on p. 3, I don't think Pan Islamism is [not readable] . . . means any of these things. Again I wonder if it is true of India as he says of Egypt (p. 6) that the only people who really take an interest in the welfare of the mass of the people are the English officials." Morley to Grey, October 12, 1906, F.O. 407, vol. 98.

9. See Cromer, "Memorandum on the present situation in Egypt," *passim;* Cromer to Grey, September 8, 1906, F.O. 371, vol. 68, file 41129, pp. 600-606; *Egypt No. 1* (1907), pp. 5-8.

10. Cromer, *Egypt No. 1* (1906), pp. 1-7; idem, *Egypt No. 1* (1907), pp. 10-26.

11. Cromer, *Egypt No. 1* (1906), p. 12.

12. Cromer, *Egypt No. 3* (1907), pp. 1, 4.

13. Cromer, *Egypt No. 1* (1907), pp. 12, 13, 32.

14. Cromer, *Modern Egypt,* 1:287-90. See especially Seikaly, "The Copts under British Rule," for a discussion of the reform movement in the Coptic community and the British efforts to use the Copts for their own ends; this is the major source for this section.

15. Seikaly, "The Copts under British Rule," pp. 47-48, 54-60, 88. The author writes that the victory of the British elicited unmitigated jubilation from the Copts, who cheered the British troops in Cairo (p. 106).

16. Ibid., pp. 29, 78.

17. Ibid., pp. 103, 171.

18. See "Memorandum on the British Occupation of Egypt: The Copts," in Clara Boyle, *Boyle of Cairo,* pp. 56-58; Seikaly, "The Copts under British Rule," p. 129.

19. Reverend MacInnes was secretary of the Church Missionary Society in Cairo from 1902 to 1903 and bishop of Jerusalem from 1914 to 1931. He was the last of a trio of young university men who were sent by the CMS in answer to "Cromer's challenge to get on or get out," and was the "master of a very simple, rather limited, quite practical, effective Arabic style." See *In Memoriam, Rennie MacInnes, D.D.* (pamphlet), CMS archives, London (p. 16).

20. MacInnes to Reverend Frederick Baylis, Cairo, April 12, 1907 (Private), CMS Archives, G 3, /05, 1907, no. 14, p. 7. This letter describes in detail an interview granted by Cromer to MacInnes on March 4, 1907. Baylis was the secretary for CMS foreign department (for Egypt) in the 1900s.

21. Ibid., pp. 5-6.

22. Ibid., pp. 10-14.

23. Ibid., pp. 10-15; MacInnes wrote Baylis: "One was

naturally anxious after the interview, at first, to write something of the sort he [Cromer] suggested, but on thinking it over
I do not see how one can write anything that would do what Lord
Cromer means, without saying what we think of the Nationalist
movement, and this would lead on to a defense of the Lord
Cromer's policy, which in the first place it is not our business,
and in the second place, we could not give it at all without at
the same time criticising his policy in the matter of exalting
the Mohammedans to the detriment of the Copts, in the matter of
Sunday, and other questions"(p. 15).

24.   Cromer to MacInnes, April 28, 1907, in MacInnes to
Baylis, Cairo, May 11, 1907, CMS archives, no. 17, Egypt/05,
1907, p. 3.

25.   MacInnes to Baylis, Cairo, May 11, 1907, CMS archives,
no. 17. Egypt/05, 1907, p. 3.

26.   Ibid., pp. 4-5.

27.   Ibid., p. 9.

28.   The khedive showed "no enthusiasm" for the appointment.   Cromer to Grey, Cairo, October 27, 1906, Cromer Papers,
vol. 13.

29.   Cromer to Grey, Cairo, November 2, 1906, Cromer
Papers, vol. 13, pp. 6-7, Grey Papers, vol. 46; see also Cromer
to Grey, Cairo, November 27, 1906, Cromer Papers, vol. 13,
pp. 182-83: "Zaghlul is a real working man, not a mere dummy.
He belongs, not to the Nationalist Party, but to the school of
bona fide Mohammedan reformers to whom I alluded in my memo"
(pp. 4-5).

30.   Cromer to Grey, Cairo, November 2, 1906, Grey Papers,
vol. 46, pp. 182-83.

31.   Cromer to Grey, Cairo, November 2, 1907, F.O. 371,
vol. 68, pp. 288-89.   Lord Hardinge, the permanent under secretary at the Foreign Office, minuted sarcastically, "It only
shows how easily public opinion in Egypt is swayed" (p. 284).

32.   Ibid.

33.   Cromer, *Egypt No. 1* (1906), pp. 36, 82, 84.

34.   Cromer to Gorst, Cairo, February 28, 1907, Grey
Papers, vol. 46, pp. 279-80; Cromer, *Egypt No. 1* (1907), p. 88.

35.   Wells had been on the faculty of the Battersea College of Technology.

36.   Cromer to Grey, Cairo, January 3, 1907, no. 1, F.O.
371, vol. 246, file 1210.

37.   Lutfi al-Sayyid, *Egypt and Cromer*, p. 178; Findlay
to Grey, Cairo, August 5, 1906, no. 140, F.O. 371, vol. 67,
file 27566.   This dispatch described a "new departure" (p.486)
by Egyptians of high standing to establish a moderate newspaper.   Reactions at the Foreign Office were pleased but pessimistic.   Gorst minuted: "Moderation and veracity are not qualities that pay in journalism, but we must hope that in spite of
this 'El Jeridah' will succeed."   Grey added, "A matter of

276   *Notes to pages 132-136*

hope rather than expectation, I fear" (p. 482).

38. Lutfi al-Sayyid, *Egypt and Cromer*, p. 189; also see
Ahmed, *The Intellectual Origins*, chapters 3-5 *passim;* Nadav
Safran, *Egypt in Search of Political Community* (Cambridge:
Harvard University Press, 1961), chapter 6 *passim;* Hourani,
Arabic Thought, pp. 171-83.

39. Grey to Cromer, London, December 6, 1906 (Private),
Cromer Papers, vol. 13.

40. Cromer to Grey, Cairo, December 18, 1906, No. 228,
F.O. 371, vol. 68, p. 675.

41. Cromer to Grey, Cairo, December 26, 1906; January 12,
17, 1907, Cromer Papers, vol. 13, pp. 19, 26, 28; Cromer to
Grey, Cairo, January 17, 1907, Grey Papers, vol. 46, p. 227.

42. Grey, "Memorandum to the Cabinet on the duration of
the occupation of Egypt," January 30, 1907, Cab 37/86, p. 2;
Cromer to H. P. Kingham, on the Nile, February 18, 1907, F.O.
371, vol. 246, file 6822. Kingham was president of the British
chamber of commerce at Alexandria. The letter is reproduced in
Cromer, *Egypt No. 1* (1907), p. 104.

43. William Brunyate, "Note on the Constitutional Reform
in Egypt," November 18, 1918, Milner Mission Papers, F.O. 848,
vol. 18. Brunyate was an official in Egypt during the Cromer
era and until 1919. He wrote: "I was much at that time in touch
with Lord Cromer, and while I cannot now recall any direct ref-
erences on his part to the feature of the situation, he gave me
very definitely the impression of a man who realized that the
situation had undergone a material change (since 1904) and who
was feeling for support for some new policy. In the main in the
new policy in 1904, 1905, and 1906 he tended to lean increasingly on the support of foreign colonies."

44. Cromer, *Egypt No. 1* (1907), pp. 43, 101.

45. Cromer, farewell address, Cairo, May 4, 1907, *The
Times* (London), May 6, 1907, p. 5, cols. 2, 4.

46. Lutfi al-Sayyid, *Egypt and Cromer*, p. 183.

47. Cromer to Lansdowne, Cairo, April 30, 1905, Cromer
Papers, vol. 6, p. 329; he also had financial problems, declaring
that he could not manage on his annual salary of sixty-five
hundred pounds, and asked for an increase, p. 330; Cromer to
Grey, Cairo, February 6, March 22, 1907, Grey Papers, vol. 46,
pp. 258-59, 344-45; Findlay to Hardinge, March 24, 1907, Grey
Papers, vol. 46, reported that Cromer was not well; Cromer to
Grey, Cairo, March 28, 1907, Campbell-Bannerman Papers, also in
Cromer Papers, vol. 13, p. 68.

48. Cromer to Grey, March 28, 1907, Cromer Papers,
vol. 13, p. 68: "If I were younger, I should rather enjoy fight-
ing the Khedive and Mustafa Kamel and his English allies, and
moreover, I think I should beat them."

49. Findlay to Hardinge, Cairo, March 30, 1907, Grey
Papers, vol. 46, pp. 361-63.

50. Ibid.

51. E. R. J. Owen, *Cotton and the Egyptian Economy, 1820-1914* (Oxford: Clarendon Press, 1969), pp. 283-87.

52. From an editorial by Mustafa Kamil in *The Egyptian Standard,* March 30, 1907, in Findlay to Hardinge, April 14, 1907, Grey Papers, vol. 46, pp. 378-84.

53. Thomas Russell to his father, April 19, 1907, Russell Papers.

54. Cromer to Grey, Cairo, April 19, 1907, Grey Papers, vol. 46, pp. 394-96.

55. Cromer to Grey, April 22, 1907, Grey Papers, vol. 46, p. 397.

56. Grey to Cromer, May 1, 1907, Grey Papers, vol. 46, p. 403.

57. Cromer to Grey, April 27, 1907, no. 72, F.O. 371, vol. 248, file 14376; Gorst to Grey, May 18, 1907, F.O. 371, vol. 248, file 17626. Gorst observed that the khedive "seemed none the worse for Lord Cromer's speech. Of course I cannot say how long the honeymoon will last."

58. Storrs to his mother, April 24, 30, May 5, 1907, Storrs Papers, box II, 1.

59. Ronald Graham, "Observations on Future British Policy with regard to Egypt," February 3, 1917, Wingate Papers, 237/10, p. 8.

60. Grey to Cromer, Cairo, April 5, 1907 (Private), Cromer Papers, vol. 13, pp. 29-31.

CHAPTER TEN

1. Gorst to Milner, Cairo (Private), November 23, 1893, Milner Papers, box 187.

2. Findlay to Hardinge, March 30, 1907 (Private), Grey Papers, vol. 46, pp. 361-63; Russell to his father, April 19, 24, 1907, Russell Papers.

3. Cromer to Grey, April 19, 1907, Grey Papers, vol. 46, p. 394.

4. Great Britain, *Parliamentary Debates* (Commons), 4th ser., 172 (1907): 1138.

5. Gorst to Grey, April 30, 1907 (Private), Grey Papers, vol. 46, pp. 399-400; Gorst Diary, April 24, 1907.

6. Gorst Notes, 2:115.

7. Russell to his father, April 24, 1907, Russell Papers.

8. Gorst to Grey, May 11, 1907, Grey Papers, vol. 46, p. 408.

9. Storrs to his mother, April 24, 1907, Storrs Papers, box II-1.

10. Gorst to Grey, May 11, 1907, Grey Papers, vol. 46, p. 408.

278 *Notes to pages 142-148*

11. Storrs to his mother, May 5, 1907, Storrs Papers, box II-1.

12. *La Bourse Egyptienne* (Cairo), May 7, 1907, Storrs Papers, box II-1: The paper noted the presence of Ronald Graham, who supervised the precautionary forces; Gorst Diary, May 6, 1907: "Streets lined with troops & immense crowd at the station"; Graham, "Observations on the Future of British Policy with Regard to Egypt," February 3, 1917, Wingate Papers, 237/10, p. 80.

13. *The Egyptian Gazette* (Alexandria), May 7, 1907, Storrs Papers, box II-1. Storrs, *Orientations*: "He drove to the station . . . through streets lined by troops armed with Ball cartridge, amid a silence chillier than ice" (p. 103).

14. Gorst to Grey, May 11, 1907, Grey Papers, vol. 46, p. 409.

15. Gorst Notes, 2:111-15.

16. Ibid., 2:111.

17. Ibid., 2:113-16.

18. Grey to Gorst, May 1, 1907, Grey Papers, vol. 46, p. 404; Gorst to Grey, May 11, 1907, Grey Papers, vol. 46, pp. 408-10.

19. Duke of Connaught, April 30, 1907, "Inspection of Troops and Defenses in Egypt," F.O. 371, vol. 248, file 15760.

20. Gorst Notes, 2:116.

21. Gorst to Grey, May 18, 1907, F.O. 371, vol. 247, file 17626; Gorst Diary, May 17, 1907.

22. Gorst to Grey, May 18, 1907, F.O. 371, vol. 247, file 17626.

23. Gorst to Grey, June 10, 1907, Grey Papers, vol. 46, pp. 413-14; George Young, *Egypt* (London: Ernest Benn, Ltd., 1927), pp. 157-58.

24. Gorst to Grey, June 10, 1907, Grey Papers, vol. 46, pp. 414-15. The prime minister and the Lord Privy Seal (the Marquess of Ripon) both initialed this dispatch.

25. Gorst Notes, 2:117.

26. Storrs, *Orientations*, p. 71; Storrs, "Sir Eldon Gorst," *The Near East* (July 19, 1911), Storrs Papers, box II-1, pp. 2-3; Carl Meyer to Lord Rothschild, July 22, 1912, "City Views on Egypt," PRO 30/57, vol. 42, pp. 1-2; Douglas Sladen, *Egypt and the English* (London: Hurst & Blockett, Ltd., 1908), pp. 155-56; Gorst to Grey, March 28, 1908, Grey Papers, vol. 47; Owen, *Cotton*, pp. 283-87, 318.

27. Grey to Gorst, May 31, 1907, Grey Papers, vol. 46, p. 411.

28. Gorst Notes, 2:117 (he first unsuccessfully approached Sir Walter Lawrence). Gorst Diary, July 16, August 10, 1907.

29. Cromer to Grey, August 2, 1907 (Private), Grey Papers, vol. 106.

30. Bowman Journal, July 17, 1907 (on vacation in England), Bowman Papers.

31. Graham to Grey, August 10, 1907, Grey Papers, vol. 46, p. 433.

32. *The Egyptian Standard* (Cairo), October 10, 1907, B.M. misc., 1335, p. 2, col. 5.

33. Arthur Goldschmidt, Jr., "The Egyptian Nationalist Party," in Holt, *Political and Social Change*, p. 321.

34. Gorst Diary, April 17, 1907.

35. Grey to Gorst, April 16, 1909, Grey Papers, vol. 47; see Stanley A. Wolpert, *Morley and India, 1906-1910* (Berkeley: University of California Press, 1967) *passim*; John Morley, *Recollections*, 2 vols. (New York: The Macmillan Company, 1917), 2:162-326.

36. Vansittart, *The Mist Procession*, pp. 85-86.

37. Storrs, *Orientations*, p. 66.

38. Cromer, *Abbas II*, pp. ix, xi.

39. Lloyd, *Egypt since Cromer*, 1:66-67. Lord Lloyd was High Commissioner in Egypt from 1925 to 1929.

40. Gorst Notes, 2:119-21, 124.

41. Gorst to Milner, Cairo, November 23, 1893 (Private), Milner Papers, box 187.

42. Gorst Notes, 2:117.

43. Gorst, "Speech Given at the Agency," November 2, 1907, Gorst Papers, pp. 3-17.

44. Ibid.

45. Ibid.

46. Ibid.

47. Gorst to Grey, November 3, 1907, Grey Papers, vol. 46, pp. 470-71; Gorst Diary, November 2, 1907.

48. Gorst to Cromer, November 16, 1907, Cromer Papers, vol. 14, p. 7.

49. Storrs to his mother, November 3, 1907, Storrs Papers, box II-1 (only the first half of the quotation [to "instructive"] is included in Storrs, *Orientations*, p. 67); Penfield, *Present-Day Egypt*, p. 131; Cromer to Sir John Scott, Cairo, March 5, 1898, Cromer Papers, vol. 8; Weigall, *Egypt from 1798 to 1914*, pp. 219-21 (Weigall was inspector general of antiquities to the Egyptian government).

50. Coles, *Recollections*, pp. 167-69; Elgood, *The Transit of Egypt*, p. 185; Russell, November 10, 1907, Russell Papers.

51. Coles, *Recollections*, pp. 167-68; see also Humphrey Bowman, *Middle East Window* (London: Longmans, Green & Company, 1942), p. 38.

52. Gorst Notes, 2:79. For civil service provisions and requirements see Appendix 1.

53. Gorst, "Speech Given at the Agency," November 2, 1907, Gorst Papers, pp. 3-4.

CHAPTER ELEVEN

1. Gorst Notes, 2:125.
2. See Thornton, *The Imperial Idea*, p. 132.
3. In 1906 at least 150 questions about Egyptian policy and administration were asked in the House, and in 1907 more than 225. During the debate over the parliamentary grant to Lord Cromer in July 1907, Dinshawai was cited as evidence of the deterioration of Cromer and a disgrace on the name of the British Empire. See Great Britain, *Parliamentary Debates* (Commons), 4th ser., 179 (1907): 866, 875-81, 883-86.
4. Grey to Cromer, London, August 13, 1907, Cromer Papers, vol. 13, p. 38 (sixteen questions on Dinshawai were asked in the House between April 30 and August 30, 1907).
5. Grey to Cromer, London, August 2, 1907, Grey Papers, vol. 46, p. 424; Cromer to Grey, London, August 2, 1907 (Private), Grey Papers, vol. 106. In this letter he petulantly asserted: ". . . to represent me as the enemy of the Egyptian national aspiration is little short of ridiculous."
6. Loreburn to Grey, London, September 14, 1907, Grey Papers, vol. 46, p. 439.
7. Grey to Cromer, London, September 14, 1907, Grey Papers, vol. 46.
8. Grey to Gorst, London, October 12, 1907, Grey Papers, vol. 46, p. 447; Gorst to Grey, Cairo, October 12, 1907, Grey Papers, vol. 46, pp. 464-65.
9. Grey to Gorst, London, November 15, 1907, Grey Papers, vol. 46. Grey declared that agitation in London makes it "essential" to release the prisoners (p. 477). Frederick Mackarness, a Liberal-Radical M.P., privately presented letters to Grey complaining about the injustice resulting from the Dinshawai incident; that of mid-December warned Grey that supporters of the Liberal government had been watching with growing anxiety the continued imprisonment of the Dinshawai villagers. "I am sure," he wrote, "you cannot realize the intensity of the feeling in this subject, though I am certain that, when Parliament meets, it will make itself known in a very emphatic manner to you." Mackarness to Grey, August 6, December 17, 1907, Grey Papers, vol. 46. Grey assured him on December 21 that his considerations were being kept in mind by the government.
10. Storrs to his mother, Cairo, October 22, 1907, Storrs Papers, box II-1.
11. Grey to Gorst, London, November 3, 6, 1907, Grey Papers, vol. 46, pp. 470, 472.
12. Gorst to Grey, Cairo, November 8, 1907, Grey Papers, vol. 46, pp. 472-74; Haldane to Grey, London, November 13, 1907, Grey Papers, vol. 46, p. 483 (Haldane, at the War Office, had been consulted and had consented to the release of the villagers); Gorst to Grey, Cairo, November 3, 1907, Grey Papers, vol. 46.

13. Grey to Gorst, London, January 8, 1908, Grey Papers, vol. 47; Gorst to Grey, Cairo, December 26, 1907, Grey Papers, vol. 47, p. 492; Graham to Tyrell, Cairo, January 11, 1908, Grey Papers, vol. 47; Gorst Diary, December 23, 1907; Gorst to Grey, Cairo, December 26, 1907, Grey Papers, vol. 46, p. 493.

14. Graham to Tyrell, Cairo, January 11, 1908, Grey Papers, vol. 47; Grey to Gorst, London, January 8, 1908, Grey Papers, vol. 47; Gorst to Grey, Cairo, January 7, 1908, no. 2, F.O. 371, vol. 448.

15. Gorst, *Egypt No. 1* (1908), p. 4.

16. The eligibility requirements can be found in *Journal Officiel*, September 18, 1909, in Foreign Office files, no. 112, September 27, 1909 (35852), F.O. 371, vol. 662. A voter had to be thirty years old and literate, and had to have paid at least twenty-five Egyptian pounds per year in land tax for the last two years and hold a *certificat d'études supérieures*. Lacking these requirements, the voter had to pay a tax of not less than fifty pounds Egyptian per year, be on the register of electors for five years, and not be a government official, an officer of the active army, or a member of another provincial council. Members were elected for six years.

17. Coles, *Recollections*, p. 173; Gorst to Grey, Cairo, November 16, 1907, Cromer Papers, vol. 14 (William Brunyate, one of his legal advisors, was an example of a staff member who objected to Gorst's scheme; Gorst wrote to Grey that Brunyate was good at objections and slow at the production of good ideas for provincial council reorganization [p. 8]); Gorst, *Egypt No. 1* (1910), pp. 27-29; see Vatikiotis, *Egypt*, p. 199, for a summary of the changes in the provincial councils.

18. Gorst to Grey, Cairo, February 7, 1909, Grey Papers, vol. 47; Gorst to Grey, Ramleh, July 1, 1909, F.O. 371, vol. 663.

19. Gorst Notes, 2:121-22, 127. Sir Reginald Wingate was Sirdar and governor-general of the Sudan from 1901 to 1916.

20. Gorst Diary, October 22, November 5, 9, 12, 1908; Gorst Notes, 2:128.

21. Gorst Notes, 1:36; Gorst to Grey, Cairo, November 8, 1908, Grey Papers, vol. 47; Seikaly, "The Copts under British Rule," p. 162; Storrs, *Orientations*, p. 85.

22. See Seikaly, "The Copts under British Rule," pp. 162-72.

23. Cromer, farewell address, Cairo, May 4, 1907, *The Times* (London), May 6, 1907: "It has been a great pleasure for me to be associated for so long with the present Minister of Foreign Affairs, Sir Ghali Boutros [*sic*], whose versatile intellect has been of the utmost service in solving many of the tangled questions to which the special political situation of this country frequently gives rise."

24. Seikaly, "The Copts under British Rule," p. 172.

25. Opinions about Kamil himself are divided, but the

popular sentiment expressed at his funeral in February 1908 was
noted by all. See Storrs, *Orientations*, p. 74; J. Alexander,
The Truth about Egypt (London: Cassell & Co., Ltd., 1911),
pp. 139-40; Gorst, *Egypt No. 1* (1908), p. 42. For a discussion
of Mustafa Kamil's ideas on religion and nationalism, see
Fritz Steppat, "Nationalismus und Islam bei Mustafa Kamil,"
Die Welt des Islams 4 (1956):266-68. Kamil's impact is described in Ahmed, *The Intellectual Origins*, pp. 78-79; Vatikiotis,
Egypt, pp. 217-18; Goldschmidt, "The Egyptian Nationalist Party,"
pp. 321-22. The program of the Nationalist Party can be found
in Alexander, *The Truth about Egypt*, pp. 121-23; Juliette Adam,
L'Angleterre en Egypte (Paris: Imprimerie du Centre, 1922),
pp. 195-97; Steppat, "Nationalismus und Islam," pp. 338-39.

    26. Goldschmidt, "The Egyptian Nationalist Party,"
pp. 322-23; Seikaly, "The Copts under British Rule," p. 160.

    27. Storrs to his mother, Cairo, November 9, 1908,
Storrs Papers, box II-1; Storrs, *Orientations*, p. 72.

    28. Gorst to Grey, Cairo, November 15, 1908, Grey Papers,
vol. 47.

    29. Ahmed, *The Intellectual Origins*, pp. 52-55.

    30. Gorst, *Egypt No. 1* (1909), p. 2; Adam, *L'Angleterre
en Egypte*, pp. 172-74 (Zaghlul, Said, Rushdi, and Sirri all
appeared on a list allegedly submitted to the British prime
minister Sir Henry Campbell-Bannerman after a meeting with
Mustafa Kamil in London); Gorst to Grey, Cairo, November 8,
1908, Grey Papers, vol. 47.

    31. Coles, *Recollections*, pp. 173, 193.

    32. Storrs, *Orientations*, p. 69; Gorst to Grey, Cairo,
November 21, 1908, no. 116, F.O. 371, vol. 452, file 40611.

    33. Gorst to Grey, Cairo, May 18, 1907, F.O. 371,
vol. 247, file 17626.

    34. Lutfi al-Sayyid, *Egypt and Cromer*, p. 178; Ahmed,
The Intellectual Origins, p. 54; Hourani, *Arabic Thought*, p. 210.
See also Elie Kedourie, "Saad Zaghlul and the British," in
St. Antony's Papers, no. 11, *Middle Eastern Affairs*, no. 2,
ed. Albert Hourani (London: Chatto and Windus, 1961), pp. 139-41.

    35. Bowman, *Middle East Window*, pp. 75-76; Lord Lloyd
(*Egypt since Cromer*, 1:161) asserted that Cromer appointed
Dunlop specifically to obstruct any dangerous schemes the inde-
pendent Zaghlul might propose. *The Egyptian Standard* (Cairo),
August 21, September 8, 1907, gives some of the complaints about
"Dunlopism" and suggestions made by the nationalist papers.

    36. Gorst to Grey, Cairo, April 10, 1910 (Private), Grey
Papers, vol. 47 (Whitehall could not find a position to offer
Dunlop).

    37. Dunlop was finally asked to leave by Allenby in 1919.
See Bowman, *Middle East Window*, pp. 41, 44.

    38. Gorst to Cromer, Cairo, March 1, 1908, Cromer Papers,
vol. 14. Gorst wrote of the strikes, demonstrations, and

activities that left the schools virtually empty when Mustafa
Kamil died. The only school that did not have trouble "by a
curious coincidence" had an Egyptian headmaster. "We seem to be
manufacturing a class of young men who will give us a very great
deal of trouble in ten or fifteen years time. Is this necessary?"

39. See information on the Egyptian University in F.O.
371, vol. 249, file 28843; *Egypt No. 1* (1908), p. 39; *Egypt
No. 1* (1909), p. 46; *Egypt No. 1* (1910), pp. 47-48; *Egypt No. 1*
(1911), p. 58.

40. *Egypt No. 1* (1909), p. 46; *Egypt No. 1* (1910), p. 48;
Egypt No. 1 (1911), p. 58: in 1908, 754 students; in 1909, 651
students; in 1910, 339 students. See also H. A. R. Gibb, "The
University in the Arab-Muslim World," Heyworth-Dunne Papers,
Hoover Institution (Stanford), box 1 (education), no. 4551,
pp. 285-86.

41. Gorst to Grey, Cairo, March 31, 1911, F.O. 371,
vol. 1113, file 13029; Morant to Grey, Whitehall, August 24,
1911, F.O. 371, vol. 1113, file 33942 (Morant told Grey the
education department would be prepared to help the Egyptian
University but it "has not yet attained such an accepted position in the world of learning as would secure for it these privileges it seeks"). Kitchener, *Egypt No. 1* (1912), p. 30.

42. Cromer to Kitchener, London, October 21, 1912, Cromer
Papers, vol. 21, p. 302; see also Cromer to Tyrell, London,
October 28, 1910, F.O. 371, vol. 895, file 47191.

43. Gorst to Grey, Cairo, December 15, 1910, F.O. 371,
vol. 895, file 47191; the director of this mission from 1907 to
1913 was Eustace Corbett, the former procurer general, an Oxford
graduate, and at one time in Egypt a tutor to Khedive Abbas
Hilmi; Humphrey Bowman succeeded Corbett in 1913. See F.O. 371,
vol. 893, files 26515, 26516, for some of Scotland Yard's reports on the students. Cromer to Tyrell, London, October 28,
1910, F.O. 371, vol. 895, file 47191; Kitchener to Grey, Cairo,
November 4, 1911, F.O. 371, vol. 1115, file 46990. He suggests
that the political activities of the students were still a problem for the British.

44. Gorst to Grey, Cairo, February 21, 1909, no. 17,
F.O. 371, vol. 247.

45. Gorst to Milner, Cairo, November 23, 1893, Milner
Papers. The letter is quoted in Lutfi al-Sayyid, *Egypt and
Cromer*, pp. 80-81.

46. Grey to Cromer, London, August 13, 1907, Cromer
Papers, vol. 13, p. 38; see Weigall, *Egypt*, pp. 231-32; Lutfi
al-Sayyid, *Egypt and Cromer*, pp. 80-81, gives some examples of
British possessiveness toward Egypt.

47. Gorst Notes, 2:122; Gorst Diary, November 9, Accounts
1907.

48. Storrs, *Orientations*, p. 71.

49. Gorst Notes, 2:130-31; Gorst Diary, April 21, 1908.

50. Gorst Notes, 2:89. Boyle's influence under Cromer
can be assessed in his papers at the Middle East Centre, Oxford,
and in two books culled from Boyle's Papers by his wife, Clara
Boyle—*A Servant of the Empire* and *Boyle of Cairo*. However,
this unusual individual deserves a more critical treatment than
his wife—who never knew him during his "salad days" in Cairo—
has given him. Storrs (*Orientations*, pp. 59-60) gives a more
balanced appreciation of his talents. See also Gorst Diary,
July 25, 1909 (the date when Storrs accepted the post).

51. Boyle to Cromer, Cairo, August 19, 1907, Cromer
Papers, vol. 11; Boyle to his mother, Cairo, February 7, 1909,
Boyle Papers.

52. Hardinge's minute on Gorst to Grey, Cairo, May 28,
1908, F.O. 371, vol. 451; see also Gorst to Grey, Cairo, May 1,
1908, F.O. 371, vol. 451; Sir Lee Stack to Wingate, Cairo,
June 14, 1908, Wingate Papers, 234/6; Gorst Diary, May 30, 1908;
Gorst Notes, 2:127-28; Gorst to Grey, Khartoum, January 3, 1908,
Grey Papers, vol. 47. Slatin and Wingate were very upset and
wanted severe sentences, for they feared leniency would have a
bad effect on the Sudan. Slatin even threatened to resign if
the British did not retaliate severely.

53. Boyle to his mother, Cairo, April 12, 1908, Boyle
Papers.

54. Russell to his father, Cairo, October 1909, Russell
Papers: "It's a fact that the English officials out here are
in a very discontented state, and Sir Eldon Gorst is . . . not
unjustly held to blame for it."

55. Cromer to Errington Baring, London, February 18,
July 21, 1909, Cromer Additional Papers, HMC A/4.

56. Hardinge to Gorst, January 29, 1909, Hardinge Papers,
vol. 17 (1909).

57. See J. N. D. Anderson, "Law Reform in Egypt," in Holt,
Political and Social Change, p. 222. Correspondence on the
judicial reforms can be found in F.O. 371, vols. 449, 661,
file 12605, vol. 662, file 18260, vol. 663, files 24428, 31575,
vol. 664, files 39914, 42234, 45304 (1909); also Grey Papers,
vols. 108, 890, files 5808, 13860, 20790. Some of these reforms are described in Gorst, *Egypt No. 1* (1910), p. 39.

58. J. F. Kershaw to C. H. Lyle, M.P., Alexandria, September 23, 1909, Grey Papers, vol. 108. This letter, from a
British judge on the Alexandria Native Tribunal, complained
that Gorst had appointed to the native tribunal a Belgian who
had never been in Egypt and did not speak Arabic: "His appointment is regarded by all English judges as a pure piece of revenge because they dared to criticize Gorst. . . . The judges
are exasperated beyond measure. The way in which Englishmen are
being treated by Gorst must end in very severe protests before
long."

59. Gorst to Mallet, Cairo, May 22, 1908, no. 26, F. O.

368, vol. 181, file 18580 (with enclosures); see also Gorst to Mallet, Cairo, May 16, 1908, F.O. 368, vol. 181, file 17971; Owen, *Cotton*, p. 284.

60. Cromer to Grey, October 29, 1909, Cromer Papers, vol. 14. See F.O. 371, vol. 663, files 25040-44952, vol. 891, files 14203, 18907, 35819 (in this correspondence are pro-Willmore articles from *The Egyptian Gazette* [Alexandria] and *The Pall Mall Gazette* [London]); Gorst to Grey, Cairo, May 19, 1910, F.O. 371, vol. 891, file 18911.

61. Gorst Notes, 2:125.

62. Gorst to Grey, Cairo, May 20, 1909, Grey Papers, vol. 47.

63. Gorst Notes, 2:129.

64. See comments in Gorst to Grey, Cairo, March 28, 1908, Grey Papers, vol. 47.

65. Abd al-Aziz Shawish apparently was the real power in the National Party after Mustafa Kamil's death. A former lecturer in Arabic at Oxford and a minor official in the Egyptian government, he resigned and turned his formidable talent for invective against the British. He was Tunisian by birth.

66. Graham to Grey, Alexandria, August 2, 1907, F.O. 371, vol. 451, files 27484, 27675. Graham reported that he had the assurance of the Cairo police chief that serious disorders were not anticipated and that the police could deal with the situation. Alexander, *The Truth about Egypt*, pp. 165-68.

67. Gorst, September 16, 1908, no. 126, Cabinet 37/95 (this memorandum was circulated to the Cabinet on October 27, 1908; it can also be found in Gorst, "The Press in Egypt," September 16, 1908, F.O. 371, vol. 451).

68. Grey to Gorst, London, November 25, December 18, 1908, Grey Papers, vol. 47; Gorst to Mallet, Cairo, December 11, 1908, F.O. 371, vol. 451, file 44332.

69. Graham to Grey, Ramleh, August 23, 1909, no. 98, F.O. 371, vol. 660, file 325399 (Dingha was the assassin of Sir Curzon Wylie).

70. Goldschmidt, "The Egyptian Nationalist Movement," p. 11; Seikaly, "The Copts under British Rule," pp. 185-86.

71. Almost the entire volume 660 of F.O. 371 (1909) was devoted to correspondence on the revival of the Press Law of 1881. France at that time was moving into a position of control in Morocco and tended to use its rights in Egypt to obtain British support for its position.

72. Mallet to Gorst, London, July 21, 1909, F.O. 371, vol. 663, file 27953.

73. Gorst Notes, 2:122-23.

74. Gorst Press Cuttings, vol. 2, April 4, 1908.

75. *The Egyptian Gazette*, April 4, 1908, Gorst Press Cuttings, vol. 2.

76. Gorst Notes, 2:129.

77. See, for example, Sladen, *Egypt and the English*, esp. pp. 1-170; Sidney Low, *Egypt in Transition* (New York: The Macmillan Company, 1914).

78. Gorst Diary, October 19, 1908.

79. The crime figures can be found in Gorst, *Egypt No. 1* (1910), pp. 21-25, 36, 56-61. Gorst to Mallet, Cairo, June 29, 1908 (Private), F.O. 371, vol. 663, file 24428; Mallet to Grey, minute on Gorst to Grey, Ramleh, July 10, 1909, F.O. 371, vol. 663.

80. Mallet, memorandum on a conversation with J. F. Kershaw, July 20, 1909, F.O. 371, vol. 663.

81. Grey, "Memorandum to the Cabinet on the Proposed Police Supervision Law," August 5, 1909, no. 106, Cabinet 37/100; Asquith to King Edward VII, August 19, 1908, Asquith Papers.

82. Gorst, *Egypt No. 1* (1910), p. 25; A. King Harmon to Crewe, October 1, 1909, F.O. 371, vol. 663, file 36380. The Colonial Office that fall received a request from the high commissioner on Cyprus, A. King Harmon, for a copy of the Criminal Deportation Act; a similar problem with violent crime apparently existed there.

83. Gorst, *Egypt No. 1* (1908), pp. 20-21; Gorst to Grey, Cairo, February 20, 1909, no. 15, F.O. 371, vol. 661, file 7791; Gorst to Grey, Alexandria, June 19, 1908, no. 60, F.O. 371, vol. 451, file 22243. The minute on this dispatch read: "We cannot tell whether it is good or bad. Assent with promulgation."

84. Gorst Diary, November 21, 1908, March 28, 1909.

85. Gorst Notes, 2:132; Gorst to Grey, Ramleh, July 1, 1909, F.O. 371, vol. 663, file 26185.

86. For the secret articles of the Anglo-French Entente see F.O. 371, vol. 68, November 26, 1906, file 39795, article 2. Gorst to Grey, Cairo, May 25, 1908, Grey Papers, vol. 47; see also Gorst to Grey, Cairo, June 6, 1908, Cromer Papers, vol. 14: "The French continue to be very tiresome locally."

87. Gorst Diary, April 20, November 22, 1907.

88. Evelyn Rudd Gorst, child's dairy (1905-1910), December 1907, Evelyn Rudd Gorst Papers, in the possession of Mrs. K. R. Thomas, Castle Combe.

89. Gorst Diary, October 2, 1909.

90. Gorst Notes, 2:130; Gorst Diary, April 21, 1907.

91. Gorst Diary, July 20, 26, 27, August 25, 27, 29, October 8, 1908; September 17, 18, 20, 1909.

92. Interview with Mrs. K. R. (Kitty) Gorst Thomas, Castle Combe.

93. Gorst Notes, 2:135; Gorst Diary, January 15, 16, December 15, 18, 1909.

94. Hardinge to Gorst, London, May 21, 1909, Hardinge Papers, vol. 17 (1909), p. 151; Grey to Gorst, August 5, 1909, Grey Papers, vol. 47.

95. Russell to his father, October 1909, Russell Papers:

"It's a fact that the English officials out here are in a very
discontented state, and Sir Eldon Gorst is . . . [not] unjustly
held to blame for it"; Storrs to his mother, Cairo, September 26,
1909, Storrs Papers, box II-1: "We are attacked with gross and
bitter injustice every single day of the year [in the native
press] and there is not save amongst the Copts (1/10 the population) the smallest trace of gratitude for what we've done here."
        96. See Goldschmidt, "The Egyptian Nationalist Party,"
pp. 322-23; Gorst to Grey, Cairo, February 16, 1908, Grey Papers,
vol. 47: Gorst wrote that the leader the nationalists had chosen
after Mustafa Kamil's death was "indolent and timid." Count de
Salis to Grey, Berlin, July 8, 1908, F.O. 371, vol. 452.
De Salis reported that the German Consul in Egypt, Baron
Oppenheim, had become frustrated by Gorst, who simply laughed at
him and treated him with contempt. Gorst, he reported, had
acted with discretion, and since the death of Mustafa Kamil and
the detachment of the khedive from the nationalist cause, Baron
Oppenheim's intrigues had been much less important.

                            CHAPTER TWELVE

        1. James Aldridge, *Cairo* (New York: Macmillan, 1969),
pp. 219-20.
        2. Owen, *Cotton,* p. 285.
        3. Sir Paul Harvey, financial advisor to the Egyptian
government, 1907-1912; unsympathetic to Kitchener, he resigned
to resume a post with the treasury, and returned to Egypt in
1919 as financial advisor. More should be learned of his career
in Egypt and his influence on policy there.
        The annual reports for this period provide a very sketchy
picture of the financial health of the late Cromer and early
Gorst regimes. See Harvey to Grey, F.O. 371, vol. 889 (1910).
        4. A question in the House on the status of the reserve
fund elicited some correspondence between the Foreign Office and
the Agency that indicated the Foreign Office wanted to conceal
the seriousness of the loss in value of the securities in the
fund. See F.O. 371, vol. 452, file 23321, July 6, 1908, file
26910, August 4, 1908.
        5. Gorst Notes, 2:128; Gorst Diary, August 16, 1908.
        6. Gorst Diary, October 23, 1908, no. 131, Cab. 37/95
(1908); Harvey to Grey, August 19, 1908, F.O. 371, vol. 452,
file 30903. "Neither popular sentiment nor the hard facts of
the situation . . . will admit of the continuance of large
capital advances to the Sudan."
        7. See especially the sultan's *Firman* of August 7, 1879;
Graham to Grey, October 10, 1909, no. 117, F.O. 371, vol. 664.
Gorst Diary, December 2, 1908; Gorst to Grey, Cairo, March 20,
1909, F.O. 371, vol. 890; Grey to Lowther, London, May 30, 1909,

Grey Papers, vol. 79.

8. See F.O. 371, vols. 664, 889, and 890.

9. The British were entitled to a total of ten directors on the Suez Canal Company's thirty-two member board; three were nominated by the British government, and seven were "unofficial" and represented the large shipping interests in Britain. Gorst lunched with Garstin, one of the directors, on October 7, 1908. Gorst Notes, 2:133; Gorst Diary, January 2, February 5, 1909.

10. Arnold T. Wilson, *The Suez Canal* (London: Oxford University Press, 1939), pp. 94-95; W. H. Cooke to Grey, May 20, 1909, F.O. 368, vol. 5654, vol. 375, file 19138 (Cooke was secretary of the British chamber of shipping); Kenrie B. Murray to the Foreign Office, April 20, 1909, F.O. 368, vol. 375, file 16313 (Murray was secretary to the London chamber of commerce). Mallet informed Murray that there was little prospect of any dues reduction at that time.

11. D. A. Farnie, *East and West of Suez* (Oxford: Clarendon Press, 1969), p. 751; Wilson, *Suez Canal*, p. 94.

12. Grey to Lloyd George, March 26, 1909, Grey Papers, vol. 101; G. H. Murray to Grey, March 17, 1909, F.O. 368, vol. 375, file 10268; Gorst Diary, April 8, 1909.

13. Cromer to Tyrell, London, May 8, 1909, F.O. 368, vol. 375, file 17945.

14. Cromer to Brodrick, Cairo, November 25, 1899 (Private), enclosed in F.O. 368, vol. 375, file 17945.

15. The exchange between Robertson and Grey is recorded in F.O. 368, vol. 375; the draft convention can be found in the Cabinet Papers, no. 141, October 19, 1909, Cab. 37/101.

16. Pierre Crabitès, *The Spoliation of Suez* (London: George Routledge and Sons, Ltd., 1940), pp. 194-203. Cromer was a member of the Debt Commission and does not mention this particular transaction in his books on Egypt, nor does his biographer, Lord Zetland.

17. Murray, August 27, 1909, no. 115, Cab. 37/100.

18. Churchill, October 25, 1909, no. 143, Cab. 37/101.

19. Grey to Gorst, November 8, 1909, no. 10, Grey Papers, vol. 93.

20. Ibid., Garstin to Tyrell, November 8, 1909, Grey Papers, vol. 107; Gorst Diary, November 4, 1909.

21. Anstruther to Montgomery, London, October 13, 1909, Grey Papers, vol. 104. The price rose from 4,500 francs to over 5,000 francs between October 8 and 13.

22. Gorst to Grey, Cairo, November 2, 1909, F.O. 371, vol. 890; Alexander, *The Truth about Egypt*, p. 287; Storrs to his mother, Cairo, October 27, 1909, Storrs Papers, box II-1.

23. Gorst to Grey, October 30, November 20, 1909, Grey Papers, vol. 47.

24. Report of the debate can be found in F.O. 371, vol. 890.

25.   Churchill to Grey, Board of Trade, October 29, November 15, 1909, Grey Papers, vol. 89.

26.   Gorst to Grey, Cairo, October 30, 1909, Grey Papers, vol. 47; Gorst Diary, October 31, 1909.

27.   Gorst Notes, 2:133; Gorst Diary, December 27, 1909: "Told Boutros I was very dissatisfied with Zaghlul and Moh. [Mohammad] Said." Lord Lloyd (*Egypt since Cromer*, 1:96) described the reaction of members of the Legislative Council: "The members merely used their increased power and opportunities in subservience to the clamour of the extremist Press. Hypersensitive to public outcry, they bombarded Ministers with obstructive questions. And, as the nationalist Press was at this time making much capital out of the question of the Sudan, they persistently opposed all the grants to be voted for that administration"; Gorst to Grey, Cairo, October 30, 1909, Grey Papers, vol. 47.

28.   Gorst to Grey, Cairo, October 30, November 20, 1909, Grey Papers, vols. 47, 890.

29.   Gorst to Grey, Cairo, November 25, 1909, no. 137, F.O. 371, vol. 664, file 44167; Alexander, *The Truth about Egypt*, p. 290.

30.   Gorst to Cromer, Cairo, February 5, 1910, Cromer Papers, vol. 14; Gorst to Hardinge, Cairo, January 29, 1910, Hardinge Papers, vol. 20, p. 42; Gorst Diary, January 30, 1910.

31.   Earl of Lytton, *Wilfrid Scawen Blunt* (London, MacDonald & Co., Ltd., 1961), p. 116; H. Hamilton Fyfe, *The Egyptian Daily Post* (Cairo), February 12, 1910, Storrs Papers, press cutting, box II-1.

32.   Wilson, *The Suez Canal*, p. 97; Alexander, *The Truth about Egypt*, p. 307; Gorst to Hardinge, Cairo, February 10, 1910, F.O. 371, vol. 895, file 47203; Gorst Diary, February 11, 1910.

33.   Gorst Notes, 2:133; Gorst to Cromer, Cairo, February 5, 1910, Cromer Papers, vol. 14, pp. 66-67: "As you know, Cassel is very hostile to the proposal, and seems to consider it a personal grievance. His attitude is like that of the Jewish money-lender when his client endeavours to borrow a small sum from another source." Gorst to Cromer, Cairo, February 26, 1910, Cromer Papers, vol. 14, pp. 68-69: ". . . one must take account of Egyptian public opinion, however stupid it may be, provided, of course, that it really is a public opinion!"

34.   Storrs, *Orientations*, pp. 72-73.

35.   Gorst to Grey, Cairo, February 20, 1910, no. 7, F.O. 371, vol. 890, no. 8, file 5946; Gorst Diary, February 21, 1910; Gorst to Grey, Cairo, March 25, 1910, F.O. 371, vol. 890, file 11091. See also Goldschmidt, "The Egyptian Nationalist Party," p. 325, and the report on the secret societies in Egypt by the secret service bureau of the ministry of the interior, Cheetham to Grey, Ramleh, June 30, 1911, no. 68, F.O. 371, vol. 1114, secret and confidential file 26809.

36. Gorst to Hardinge, Cairo, March 5, 1910, F.O. 371, vol. 895, file 47204.
37. Seikaly, "The Copts under British Rule," pp. 208-9.
38. Gorst Diary, February 22, 1910; Gorst to Cromer, Cairo, February 26, 1910, Cromer Papers, vol. 14, p. 69.
39. Gorst to Grey, February 21, 1910, F.O. 371, vol. 891, file 6194 (a minute on the dispatch reads "We are quite ignorant here of his merits or otherwise—there is always the safeguard that he can be got rid of if he proves unsatisfactory"; the initials were APN for A. P. Norman); see also Gorst Diary, February 21, 1910.
40. Gorst to Grey, Cairo, February 26, March 12, 1910, Grey Papers, vol. 47; Gorst, *Egypt No. 1* (1910), p. 2; Gorst to Cromer, Cairo, February 26, 1910, Cromer Papers, vol. 14, p. 68.
41. Clayton to Wingate, Cairo, March 6, 1910, Clayton Papers, Durham.
42. Gorst to Grey, Cairo, February 26, 1910, Grey Papers, vol. 47 (Gorst informed Grey privately that the prince resigned from fear that he too would be murdered); Blunt, *My Diaries,* 2:294; Gorst Diary, February 23, 1910.
43. See Wilson, *Suez Canal,* pp. 98-101; Alexander, *The Truth about Egypt,* pp. 325-26 (this version of the committee recommendations differs slightly from Wilson's).
44. Gorst to Grey, Cairo, April 23, 1910, F.O. 368, vol. 502, file 13865.
45. Gorst Diary, April 9, 1910; Gorst to Grey, Cairo, April 10, 1910, Grey Papers, vol. 47.
46. Wilson, *Suez Canal,* p. 101.
47. Gorst to Grey, Cairo, April 10, 1910, Grey Papers, vol. 47.
48. Grey to Gorst, Foreign Office, April 24, 1910, Grey Papers, vol. 47; Hardinge to Gorst, April 22, 1910, Hardinge Papers, vol. 21, p. 67.
49. Gorst to Grey, Cairo, April 10, May 6, 1910, Grey Papers, vol. 47; Gorst Diary, April 30, 1910. Gorst consulted with General Maxwell, chief of the occupying army, and Ronald Graham, advisor to the interior ministry.
50. See F.O. 371, vols. 889, 895: files 43955-47000; Gorst to Grey, Cairo, February 25, 1911, no. 13, F.O. 371, vol. 1112, file 7915.
51. Report on secret societies in Egypt in Cheetham to Grey, Ramleh, June 30, 1911, no. 68, F.O. 371, vol. 1114; see F.O. 371, vol. 892, files 15651, 19673; Gorst Diary, May 14, 19, 22, 1910; Gorst to Grey, Ramleh, June 19, 1910, F.O. 371, vol. 893, file 22962.
52. Gorst Diary, April 21, May 8, 1910.
53. Gorst to Grey, Cairo, April 23, 30, 1910, Grey Papers, vol. 47; Storrs to his mother, Cairo, April 23, 1910, Storrs Papers, box II-2; Russell to his father, April 24, 1910,

Russell Papers; see Asquith to Edward VII, London, May 12, 1910, Asquith Papers; Grey to Gorst, London, May 12, 1910, F.O. 371, vol. 390, file 16950; Ronald Graham, "Note on the Imprisonment and Execution of Ibrahim Nassif el-Wardani," July 11, 1910, F.O. 371, vol. 890, file 24961; see also Gorst Diary, June 28, 1910.

54. Ziadeh, *Lawyers*, p. 68; Faris Nimr to Boyle, Cairo, May 8, 1910, Cromer Papers, vol. 14. Nimr, one of the proprietors of *al-Muqattam*, informed Boyle that Gorst had admitted that his policy had failed and that the Egyptians were "perfectly hopeless." Nimr thought that Egypt was drifting toward disorder after the assassination of Butrus. Seikaly, "The Copts under British Rule," pp. 208-9.

55. *The Saturday Review*, July 10, 1909, in Gorst Press Cuttings, vol. 3.

56. Hardinge to Gorst, London, May 13, 1910 (Private), Hardinge Papers, vol. 21, p. 71; Vansittart, *The Mist Procession*, p. 87.

57. "The Case of Sir Eldon Gorst," *The Saturday Review*, April 16, 1910, pp. 485-86, in Gorst Press Cuttings, vol. 3, and Wingate Papers, box 235/1.

58. Gorst Diary, March 14, April 24, 25, May 2, 1910. The Sykeses left for Syria with Eva Gorst on March 14, 1910.

59. William Congreve, *The Mourning Bride*, act 3, scene 8; Italian adage quoted in Mario Puzo, *The Godfather* (Greenwich, Conn.: Fawcett Crest Book, 1969), p. 404; the articles in these papers were collected in Gorst Press Cuttings, vol. 3.

60. Gorst to Grey, April 24, 29, 1910; Hardinge to Gorst, April 28, 1910, Grey Papers, vol. 47.

61. Gorst to Mallet, Ramleh, June 5, 1910, F.O. 371, vol. 893, file 21418.

62. Seikaly, "The Copts under British Rule," pp. 159, 344-46; Sladen, *Egypt and the English*, pp. 132-34.

63. This group's program can be found in Alfred Cunningham, *To-Day in Egypt* (London: Hurst & Blackett, Ltd., 1912), pp. 260-64.

64. Seikaly, "The Copts under British Rule," p. 192.

65. Gorst Notes, 2:112.

66. Gorst to Hardinge, March 5, 1910, F.O. 371, vol. 895, file 47204; Hardinge to Grey, April 26, 1910, Hardinge Papers, vol. 21, p. 137. "It looks as though there is in preparation a press campaign against Gorst and the Government policy in Egypt."

67. Gorst to Grey, Cairo, April 29, 1910, Grey Papers, vol. 47.

68. Seikaly, "The Copts under British Rule," pp. 212-13; Alexander, *The Truth about Egypt*, pp. 337-38.

69. Gorst to Hardinge, Cairo, April 1, 1910, F.O. 371, vol. 895, file 47205; Gorst to Grey, Cairo, April 1, 1910, F.O. 371, vol. 895, file 47205. The dispatch quotes from a nationalist paper, *El Masonier* [*sic*], which asserted that

Roosevelt was a son of a whore and prostitute who should get out
of Egypt and stop giving unwanted advice.

70. Gorst Diary, March 28, 1910; Wingate to Clayton,
Cairo, March 29, 1910, Clayton Papers, p. 2.

71. The speech can be found in *The Times* (London), June 1,
1910.

72. Hardinge's minute on Gorst to Mallet, Ramleh, June 5,
1910, F.O. 371, vol. 893, file 21418.

73. Gorst to Mallet, Ramleh, June 5, 1910, F.O. 371,
vol. 893, file 21418; Gorst to Grey, Ramleh, June 26, 1910, Grey
Papers, vol. 47; Gorst Diary, June 1, 1910. Gorst noted, unhap-
pily: "Roosevelt seems to have been again disporting himself as
the bull in the china shop—this time at my expense." He felt
T. R.'s manner of expression was "most unfortunate" and said
Roosevelt derived most of his information from American missionary authorities, "a worthy but prejudiced and narrow-minded
body," subject to the influence of the native Christians.

74. Elgin to Grey, Watford, June 5, 1910 (Confidential),
Grey Papers, vol. 91.

75. Grey to Crewe, June 3, 1910, Grey Papers, vol. 91.

76. Cromer to Gorst, May 12 (Private), May 30, 1910,
Cromer Papers, vol. 14, pp. 109, 114. This correspondence belies
Cromer's assertion that he was never consulted by the Foreign
Office regarding Egyptian affairs.

77. Gorst to Cromer, Cairo, February 26, 1910, Cromer
Papers, vol. 14, p. 68.

78. Grey to Gorst, May 3, 1910, Grey Papers, vol. 47.

79. Gorst's memorandum of May 22, 1910, can be found in
Cab. 37/102, no. 19, pp. 1-3, and F.O. 371, vol. 890, file 19674.
Grey to Gorst, June 1, 1910 (Private), F.O. 371, vol. 890.

80. Gorst memorandum of May 22, 1910, Cab. 37/102, no. 19.

81. Ibid.

82. Gorst to Grey, Ramleh, June 13, 1910, Grey Papers,
vol. 47.

83. Grey to Gorst, June 7, 1909, Grey Papers, vol. 47.

84. Cromer to Gorst, May 30, 1909, Cromer Papers, vol. 14,
p. 115.

85. Great Britain, *Parliamentary Debates* (Commons), 5th
ser., vol. 17 (1910): 1106-11, 1125-38.

86. Ibid., cols. 1111-19.

87. Ibid., cols. 1123, 1142-43.

88. Ibid., cols. 1144-46.

89. Ibid., col. 1146.

90. Ibid., cols. 1151-53.

91. Ibid., col. 1154.

CHAPTER THIRTEEN

1. Lawrence Durrell, *Mountolive* (London: Faber and Faber, Limited, 1965), p. 93.

2. See Cheetham to Mallet, Ramleh, July 17, 1910, F.O. 371, vol. 894. The ministry of the interior had subsidized subscriptions to an Islamic magazine to be sent to the mosques and all *Umdahs;* Cheetham wrote that the government was convinced this was one of the most effective means of influencing the ignorant peasantry. The magazine contained sermons on obedience to the authorities, honesty, and truthfulness in bearing witness in the courts—all virtues thought good for the British cause.

3. Gorst Diary, May 29, June 10, July 28, 1910; see also Cheetham to Allen, Cairo, April 13, 1911, Cheetham Papers; Cheetham to Gorst, Cairo, May 7, 1911, Cheetham Papers; *The Near East* (London), vol. 4 (1910):237, 245, 247, 248.

4. See F.O. 371, vol. 892 (1910), files 13975, 14654, 16547, 17049, 20009, 20667, 30817, 34292, for some of the correspondence on nationalist activities inside and outside Egypt. Gorst to Grey, Cairo, November 6, 1910, F.O. 371, vol. 895, file 47211.

5. Seikaly, "The Copts under British Rule," pp. 228-30, 244-45; Gorst to Mallet, Ramleh, June 10, 1910, F.O. 371, vol. 893, file 21418. Gorst mentioned the personal "canards" planted in English papers by Copts and Syrian [Lebanese] Christians. He asserted that most of the correspondents for the minor English newspapers in Egypt were Copts and Syrians "anxious to stir up trouble and make out they are in constant danger of massacre." See F.O. 371, vol. 1111 (1911), files 5672, 5674, 5779, 7113.

6. Gorst to Grey, Cairo, March 10, 11, 18, 1911, F.O. 371, vol. 1111, files 8011, 9057, 10869. Gorst wrote: "The figures indicate that the Copts are represented in the Egyptian Civil Service both as to numbers and salaries to altogether disproportionate extent." Gorst, *Egypt No. 1* (1911), pp. 6-7.

7. The speeches at the Coptic congress can be found in translation in F.O. 371, vol. 1111, file 13807.

8. Cheetham to Nicolson, Cairo, April 29, 1911, Carnock Papers, F.O. 800, vol. 345; Cheetham to Grey, Cairo, May 6, 1911, no. 43, F.O. 371, vol. 1113, file 18097.

9. Seikaly, "The Copts under British Rule," p. 317.

10. Durrell, *Mountolive,* pp. 36-39.

11. Ibid.

12. Owen, *Cotton,* p. 346; Gorst to Grey, Cairo, April 16, 1910, no. 45, F.O. 371, vol. 891, file 13861; Gorst to

C. W. Macera, Ramleh, June 24, 1910, F.O. 368, vol. 400; Gorst
to Grey, Cairo, November 6, 1910, F.O. 371, vol. 895, file 47211.
    13. Gorst to Grey, Ramleh, June 13, 1910, Grey Papers,
vol. 47; Gorst to Nicolson, Cairo, December 24, 1910 (Private),
F.O. 371, vol. 895, file 47209.
    14. Gorst to Nicolson, Cairo, January 4, 1911 (Private),
Grey Papers,vol. 347.
    15. Kitchener, *Egypt No. 1* (1912), pp. 42-43; Lloyd,
Egypt since Cromer, 1:105-6.
    16. Lloyd, *Egypt since Cromer*, 1:29; Vatikiotis, *Egypt*,
pp. 296-97.
    17. H. P. Harvey, "Note by the Financial Advisor on the
Budget for 1911," December 21, 1910, Milner Papers, p. 1.
    18. Gorst Notes, 2:110, 130.
    19. Gorst Notes, 2:135; Gorst to Grey, January 21, 1909,
Grey Papers, vol. 47; Boyle to his mother, Cairo, April 7, 1909,
Boyle Papers; Grey to Hardinge, Foreign Office, June 10, 1911,
Hardinge Papers, vol. 69, p. 247.
    20. Vansittart, *The Mist Procession*, p. 85; Gorst to Grey,
Ramleh, June 26, 1910; Grey Papers, vol. 47; Cheetham to Mallet,
June 20, 1910, F.O. 371, vol. 893, file 23639.
    21. Gorst Diary, February 12, 16, 25, March 4, June 9, 12,
14, 15, 1910.
    22. Ibid., July 7, 8, 24, 27, 29, 1910.
    23. Ibid., August 2, 12, September 13, October 1-3, 1910.
The will was signed September 1, 1910.
    24. Ibid., October 4, 6, 7, 10, 1910.
    25. Gorst to Grey, Cairo, November 6, 1910, F.O. 371,
vol. 895, file 47211.
    26. Gorst Diary, November 7, 17, December 7, 14, 28,
1910.
    27. Ibid., February 19, 20, 24, 25, 1910.
    28. Gorst to Grey, Cairo, March 25, 1911, Grey Papers,
vol. 47.
    29. Gorst Diary, March 31, April 4, 1911.
    30. Ibid., April 14, 15, 19, June 2, 8, 9, 10, 1910.
    31. Cromer to Cheetham, London, June 19, 1911, Cheetham
Papers; interview with Mrs. K. R. Thomas, August, 1975.
    32. Garstin to Gorst, Bagshot Park, 1911, Gorst family
papers.
    33. Abbas Hilmi to Sir John Gorst, London, July 8, 1911,
Gorst family papers.
    34. Abbas Hilmi to Sir John Gorst, Paris, June 30, 1911,
Gorst family papers; interview with Archibald Hunter, Gorst's
nephew, summer 1971; Harold Gorst, *Much of Life is Laughter*,
p. 204.
    35. Ronald Robinson and John Gallagher with Alice Denny,
Africa and the Victorians (New York: St. Martin's Press, 1971).

36.   Elizabeth Monroe, *Britain's Moment in the Middle East* (Baltimore: The Johns Hopkins Press, 1963), p. 58.

37.   Hynes, *Edwardian Turn of Mind*, p. 234.

38.   Storrs, *Orientations*, p. 477; Harold Gorst, *Much of Life is Laughter*, p. 204 (his brother blamed the anonymous attacks on Gorst as contributing to Sir Eldon's fatal illness).

BIBLIOGRAPHY

Archival Sources

Manuscripts

Earl of Oxford and Asquith Papers. Bodleian Library, Oxford.
Charles Moberley Bell Papers. The Archives of *The Times*, London.
Sir Francis Bertie Papers. Public Record Office, London.
Humphrey Bowman Papers. Middle East Centre, Oxford.
Harry Boyle Papers. Middle East Centre, Oxford.
The Cabinet Papers. Cab. 37, Public Record Office, London.
Sir Henry Campbell-Bannerman Papers. British Museum, London.
Sir Milne Cheetham Papers. Middle East Centre, Oxford.
Sir Valentine Chirol Papers. The Archives of *The Times*, London.
Church Missionary Society Papers. Church Missionary Society
    Archives, London.
Sir Gilbert F. Clayton Papers. Sudan Archive, Durham.
The Committee of Imperial Defense Papers. Cab. 38, Public
    Record Office, London.
Earl of Cromer Papers. F.O. 633, Public Record Office, London.
    Autographs. Historical Manuscripts Commission, London.
    "Cromer Additional Papers." Historical Manuscripts Commis-
        sion, London.
    Cromer Letters. Archives of *The Times*, London.
Viscount D'Abernon Papers. British Museum, London.
Phillip Gell Papers. Historical Manuscripts Commission, London.
Sir Eldon Gorst Papers:
    Autobiographical Notes. Middle East Centre, Oxford.
    Press Cuttings. Middle East Centre, Oxford.
    Diaries, 1890-1911. Castle Combe, Wiltshire.
Evelyn Rudd Gorst Papers. Castle Combe, Wiltshire.
Viscount Edward Grey of Fallodon Papers. F.O. 800, Public Record
    Office, London.
Sir Charles Hardinge Papers. Cambridge University Library,
    Cambridge.
J. Heyworth-Dunne Papers. Hoover Institution, Stanford.
W. E. Jennings-Bramly Papers. Royal Geographical Society, London.
Earl Kitchener of Khartoum Papers. Public Record Office, London.
Sir Gerald Lowther Papers. Public Record Office, London.

Viscount Alfred Milner Papers. Bodleian Library, Oxford.
Public Record Office Papers. London.
    F.O. 141, Consular Correspondence.
    F.O. 368, Commercial Correspondence.
    F.O. 369, Consular Correspondence.
    F.O. 371, Political Correspondence.
    F.O. 407, Confidential Prints.
    F.O. 848, "The Special Mission Appointed to Inquire into the
      Situation in Egypt" [The Milner Mission].
Baron Rennell of Rodd Papers. The Rodd, Prestigne.
Sir Thomas Russell Pasha Papers. Middle East Centre, Oxford.
Sir Ronald Storrs Papers. Pembroke College, Cambridge.
Archives of *The Times*, London:
    Managers' Letters, 1890-1908.
    Foreign Editors' Letter Book, 1891-1910.
General Sir Francis R. Wingate Papers. Sudan Archive, Durham.

Printed Documents

Great Britain, *Parliamentary Debates* (Commons), 4th series,
    1906-1908; 5th series, 1909-1911.
Great Britain, *Parliamentary Papers* (Accounts and Papers).
    Egypt No. 1 (1890), "Report on the Finances of Egypt," vol. 83,
      Cd. 5973.
    Egypt No. 3 (1899), "Report on the Finances, Administration,
      and Condition of Egypt and the Sudan in 1898," vol. 112,
      Cd. 9231.
    Egypt No. 1 (1906), "The Annual Report for 1905," vol. 137,
      Cd. 2817.
    Egypt No. 2 (1906), "Correspondence on the Turco-Egyptian
      Frontier," vol. 137, Cd. 3006.
    Egypt No. 3 (1906), "The attack on British Officers at
      Denshawai," vols. 137, 138, Cd. 3086.
    Egypt No. 4 (1906), "Further Correspondence on . . .
      Denshawai," vol. 137, Cd. 3091.
    Egypt No. 1 (1907), "The Annual Report for 1906," vol. 100,
      Cd. 3394.
    Egypt No. 2 (1907), "Proposals of the Egyptian General
      Assembly," vol. 100, Cd. 3451.
    Egypt No. 1 (1908), "The Annual Report for 1907," vol. 125,
      Cd. 3966.
    Egypt No. 1 (1909), "The Annual Report for 1908," vol. 105,
      Cd. 4580.
    Egypt No. 2 (1909), "The Egyptian Criminal Deportation Law
      of 1909," vol. 105, Cd. 4734.
    Egypt No. 1 (1910), "The Annual Report for 1909," vol. 112,
      Cd. 5121.

Egypt No. 1 (1911), "The Annual Report for 1910," vol. 103, Cd. 5633.

Egypt No. 1 (1912), "The Annual Report for 1911," vol. 121, Cd. 6149.

Egypt No. 1 (1921), "Report of the Special Mission to Egypt" [The Milner Mission], vol. 42, Cmd. 1131.

Books and Articles

Abdel-Malek, Anouar. *Egypt: Military Society*. New York: Random House, 1968.

Abu-Lughod, Janet L. *Cairo: 1001 Years of the City Victorious*. Princeton: Princeton University Press, 1971.

Adam, Juliette (Lambert). *L'Angleterre en Egypte*. Paris: Imprimerie du Centre, 1922.

Adams, Charles C. *Islam and Modernism in Egypt*. London: Oxford University Press, 1933.

Adelson, Roger. *Mark Sykes: Portrait of an Amateur*. London: Jonathan Cape, 1975.

Ahmad, Feroz. "Great Britain's Relations with the Young Turks, 1908-1914." *Middle Eastern Studies* 2 (1966): 303-29.

Ahmed, Jemal Mohammed. *The Intellectual Origins of Egyptian Nationalism*. London: Oxford University Press, 1960.

Aldridge, James. *Cairo*. New York: Macmillan, 1969.

Alexander, J. *The Truth about Egypt*. London: Cassel & Co., Ltd., 1911.

Amin, Osman. *Muhammad Abduh*. Washington, D.C.: American Council of Learned Societies, 1953.

Anderson, J. N. D. "Law Reform in Egypt." In *Political and Social Change in Modern Egypt*, edited by P. M. Holt. London: Oxford University Press, 1968.

Arthur, Sir George. *Life of Lord Kitchener*. London: Macmillan & Co., Ltd., 1920.

Baedeker, Karl, ed. *Egypt, 1902*. Leipsic: Karl Baedeker, 1902.

————. *Lower Egypt*. London: Dulac & Co., 1885.

Beaman, Arden Hulme. *The Dethronement of the Khedive*. London: George Allen & Unwin, Ltd., 1929.

————. "Egypt Revisited." *The Standard* (London), September 5-13, 1910.

Bell, Gertrude L. *Amurath to Amurath*. London: Macmillan & Co., Ltd., 1924.

Berque, Jacques. *L'Egypte*. Paris: Gallimard, 1967.

Blunt, Wilfrid Scawen. *Atrocities of Justice under British Rule in Egypt*. London: T. Fisher Unwin, 1906; 2d ed., 1907.

————. *My Diaries*. 2 vols. London: Martin Secker, 1921.

————. *The New Situation in Egypt*. London: Burns & Oates, 1908.

————. *Secret History of the English Occupation of Egypt.*
2d ed. London: T. Fisher Unwin, 1907.
Boktor, Amir. *School and Society in Valley of the Nile.* Cairo:
Elias' Modern Press, 1936.
Bourne, H. R. Fox. *The Administration of Justice in Egypt.*
London: P. S. King & Son, 1909.
————. *The Case for Constitutional Reform in Egypt.* London:
P. S. King & Son, 1907.
————. *Egypt under British Control.* London: P. S. King & Son,
1907.
————. *Local Government in Egypt.* London: P. S. King & Son,
1908.
————. *Lord Cromer's Supremacy.* London: P. S. King & Son, 1907.
————. *Military Control in Egypt.* London: P. S. King & Son,
1907.
————. *Political Institutions in Egypt.* London: P. S. King &
Son, 1907.
Bowman, Humphrey. *Middle East Window.* London: Longmans, Green
& Co., 1942.
Boyle, Clara. *Boyle of Cairo.* Kendal: Titus Wilson & Son,
Ltd., 1965.
————. *A Servant of the Empire.* London: Methuen & Co., Ltd.,
1938.
Brinton, Jasper Yates. *The Mixed Courts of Egypt.* New Haven:
Yale University Press, 1930.
Budge, E. A. Wallis. *Cook's Handbook for Egypt and the Sudan.*
2d ed. London: Thos. Cook & Son, 1906.
Cecil, Lord Edward. *The Leisure of an Egyptian Official.*
London: Hodder and Stoughton Limited, 1921.
Chapman, Robert, and Sinclair, Keith, eds. *Studies of a Small
Democracy.* Auckland: Blackwood & Janet Paul, Ltd., 1963.
Charles-Roux, F. "L'Egypte de l'occupation anglaise à l'indé-
pendance égyptienne." In *Histoire de la nation égyptienne,*
vol. 7, edited by Gabriel Hanotaux. Paris: Librairie Plon,
1937.
Chirol, Sir Valentine. *The Egyptian Problem.* London: Macmillan
& Co., Ltd., 1920.
Coles, C. E. *Recollections and Reflections.* London:
St. Catherine Press, 1918.
Collins, Robert O. *King Leopold, England and the Upper Nile,
1899-1909.* New Haven: Yale University Press, 1968.
Connolly, Cyril. *Enemies of Promise.* Garden City: Doubleday &
Company, Inc., 1960.
Crabitès, Pierre. *The Spoliation of Suez.* London: George
Routledge and Sons, Ltd., 1940.
Cromer, Earl of. *Abbas II.* London: Macmillan & Co., 1915.
————. *Ancient and Modern Imperialism.* London: John Murray,
1910.

————. "Farewell Address." *The Times* (London), May 6, 1907.

————. *Modern Egypt*. 2 vols. London: Macmillan and Co.,
    Limited, 1908.

Cunningham, Alfred. *To-Day in Egypt*. London: Hurst & Blackett,
    Ltd., 1912.

Curtis, Myra. "John Gorst." *Dictionary of National Biography*.
    Oxford University Press, 1927.

D'Abernon, Viscount [Edgar Vincent]. *Portraits and Appreciations*.
    London: Hodder and Stoughton, Ltd., 1931.

Daniel, Norman. *Islam, Europe and Empire*. Edinburgh: The Uni-
    versity Press, 1966.

Deighton, H. S. "The Impact of Egypt on Britain: A Study of
    Public Opinion." In *Political and Social Change in Modern
    Egypt*, edited by P. M. Holt. London: Oxford University Press,
    1968.

————. "Some English Sources for the Study of Modern Egyptian
    History." In *Political and Social Change in Modern Egypt*,
    edited by P. M. Holt. London: Oxford University Press, 1968.

Dicey, Edward. "Lord Cromer's Resignation." *Empire Review*,
    May 19, 1907, pp. 321-25.

Durrell, Lawrence. *Mountolive*. London: Faber and Faber Limited,
    1965.

Dust, Muhammad [Mohammed Duse]. *In the Land of the Pharaohs*.
    London: Stanley Paul & Co., 1911.

Elgood, P. G. *Egypt and the Army*. London: Oxford University
    Press, 1924.

————. *The Transit of Egypt*. London: Edward Arnold & Co., 1928.

Farnie, D. A. *East and West of Suez*. Oxford: Clarendon Press,
    1969.

Feuchtwanger, E. J. "J. E. Gorst and the Central Organization of
    the Conservative Party, 1870-1882." *Bulletin of the Institute
    of Historical Studies* 32 (1959): 192-208.

Finch, Edith. *Wilfrid Scawen Blunt*. London: Jonathan Cape, 1938.

Galt, Russell. *The Conflict of French and English Educational
    Philosophies in Egypt*. Cairo: American University, 1933.

Gilbert, Bentley Brinkerhoff. "Sir John Eldon Gorst: Conserva-
    tive Rebel." *The Historian* 18 (1956): 151-69.

Goldschmidt, Arthur, Jr. "The Egyptian Nationalist Party." In
    Political and Social Change in Modern Egypt, edited by P. M.
    Holt. London: Oxford University Press, 1968.

Gollin, A. M. *Proconsul in Politics*. New York: The Macmillan
    Company, 1964.

Gorst, Sir Eldon. "The Anglo-Egyptian Official." Work and
    Workers Series, *Time* (1889).

————. "Egyptian Finance." *Encyclopaedia Britannica*, 1899-1900.

————. "Egypt in 1904." In *England in Egypt*, edited by
    Viscount Milner. 4th ed. London: Edward Arnold, 1907.

————. "Egypt: The Old Problem and the New." *Edinburgh Review* 205 (1907): 48-77.

————. "The English in Egypt." *Edinburgh Review* 188 (1890): vol. 171, pp. 267-306.

————. "The French Occupation of Egypt." *Edinburgh Review* 189 (1891): vol. 173, pp. 144-74.

————. "Lord Cromer in Egypt." In *The Empire and the Century*. London: John Murray, 1905.

————. "The Oriental Character." *Anglo-Saxon Review* 2 (1899): 47-55.

Gorst, J[ohn] E[ldon] [father]. *The Maori King*. London: Macmillan & Co., 1864.

————. *New Zealand Revisited*. London: Sir Isaac Pitman and Sons, Ltd., 1908.

Gorst, Harold E. *The Fourth Party*. London: Smith, Elder & Co., 1906.

————. *Much of Life is Laughter*. London: George Allen & Unwin, Ltd., 1936.

Grey of Fallodon, Edward, Viscount. *Twenty-Five Years*. 2 vols. London: Hodder & Stoughton, Ltd., 1925.

de Guerville, A. B. *New Egypt*. London: William Heinemann, 1905.

Hardy, Patrick Steel. *Thirty-Five Years of British Rule in Egypt*. Lausanne: Librairie Nouvelle, 1918.

Harris, Christina Phelps. *Nationalism and Revolution in Egypt*. The Hague: Mouton & Co., 1964.

Harris, Murray. *Egypt under the Egyptians*. London: Chapman & Hall, Ltd., 1925.

Hayter, Sir William. *Recent Constitutional Developments in Egypt*. Cambridge: The University Press, 1924.

Hertslet, Godfrey P. *The Foreign Office List(s), 1906-1914*. London: Harrison & Sons, 1906-1914.

Heyworth-Dunne, J. *Religious and Political Trends in Modern Egypt*. Washington, D.C.: by the author, 1950.

————. "Society and Politics in Modern Egyptian Literature." *Middle East Journal* 2 (1947): 306-18.

Hill, Richard. *A Biographical Dictionary of the Anglo-Egyptian Sudan*. Oxford: Clarendon Press, 1951.

————. *Slatin Pasha*. London: Oxford University Press, 1965.

The History of the Times, 1884-1912. Vol. 3: *The Twentieth Century Test*. London: Printing House Square, 1947.

Hogarth, D. G. "Lord Cromer Today." *Fortnightly Review* 110 (1921): 470-76.

Holt, Peter Malcolm. *Egypt and the Fertile Crescent, 1516-1922*. London: Longmans, Green & Co., Ltd., 1966.

————. *A Modern History of the Sudan*. 3d. ed. London: Weidenfeld & Nicolson, 1967.

————, ed. *Political and Social Change in Modern Egypt*. London: Oxford University Press, 1968.

————. "The Source-Materials of the Sudanese Mahdia."
St. Antony's Papers, no. 4, *Middle Eastern Affairs,* no. 1,
edited by Albert Hourani. London: Chatto and Windus, 1958.

Hourani, Albert. *Arabic Thought in the Liberal Age.* London:
Oxford University Press, 1962.

————, ed. *St. Antony's Papers,* nos. 4, 11, *Middle Eastern
Affairs,* nos. 1, 2. London: Chatto and Windus, 1958, 1961.

Hurewitz, J. C. *Diplomacy in the Near and Middle East.* vol. 1.
Princeton: D. Van Nostrand, Inc., 1956.

Hynes, Samuel. *The Edwardian Turn of Mind.* Princeton: Princeton
University Press, 1968.

Issawi, Charles. "Asymmetrical Development and Transport in
Egypt, 1800-1914." In *Beginnings of Modernization in the
Middle East,* edited by William R. Polk and Richard L. Chambers.
Chicago: University of Chicago Press, 1968.

————. *Egypt: An Economic and Social Analysis.* London: Oxford
University Press, 1947.

James, Robert Rhodes. *Lord Randolph Churchill.* London:
Weidenfeld & Nicolson, 1959.

————. *Rosebery.* London: Weidenfeld & Nicolson, 1963.

Jarvis, C. S. *Desert and Delta.* London: John Murray, 1938.

Jarvis, H. Wood. *Pharaoh to Farouk.* London: John Murray, 1955.

Jenkins, Roy. *Asquith.* London: Collins, 1964.

Judd, Denis. *Balfour and the British Empire.* New York:
St. Martin's Press, 1968.

Kedourie, Elie. "Saad Zaghlul and the British." *St. Anthony's
Papers,* no. 11, *Middle Eastern Affairs,* no. 2, edited by
Albert Hourani. London: Chatto and Windus, 1961.

Khouri, Mounah A. *Poetry and the Making of Modern Egypt (1882-
1922).* Leiden: E. J. Brill, 1971.

Kitchen, Helen A. "Al Ahram--*The Times* of the Arab World."
Middle East Journal 4 (1950): 155-69.

Landau, Jacob M. *Parliaments and Parties in Egypt.* Tel-Aviv:
Israel Publishing House, 1953.

Leslie, Shane. *Mark Sykes: His Life and Letters.* London:
Cassell and Company, Ltd., 1923.

Little, Tom. *Egypt.* London: Ernest Benn, Ltd., 1958.

————. *Modern Egypt.* New York: Frederick A. Praeger, 1967.

Lloyd, Lord [George A. L.]. *Egypt since Cromer.* vol. 1.
London: Macmillan & Co., 1933.

Low, Sidney. *Egypt in Transition.* New York: The Macmillan
Company, 1914.

Lutfi al-Sayyid, Afaf. *Egypt and Cromer.* New York: Frederick
A. Praeger, 1969.

Lytton, Earl of. *Wilfrid Scawen Blunt.* London: MacDonald & Co.,
Ltd., 1961.

McIlwraith, Sir Malcolm. "Egyptian Administration." *United
Empire* 10 (1919): 161-72.

————. "Three Egyptian Proconsuls." *Fortnightly Review* 105

(1919): 566-77.

McLeave, Hugh. *The Last Pharaoh: Farouk of Egypt.* New York: The McCall Publishing Company, 1970.

Magnus, Philip. *King Edward the Seventh.* New York: E. P. Dutton & Co., Inc., 1954.

————. *Kitchener.* New York: E. P. Dutton & Co., Inc., 1968.

Mannoni, O. *Prospero and Caliban.* Translated by Pamela Powerland. London: Methuen & Co., Ltd., 1956.

Mansfield, Peter. *The British in Egypt.* New York: Holt, Rinehart and Winston, 1971.

Marlowe, John. *Anglo-Egyptian Relations, 1800-1956.* 2d. ed. London: Frank Cass & Co., Ltd., 1965.

————. *Cromer in Egypt.* London: Elek Books, 1970.

Marshall, J[ohn] E[dwin]. *The Egyptian Enigma, 1890-1928.* London: John Murray, 1928.

Marshall-Cornwall, General Sir James. "An Enigmatic Frontier." *The Geographical Journal* 125 (1959): 459-62.

El-Mesaddy, Mohamad. "The Relations between Abbas Hilmi and Lord Cromer." Ph.D. dissertation, University of London, 1966.

Milner, Alfred, Viscount. *England in Egypt.* 4th ed. rev. London: Edward Arnold, 1907.

Monger, George. *The End of Isolation.* London: Thomas Nelson and Sons, Ltd., 1963.

Monroe, Elizabeth. *Britain's Moment in the Middle East, 1914-1956.* Baltimore: The Johns Hopkins Press, 1963.

————. "Review of *Modernization and British Colonial Rule in Egypt,* by Robert L. Tignor." *Middle East Journal* 22 (1968): 95-96.

Morley, John, Viscount. *Recollections.* 2 vols. New York: The Macmillan Company, 1917.

Morris, James. "A Wishful Good-By to All That." *New York Times Magazine,* February 18, 1968, pp. 32-33, 96-103.

Moseley, Sydney A. *With Kitchener in Cairo.* London: Cassell and Company, Ltd., 1917.

Newman, E. W. Polson. *Great Britain in Egypt.* London: Cassell and Company, Ltd., 1928.

Nicolson, Harold. *Portrait of a Diplomatist.* New York: Harcourt, Brace & Co., 1930.

O'Brien, Patrick. *The Revolution in Egypt's Economic System.* London: Oxford University Press, 1966.

Owen, E. Roger J. *Cotton and the Egyptian Economy, 1820-1914.* Oxford: Clarendon Press, 1969.

————. "The Influence of Lord Cromer's Indian Experience on British Policy in Egypt, 1883-1907." *St. Antony's Papers,* No. 17, *Middle Eastern Affairs,* No. 4, edited by Albert Hourani. London: Oxford University Press, 1965.

————. "Lord Cromer and the Development of Egyptian Industry, 1883-1907." *Middle Eastern Studies* 2 (1966): 282-301.

Panday, B. N. *The Break-up of British India.* New York:
St. Martin's Press, 1969.
Pelling, Henry. "British Labour and British Imperialism." In
Popular Politics and Society in Late Victorian Britain.
London: Macmillan & Co., Ltd., 1968.
Penfield, Frederick Courtland. *Present-Day Egypt.* New York:
The Century Co., 1903.
Piper, David. *The Companion Guide to London.* London: Fontana
Books, 1970.
Porter, Bernard. *Critics of Empire.* London: Macmillan & Co.,
Ltd., 1968.
Priestley, J. B. *The English.* Harmondsworth: Penguin Books,
Ltd., 1975.
Rifaat Bey, Muhammad Ali. *The Awakening of Modern Egypt.*
London: Longmans, Green & Co., 1947.
Rifat, Mansur Mustafa. "Lest We Forget . . . ." Pamphlet in
the Hoover Institution Middle East Collection, May 1915.
Robinson, Ronald; Gallagher, John, and Denny, Alice. *Africa and
the Victorians.* New York: St. Martin's Press, 1961.
Rodd, Sir James Rennell. *Social and Diplomatic Memories, 1894-
1901.* 2 vols. London: Edward Arnold & Co., 1923.
Ronall, Joachim O. "Julius Blum Pasha: An Austro-Hungarian
Banker in Egypt, 1843-1919." *Tradition: Zeitschrift für
Firmengeschichte und Unternehmerbiographie* 2 (1968): 57-80.
Rowland, Peter. *The Last Liberal Governments.* New York: The
Macmillan Company, 1968.
Rowlatt, Mary. *A Family in Egypt.* London: Robert Hale, Ltd.,
1956.
Royal Institute of International Affairs (Information Department).
Paper No. 19: *Great Britain and Egypt, 1914-1936.* London:
Chatham House, 1936.
Russell Pasha, Sir Thomas. *Egyptian Service, 1902-1946.* London:
John Murray, 1949.
Safran, Nadav. *Egypt in Search of Political Community.*
Cambridge: Harvard University Press, 1961.
Sanderson, G. N. *England, Europe and the Upper Nile (1882-1899).*
Edinburgh: The University Press, 1965.
Seikaly, Samir. "Coptic Communal Reform: 1860-1914." *Middle
Eastern Studies* 6 (1970): 247-75.
————. "The Copts under British Rule, 1882-1914." Ph.D.
dissertation, University of London, 1967.
Semmel, Bernard. *Imperialism and Social Reform.* Garden City:
Doubleday & Doubleday, Inc., 1968.
Seth, Ronald. *Russell Pasha.* London: William Kimber, 1966.
Shaw, George Bernard. *John Bull's Other Island and Major
Barbara.* New York: Brentanos, 1907.
Sinclair, Keith. *A History of New Zealand.* Harmondsworth:
Penguin Books Ltd, 1959.

————. *The Origins of the Maori Wars*. Wellington: New Zealand University Press, 1957.

Sladen, Douglas. *Egypt and the English*. London: Hurst & Blackett, Ltd., 1908.

Spender, J. A. "Egypt." In *Essays on Liberalism*. London: W. Collins & Son Ltd., 1922.

————. *The Life of the Right Honourable Sir Henry Campbell-Bannerman*. 2 vols. London: Hodder and Stoughton, Ltd., 1923.

Steiner, Zara S. *The Foreign Office and Foreign Policy, 1898-1914*. Cambridge: Cambridge University Press, 1969.

Steppat, Fritz. "Nationalismus und Islam bei Mustafa Kamil." *Die Welt des Islams* 4 (1956): 241-341.

Storrs, Ronald. *Orientations*. London: Nicholson & Watson, 1945.

Symond, M. Travers. *The Riddle of Egypt*. London: Cecil Palmer, 1913.

Thornton, A. P. *Doctrines of Imperialism*. New York: John Wiley & Sons, Inc., 1965.

————. *The Habit of Authority*. Toronto: University of Toronto Press, 1966.

————. *The Imperial Idea and Its Enemies*. London: Macmillan & Co., Ltd., 1959.

Tignor, Robert L. "Indianization of the Egyptian Administration under Britain." *American Historial Review* 68 (1963): 636-61.

————. *Modernization and British Colonial Rule in Egypt, 1881-1914*. Princeton: Princeton University Press, 1966.

Vansittart, Baron [R. G.]. *The Mist Procession*. London: Hutchinson & Company, Ltd., 1958.

Vatikiotis, P. J. *The Modern History of Egypt*. New York: Frederick A. Praeger, 1969.

Waldberg, Jorge Nelken Y. *Régime de félonie et de crime inaugurée en Egypte sous Evelyn Baring, Earl Cromer*. Le Caire: Imprimerie Américaine, 1906.

Warburg, Gabriel. *The Sudan under Wingate*. London: Frank Cass & Co., Ltd., 1971.

Weigall, Arthur E. P. Brome. *A History of Events in Egypt from 1798 to 1914*. London and Edinburgh: William Blackwood & Sons, 1915.

White, Arthur Silva. *The Expansion of Egypt under Anglo-Egyptian Condominium*. London: Methuen and Co., 1899.

Willcocks, Sir William. "In Egypt during the Forty Years of British Occupation." *Bulletin d'Institut d'Egypte* 8 (1925-26): 19-37.

————. *Sixty Years in the East*. Edinburgh: William Blackwood & Sons, Ltd., 1935.

Wilson, Arnold T. *The Suez Canal*. London: Oxford University Press, 1939.

Wilson, John. *CB: A Life of Sir Henry Campbell-Bannerman*. New York: St. Martin's Press, 1973.

Wolpert, Stanley A. *Morley and India, 1906-1910.* Berkeley: University of California Press, 1967.

Wrench, John Evelyn. *Alfred Lord Milner.* London: Eyre & Spottiswoode, Ltd., 1958.

Young, George. *Egypt.* London: Ernest Benn, Ltd., 1927.

Youssef Bey, Amine. *Independent Egypt.* London: John Murray, 1940.

Zayid, Mahmud Y. *Egypt's Struggle for Independence.* Beirut: Khayats, 1965.

Zebel, Sydney H. *Balfour: A Political Biography.* Cambridge: Cambridge University Press, 1973.

Zetland, Marquess of. *Lord Cromer.* London: Hodder and Stoughton, Ltd., 1932.

Ziadeh, Farhat J. *Lawyers and the Rule of Law and Liberalism in Modern Egypt.* Stanford: Hoover Institution Publications, 1968.

Index

Capitulations, the, 16-17, 36;
  proposed reforms of, 89,
  122, 187-88, 228-29
Cassel, Sir Ernest, 71, 85, 197
Cecil, Lord Edward, 149
Chamberlain, Joseph, 31
Cheetham, Sir Milne, 231-32,
  235
Chirol, Valentine, 70, 225
Chitty, Sir Arthur, 175, 185
Church Missionary Society, 93-
  94, 124-28, 202, 226. *See
  also* MacInnes, Rennie
Churchill, Lord Randolph, 8-9,
  11, 12, 21
Churchill, Winston, 71, 196,
  197
Clarence, Prince Albert Victor,
  26-27
Clayton, Gilbert F., 204, 214
Coffin, Major Pine, 111
Coles Pasha, C. E., 103, 157,
  168-69
Connaught, Duke of, 145
Conservative Party, 2, 8-10,
  52, 220-22
Copts, 124, 202, 208, 211-13,
  226-28. *See also* Ghali
  Pasha, Butrus
Corbett, Eustace, 175
Corbett, Sir Vincent, 143, 147,
  149, 173, 174
Crewe, Lord, 216
Criminal Deportation Act (1909),
  180, 185-86, 239
Cromer, Earl of (Sir Evelyn
  Baring): career of, xxiii-xxv,
  14-21 *passim*, 31-45 *passim*,
  50-54 *passim*, 96-110, 120-38
  passim, 142-43, 150-51; and
  Gorst, 18-19, 47-49, 67, 71-
  72, 78-80, 220, 231, 235; on
  Gorst as successor, 73-74,
  83, 90-91, 135; news management, 32-38; and nationalism,
  101, 122, 132, 134; on Dinshawai incident, 113, 116-19,
  159-63 *passim*; and Copts,
  124-25, 212; on judicial

reforms, 178-79; on Suez
  Canal proposal, 194-95
Cromer, Lady (Ethel Errington),
  21, 135
Cust, Harry, 201-2

D'Abernon, Viscount, *see*
  Vincent, Edgar
Dawkins, Clinton, 41, 47, 51-
  57 *passim*, 67
Dillon, John, 169
Dinshawai incident: and Cromer,
  104; events of, 111-12;
  special tribunal for, 113-
  19; Gorst on, 144; prisoners
  from, 159, 161-63
diplomatic service, entry into,
  10-11
Dudgeon, G. C., 228
Dunlop, Douglas, 50, 70, 129-
  31, 146, 149

education department, 128-31,
  168-73
education: reforms in, 88, 143,
  146, 167, 169-73; Cromer on,
  128-31; and religion, 226
Edward VII, 74
Egyptian army, 86, 98, 109-10,
  146
Egyptian character, 43, 87
Egyptian civil service, 44-50,
  97, 101-2, 153-58
Egyptian Committee, in House
  of Commons, 163
Egyptian economy, 136, 140,
  143-44, 192
Egyptian finances, 18, 31, 97,
  146, 230; and crisis of
  1907, 140, 147-48, 179, 192
Egyptian Gazette, The, 37,
  113-14, 143; on Gorst, 184,
  226
Egyptian internal policy, 150,
  152, 154
Egyptian National Bank, 85
Egyptian social structure,
  Gorst's views on, 86-87
Egyptian Standard, The, 137,

149. See also *al-Liwa*
Egyptian University, 170-71
Elgin, Lord, 215-16
Elgood, P. G., 100, 156-57
engineering school, 172
England in Egypt (Milner), 32, 85
Eton College, 3-6

Fahmi, Mustafa, 41, 134, 165-66
Fakhri Pasha, 165
Fanus, Akhnukh, 211
Felix, Frau, 59
fellahin, 110-15, 121, 136, 226
finance ministry, 38-39, 168, 204
finances, *see* Egyptian finances
Findlay, Charles de Mansfeld, 108-9, 119-20, 135-36
Fitzmaurice, Sir Edmond, 10
Foreign Office: Gorst and, 10-12, 35, 79-91, 148, 176, 179, 190; and Dinshawai incident, 115-19; and Press Law, 181; on Criminal Deportation Act, 185-86; and Suez Canal negotiations, 195-200; on Said, 203. *See also* Grey, Sir Edward
foreign residents in Egypt, 122, 131, 144, 179, 228-29. *See also* Capitulations
Fourth Party, the, 8-10, 21
French, in Egypt, 50, 182, 207, 229
Fuad, Prince Ahmad, 171
Fyfe, H. Hamilton, 200

Garstin, Sir William, 135, 174, 194, 235-36
General Assembly, 123, 164, 208, 217-18; on Suez Canal Company, 197, 204-5, 224, 230
German Empire, and Tabah Crisis, 106-7
Ghali Pasha, Butrus, 113, 124-25, 134, 182; and Gorst, 45,

164, 187, 197-99; assassination of, 163, 202-8 *passim*, 212-13, 224; as prime minister, 165-67, 238
Gorst, Edith, 60, 210
Gorst, Sir Eldon (John Eldon Gorst, the younger): early life of, 1-40, 45-48, 70-74, 78-91; and Cromer, 18-19, 47-49, 67, 71-74, 78-80, 220, 231, 235; and Lady Sykes, 24-29, 58, 60-63; Khedive Abbas and, 42, 44-46, 71-73, 145, 167, 186-87, 233, 236; and Romaine Turnure, 57-69, 73, 82, 188-89; Evelyn Rudd and, 71, 77, 79, 81-82, 188-90, 235; as British Agent and Consul General in Egypt, 92-95, 140-239; conciliation policy of, 154-206, 237-39; educational reforms of, 169-73; discontent with policies of, 173-87, 226-28; on Suez Canal Company concession, 192-204; on British occupation of Egypt, 208-30; ill health of, 230-36
Gorst, Eva ("Dolly"), 60, 71, 190, 235
Gorst, Evelyn Rudd ("Doll"), 71, 77, 79, 81-82, 188-90, 235
Gorst, Harold, 75, 84-85
Gorst, Hylda, 60
Gorst, Sir John Eldon, the elder, 1-3, 5, 8-12, 52, 55, 94
Gorst, Katherine Rachel ("Kitty"), 81, 188, 232, 235
Goschen, C. J., 32
government, in Egypt, 96-99, 133-34, 143-44; Gorst's reforms of, 146-47, 164
Graham, Ronald, 138, 148-49, 163, 182
Grey, Sir Edward, 163, 167-69, 173, 179-80, 186, 207,